Jamaica

**APA** PUBLICATIONS
Part of the Langenscheidt Publishing Group

ABOUT THIS BOOK

Editorial

Editor
Lesley Gordon
Editorial Director
Brian Bell

Distribution

UK & Ireland
GeoCenter International Ltd
The Viables Centre , Harrow Way
Basingstoke, Hants RG22 4BJ
Fax: (44) 1256-817988

United States
Langenscheidt Publishers, Inc.
46–35 54th Road, Maspeth, NY 11378
Fax: (718) 784-0640

Canada
Prologue Inc.
1650 Lionel Bertrand Blvd., Boisbriand
Québec, Canada J7H 1N7
Tel: (450) 434-0306. Fax: (450) 434-2627

Australia & New Zealand
Hema Maps Pty. Ltd.
24 Allgas Street, Slacks Creek 4127
Brisbane, Australia
Tel: (61) 7 3290 0322. Fax: (61) 7 3290 0478

Worldwide
**Apa Publications GmbH & Co.
Verlag KG (Singapore branch)**
38 Joo Koon Road, Singapore 628990
Tel: (65) 865-1600. Fax: (65) 861-6438

Printing

Insight Print Services (Pte) Ltd
38 Joo Koon Road, Singapore 628990
Tel: (65) 865-1600. Fax: (65) 861-6438

©2000 Apa Publications GmbH & Co.
Verlag KG (Singapore branch)
All Rights Reserved
First Edition 1983
Seventh Edition 2000

CONTACTING THE EDITORS
Although every effort is made to
provide accurate information, we
live in a fast-changing world and
would appreciate it if readers
would call our attention to any
errors or outdated information
that may occur by writing to:
**Insight Guides, P.O. Box 7910,
London SE1 1WE, England.
Fax: (44 20) 7403-0290.
e-mail:
insight@apaguide.demon.co.uk**

NO part of this book may be repro-
duced, stored in a retrieval system or
transmitted in any form or means elec-
tronic, mechanical, photocopying,
recording or otherwise, without prior
written permission of *Apa Publications*.
Brief text quotations with use of
photographs are exempted for book
review purposes only. Information has
been obtained from sources believed to
be reliable, but its accuracy and
completeness, and the opinions based
thereon, are not guaranteed.

This guidebook combines the interests and enthusiasms of two of the world's best known infor-mation providers: Insight Guides, whose titles have set the standard for visual travel guides since 1970, and Discovery Channel, the world's premier source of nonfiction tele-vision programming.

The editors of Insight Guides pro-vide both practical advice and general understanding about a des-tination's history, culture, institu-tions and people. Discovery Channel and its Web site, www.discovery.com, help millions of viewers explore their world from the comfort of their own home and also encourage them to ex-plore it first hand.

This updated edition of *Insight Guide: Jamaica* is carefully structured to convey an understanding of the island and its culture as well as to guide readers through its varied sights and activities:

◆ The **Features** section, indicated by a yellow bar at the top of each page, covers the history and culture of the country in a series of infor-mative essays.

◆ The main **Places** section, indi-cated by a blue bar, is a complete guide to all the sights and areas worth visiting. Places of special interest are coordinated by number with the maps.

◆ The **Travel Tips** listings section, with an orange bar, provides a handy point of reference for information on travel, hotels, shops, restau-rants and more. An index is printed on the back cover flap, which serves as a bookmark.

The contributors

This edition of *Insight: Jamaica* was edited by London-based Insight Guides editor **Lesley Gordon**. A talented team contributed to the update of the original book, edited by **Paul Zach** and **Mike Henry**, which became a classic amongst visitors and locals.

James Ferguson author of *A Traveller's History of the Caribbean* wrote *Tales From "Back 'A' Yard"* and updated the in-depth history written by the late **Clinton V. Black** who surveyed Jamaica from Taino times. He wrote the standard history text, *The Story of Jamaica*.

Journalist **John Maxwell** updated *Transition to Independence*, **Ken Maxwell's** *Cockpit Country* and *The Political Canvas*, the modern politics chapter by the late **Dr Carl Stone**. Jamaican-educated journalist and

novelist, **Leone Ross**, defined modern culture for *The Jamaicans* based on the work of the late **Victor Stafford Reid**, who also wrote about Jamaica's vibrant religious life.

Sonia Mills updated award-winning author, Olive Senior's essay on *Kingston* and its surrounds and also produced the Travel Tips section. **Alan Ross** updated the remainder of Senior's chapters including *Port Royal*, *Port Antonio*, and the *East Coast*. Ross also updated **Dr Ian Sangster's** *High in the Blue Mountains* and Ken Maxwell's *Negril and South Cornwall*. Maxwell also wrote the feature on language, *Pardon My Patois*.

Andrea Hutchinson updated Sangster's *Ocho Rios* chapter, **Dr Heather Royes'** essay on the arts, **Barbara Gloudon's** *Dance and Drama: Everybody Is a Star* and the seminal music feature *The Red-Hot Rhythms of Reggae* written by radio broadcaster **Dermott Hussey** and Zach. **Gertrude M. Trox** updated Sangster's Montego Bay chapter and Ken Maxwell's Spanish Town chapter, provided text for the architecture and flora and fauna features, and supplied new pictures.

Canute James, updated **Sonia Gordon's** *Education, Migration and Trade* and also expanded **Jimmy Carnegie's** chapter on cricket.

Lloyd Williams penned the mandatory piece on the island's infamous ganja trade.

Principal photography from Zach, Hans Höfer and David Stahl was added to by Bill Wassman and Paul R. Turnbull. The archives of the National Library at the Institute of Jamaica were invaluable. Thanks to the Jamaica Tourist Board and to **Caroline Radula-Scott** for her editorial assistance. The final text was proofread and indexed by **Laura Hicks**.

Map Legend

	County Boundary
	Parish Boundary
	National Park/Reserve
	Ferry Route
✈	Airport: International/Regional
🚌	Bus Station
P	Parking
ℹ	Tourist Information
✉	Post Office
†	Church/Ruins
†	Monastery
☾	Mosque
✡	Synagogue
	Castle/Ruins
∴	Archeological Site
∩	Cave
ⅼ	Statue/Monument
★	Place of Interest

The main places of interest in the Places section are coordinated by number with a full-colour map (e.g. ❶), and a symbol at the top of every right-hand page tells you where to find the map.

CONTENTS

Gazebo at
sunset in
Montego
Bay

Insight on ...

Information panels

Travel Tips

Places

PORTRAIT OF AN ISLAND

Beautiful beaches, spectacular mountains, exotic scenery
and warm, witty people. This is the Caribbean with attitude

There's something sensuous in the undulating lines of this island's contours, in the way the winds tease the palm trees and the seas massage the sands. There's a hypnotic quality to its people's lilting patois and musical rhythms, to the deafening hush that hangs in the heights of the Blue Mountains, to the hum and whistle of the birds. So "walk good", but be wary. Once it grabs you, Jamaica might not let go.

Few islands or countries of Jamaica's size have such a diversity of skin tones and facial features, of landscapes and seascapes, of plant and animal life. With a total land area of 11,424 sq. km (4,411 sq. miles) the island stretches about 235 km (146 miles) east to west from Morant Point to Negril, and bulges to 82 km (51 miles) at its widest point. About 2½ million people live here, handsome blends of African, European, Arabic, Chinese and eastern Indian stock who account for their national motto: "Out of Many, One People."

Jamaica floats in the Caribbean Sea at a latitude 18° north of the Equator. Its reputation has grown around its fine beaches, and hotels and resorts crowd powdery slivers of sand along the north coast yet rugged highlands dominate the landscape.

More than half of Jamaica hovers 305 metres (1,000 ft) above the Caribbean. The highest point, the Blue Mountain Peak, punctures the clouds at 2,256 metres (7,402 ft) just 16 km (10 miles) from the coastal plain east of Kingston. In the middle of the island sits cool Mandeville on a plateau in the Don Figueroa Mountains, rising 610 metres (2,000 ft) above the check-patterned agricultural slopes.

The northwest is pockmarked by the surreal karst landscapes of the Cockpit Country – the "Me No Sen, You No Come" land of the free-spirited Maroon people. Sinkholes have settled in the limestone surface, forming a pitted woodland. Where the highlands plummet to the sea, spectacular cliffs have been created, like Lovers' Leap on the south coast. Some 120 rivers and streams gush from mountain ravines to carve gashes in the coastal plains.

The evolution of paradise

Geologists believe that Jamaica and its neighbouring islands in the Caribbean evolved from an arc of volcanoes that bubbled up from the seas billions of years ago. Lower lands surrounding the peaks eased out of the waters over 30 million years ago. A cap of white limestone, the residue of the skeletons of sea creatures and marine organisms, still covers about two-thirds of the island. This land-building process climaxed about 20 million years ago when the island emerged from the Caribbean.

The Cockpit Country and innumerable cave systems betray the country's oceanic origins. The systems include Twin Sisters on the

PRECEDING PAGES: a south-coast beach scene; University of West Indies mural; Ocho Rios hat stand; Ziggy Marley.
LEFT: colourful carnival character in Kingston.

Hellshire Coast near Kingston and a series of spectacular chambers in the Cockpit area, called Windsor Cave, nearly 3 km (2 miles) long.

When the Europeans arrived the only native fruits were guava, pineapple, the sweetsop and possibly the star apple. Virtually everything that blooms today was imported by either the hands of humans or the droppings of birds. The Europeans introduced sugar cane, bananas and citrus, and Spanish traders brought coconuts from Malaysia in the 17th century. The ackee that is the staple of most Jamaican breakfasts arrived on slave ships from West Africa in 1778. Pimento is a native plant, as is the mahoe, Jamaica's national tree. The lavender-coloured blossom of the *lignum vitae* is the national flower.

Nearly 3,000 varieties of flowering plant have been identified, including 800 species found only in Jamaica. Indigenous plants include 200 species of wild orchid, 60 species of bromeliad, called "wild pine" by Jamaicans, and about 550 ferns. Bamboo imported from China flourishes throughout the island.

Tales of mermaids

There are rats, of course, and mongooses introduced by 19th-century plantation owners to combat the rats. The rare native Jamaican coney resembles a large guinea pig but is a relative of the rat. Bats are numerous; about 25 varieties flitter through island belfries. The enormous gentle manatee that inspired tales of mermaids is another mammal still inhabiting lonely waters along the south and east coasts. Jamaica's crocodile community is dwindling. The ubiquitous gecko keeps the insect population in check. Around 100 large Jamaican iguanas, for a long time thought to be extinct, still live in the Hellshire hills. Jamaica has few snakes, all harmless.

There are more than 200 species of bird, including 25 endemic ones. The national bird, the Doctor Bird, a streamer-tailed hummingbird found only in Jamaica, darts about the island's flower gardens, and bright yellow, orange and green parrots, parakeets and finches sing in the forest. The John Crow turkey buzzards scavenge garbage and the entrails of dead animals.

Warm breezes

Jamaica's climate has always been its biggest attraction. The warmth that lured its earliest residents now brings more than 1 million sun-worshipping visitors each year. Seasons are non-existent, with annual average temperatures of 27°C (80°F) on the coast, dropping to the low 20s and a little below in higher mountain elevations. Peaks in the Blue Mountains have been known to sustain "frigid" conditions below 10°C (50°F) on rare occasions.

Mostly the weather is perfect. Cooling trade winds that Jamaicans call the "Doctor Breeze" blow in from the seas to lessen the heat of the daytime hours. Night brings the "Undertaker's Breeze" from the mountains; Jamaicans used to bundle up against it for fear of catching their deaths of cold. As the artist-historian Howard Pyle wrote in 1890: "The Air here, notwithstanding the heat, is very healthy. I have known blacks one hundred and twenty years of Age, and one hundred years old is very common amongst Temperate Livers." ❏

RIGHT: Surrey in the east is rich in tropical mountain vegetation.

Decisive Dates

c. AD 650 Arrival of the "Redware People", a branch of the Amerindian Tainos, originating from the Orinoco region of South America. They travel up through the Lesser Antilles in dugout canoes.

c. 850 Second wave of Taino migration.

1494 Christopher Columbus sights Xaymaca on his second voyage of discovery and claims it for Spain after a skirmish with indigenous Tainos.

1503 On his fourth voyage, Columbus is forced to spend a year stranded in Jamaica after his ships founder off the north coast.

SPANISH RULE

Jamaica was a quiet backwater in Spain's American empire, but it soon attracted the attention of competing European nations and pirates.

1510 First permanent settlement, Sevilla la Nueva, founded at St Ann's Bay by Spanish Governor Juan de Esquivel.

1517 Arrival of first African slaves.

1524 Sevilla la Nueva is abandoned in favour of the new settlement of Villa de la Vega (later to be known as Spanish Town) on the island's south coast.

1555 First raid by French pirates on Jamaica is successfully repulsed by colonists.

1596 English force under Sir Anthony Shirley raids and plunders Spanish Town.

1643 Captain William Jackson's English expedition captures and loots Spanish Town.

BRITISH COLONISATION AND CONQUEST

After several attempts, England seized the island, allowing it to become home to many much-feared pirates.

1655 Jamaica invaded and captured by 8,000-strong force under Admiral William Penn and General Robert Venables.

1658 Spanish attempt to retake Jamaica fails.

1660 Mutiny of English troops is quelled by Colonel Edward D'Oyley.

1660 Jamaica becomes main base of buccaneers and pirates, who attack Spanish shipping and coastal towns in the Caribbean.

1664 Governor Sir Thomas Modyford encourages development of Jamaican sugar industry.

1670 Treaty of Madrid officially cedes the island to England.

1692 Earthquake and tidal wave destroy the pirate capital of Port Royal, killing 3,000 people.

1690 Start of the First Maroon War, pitting former and recently escaped slaves against colonial militia.

1694 Attempted French invasion of Jamaica causes large-scale loss of life and damage.

SUGAR AND SLAVERY

In the second half of the 18th century Jamaica became one of Britain's most valuable colonial possessions, largely because of its sugar exports. But instability and conflict were ever-present.

1739 Peace treaty ends the First Maroon War by granting the Maroons land, freedom and autonomy in return for assistance in suppressing slave revolts.

1760 Tacky's Rebellion is put down with the help of Maroon forces.

1765 Another serious slave uprising is savagely repressed.

1791 Beginning of slave rebellion in neighbouring French colony of St Domingue.

1795 Second Maroon War takes place, provoked by ill-treatment of Maroons and, allegedly, by French *agents provocateurs*. The Maroons surrender after five months.

FREEDOM AND HARDSHIP

Emancipation brought freedom and escape from the plantations for many, but it did little to address social inequalities and poverty.

1804 Independent state of Haiti is born, hastening the end of slavery throughout the Caribbean.

1807 Britain abolishes the slave trade.

1831 Samuel Sharpe leads slave revolt, causing widespread damage and leading to severe reprisals.

1833 British Parliament votes for the abolition of slavery after a period of "apprenticeship".

1838 Full emancipation frees some 300,000 slaves in Jamaica, many of whom become peasant farmers.

1846 The British government introduces the Sugar Duties Act, removing preferential treatment given to sugar from colonial suppliers and irreversibly damaging Jamaica's industry.

1862 First banana exports from Jamaica to the US.

1865 Morant Bay Rebellion erupts, caused by poverty and land shortages. Governor Edward John Eyre orders ruthless repression and the execution of more than 400 rebels. In the aftermath Jamaica loses much autonomy and becomes a Crown Colony, governed from London.

1872 Kingston becomes the island's capital.

1907 An earthquake destroys much of Kingston.

INDEPENDENCE AND TWO-PARTY POLITICS

The social turmoil of the 1930s gave rise to the island's two modern-day political parties and also hastened the movement towards independence.

1938 Widespread unrest and political mobilisation in the wake of the Depression lead to the formation of the People's National Party (PNP) and Jamaica Labour Party (JLP) as well as affiliated trade unions.

1944 Introduction of new constitution ends Crown Colony rule and introduces universal suffrage.

1950–60 A quarter of a million Jamaicans emigrate to Britain in search of work.

1958 Creation of short-lived West Indies Federation, which collapses two years later after Jamaicans vote to leave.

1962 Jamaica becomes fully independent, led by William Alexander Bustamante's JLP.

1966 Emperor Haile Selassie of Ethiopia visits the island and is greeted by thousands of Rastafarians.

1967 The JLP wins a second term of office.

1972 The PNP takes power in elections, led by the radical Michael Manley.

1976 The PNP wins elections amidst intense political violence, a month before economic crisis breaks.

1980 Edward Seaga's JLP wins a landslide electoral victory, promising "deliverance" from Manley's experiment with socialism.

1981 Death of reggae star Bob Marley, one of the world's most influential musicians.

1983 Seaga wins a second term despite increasing economic problems and unpopular austerity programmes; the PNP boycotts the election.

LEFT: slaves celebrate their freedom.
RIGHT: P. J. Patterson.

1988 Hurricane Gilbert devastates the island, leaving a quarter of Jamaicans homeless.

1989 Michael Manley is returned to power, but on a much more conservative political platform.

MODERN JAMAICA

The 1990s witnessed the dominance of the PNP and a reduction in political violence, but economic difficulties and social tensions continued to plague the island.

1990 The Jamaican dollar is "floated" on the international market, resulting in massive devaluation.

1992 Manley announces his retirement on health grounds, handing over the PNP leadership and post of

prime minister to Percival J. Patterson.

1993 Patterson leads the PNP to victory in general election with a record 60 percent of the vote.

1995 Factional splits within the JLP lead to the formation of a new political party, the National Democratic Movement (NDM), led by former JLP Chairman Bruce Golding.

1997 Death of Michael Manley precedes another electoral success for the PNP, which takes power for a record third consecutive term.

1998 Jamaica's soccer team takes part in the World Cup in France, creating "Reggae Boyz" hysteria.

1999 Government plans to raise fuel taxes lead to widespread rioting and looting across the island, and several deaths. ❏

THE EARLIEST ISLANDERS

The first known Jamaicans were the peaceful Tainos, an Arawak-speaking
people, but their paradise would not endure...

When Christopher Columbus "discovered" Jamaica on 5 May 1494, during his second voyage to the New World, he found a thriving colony of Taino Indians such as he had already met in the neighbouring islands of Cuba and Haiti.

From an ancestral home in the Orinoco

region of the Guianas and Venezuela, the Tainos – members of an Amerindian Arawak-speaking people – had long before sailed northwards in their dugout canoes, settling in each of the islands of the Antilles from Trinidad to Cuba. They are believed to have arrived in Jamaica in two waves – the first (the so-called "Redware People") around AD 650, the second between 850 and 900.

Some centuries later, the Tainos' calm and peaceful lives were rudely disturbed by the arrival of another Amerindian people, the Kalinas, whom Columbus called Caribs, giving their name to the surrounding sea. Probably also originating in the Guiana region of South

America, this less-sophisticated, warlike people began to spread through the islands, slaughtering the Taino men and abducting their women to run their new settlements.

Farther and farther north they came, until, by the time Columbus had reached the West Indies in 1492, they had taken the entire Lesser Antilles and were raiding the eastern end of Puerto Rico. They were known and feared by other Amerindians in Haiti and from time to time made murderous attacks even on Jamaica. But for the arrival of the Spaniards, the Caribs might have exterminated those early Jamaicans. As it happened, the newcomers from Europe were shortly to complete the work of destruction themselves.

The Tainos' way of life

Somewhere between 100,000 and 500,000 Tainos at one time lived on the island. Aboriginal remains show that they lived in most parts of Jamaica, even as far inland as Ewarton and Moneague, and in such upland areas as the Long Mountain and Jack's Hill. The majority of their villages were close to the coast or near rivers, as the Tainos were seagoing people and lived chiefly on seafood.

An interesting village site, and one of the most accessible, is that at the White Marl, near Central Village, 5 km (3 miles) outside Spanish Town. On a hill adjacent to the site now stands the Taino Museum.

The Tainos were brown-skinned, short and slightly built, with straight, coarse black hair, broad faces and flat wide noses. Their only breadstuff, cassava, was doubtlessly brought by them to the island in their migration from the South American mainland. In addition they grew sweet potatoes, fruits, vegetables, cotton and tobacco.

In Jamaica they excelled in the cultivation of cotton. Much of the women's time was spent spinning and weaving. The island supplied hammocks (believed to be a Taino invention) and cotton cloth to the neighbouring islands of Cuba and Haiti, and the conquering Spaniards themselves had their sailcloth made in Jamaica.

The Jamaican Tainos were skilled artisans who left their paintings on the walls of many island caves. They were superb stoneworkers, and their implements were particularly well shaped, smooth and beautifully finished. They fashioned their dugout canoes from the trunks of cedar and silk-cotton trees, hollowing out the trunks first by charring, then by chipping with their stone axes and chisels. These canoes, which took months to make, varied greatly in

MEN OF THE GOOD

The peace-loving Caribbean descendants of the Arawak-speaking people of the Orinoco are referred to by historians as Tainos, meaning "men of the good", the name they gave themselves.

respected; they alone enjoyed the privilege of polygamy, and they occupied the best houses, in which the family idols were kept. If a *cacique* was dying he would be strangled as a mark of special favour.

The Tainos explained the mysteries of everyday life in their myths and worshipped both spirit gods and their images, called *zemis*. Very few of the original *zemis* survive, but three found in a cave in the Carpenter Mountains, Manchester, are now in the British Museum. Five casts of these

size: some held one person, others 50 or more.

Smoking was both a pastime and a religious ritual with the Tainos. The word "tobacco" comes from the name of their pipe, but another similar word, *tabaco,* was used to describe a particular type of cigar. They were a pleasure-loving people and enjoyed dancing, singing, and playing a ball game called *batos.*

As in Cuba, Jamaica's inhabitants divided their island into provinces, each ruled over by a *cacique* – male or female – assisted by village headmen or sub-chiefs. *Caciques* were much

LEFT: an artist's impression of early Amerindian life.
ABOVE: Columbus meets an Amerindian chieftain.

images are in the museum of the Institute of Jamaica. There is also one in the small Arawak museum at Coyaba in Ocho Rios.

The Tainos were encouraged by their priests to believe that some *zemis* could speak, although this was exposed by the Spaniards as a hoax used to control the people. The priests were also the medicine men of the tribe, using herbs for treatment. The souls of the departed were believed to go to *coyaba*, a place of ease and rest where there were no droughts, hurricanes or sickness, and time was spent in feasting and dancing. The Tainos often buried their dead in pots in caves, where some of the best preserved skulls and examples of pottery have been found. ❏

SPANISH DISCOVERY AND COLONISATION

For 160 years after Columbus arrived, Jamaica remained a distant outpost of the Spanish Empire

"Jamaica, like many other of the West India Islands, is like a woman with a history. She has had her experiences, and has lived her life rapidly. She has enjoyed a fever of prosperity founded upon those incalculable treasures poured into her lap by the old-time buccaneer pirates. She has suffered earthquake, famine, pestilence, fire, and death: and she has been the home of a cruel and merciless slavery. Other countries have taken centuries to grow from their primitive life through the flower and fruit of prosperity into the seed-time of picturesque decrepitude. Jamaica has lived through it all in a few years."

– Howard Pyle, *Jamaica New and Old*, *New Monthly Magazine*, January 1890.

A s the 15th century drew to a close, Jamaica was still primitive, its years of hardship and glory still ahead. In Europe, meanwhile, civilised man was entering the Renaissance. One of the most outstanding figures of the age was the Genoese seafarer Christopher Columbus (1451–1506), the man who was to discover the New World.

On 3 August 1492, Columbus – in his flagship *Santa Maria*, accompanied by two caravels, the *Niña* and the *Pinta*, with a total crew of 90 – sailed from Palos de la Frontera, Spain, on his first great voyage. On 12 October, he landed on one of the islands of the Bahamas, today's Watling Island. In gratitude to the Lord for bringing him safely to port, Columbus named it San Salvador, or "Holy Saviour".

It was on his second voyage that Columbus discovered Jamaica. He first heard of the island of Xaymaca (an indigenous name of disputed meaning) from the Cuban Indians, who described it as "the land of the blessed gold". But Jamaica had no gold – a disappointment not

only to Columbus but also to those other adventurers and prospectors who followed him.

On 5 May 1494 Columbus arrived at St Ann's Bay, and named it Santa Gloria – "on account of the extreme beauty of its country",

according to his biographer, Samuel Eliot Morison (1887–1976). Columbus thought Jamaica itself "the fairest island that eyes have beheld... all full of valleys and fields and plains". But, finding the Amerindians hostile, he anchored off the port for the night, and the following day sailed down the coast to a harbour "shaped like a horse-shoe".

Here also the Amerindians were unfriendly, but Columbus was determined to land; he needed wood and water and a chance to repair his vessels. The islanders scattered before the advance of a fierce dog and the Spanish crossbow men, leaving some of their number killed and wounded on the beach. Columbus claimed

LEFT: the Columbus family contemplates the West Indies in an 18th-century engraving.
RIGHT: ships on Black River around 1830.

Jamaica in the name of his patron sovereigns, Ferdinand and Isabella of Spain. He called it "St Jago" or "Santiago" after his country's patron saint. For the rest of the admiral's stay the Amerindians regularly supplied him and his men with provisions, in exchange for trinkets and other trade goods.

Marooned in St Ann's Bay

On 9 May the fleet sailed westwards to Montego Bay – El Golfo de Buen Tiempo, as Columbus called it, "Fair Weather Gulf". He then continued his cruise along the Cuban coast to the north before crossing back to Jamaica

beset by hardship, hunger, doubts and sickness, abandoned by the Amerindians and deserted by many of his followers – some of whom even staged an abortive mutiny.

Eventually two of his company made the arduous sea journey in a small canoe to Hispaniola, where they managed to charter a caravel. Towards the end of June 1504 the little vessel arrived at St Ann's Bay, and the desperate year-long wait was at an end. On the 29th she left for Hispaniola with Columbus and the survivors of his crew, about 100 in all. In September, Columbus sailed for Spain. He was never to see the New World again.

to complete the exploration of this island.

Nine years later, on his fourth voyage, Columbus visited Jamaica again – this time in tragic circumstances. After he left the American mainland, it became clear that his two battered, worm-eaten caravels were not fit for the Atlantic crossing. He tried to make for Hispaniola but got no further than St Ann's Bay before the ships were stranded side by side, a bow's shot from the shore. With heavy hearts, the admiral and his company – including his young son Ferdinand and his brother Bartolomé – watched the vessels fill with water and settle for good in the soft sand of the bay.

Here Columbus was to spend 12 months,

Serious settlers

It was not until 1510 that colonists arrived in Jamaica, under the island's first Spanish governor, Juan de Esquivel. Sevilla la Nueva, or "New Seville", as they called their settlement in St Ann's Bay, was conceived on a large and not unimpressive scale. It included among the principal buildings a fort, a castle and a church. But the location, close to swamps, proved unhealthy; it was soon abandoned in favour of a new site on the south side of the island, in what is now Spanish Town.

Little survives today of New Seville. Finely carved stone panels, semi-columns, door jambs, friezes and other artefacts which have been found on the site are now in the possession of the Institute of Jamaica.

Spanish Town (the Villa de la Vega of the Spaniards) quickly became a centre of activity. In a convenient location – sufficiently near to two harbours and enjoying protection from direct sea attack – and with its healthy situation featuring an ample water supply and fertile surroundings, Spanish Town had attracted the colonists' attention.

A number of interesting accounts of the town

AMERINDIAN HERITAGE

Barbecue, hurricane, maize, canoe, tobacco, hammock, savannah, guava and the name Jamaica itself are all words that have originated from an Arawak Amerindian language.

today, having deteriorated well beyond repair.

The Spaniards enslaved the native Tainos, and so overworked and ill-treated them that in a short time they had all died out (*see page 28*). The process was doubtlessly aided by the introduction of European diseases to which they would have had little or no immunity. Upon the demise of the Amerindians the Spaniards began to import black slaves from Africa. The first of them arrived in 1517, the earliest ancestors of Jamaica's majority race today.

were written during the Spanish period. A Carmelite missionary, Antonio Vázquez de Espinosa, writing around 1628, says the site was "marvellously attractive… very well built and laid out". An unwelcome English visitor, Captain William Jackson, who plundered Spanish Town some 15 years later, thought it a fair town, consisting of 400 or 500 houses, five or six stately churches and chapels, and one monastery of Franciscan friars. Unfortunately, no Spanish buildings from that period remain

LEFT: King's House in Spanish Town.
ABOVE: work on and around the plantations was relentless.

A neglected outpost

Jamaica as a Spanish colony was largely a failure. Its main use to Spain was that of a supply base. In the early days of colonisation, men, horses, arms and food from here helped in the conquest of Cuba and much of the American mainland, but after that the island's significance waned until it sank to the position of an unimportant, badly governed and largely neglected outpost.

Almost nothing was done to develop the natural resources of Jamaica. The chief trades were the supply of fresh provisions to passing ships and the export of hides and lard to Havana and the mainland. In exchange the ships that touched here brought supplies of clothing, oil, wine, wheaten flour and a few luxury items.

The colonists devoted themselves chiefly to pastoral and agricultural pursuits. From Spain they brought all the familiar varieties of citrus (except grapefruit), and they carried the banana and plantain to Jamaica from the Canary Islands via Hispaniola. They also introduced cattle, horses and swine, which they kept in *hatos*, or ranches, on the open savanna. Chief among the *hatos* were Morante (the name lingers in Morant Bay), Liguanea (in lower St Andrew) and Guanaboa Vale (in St Catherine).

Roads in Spanish times were mostly bridle

paths. Settlements, with the exception of the capital, were scarcely better than townships. These included Caguaya (Passage Fort), Oristano (Bluefields), Las Chorreras (near Ocho Rios), Savanna-la-Mar and Puerto Antón (Port Antonio).

Strictly speaking, although the island was under the control of Spain, it was to some extent self-governing. The Spanish governor ruled with the aid of a *cabildo*, a council of nominated members. A strong governor ruled largely by himself; a weak one was controlled by the *cabildo*. A tactless governor quickly ran into trouble with Church authorities.

In fact, the Church played an important part in the life of the colony. There is still a Red Church Street and a White Church Street in Spanish Town, both named after Spanish chapels, as well as a Monk Street – a reminder of the dark-robed, sandalled figures who were once a familiar feature of the old town.

The end of Spanish control

By the last years of the Spanish occupation, internal strife had weakened the colony. The governors were not properly supported from home, and quarrels with the Church authorities undermined their control. Frequent attacks by pirates were another corrupting influence. These were not limited to Jamaica, but formed part of a general effort on the part of certain European nations to loosen Spain's grip on the region.

When Columbus discovered the New World, the Pope issued proclamations neatly dividing the Indies between Spain and Portugal, but it was not long before other European nations began to challenge the justice of this division;

THE DISAPPEARANCE OF THE AMERINDIANS

Within 50 years of the Spanish colonising the Greater Antilles, the race of Amerindian Tainos had died out. Those who had survived the initial gold rush, when they had been forced to produce a certain amount of gold (none was found in Jamaica) or be killed, were felled by the new European diseases such as smallpox and measles, or in despair committed suicide by eating the poisonous juice of the cassava.

The Spanish Crown forbade the enslavement of the Tainos, recognising them as a peaceful people, but permission was given to take the fearsome "Caribs", who they believed were cannibals (today this is largely considered to be a myth exaggerated by the Spanish to justify their ill-treatment of them) and past redemption. Nevertheless, the colonists provoked the Tainos to rebel and massacred or enslaved them just the same.

The Spanish colonies were divided into *encomiendas*, each large area under the charge of a settler, and the Amerindians were shared out between them as slave labour. Overworked, often to the point of death, they were unable to tend their own crops in their villages, and whole families succumbed to malnutrition and disease. Even the lifelong efforts of Friar Bartolomé de las Casas (1474–1566) to return their freedom could not save them.

"I should like to see the clause of Adam's will that excludes me from a share of the world," declared Francis I, King of France.

Rival European nations

Rivalries among nations in Europe spread to distant lands, and from the mid-1500s to the end of the 18th century the rich countries of the Caribbean were the scene of international and commercial competition. As early as 1506 French ships appeared in the Caribbean, attacking small Spanish settlements and capturing vessels. In 1555 the Jamaican colonists chased two French ships away. But other Frenchmen largely because of their rugged terrain and fierce Carib inhabitants. The British established a foothold in St Kitts in 1622, moving slowly to build settlements in Nevis, Montserrat and Antigua. But the biggest British prize was Barbados, claimed for England in 1625.

The French were not far behind, forming a rival encampment in St Kitts and beginning the colonisation of Martinique and Guadeloupe in 1635, while the Dutch added to the inter-European competition by helping themselves to islands such as Curaçao and St Maarten.

Motivated partly by Protestant anti-Catholicism but mostly by old-fashioned greed, the

followed, as did Dutch, Italian, Portuguese and English, all bent on trade and plunder. In 1596 the Elizabethan adventurer Sir Anthony Shirley raided the island. More raids by English forces took place in 1603, 1640 and 1643.

Meanwhile, the rival European powers were also putting down more permanent roots, challenging Spain's increasingly shaky monopoly in the region. The Spanish had long been indifferent to the smaller islands of the Eastern Caribbean – although they claimed them –

new colonising nations began to eye Spain's larger island possessions. The Spanish made attempts to drive the interlopers away, but traders from London, Bordeaux or Amsterdam proved popular with the colonists in places such as Cuba and Jamaica which depended on irregular supply fleets from Spain. Smuggling was rife, and Spain, battered by wars in Europe, began to look vulnerable.

The question was: how long would it be before some foreign power attempted to take and hold Jamaica? The answer came on 10 May 1655, when a large English expeditionary force sailed into Caguaya (today's Passage Fort), spelling the end of Spanish rule in Jamaica. ❑

LEFT: a romantic interpretation of Columbus.
ABOVE: merchant ships like these in Port Royal harbour were a common sight in Jamaican waters.

THE BRITISH TAKEOVER

The English captured Jamaica almost as an afterthought,
but it was to become the jewel in the British colonial crown

The English expeditionary force which captured Jamaica in 1655 had been sent out by the Lord Protector, Oliver Cromwell (1599–1658), as part of a plan known as his "Western Design", aimed against Spain's power and trade monopoly. Cromwell had hastily assembled a fleet under Admiral William Penn and General Robert Venables. He also appointed a council of three commissioners to accompany the important expedition.

But the omens for success were not favourable. "No worse prepared and equipped expedition ever left the English shores," wrote Sir Charles Firth, the Cromwellian scholar, "and the consequences of these initial mistakes and negligences were all aggravated by the mistakes and quarrels of those charged with its command." Ruffians and thieves made up the majority of the troops, with a sprinkling of good soldiers, seasoned and better principled.

Sailing from Portsmouth at the end of December 1654, the expedition stopped first at Barbados to raise levies from the plantations and take on provisions. In the Leeward Islands additional recruits were also signed on. Then the party sailed for Hispaniola on its great mission to attack the capital city of Santo Domingo.

But there the expedition met disaster. Its forces were roundly defeated, a complete massacre being averted only by the landing of a party of sailors to cover their flight back to the ships. As it was, a third of them were killed.

The assault on Spanish Town

Fearful of Cromwell's rage at the failure at Santo Domingo, the British decided to attack another Spanish settlement. Jamaica, known to be thinly populated and weakly defended, was chosen as the target for invasion.

On 10 May 1655, the fleet of 38 ships and about 8,000 men anchored off Caguaya, later to be known as Passage Fort, the landing-place

for Spanish Town. A few shots fired into the little fort dispersed the defenders, and soon the English flag was waving above its walls. The expedition commanders may have had plans to attack some stronger place from here later; however, Jamaica was to prove the end of Cromwell's ambitious "Western Design".

An early opportunity to occupy Spanish Town itself, the capital, was missed. Combined with a further delay by the Spaniards, on the plea of considering surrender terms, this gave most of the inhabitants the opportunity to escape with their valuables to the north side of Jamaica and on to Cuba. When the English finally marched into the town they found it empty. Angry and disappointed, they destroyed much of the place, burning the churches and melting the bells down to make shot.

Confident that they would in time recover the island, the fleeing Spaniards had freed and armed their slaves and left them behind in the trackless interior. The plan was that these freed

---

LEFT: portrait of Oliver Cromwell at the time of England's takeover of Jamaica.
RIGHT: an English cannon guards Spanish Town.

men would harry the invaders with guerilla warfare until an army for the Spanish reconquest could be collected. Instead, these people and their descendants later won fame as the redoubtable Maroons.

Although disappointed over the Santo Domingo fiasco, Cromwell decided to make the most of the new colony, the only non-Spanish one in the Greater Antilles, offering very attractive terms in the way of land grants and other requisites to "such as shall transplant themselves to Jamaica".

> **UNPREPARED FOR BATTLE**
>
> "... little wine with much water, the one losing its proper strength and vigour and the other thereby little bettered" – a ship's captain describing the expeditionary force sent to Hispaniola and Jamaica.

D'Oyley offered Ysasi honourable surrender terms, but received in reply a jar of sweetmeats and a courteous refusal.

The battle that took place on 27 June made amends for the failure at Santo Domingo. More than 300 Spaniards were killed, and valuable supplies of food and arms were captured, together with the Spanish royal standard and 10 colours. It was the most important battle ever fought in Jamaica, and it put an end to Spanish hopes of reconquest, although the war was to drag on

The Battle of Jamaica

Meanwhile, under the courageous and determined Governor Cristóbal Arnaldo de Ysasi, stout but unsuccessful efforts were made by the displaced Spanish to recapture the island. The decisive battle was fought in June 1658. A large force consisting mainly of Mexican contingents landed at Rio Nuevo and dug in behind a strong fort, armed with cannon, on a cliff near the river's west bank.

The English commander, Colonel Edward D'Oyley, proved equal to the challenge. As soon as news of the landing reached him he called out 750 of his best officers and men. They sailed around the island to the attack.

for two more years. Ysasi held out in the mountains to which he had fled, always hoping for the relieving force which never arrived. With his eventual escape by canoe to Cuba, all Spanish influence in Jamaica ended, and the island was officially ceded to the English Crown under the Treaty of Madrid in 1670. Apart from the Seville carvings and some names of places and rivers, almost no visible traces of Spanish occupation are left.

The defeat of the Spaniards removed the immediate danger of foreign invasion. But in August 1660 the threat of internal rebellion arose in the form of a mutiny of troops led by two colonels, Raymond and Tyson, the latter in command of a regiment quartered at Guanaboa Vale, 9 miles (14 km) from Spanish Town.

The reasons for the mutiny are not clear. Dislike of D'Oyley and his iron-handed methods played a part, as did rivalry between those who favoured the monarchy and those who preferred the Commonwealth. But the root cause may have been impatience with the continuation of military rule and a longing to settle as colonists.

Court martial

D'Oyley acted with characteristic promptness to meet this new danger. He tried fair words at first. When these failed, he brought reinforce-

who were to guide the destiny of the island.

It is ironic that D'Oyley's instructions conferred, in effect, the very privileges which the rebellious colonels had tried to grasp too soon. He was ordered to release the army and encourage planters, merchants and traders. Civil government was established, and law courts set up. This was the groundwork that in time would lead Jamaica to become one of the most valuable possessions in the New World.

Under D'Oyley and his successors, Jamaica gradually elevated itself to relative prosperity by the early years of the 18th century. Despite war conditions in the Caribbean and some

ments into Guanaboa Vale and persuaded the troops to hand over their leaders and disperse in exchange for a complete pardon. A court martial was quickly convened, and the colonels were condemned to death. Without delay, they were executed in full view of both the government and their troops.

News of the restoration of the monarchy in England arrived soon after. Within a year Colonel D'Oyley was appointed Jamaica's governor – the first of more than 60 administrators

serious internal difficulties, island-born proprietors rose in power and wealth. Politics and the island economy were put on a sound footing as sugar production increased rapidly and cattle breeding, logging and coffee cultivation proved more and more profitable.

The British abandoned Spanish Town and shifted their colonial government to the Liguanea Plain with its excellent access to the sea. It was here that they moulded King's Town into a proper English port city. Kingston, as it came to be called, increased dramatically in size and importance, with good entertainment contributing to a lavish lifestyle for the privileged rich. By 1872 it was the capital of Jamaica.   ❏

LEFT: the British flag flies over Kingston's King Street.
ABOVE: an 18th-century cartoon depicting the supposed lifestyle of expatriates.

PIRATES AND BUCCANEERS

The 17th century was the golden age of piracy
in the Caribbean, and Jamaica's Port Royal was its capital

Although the war with Spain, sparked by Cromwell's "Western Design", ended with the restoration of King Charles II to the English throne, the fighting never really ceased in the West Indies. Jamaica, as it turned out, was even better situated than Hispaniola for harassing the Spaniards. Early on, official English encouragement was given to the buccaneers – a rough, wild and ruthless collection of sea-rovers – to continue hostilities against Spain's West Indian possessions. They played a role of the first importance in the history of Jamaica, and of the Caribbean as a whole.

An odd lot, these early rebels included runaway bondsmen, castaways, escaped criminals and political and religious refugees, who had gravitated in time towards the small, rocky island of Tortuga, off the northern coast of Hispaniola, where they set up a sort of international port. Their early activities were limited to hunting the wild pigs and cattle in the forests of western Hispaniola, to provide meat, hides and tallow. These they bartered to passing ships for ammunition and rough stores. They usually worked in pairs, the partners sharing everything. Armed with knives and long-barrelled muskets, they tracked their quarry with the help of dogs. From their method of curing the meat on a wooden frame called a *boucan* (the French adaptation of an Amerindian word) they earned the name *boucaniers* – buccaneers.

Buccaneers unite

Spain, of course, resented their presence on Spanish soil and hunted them relentlessly from the Hispaniolan forests. Driven by both desperation and the realisation that survival lay in unity, this scattered, ragged bunch of men banded together as the "Confederacy of the Brethren of the Coast" and took to the sea. At first they used whatever craft were available –

PRECEDING PAGES: Captain Henry Morgan blasts a Spanish armada.
LEFT: Morgan, the vaunted governor and buccaneer.
RIGHT: the execution of a bandit, Three-fingered Jack.

chiefly canoes – but as they seized Spanish ships by surprise attacks, their fleet soon swelled in size. With captured guns and arms they fortified Tortuga. Each success brought new recruits, and the stronger and bolder they grew, the farther they raided.

These buccaneers were a hardy breed.

Immune or seasoned to the climate and its ills, they were ruthless, fearless and – except in their communal dealings – lawless. As Brethren they were welded together by a stern code of discipline which accounted for much of their success. They usually sailed under strict articles, the first of which was: "No prey, no pay."

All plunder went into a common pool to be divided according to the share-out scales and disability pensions laid down in the articles. The loss of a finger, for example, rated a payment of 100 pieces-of-eight or one slave, while compensation for the loss of both eyes was 1,000 pieces-of-eight or 10 slaves.

Sir Thomas Modyford began his term as

governor of Jamaica in June 1664 by suppressing buccaneering, but the outbreak of the Second Dutch War in the following March caused an about-face in policy. The hard-pressed Admiralty could not spare a fleet for the West Indies, and its defence was placed in the hands of the wild Brethren. Historian Edward Long wrote later: "It is to the Bucaniers that we owe the possession of Jamaica at this hour."

In Port Royal the buccaneers found a ready market for their Spanish loot, facilities for their vessels and ample opportunities for amusement, and they flocked there in increasing numbers. "Such of these Pirates", wrote the historian

man, the buccaneers and Port Royal were to reach the pinnacle of their infamy.

Morgan – whose later career was crowned by a knighthood, the governorship of Jamaica, and other official appointments – started humbly enough. Born about 1635, the son of a Welsh land-owning farmer, he went to Barbados, possibly as an indentured servant, and then made his way to Tortuga where he joined the Brethren and became Governor Modyford's strongest ally. The ruthless, resourceful buccaneer leader was the one man who could hold the wild Brethren together and direct their main efforts towards the defence of the island.

John Esquemeling, "are found who will spend two or three thousand pieces-of-eight in one night… I saw one of them give unto a common strumpet five hundred pieces-of-eight only that he might see her naked."

Nourished by such wealth, Port Royal grew and prospered at such a rate that within a decade and a half it had earned the title of the richest – and wickedest – city in the world.

Sir Henry Morgan

It was about this time that a new buccaneer-captain appeared on the scene and instantly claimed the limelight. Under the leadership of Henry Morgan, a tough, thick-set young Welsh-

The sacking of Puerto Principe (near Camagüey, Cuba), Porto Bello (Panama) and Maracaibo (Venezuela) stand out as incredible milestones in Morgan's equally incredible career. That he was a hater of Spaniards, not averse to extremes of violence and debauchery, is clear in this description by Esquemeling of the sacking of Porto Bello: "Having shut up all the Soldiers and Officers, as prisoners, into one room, they instantly set fire unto the powder (whereof they found great quantity) and blew up the whole Castle into the air, with all the Spaniards that were within. This being done, they pursued the course of their victory, falling upon the City… They fell to eating and drinking, after their usual manner, that is to say, committing in both these things all manner of debauchery and excess. These two vices were immediately followed by many insolent actions of Rape and Adultery committed upon many very honest women, as well married as virgins…"

Morgan's crowning achievement was the destruction of Spain's supreme New World city of Panama. Peace had previously been sealed between Spain and England by the Treaty of Madrid, and Morgan's exploits –

PIRATE POWER

The pirates marauding throughout the Caribbean were hated and feared by most people as "lewd and wicked men". But several were actually cross-dressing women, living their lives as men.

port. On 7 June 1692 a violent earthquake broke under the town, plunging the better part of it, together with Morgan's grave, beneath the sea.

Meanwhile the Jamaican government had been cracking down on buccaneering, which had achieved its end and was now going out of fashion. A decision was made to abandon the stricken port and found a new settlement, King's Town, soon to be known as Kingston, across the harbour. But in spite of the earthquake, and subsequent disastrous

which shattered the treaty – earned both himself and Modyford the deep displeasure of their monarch in England. Eventually, however, the two daring and far-sighted friends were cleared of all disgrace and reunited in Jamaica, Morgan as governor and Modyford as chief justice.

Although Morgan was a rich landowner in his own right, his spiritual home and favourite stamping-ground remained Port Royal. His body was entombed here in 1688, and his death presaged the end of Port Royal as a buccaneering

LEFT: a later artist's impression of Anne Bonney and Mary Read taking a break from pillaging.
ABOVE: Kingston in the 19th century.

fires and hurricanes, Port Royal survived to become an important naval station.

The French invade

As a prelude to 100 years of wars and alarms, the 17th century closed with the only real invasion attempt that Jamaica was to know. Taking advantage of the damage and confusion caused by the Port Royal earthquake, a large French force under Admiral Jean du Casse descended on the eastern part of the island and ravaged the countryside in true and terrible buccaneer fashion. But at Carlisle Bay, Clarendon, where the next landing was made, Jamaica's scanty but gallant forces engaged the invaders and killed 700 of them. Although the island was saved, it suffered severely from the attack. About 100 settlers had been killed or wounded, scores of plantations burnt, 50 sugar works destroyed and some 1,300 slaves as well as quantities of loot carted away.

The war petered out in September 1697 with the Treaty of Ryswick. Spain recognised French claims to the western part of Hispaniola, and renamed its part Santo Domingo. Today the island is still shared by two independent states, French-speaking Haiti and the Spanish-speaking Dominican Republic.

The 18th century was only two years old

when the War of the Spanish Succession broke out in Europe, and England, The Netherlands and the Holy Roman Empire allied themselves against France and Spain. Although Europe was the main theatre of war, the Caribbean saw some naval activity, including Admiral John Benbow's memorable engagement of a French fleet under the redoubtable Admiral du Casse. On 19 August 1702, Benbow, in the 90-gun *Breda,* sighted du Casse's squadron off Santa Marta, Colombia. The ensuing six-day battle, though indecisive, was notable for Benbow's obstinate courage in carrying on the running fight in spite of the desertion of four of his captains. At one point the gallant admiral engaged

the entire French squadron single-handed and succeeded in recapturing a British galley. But at length, with the *Breda* badly damaged, his own right leg shattered by chainshot, and his captains refusing to engage the enemy, Benbow was forced to return to Port Royal. On arrival he immediately court-martialled the defecting captains, two of whom were sentenced to be shot. He himself died of his wounds at the old port and was buried in Kingston Parish Church, where his tomb may still be seen.

Notorious pirates

The war was brought to an end in 1713 by the Treaty of Utrecht, and Britain was awarded France's *asiento*, or contract, for the supply of slaves to Spanish New World settlements. Jamaica quickly became the entrepôt for the trade, most of the slaves being shipped from here to Spanish ports in locally owned vessels.

But all was not well with the island. Pursuing its aggressive policy, the House of Assembly was constantly at loggerheads with the governors representing the Crown, especially over money matters. Epidemics raged, violent hurricanes caused grievous loss of life and property, and troubles with the Maroons added to the general confusion.

So did attacks by pirates, who were now plaguing the Caribbean in growing numbers. Coastal vessels were constantly being molested and isolated plantations plundered. On one occasion Nicholas Brown, the "Grand Pirate", and his companion Christopher Winter burnt down a house near the coast in St Ann with 16 people locked inside. A reward of £500 for his capture was earned by one John Drudge, who captured Brown after a fight on one of the South Cays of Cuba. Brown died of his wounds on the way to Jamaica, but Drudge, not to be cheated of the reward, cut off the pirate's head, pickled it in a keg of rum, and produced it in Jamaica in support of his claim.

Among the pirates who flourished at this time was Edward Teach, better known as "Blackbeard", believed by some to have been born in Jamaica. He was eventually killed in a sea fight off North Carolina in 1718. Captain Charles Vane, another notorious pirate of this period, was captured after a successful career of robbery and murder and brought to Port Royal, where he was hanged on Gallows Point. But perhaps the most romantic of the lot was Captain

Jack Rackham, called "Calico Jack" because of his penchant for calico underwear. He started his career as a member of Vane's crew, rising to be its leader.

After terrorising the Caribbean for more than two years, he made the mistake of lingering on Jamaica's north coast during November 1720. News of his presence at Ocho Rios reached Governor Sir Nicholas Lawes, who immediately dispatched a Captain Barnet and a swift sloop in pursuit. Barnet found Rackham anchored in Negril Bay,

BLACKBEARD

A powerful giant of a man, Edward Teach, otherwise known as Blackbeard, is said to have struck terror into the hearts of his enemies by going into action with flaming matches plaited into his flowing black beard and hair.

body was squeezed into an iron frame and hung off Port Royal, on a sandy islet still called Rackham's Cay, as a grim warning to other pirates.

The War of Jenkins' Ear

But the pirates, of course, were not the only people raising their pistols at sea. Old rivalries between Britain, Spain and France meant almost continuous conflict in the Caribbean.

One of the more notable tiffs of the time was the so-called War of Jenkins' Ear, which broke

enjoying a rum-punch party. After a short fight he captured the pirate and his crew.

At the trial at the Court of Vice-Admiralty in Spanish Town, the startling discovery was made that two of Rackham's toughest crew members were women. Both Anne Bonney and Mary Read were condemned to death, but Bonney managed to escape punishment, and Read died in prison, of fever, before sentence could be carried out. "Calico Jack" was executed. His

LEFT: Edward Teach, known as "Blackbeard", started his pirate career in Jamaica.
ABOVE: Sir George Rodney bombards the French fleet on 12 April 1782.

out in 1739 over the old argument of illegal trade. The stopping of British ships and ill-treatment of their crews by Spanish *guarda costas*, patrol vessels whose captains claimed the right of search, led to reprisals by the British.

A seaman named Robert Jenkins added fuel to the fire. He had been captured by a *guarda costa* whose captain, he said, had slashed off one of his ears and told him to take it to England as a warning of the fate awaiting others who broke Spain's trade laws. Jenkins appeared before a committee of the House of Commons in London and waved a shrivelled leathery object which he claimed was his ear. Those in the Caribbean who knew Jenkins to be a scallywag insisted that he had both his ears safely under his wig – but the clamour he created in Parliament was more than enough to incite a declaration of war against Spain.

The war itself was not a happy one for the British. Admiral "Old Grog" Vernon (1684–1757) mounted one disastrous campaign after another from Jamaica, costing the lives of some 20,000 men.

> ### OLD GROG
>
> Admiral Edward Vernon was called "Old Grog" because of the grogram coat he wore. When he ordered the sailors' rum ration to be diluted with water in 1740, to reduce drunkenness, the drink became known as "grog".

The peace which followed the Treaty of Aix-la-Chapelle in 1748 was a fragile one, and by

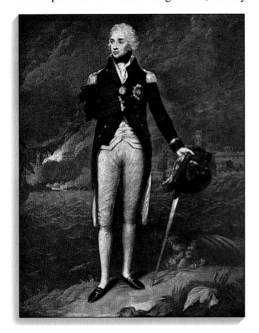

1756 the old rivals were embroiled in the Seven Years War. This ended with the Treaty of Paris in 1763 and the loss of almost every French West Indian island to the British.

Tensions were running high in Jamaica in the late 18th century. The famous bandit Three-fingered Jack caused alarm everywhere. Fires and hurricanes ravaged the island, taking a heavy toll on life and property; a storm in October 1780 destroyed the town of Savanna-la-Mar.

Of more long-term effect was the War of American Independence (1775–83). Britain's West Indian colonies did not sympathise with the motherland over this war, and, the Jamaica House of Assembly made its sentiments abundantly clear in a petition to the king, justifying the actions of the American colonists. France and Spain, meanwhile, were anxious to avenge their losses, and by 1782 only Jamaica, Barbados and Antigua remained in British hands.

Rodney saves the day

The Comte de Grasse, Admiral of France, joined forces with the Spanish and launched an invasion of Jamaica in April 1782, but they were intercepted by Admiral George Rodney on 9 April off the island of Dominica.

In a three-day running engagement Rodney skillfully manoeuvred his 36-ship fleet to break the enemy lines near the tiny Iles des Saintes, between Dominica and Guadeloupe. To this day, the conflict is remembered as "The Battle of the Saints".

When the victorious Admiral Rodney sailed into Kingston harbour with his spoils of war in tow, the island went wild with jubilation. The splendid French flagship *Ville de Paris*, with the count himself aboard as prisoner, was in British hands. Rodney was honoured by the Crown with a barony and a pension of £2,000 a year. Today a monumental statue of Rodney, sculpted by John Bacon, dominates the square in Jamaica's Spanish Town. The statue is flanked by two of de Grasse's cannons.

Toward the end of the 18th century, the youthful Horatio Nelson visited Jamaica. While awaiting the arrival of his ship, the *Hinchinbrooke*, he was put in command of the batteries at Port Royal's Fort Charles in preparation for a threatened French invasion which never materialised. Later he led an expedition from Jamaica to Nicaragua; it failed when yellow fever wiped out two-thirds of his forces.

But Nelson went on to become one of the greatest of all British naval commanders, and his residence in Jamaica is commemorated by a marble tablet fixed to the wall of Fort Charles. It reads:

IN THIS PLACE DWELT HORATIO NELSON
You who tread his footprints
Remember his glory. ❏

LEFT: British naval commander Horatio, Lord Nelson.
RIGHT: France's Comte de Grasse surrenders to Britain's Admiral Rodney (left): an 18th-century engraving.

Hamilton delin.   Thornton sculp.

The French Admiral COUNT De GRASSE Delivering his Sword to ADMIRAL (now LORD) RODNEY,
(Being a more Exact Representation of that Memorable Event than is given in any other Work of this kind)
On Board the Ville de Paris, after being Defeated by that Gallant Commander on the Glorious 12.th of April 1782.
— in the West Indies —

JOHNNY NEW-COME in the ISLAND of JAMAICA.

London Published by Will.ᵐ Holland, N.º50 Oxford Street Oct.ᵣ 1.1800.

Johnny New-come.

Johny accustom'd, and believes himself Seasond

Thinks all Mosquitoes, and calls em Sand-flies.

Feels his Pulse and trembles.

Ussumbequa shifts a Train of Ammonial Urine.

Johny feels Quaimy, and begins to cume out.

Johny Poor, of Ammonial Urine

Johny glumms the Planters.Agent relating as Game Johny Cropsick, and puffs feeling's away.

John gets sick, plays the Devil, with Quafhie.

John fruits for N.º Catskill Respects his Bill.

John writes to the Packet a State of his case

Blung Cook, Quamy, and Quaco he comes out.

Johny ravis, spews, and demonstrates.

Th.ᵉ Colonel feels the Pulse of N.º Commercial Makes his head.

John puts Johnny, in a hubaricum or the time of Morgan Rattlecher.

Johns hearts a lone of Hair says John thinks himself better

Th.ᵉ Follow Glass of Three, gives Johny a moderate rich

The Soul ʇ Body of John are consigned to th.ᵉ Pit.

Johny takes himself for the Corn.

Taking of John is packed up for the Corn.

The last Scene's Scene come.

JOHNNY NEWCOME IN LOVE IN THE WEST INDIES.

Smitten with the charms of Mimbo Wampo, a sable Venus, daughter of Wampo Wampo, King of the Silver Sand Hills in Congo.

Delicately declaring his Love to the amiable Mimbo Wampo, while she is picking his Dagoes.

"You tub me Masfa' eh eh! ?"

Consulting Old Mumbo Jumbo the Oby Man, how to get possession of the charming Mimbo Wampo.

"Leb me alone for dat Masfa'."

A few of the Hopeful young Newcomes

1	2	3
4	5	6
7	8	9

M.r Newcome taking leave of his Ladies & Pickaninees, previous to his departure from Prying Pan Island, to graze a title in his Native Land.

M.r Newcome happy. — Mimbo made Queen of the Harem.

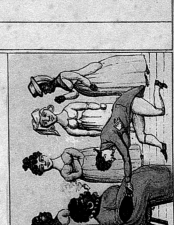

1. Lucretia Diana Newcome, a delicate Girl very much like her Mother, only that she has a great antipathy to a pipe, and cannot bear the smell of Rum. - 2 Penelope Mimbo Newcome. -
3. Quaw Dush Newcome prodigiously like his father. - 4. Cuffy Cato Newcome. - 5. Cæsar Cudjoe Newcome. - 6. Hslaw Quashebah Newcome. - 7. Aristida Juba Newcome. - 8. Hector Sammy Newcome. -
9. Hannibal Pompy Wampo Newcome.
a child of great spirit, can already Damnme, Liberty and Equality and promises fair to be the Toujours of his Country.

Published April 1808. by William Holland, Cockspur Street, London.

TO BE SOLD & LET

BY PUBLIC AUCTION,

On MONDAY the 18th of MAY. 1829,

UNDER THE TREES.

FOR SALE,
THE THREE FOLLOWING

SLAVES,

viz.

HANNIBAL, about 30 Years old, an excellent House Servant, of Good Character.
WILLIAM, about 35 Years old, a Labourer.
NANCY, an excellent House Servant and Nurse.

The MEN Belonging to "LEECH'S" Estate, and the WOMAN to Mrs. D. SMIT

TO BE LET,

On the usual conditions of the Hirer finding them in Food, Clothing and Medical ance,

THE FOLLOWING

MALE and FEMALE

SLAVES,

OF GOOD CHARACTERS.

ROBERT BAGLEY, about 20 Years old, a good House Servant.
WILLIAM BAGLEY, about 18 Years old, a Labourer.
JOHN ARMS, about 18 Years old.
JACK ANTONIA, about 40 Years old, a Labourer.
PHILIP, an Excellent Fisherman.
HARRY, about 27 Years old, a good House Servant.
LUCY, a Young Woman of good Character, used to House Work and the Nursery.
ELIZA, an Excellent Washerwoman.
CLARA, an Excellent Washerwoman.
FANNY, about 14 Years old, House Servant.
SARAH, about 14 Years old, House Servant.

Also for Sale, at Eleven o'Clock,

Fine Rice, Gram, Paddy, Books, Muslins, Needles, Pins, Ribbons, &c. &c.

AT ONE O'CLOCK, THAT CELEBRATED ENGLISH HORSE

BLUCHER,

CRDAW NO. 12 THE SLAVE TRADE AND ITS ABOLITION — ADDISON PRINTER GOVERNMENT OFFICE. — PRINTED IN GREAT BRITAIN

THE PLANTATION ERA

Dogged for a while by Maroon warfare, "King Sugar" ruled in the
18th century, but its might faded with the struggle for slave emancipation

Not long after the English takeover of Jamaica in 1655, one of the commissioners – Major-General Robert Sedgwick – predicted that the Maroons would become "a thorn in the sides of the English". His words proved truer than perhaps even he himself expected.

These former slaves who had escaped to the wild mountain country, and earned the name *cimarrón*, Spanish for "wild" or "untamed", entrenched themselves there for centuries, even developing a culture of their own.

As the island became more settled, and English plantations spread further inland, the Maroons found it easier to swoop from the hills at night, set fire to the fields and steal cattle and other stock. Runaway slaves from the new plantations swelled their numbers and gave them greater confidence. In 1663 they ignored an offer of land and full freedom to every Maroon who surrendered to authorities, and for the next 76 years irregular warfare resulted in government expenditure of nearly £250,000 and the passing of 44 Acts of the Assembly.

The First Maroon War

In time the original Maroons settled chiefly in the eastern and northern parts of the island. In 1690, however, the Clarendon slaves – consisting mainly of Coromantees, an extremely brave and warlike people from Africa's Gold Coast – rebelled and escaped into the woods. Led by a general named Cudjoe, they joined forces with the Maroons and launched a campaign known as the First Maroon War. Cudjoe's brothers, Accompong and Johnny, carried the war in the west, and sub-chiefs Quao and Cuffee controlled affairs in the east.

Concentrated on the northern slopes of the Blue Mountains and in the forested interior, including the weird and trackless Cockpit

---

PRECEDING PAGES: William Holland's biting Johnny Newcome cartoons of 1800.
LEFT: a sign typical of pre-emancipation Jamaica.
RIGHT: Maroon chief Cudjoe makes peace.

Country, the Maroons developed guerrilla warfare. Skilled in woodcraft and familiar with the untracked forests, they avoided open fights. Instead, disguised from head to foot with leaves and tree boughs, they preferred ambush. What's more, it was almost impossible to surprise them in their settlements. Keen-eyed lookouts spotted

approaching forces hours before their arrival, and spread the warning by means of an *abeng*, a cow's-horn bugle.

British troops, unaccustomed to the country and climate, suffered heavily in their early clashes with the Maroons. But as more and more troops were thrown into the campaign, including Mosquito Coast Indians, tracker dogs and companies of *mestizos* and free blacks, the tide began to turn. The pivotal point may have come with the successful storming of Nanny Town, the stronghold of Queen Nanny and her Windward Maroons, high in the vast wilderness of the Blue Mountains. The town was destroyed and never rebuilt, and to this day the site is believed to be haunted by the ghosts of those who died in the bloody engagement.

Pressured on all sides and faced with starvation, as most of their "provision grounds" had been systematically destroyed, the Maroons agreed to listen to surrender terms. The English commissioned a Colonel Guthrie to seek out the great old warrior Cudjoe in his Cockpit Country hideout and conclude a treaty of peace. This was achieved on 1 March 1739, under a cotton tree amid a cluster of Maroon

> ### KEEPING THE PEACE
>
> Under the terms of the peace treaty which ended the First Maroon War, two white men, named by the governor, had to live permanently with the Maroons to maintain friendly contact.

hostilities against the British. They were to reject asylum pleas from runaway slaves, helping instead to recapture them in exchange for a reward, and they were to assist the government as necessary in suppressing local uprisings or foreign invasions.

A similar treaty was concluded with Quao, chief of the Maroons left in the Blue Mountains, and more than 50 years of peace were to follow.

The first settlers in the West Indies had concerned themselves with tropical crops which

huts at the entrance of the passage to Petty River Bottom in the Cockpit.

Under the terms of the treaty, the Maroons were guaranteed full freedom and liberty, and were allotted 1,500 acres (610 hectares) of land between Trelawny Town and the Cockpits. Cudjoe was appointed chief commander in Trelawny Town, and his successors were named in order, beginning with his two brothers, Accompong and Johnny. The chief was empowered to impose any punishment he regarded as fitting for crimes committed by his own people, except the death sentence; these cases had to be referred to a government judge. The Maroons, on their part, were to cease all

could easily be sold in Europe or North America. Tobacco, indigo and cocoa all achieved modest success, but sugar turned out to be the most profitable of all.

When sugar was king

The African slave trade to the West Indies grew out of the need for a large labour force for sugar production. At the same time the small-scale farmers started to disappear as ever-larger areas of land came into the hands of a few powerful and extremely rich sugar planters with their armies of slaves.

The English first started the systematic cultivation of sugar cane in Barbados in 1640. So profitable was the crop that within 10 years the wealth of the planters had multiplied 20-fold, and the slave population was more than 20,000.

The capture of Jamaica opened up a piece of land over 26 times larger than Barbados. Governor Sir Thomas Modyford, upon his appointment in 1664, promptly set about establishing a sound footing for Jamaica's sugar industry. It grew prodigiously: by 1673 there were 57 estates, and another 66 years later the island had 430. Jamaica was on its way to becoming the world's single largest producer of sugar.

During their 18th-century heyday the West Indies "sugar colonies" were extremely valu-

the planters liked to make a great show of their riches, especially in Europe. Such displays strengthened belief in the great wealth of the sugar colonies.

Slaves strike back

Despite this ostentation, a spectre of fear walked the sugar estates day and night. Eighteenth-century plantation life was founded on force, but despite the tyranny which held him in bondage, the slave did not accept his lot without a struggle. Whenever he saw a way the slave rebelled, killing his white masters and destroying their hated plantations. Many African

able. They were fiercely fought over in every war and fiercely bargained for at every peace conference. For a while, the British West Indies actually had more political influence with the Crown than did all 13 of the American mainland colonies.

The ambition of most planters was to be absentee proprietors, living in Europe in luxury on their estate profits and leaving the cares and troubles of management to paid attorneys and overseers. Generous, hospitable and hearty,

LEFT: Maroons demonstrate guerrilla tactics as they prepare for an ambush on an estate in 1796.
ABOVE: slaves toiling on a West Indian sugar plantation.

blacks did not even wait until they had arrived in the new land to start their resistance; slave-trading voyages often ended in failure because of an uprising among the slaves.

In the early days of the slave trade, Africans shipped to the West Indies were mainly prisoners of war or criminals, bought from local chiefs in exchange for European goods. But as the slave traffic increased, other means had to be found to maintain the supply. African tribal wars were stirred up, for no other reason than to replenish the supply of prisoners who could later be sold as slaves. Stragglers were captured from neighbouring villages for the same purpose, and regular manhunting raids were organised by tribes with the help of white hunters. Slaves so taken were usually chained to one another and brutally driven to the coast, where they were stored in "factories" – large fortified castles built especially for the purpose – until the slave ships arrived for the dreaded "Middle Passage" to the West Indies.

Lasting from 6 to 12 weeks, the Middle Passage was perhaps the most dreadful of all experiences a slave endured. On arrival he was put ashore, exhibited and auctioned to planters and local dealers. The price range normally varied from £25 to £75 (US$40–120). Of the tens of thousands of black Africans imported into Jamaica during the 18th century, about 5,000 were retained each year as slaves. The rest were re-exported.

Life on the plantations

The majority of plantation slaves were *predial* (field workers); others did domestic duties in the Great Houses and overseers' residences as cooks, maids, butlers and grooms. Domestic service was generally much lighter than field labour under the driver's lash, and domestic slaves dreaded being transferred to the fields.

Punishment was a regular part of estate life. A planter could do much as he liked with his slaves. In time, a revision of slave laws brought

JAMAICAN SUGAR ESTATES

Villages in themselves, the large Jamaican sugar estates consisted of overseers' houses and offices; the sugar works and mills; boiling houses, curing houses and still houses; the stables which housed the grinding cattle; lodging for the white book-keepers; workshops for the blacksmiths, carpenters and coopers; and streets of houses for the slaves.

On rising ground – usually some distance away from the sugar works – the planters built their great houses. Constructed of finely cut stone blocks and seasoned timber, with handsome carved woodwork and highly polished floors, they set the elegant style of the day.

stricter controls, but life was still brutal, as the masters believed that only by terrorism could the slaves, who greatly outnumbered them, be prevented from rising and killing them.

The slaves were given patches of land on which to grow their own yams, potatoes, plantains and other foodstuffs. They worked their "provision grounds" in the few free hours allowed daily, producing almost all the food they needed to survive. They sold their surplus produce in Sunday markets, earning a little extra money which they hoped might in time be sufficient to buy their freedom. A planter could set a slave free, either in his own lifetime or by his will.

The lot of a slave, dependent as it was on the whims and fancies of others, could be terrible indeed. But he wasn't alone in his struggle for rights. Among his friends were the early church missionaries – first the Moravians and later the Wesleyan Methodists and the Baptists. They taught the slave Christianity, did what they could to protect him from cruelty, and later took part in the struggle for the abolition of slavery itself.

Slaves had few opportunities for recreation, but they learned to make the most of them.

cies like grapes, melons and strawberries from the high, cool St Andrew mountains.

There were nightly gatherings outside the huts when the day's work was over. Then there were singing, dancing and storytelling.

Tacky's Rebellion

In 1760 the most serious slave revolt in the island's history broke out, and the government called upon the Maroons' assistance, as provided for in their 1739 treaty.

Known as Tacky's Rebellion, the revolt

During the Christmas and New Year holidays, colourful John Canoe (*see page 145*) bands roamed the streets, and teams of pretty Set Girls dressed in the rich clothes and jewellery of their mistresses to compete with one another in the lavishness of their costumes. And once a week there was the Sunday Market. A carnival atmosphere prevailed as thousands of people came to sell or trade pigs, goats and fowls; yams and other vegetables; small homemade articles like mats, baskets, bark ropes and jars; and delica-

---

LEFT: a typical West Indian "Negro Market" in 1806.
ABOVE: a British emancipation society's view of slaves being tortured in *A Jamaica House of Correction*.

began in the parish of St Mary. Tacky, its leader, was a Coromantee slave who had been a chief in Africa. He gathered a small party of trusted followers, mostly Coromantees like himself, from the Frontier and Trinity plantations, and laid his plans.

Before daybreak on Easter Monday, Tacky and his band stole down to Port Maria, murdered the fort's drowsy storekeeper, and made off with a supply of muskets, powder and shot. By dawn hundreds of slaves had joined Tacky and moved swiftly inland, overrunning the estates and killing the sleeping white settlers.

But a slave from the overrun Esher plantation had slipped away and spread the alarm. As soon as he heard the news, the governor in Spanish Town dispatched two companies of regular troops and called out the Maroons from their Scott's Hall settlement.

The battles that followed were fought with great skill and daring by the slaves, but as the conflict wore on the prospect of success grew dim, and a number of them lost heart and returned to their plantations. Not so Tacky; he and a band of about 25 men held out, and eventually took to the woods. There they were pursued by the Maroons, one of whom – a sharpshooter named Davy – shot the rebel leader dead. The rest of Tacky's band were later found

republic of Haiti out of the French colony of St Domingue in Hispaniola, inspired the disaffected. From the time it began, in 1789, there was fear in Jamaica that the spirit of subversion might spread to the slaves. European refugees poured onto the island, bringing slaves who carried the news of what was taking place in Hispaniola, only 100 miles away. This flow of refugees, and later of French prisoners of war, was a danger to Jamaica's security: it gave spies and agents of the Revolution an opportunity to enter and create disorder.

The events also caused alarm to the Spanish government in Santo Domingo, which shared a

in a cave. They had committed suicide rather than be captured.

Meanwhile slave revolts were breaking out in parishes throughout the island. An uprising of Coromantees in Westmoreland proved almost as serious as Tacky's Rebellion, and again the Maroons were called upon to help.

Inspiration from abroad

In the late 18th century, the effects of two events of worldwide importance began to be felt in Jamaica: the French Revolution, and the anti-slavery movement in Britain.

The revolution in France, and the ensuing conflict which led to the formation of the black

common border with St Domingue. In 1793, when Spain and England both went to war with revolutionary France, they sent separate expeditions to invade St Domingue. The British captured Port-au-Prince in March 1794 and hung on to it for four years, but the invasion was eventually foiled by yellow fever and by the military skill of Toussaint l'Ouverture, the first of many remarkable black Haitian leaders.

Jamaica was unable to send assistance to the British troops in Haiti: there were problems enough at home. In 1795 the Second Maroon War broke out, encouraged by the example of the French islands and – said some – promoted by actual French agents.

The Second Maroon War

The immediate cause of this Maroon War is said to have been the flogging in Montego Bay of two Trelawny Town Maroons for pig-stealing, but it was well known that trouble had been brewing among the Trelawnys for some time. The flogging, carried out under sentence of court, was not objected to; in fact, the men would have been far more severely dealt with by their own people for such an offence.

The real rub was that the work-house driver who wielded the whip, and most of the prisoners who were allowed to look on and mock, were runaway slaves whom the Maroons themselves had previously captured.

This was a harsh blow to Maroon pride. When word of the incident reached Trelawny Town there was an instant uproar, and wild threats of vengeance against the people of Montego Bay were voiced. Alarmed by this reaction, magistrates asked for troops to reinforce the local militia – and thus the tragedy began.

Strong measures

The Earl of Balcarres, who had recently arrived as Jamaican governor, treated the matter most seriously. A veteran of the War of American Independence, he was a firm believer in strong measures. He declared martial law, took command of all forces, and set up headquarters at Montego Bay.

One of his first moves was to send a detachment of men inland to destroy the Trelawny Town provision grounds. However, when the detachment reached its destination it found them already razed and the Maroons vanished. But not for long – on the return march to Montego Bay the detachment was ambushed by the Maroons. The colonel and a number of officers and other men were killed or wounded, and the survivors fled in disorder.

As the war dragged on, the whole island was disrupted. Jamaica, in the words of a writer of the time, seemed "more like a garrison… than a country of commerce and agriculture".

It became increasingly clear to Lord Balcarres that no one could search out a Maroon but another Maroon – or a dog. So the governor and his council decided to call in the dogs. A shipload of 100 terrifying beasts was imported from Cuba, where they were used for hunting runaway slaves and robbers, together with 40 handlers called *chasseurs*, strong men who were accustomed to great exertion and hardship.

The news of the dogs' arrival caused panic among the Maroons. In the wild and uncharted Cockpit Country, the mountain men had shown

that they could elude almost any number of troops sent against them, but there was no escape from savage bloodhounds that tracked by scent. Before the dogs were released the Trelawnys sued for peace.

One of the terms of surrender was that the Maroons would not be transported from the island, but, using a slim technical pretext as a loophole, the determined Balcarres secured the transportation of some 600 Trelawnys to Nova Scotia, from where they were later removed to Sierra Leone. Trelawny Town was turned over to a detachment of British troops, for whom barracks were built on the site. The Maroon menace had been laid aside for ever.

LEFT: cartoons like this one published in London in 1838 played a role in freeing the Jamaican slaves.
RIGHT: abolitionist William Wilberforce.

An end to slavery

The end of the 18th century saw the beginning of the end of the system of plantation slavery. In Great Britain, changes in industrial and commercial life were causing doubts about the soundness of supporting the West Indies' slave-based economy. More importantly, a wave of humanitarian reform was sweeping Britain, part of a new demand for liberty being voiced throughout Europe.

A movement led by William Wilberforce (1759–1833) secured the abolition of the slave trade in 1807, and complete emancipation from slavery in 1838. In Jamaica, abolitionists found

valuable allies in the missionaries of non-conformist churches, by now well established and making heartening Christian progress among the black population. It was a different matter with the planter-dominated House of Assembly and with the majority of slave owners, who fiercely opposed the measures.

In the end the planters defeated themselves by exhausting the patience of the British Parliament. It only required one more slave uprising to hurry the day of freedom. As it turned out, that final uprising was the most serious in the island's history. It broke out during the 1831 Christmas holidays, and its influence was felt far and wide. Samuel "Daddy" Sharpe, a

Baptist leader who sparked the revolt, is now regarded as a National Hero. He was hanged in the Montego Bay square that today bears his name. So slavery came to an end in Jamaica.

With emancipation, sugar production fell sharply. The old plantation economy slowly died, and estates were sold for whatever they would fetch. An attempt was made in the 1840s to provide labour with indentured workers from eastern India, with poor results.

Although the original white planter class had gradually given way to a new class of owners – chiefly mixed-bloods and Jews – the old oligarchic system of government remained unchanged. The legislature of the island was still elected by a handful of voters: those who met qualifications of property and income. The magistrates did the will of those in power, and the black peasantry was left to manage as best it could. To add to the distress of the latter, the American Civil War had cut off supplies of their staple foods, while severe droughts at home ruined their own crops. Edward John Eyre, who became governor in 1862, did almost nothing to assist them.

The Morant Bay Rebellion

Matters came to a head in October 1865 with an uprising in St Thomas-in-the-East. Known as the Morant Bay Rebellion, and led by Paul Bogle, a Baptist deacon and champion of the poor, it resulted in the killing of a number of whites. The uprising was put down by Governor Eyre with great severity. More than 430 people were executed or shot, hundreds were flogged, and 1,000 homes were destroyed.

Bogle and George William Gordon, a prominent mulatto legislator of the day, were hanged. Gordon was blamed by Eyre for the trouble; in retrospect, he appears to have been a scapegoat. A century later both were declared National Heroes, and a statue of Bogle stands in the courthouse square where the rebellion started.

Eyre's handling of the uprising caused an outcry in Britain that led to his eventual recall, but before leaving Jamaica he got the frightened members of the Assembly to surrender their constitution in exchange for the Crown Colony form of government. ❏

LEFT: Paul Bogle, Jamaican National Hero.
RIGHT: a statue of Bogle by Edna Manley stands in Morant Bay's town square.

The Daily Gleaner

LARGEST CIRCULATION   ESTABLISHED 1834   Price: THREEPENCE

Vol. CXXVIII No. 189.   KINGSTON, JAMAICA, W. I. WEDNESDAY, AUGUST 8, 1962.   THIRTYTWO PAGES

JAMAICA CELEBRATES INDEPENDENCE
Princess opens first Parliament

'...News received with satisfaction...'
Khrush's telegram to Busta

MOSCOW, Aug. 6 (Reuter).
Mr. Khrushchev has sent a message to Sir Alexander Bustamante, Prime Minister of Jamaica, congratulating the people of Jamaica on achieving their independence, the Soviet news agency Tass reported last night.

On the same time the Soviet Government has declared its recognition of Jamaica as an independent and sovereign state and has expressed its readiness to establish diplomatic relations with it, the agency said.

In his message, Mr. Khrushchev said: "Abiding by the great principle of equality and self-determination of the people, the Soviet Government has resisted with satisfaction news of the proclamation of the independence of the Jamaican people."

The telegram declared that the Soviet Government was ready to co-operate with Jamaica in the economic, cultural and other fields...

From China

TOKYO, Aug. 5 (AP). Both Nationalist and Communist China announced Sunday their recognition of Jamaica which became independent Monday.

President Chiang Kai-Shek, wired congratulations to Sir Kenneth Blackburne, the Governor of Jamaica and named Councillor Yu Fong of the Nationalist Embassy in Lima, Peru, as special envoy to attend the Independence Day ceremonies...

Her Royal Highness in Throne speech:
UK and Jamaica wish to maintain bonds of friendship

THE FIRST PARLIAMENT of the independent Jamaica, summoned to a joint sitting by proclamation of Her Majesty the Queen, was opened in state at Gordon House yesterday morning by the Queen's sister, Her Royal Highness the Princess Margaret.

Before a full house of the bewildered Senators and of the Members of the House of Representatives and at a glittering gathering of dignitaries from home and from abroad, Princess Margaret read the Speech from the Throne in a vivid and natural voice, and, with the assembly standing, read the Queen's personal message.

Multi-coloured

Queen's message:
I warmly welcome Jamaica to Commonwealth

(Please turn to Page 2, col. 3)

Busta on taxes:
Those who can pay will have to pay more

That taxation is likely to be increased among people in the higher income brackets, was indicated at the Prime Minister's first Press conference yesterday afternoon at Strata Hall, University of the West Indies.

In answer to a question from a foreign correspondent about the "heavy" and "burden" duty" and "report" that the Government to tax the rich in order to help the poor, Sir Alexander replied that he was ready to put a little more taxes" on those who could afford it...

Ashenheim Ambassador to Washington

Mr. Neville N. Ashenheim, C.B.E. is to be the first Jamaican Ambassador to Washington. It was announced last night from the Premier's Office.

Midnight...then bonfires, fireworks...
Down the Union Jack, up the Black, Gold and Green

With pomp and ceremony, and in an atmosphere of general rejoicing all over the country, Jamaica became an independent nation at midnight Sunday.

More than 20,000 people crowded the National Stadium Sunday night to see the Union Jack hauled down and the Jamaica National Flag hoisted in its place to the joy of the flagstaff while eager voices sang the Jamaica National Anthem.

From Macmillan —
Jamaica equal partner with UK

The Hon. Hugh Fraser, Air Minister and former Under-Secretary of State for the Colonies, handed the following message from the Rt. Hon. Harold Macmillan, Prime Minister of Britain, to Sir Alexander Bustamante, the Premier of Jamaica on Sunday morning, August 5:

"I have asked Mr. Fraser, who is leading the British Delegation to the Jamaican Independence Celebrations, to deliver to you, my Prime Minister, this message of goodwill from Her Majesty's Government and people..."

'Out of many...'

Prime Minister's message:
I know you will respond to the challenge

Sir Alexander Bustamante, Prime Minister of Jamaica, in a special message to the people of Jamaica on the occasion of the country's attainment of Independence, said:

"I want to Jamaicans, both at home and overseas, on this Prime Minister of the Government of Jamaica at this historic moment when we attain our independence...

LAUGH IT OFF

"She's the lucky man"

MARILYN MONROE FOUND DEAD
Sleeping pills nearby

HOLLYWOOD, Aug. 5 (AP): Blonde and beautiful Marilyn Monroe, a glamorous symbol of the gay, exciting life of Hollywood, died tragically Sunday.

The world may never know whether she deliberately took her life—but a special "suicide team" will have a difficult time before it makes a final probe into her death.

Her body was found nude in bed, a printable suicide, Sine was...

FOLLOW
ME TO 59 H.W.T. RD.

Come into our showrooms.... inspect the dazzling range of General Motors cars now on display and make your choice.

Plea for UN membership

THE TRANSITION TO INDEPENDENCE

Jamaica followed a rocky road to independence, from
cruel governors to emancipation and the rise of the black middle class

Almost 200 years after the Assembly first met, the mostly white group was stampeded into surrendering Jamaican self-government to the Colonial Office in Whitehall, and Governor Edward John Eyre finally got his way. The Assembly had not always been so timid; 13 years after it had first been convened it had indignantly rejected an attempt by the British government to curtail its power to legislate for Jamaica. In 1678 Chief Justice Long and the President of the Assembly, Colonel William Beeston, were taken to England to be tried for treason. Long's persuasive arguments before the king in Council, defending the rights and privileges of the members as Englishmen, resulted in victory.

Elected in 1863, the Assembly consisted of 27 white and 10 coloured members, including George William Gordon, Robert Osborn and Edward Jordon, who had been powerful forces for the emancipation of the coloured middle class and, by extension, for the black Jamaicans. The rapid growth of black and coloured enterprise since emancipation had scared some of the white planters, and visions of the nearby Haitian revolution frightened them even more. It was obvious that economic progress would soon produce a coloured, if not black, majority in the governing body.

The new professionals

By the mid-1860s black and coloured men had attained positions of prominence, not only as merchants and property owners but also as members of the Assembly, magistrates, barristers, schoolteachers, newspaper editors, clergymen and occupants of important public office, as Professor Douglas Hall pointed out in his book *Free Jamaica*.

After the imposition of Crown Colony status and government on Governor Eyre's depar-

ture in 1866, following the Morant Bay Rebellion, Hall reports that a former coloured man who had been a member of the Assembly said to a member of the newly installed Legislative Council: "You and I have been equals, but what will be the respective position of our children? Yours will hardly speak to mine!"

John Stuart Mill and other formidable liberals were outraged by Eyre's harsh response to the rebellion, and launched a prosecution for murder against the former governor of Jamaica. Eyre fought back with support from the likes of Thomas Carlyle and James Anthony Froude, whose opinion it was that "Black insurrection could not be treated in the same way as a white one, because the Negro in Jamaica is pestilential… a dangerous savage at best."

A clean sweep

Eyre's trial ended in his acquittal, but the affair had put Jamaica again squarely on the map. To govern this troublesome colony the British

---

PRECEDING PAGES: Jamaicans spill into the streets of Kingston for pre-Independence celebrations.
LEFT: the key issue of the *Daily Gleaner* newspaper.
RIGHT: 19th-century Montego Bay.

chose one of their ablest administrators, Sir John Peter Grant. On his arrival he declared that he would so change Jamaica that, when he was finished, if the dead returned they would not recognise the island.

Grant brought with him a new constitution. It made him virtual dictator of Jamaica, assisted by a Legislative Council of nine: mainly civil servants and all hand-picked by him. He took advice from a Privy Council, also appointed by him. His administration did not bring democratic satisfaction to the majority, but it did bring better social services: state schools, a health service, a Jamaica Constabulary and a judicial

was bought out by the government, and the track was extended halfway across the island before a US company took over in 1890. It was then further extended, to Montego Bay in 1894 and Port Antonio in 1896.

The decline of sugar

Grant's administration, and those of Sir William Grey and Sir Anthony Musgrave which followed, did a great deal to bring Jamaica out of its post-emancipation economic doldrums. Land settlements gave legal title to the descendants of the slaves, and the Jamaica Agricultural Society (JAS) provided the "small

system, the latter two both run by imported Englishmen. The new Public Works Department began a network which eventually provided 1 mile (1.5 km) of first-class road for every square mile of Jamaica's mountainous land.

The penny banks

When the Government Savings Bank (GSB) was set up in 1870, the British administrators were so distrustful of the Jamaican élite that its charter forbade the bank to make any investments in Jamaica itself. Subsequently a number of churches organised a penny-bank movement, to take smaller deposits than the GSB would accept. In 1879 the private railway company

settlers", as they were called, with technical expertise and a voice in public affairs. The Jamaica Union of Teachers (JUT), which was formed in 1895, the same year as the JAS, became a powerful voice of the re-emerging black middle class.

The banana trade with the United States, begun in 1868, assumed increasing economic importance, while sugar continued to decline. The reduction in the importance of sugar started after emancipation, initially because of labour shortages; it was exacerbated by free trade and the abolition of preferential duties,

Kingston, now the commercial centre of Jamaica, became the administrative capital in

1870. Tramcars were introduced there in 1876; the electric lighting system was extended, municipal water supplies began to be built, and by 1891 the prosperity and tranquillity of Jamaica resulted in an International Exhibition of the island's produce. Officially opened by the Prince of Wales, it attracted more than 300,000 visitors in five months.

Meanwhile, the disenfranchised black middle class continued to agitate for a real voice in the affairs of the colony. Debating clubs, as they were called, were impotent

BLACK, GREEN AND GOLD

The national flag incorporates three colours: black representing hardship and the majority race in Jamaica; green for the land, and gold representing the sun.

The new planter hegemony was backed by the election in Britain of Conservative governments no longer interested in their former crown jewel in the Caribbean. Many early advances were reversed, and by the time World War I broke out in 1914 the Jamaican Legislature was almost lily-white once more.

The mini-boom of the 1890s did not last. A disastrous earthquake in 1907, followed by an even more devastating fire, caused immense financial loss, and the island was regularly disturbed by riots and strikes. One of these, in

parliaments for the majority, and, as British official interest declined, the planters again re-asserted their control.

Disenfranchised and dissatisfied

In 1895 the franchise had been limited to property-owners who paid the equivalent of 10 shillings (50p/US80¢) annually in tax or earned £50 (US$80) a year. Voters also had to be able to read and write; since there had been no education for the masses, many who qualified under the property criterion were disenfranchised by illiteracy.

LEFT: Coke Chapel crumbles during the 1907 earthquake.
ABOVE: King Street in 1920.

Montego Bay in 1902, was regarded by the authorities as almost as serious as the uprising linked to Paul Bogle in 1865 (*see page 54*).

Economic hardship was somewhat alleviated by significant migrations of Jamaicans to Central America for work on the American banana plantations and railways, and then to construct the Panama Canal.

After World War I, unemployment and its effects were intensified by the return of the workers, along with Jamaican soldiers from Europe who never received the lands promised as a form of military pension.

The unequal character of the Jamaican economy contributed to a rapid decline in the social situation because, despite the land settlement schemes, fewer than 1,000 large landowners still owned more than half the cultivable land, and most of that was in "ruinate" – a Jamaican word meaning uncultivated, unworked, idle.

White supremacy

Despite the fact that they comprised only 1.7 percent of the population, by 1921 the white or (very) light-brown classes still provided the majority of the legislators, top civil servants and heads of all the leading societies, businesses and other enterprises and organisations. Social services were almost non-existent, and

the taxation system, based mainly on customs and excise taxes, bore heavily on the poor.

Sugar production, which had enjoyed a brief resurgence after the war, was hit by the Great Depression; along with a rising birth rate and reduced government spending, the result was even greater poverty and an increasingly unhealthy population, afflicted by yaws, tuberculosis, malaria and malnutrition.

Political unrest

In the 1920s and 1930s the Jamaican black political activist Marcus Garvey (*see below*) was blamed for many a riot and political unrest,

MARCUS GARVEY – A NATIONAL HERO

Marcus Mosiah Garvey was born in St Ann's Bay in 1887, not quite 50 years after emancipation, and made his mark on the world as a black nationalist, instigating a "back to Africa" movement. In 1914 he founded the Universal Negro Improvement Association (UNIA), advocating black unity and pride, and two years later launched it in New York.

Garvey's influence on Jamaica, though significant, was less obvious than in the United States. While he was there, he supported the Jamaican Federation of Labour in a police strike in 1920, and on a visit home the following year he advocated the unionisation of Jamaican labour.

His political activities, including the establishment of the Black Star Line, a steamship company, led to his deportation from the USA, while his daily newspaper, *The Negro World*, became a forum for labour and other grievances in Jamaica. The manifesto of his People's Political Party (1929) demanded a national minimum wage, and he campaigned for an eight-hour working day.

Ho Chi Min and Nelson Mandela have both acknowledged that they were influenced by Garvey and his ideas, but in Jamaica his importance was played down by the establishment, and he died in obscurity in London in 1940. It was only after Independence that his body was brought home, and he was made a National Hero.

but after he lost the 1930 election he moved to London (in 1935) and played no part in the momentous events of 1938. Riots, demonstrations and strikes, which had been spreading throughout the British West Indies, eventually forced the British government to begin concessions to the workers, changes which inexorably were to culminate in independence.

The disturbances of 1938, including those at Frome in Westmoreland, provided the platform for a new national movement in Jamaica, with Norman Washington Manley leading the political wing of the movement and his cousin, William Alexander Bustamante, the trade-union

mante led the party to victory in elections held under a new constitution, which was based on full adult suffrage and owed much to the agitation of Manley and his party. This ended the Crown Colony period. The JLP won again in 1949.

Keeping it in the family

The political philosophies of Bustamante and Manley were very different, but these two party leaders sowed the seeds of a political dynasty which spanned almost 40 years. Three of Jamaica's first five prime ministers hailed from the same family – Bustamante, Michael Manley (Norman's son) and Hugh Shearer.

wing. The rise of labour to political power was a new and dramatic development. Its leaders pressed for not only increased wages and better working conditions, but also political reform.

But this unity did not last, and Bustamante split from the Manley-led socialist People's National Party (PNP) in 1941. Three years later, he formed the Jamaica Labour Party (JLP), an unlikely coalition between merchant interests and his agricultural labourers. In 1944, Busta-

LEFT: King's House, circa 1890.
ABOVE LEFT: Marcus Garvey inspired African pride.
ABOVE RIGHT: JLP leader Alexander Bustamante rides into Kingston.

Manley's chance finally came in 1955, and his new government rapidly moved Jamaica towards independence. In 1957 Jamaica became independent in all but name, and in 1958 it combined with other islands in a West Indian Federation. Beset by problems, the federal dream was finally shot down in a referendum in 1961, when Jamaicans voted in favour of individual independence instead.

In the general election which followed on 10 April 1962, Bustamante narrowly beat his cousin to become independent Jamaica's first prime minister. Independence Day was set for 6 August, the day before the first session of the new parliament. ❑

THE POLITICAL CANVAS

Jamaica has a colourful two-party history spiced with political associations with

Cuba, Russia and the USA. Today three-party politics is finally emerging

On 6 August 1962 Jamaica became the first of Britain's West Indian colonies to achieve independence. The island had in fact been self-governing and independent in all but name for four years, since 1958, when the British conceded home rule to the Norman Manley-led government. The delay in finally severing colonial ties had been caused by the hope that Jamaica would gain its independence as a member of a new West Indian Federation with neighbouring nations. The Federation floundered on the Jamaican referendum of 1961, when voters decided, by a very slim majority, to go it alone.

The referendum had been provoked by the opposition of Sir Alexander Bustamante and the Jamaica Labour Party (JLP), who felt that Jamaica in federation would be drained by its association with the smaller Caribbean islands.

Norman Manley had driven the island from Crown Colony status in 1955 to a 1958 constitution which gave it autonomy in everything save defence and foreign policy. As soon as Manley's government installed the constitution it decided – against British advice and pressure – to ban trade with the apartheid regime in South Africa, beginning a four-decade-long struggle against apartheid which gained Jamaica many friends in the Third World but also created some powerful enemies.

British political advisers informed Manley that the constitution did not allow him to interfere in foreign affairs. He retorted that if Jamaicans were unwelcome in South Africa because of their race, Jamaica had the right to make South African goods unwelcome in Jamaica.

So, by the time Jamaica became fully independent, it had the beginnings of a foreign policy, plus many of the institutions of an independent country, including a national bank – the Bank of Jamaica – a central planning

authority, and a public broadcasting corporation modelled on the Canadian CBC. The Independence celebrations were held in the new National Stadium, for the construction of which Manley had been severely criticised.

Although Manley helped to guide Jamaica to the dawn of a new age he was defeated in the

General Election of April 1962; this left Alexander Bustamante and the JLP to lead the country over the threshold. As the political commentator Professor Carl Stone pointed out in his book *Politics versus Economics*: "Manley lost power while presiding over the modernising of the Jamaican economy in a period characterised by the highest rates of growth in consumption, investment, exports and imports experienced in Jamaica in the twentieth century."

Ironically, Manley, the father of independence, now found himself in opposition to the first government of independent Jamaica, led by his cousin, and lifelong antagonist, Alexander

LEFT: Sir Alexander Bustamante and Princess Margaret celebrating Independence Day, 1962.
RIGHT: Norman Manley, People's National Party (PNP) founder, in a reflective mood.

Bustamante, née Clarke. Bustamante, who had on many occasions questioned the value of independence, professed himself an Empire loyalist, and revelled in the trappings of the old regime.

Parliament was the place in which Jamaica demonstrated its 300 years of British heritage, with all the trappings and paraphernalia of the British House of Commons, complete with a mace – a gift from the British parliament. *May's Parliamentary Practice*, the bible of the British parliament, fulfils the same function in Jamaica.

> **BRITISH HERITAGE**
>
> The Jamaican parliament is based on the British model. The mace was a gift from the British, and the Speaker of the House wears a wig and gown similar to a judge's.

However, the new parliament was very unlike the old in many respects. The JLP had recruited a largely new and younger group of leaders for the 1962 elections, and they were not only youthful but also more middle class and representative of the Jamaican élite. This may have helped precipitate some of the government's clashes with various sectors of society: first with the police and the teachers, later with the Press and the University academics.

Structural economic problems, previously concealed by Commonwealth Development and Welfare aid from Britain, began to emerge. Sugar production, which had been increasing since the late 1950s, reached a peak in the early 1960s, just as world market prices began to decay. Big foreign investments in both bauxite and tourism managed for a time to conceal the fact that Jamaica was living beyond its means. The tailing-off of foreign investment and official aid towards the end of the decade was not conducive to either budgetary stability or social peace.

Meanwhile, the new leaders of the JLP seemed to prefer a more confrontational approach to government and began to antagonise sections of the establishment. Government interference with the Jamaica Broadcasting Corporation (JBC), especially the newsroom, caused a prolonged strike in 1964, an event which propelled Michael Manley into greater prominence as a labour leader and possible political successor to his father Norman.

The collision with the University academics came about because of Cold War politics. Bustamante had declared "We are with the West" at his first press conference after independence. He refused to have any dealings with Cuba, Jamaica's nearest neighbour, and academics who visited Cuba had their passports confiscated. American Black Power leaders such as Stokely Carmichael were barred, and Alex Haley's *Autobiography of Malcolm X* was banned. Church sermons considered critical of the Government were banned from being broadcast on the radio, and songs criticising it were refused airtime.

The rise of political protest

Concurrently, a new kind of political violence began to develop, particularly in West Kingston. The situation became so charged that in 1967 the Government declared a State of Emergency in West Kingston.

In 1968 the world seemed on fire with political protest, such as the Black Power and anti-Vietnam war violence in the USA, barricades in Paris and revolution in Czechoslovakia. Jamaica was not to be left out. The Rodney Affair, as it became known, developed out of the deportation of Dr Walter Rodney, a university lecturer of Guyanese origin and a Black Power advocate. When a student protest against his deportation resulted in a demonstration which was broken up by the police, it precipitated an outbreak of looting, arson and damage to property.

The JLP's unpopularity resulted in a crushing defeat at the polls in 1972. Carl Stone, in accounting for the failure, perceived a break in the party's traditional relations with the business sector as a result of the Government's tax policies and its attempts to control and regulate the manufacturing sector. In addition, Stone said, the JLP had managed to "antagonize the entire government bureaucracy… the dissatisfied bureaucracy, younger businessmen and upwardly mobile professionals provided a ready pool of voluntary labour" which the People's National Party (PNP) used to organise its campaign.

Joshua and the Promised Land

Michael Manley had succeeded his father as leader of the PNP in 1969, defeating Vivian Blake, a candidate whose supporters claimed that he was more like Norman Manley than Michael was. He led the PNP to an overwhelming victory in 1972 and immediately began a programme to make the Government more responsive to the needs of the people. He had after all won on the slogan "Power for the People".

A graduate of London University, Manley Jr entered politics after a stint as a labour union negotiator. He was a great orator whom people travelled miles to hear. Manley even visited Ethiopia and had an audience with Emperor Haile Selassie. He received a staff from Selassie, a "rod of correction" which he said he would wave to right wrongs and transform the country's deteriorating social fabric. The PNP then promoted him as a modern-day "Joshua" who would lead the people to the Promised Land.

The new Government passed several important pieces of social legislation: creating a national minimum wage, equal pay and status for women, and maternity leave; abolishing the stigma of illegitimacy; and abolishing the hated Master and Servants Act, a 19th-century hangover designed to keep ex-slaves on the sugar estates, or at least accountable to the constabulary. A Labour Relations and Industrial Disputes Act gave new rights to workers and their unions, and the National Housing Trust provided the means for most employed people to own their own homes. More than 40,000 houses were built in the last six years of PNP

rule, more than had been built over any comparable period in Jamaican history.

Despite this record, Manley's rhetoric soon got him into trouble. His statement about walking to the mountain-top with Fidel Castro of Cuba gave his opponents the opportunity to brand him a communist.

In 1974 a serious outbreak of violence, apparently directed at important middle-class figures, provoked the hasty imposition of the draconian Suppression of Crimes Act. This Act was an assault on personal liberty as it gave the police the right to search and detain people without any stated reason. The creation of a

Gun Court – specifically aimed at dealing with firearms crimes – was meant to strike terror into the hearts of gunmen. It had little effect.

Reams of unfavourable publicity began to be generated in the foreign press, and Jamaica's tourist trade, which was rising steadily until 1974, stagnated and began to slip. Growing unemployment, severe shortages of even basic necessities, dwindling foreign exchange reserves and successive years of negative growth bred a sense of despair. Meanwhile oil prices shot up in 1973, and this caused serious hardship for Jamaica, which depended almost entirely on imported energy.

Manley's response – placing a levy on the

LEFT: The late Michael Manley, former PNP leader and prime minister.
RIGHT: Cuban leader Fidel Castro.

bauxite companies – meant that Jamaica could at least pay for its oil. But the levy provoked even greater international disapproval. Manley's foreign interests leaned increasingly towards Cuba and the Soviet Union, and he became a popular spokesman for Third World "have-not" countries. Consequently, the US aid upon which Jamaica had been dependent dwindled.

In the middle of all this the JLP elected a new leader, Edward Seaga. Minister of finance in the previous JLP government, he had a much more confrontational stance than his predecessor, Hugh Shearer.

Seaga's leadership increased the tension lev-els between the parties. He denounced the PNP as communist-inspired and led the JLP into the 1976 elections with the slogan "Turn Them Back". But Manley and the PNP again over-whelmed the JLP in an election held during a State of Emergency designed to shut down the increasing political violence.

Silencing the guns

Even the reggae star Bob Marley became a tar-get. A gang of gunmen burst into his Kingston home, now the Bob Marley Museum, and shot Marley, his road manager and others two days before a scheduled free "Smile Jamaica" concert

NATIONAL HEROES OF JAMAICA

Jamaican National honours and awards were introduced in 1969. There are five Orders: Order of National Hero, the highest honour of the land; the Order of the Nation (ON); the Order of Merit (OM); the Order of Jamaica (OJ);, and the Order of Distinction, with Commander and Officer ranks (OD and CD). Jamaica has seven National Heroes:

● **Nanny of the Maroons** led a guerilla war against the colonisers during the First Maroon War, 1720–39.

● **Samuel Sharpe** instigated the 1831 slave rebellion which contributed to the abolition of slavery seven years later.

● **George William Gordon**, the son of a slave mother and a planter, led the movement in the 19th century campaign-ing for political rights for freed slaves.

● **Paul Bogle** demonstrated against poverty and injustice, preparing the way for the establishment of fair treatment in courts and improvements in social and economic conditions.

● **Marcus Mosiah Garvey** was the earliest proponent of black nationhood, pride and self reliance; in 1914 he founded the Universal Negro Improvement Association (UNIA), a large black Pan-African movement.

● **Sir William Alexander Bustamante**, an advocate of the labour movement in 1942; founder of the Jamaica Labour Party (JLP); Jamaica's first independent prime minister.

● **Norman Washington Manley**, founder of the People's National Party (PNP); he led the negotiations for Jamaica's independence from Britain.

which Marley hoped would help cool the over-heated political climate. Marley later wrote about the attack in his song "Ambush in the Night". He bandaged his wounds and went through with the concert, albeit reluctantly, and Manley later met Seaga to sign a "Pledge of Peace". But the truce proved temporary. The stakes were much too high.

By 1978 clashes between supporters of the PNP and JLP were again on the increase. Marley, now an international musical superstar, again tried to intervene. He staged a "One Love" concert in April to commemorate the 12th anniversary of the 1966 visit to Jamaica by Haile Selassie. More than 25,000 Jamaicans watched Marley call JLP leader Seaga and Prime Minister Manley to the stage, lock hands with both in a raised pyramid, and sing:

One Love, One Heart
Let's get together and feel all right.

Again, the guns were silenced. Again, the truce proved temporary.

A flight of capital and businessmen from the island soon had a severe effect on the economy, and when Manley went to the International Monetary Fund (IMF) for balance of payments support, the multilateral agency exacted heavy penalties. Devaluation, the slashing of subsidies to the poor and other belt-tightening measures were seen by the left as foreign interference in Jamaica's politics. The US security agency, the CIA, came in for its share of criticism when it was accused of trying to destabilise Jamaica. The increasing violence after the end of the State of Emergency, the increasing unemployment and the closure of many businesses persuaded Manley to call an election, more than a year early, to settle the question of who was going to run Jamaica.

In the October 1980 General Election Edward Seaga and the JLP triumphed after a year-long campaign in which nearly 1,000 Jamaicans died violently. Seaga's massive majority in Parliament seemed to promise smooth running, but within 18 months his government's popularity had dwindled and the political commentator Carl Stone was forecasting a PNP victory in the next elections.

Providence, in the form of the political coup

in Grenada, rescued the JLP, as the news of socialists killing socialists reflected adversely on the PNP in Jamaica. Seizing the propitious moment, Seaga called an election in 1983 – two years early.

Dissatisfaction with the JLP could have meant a PNP win, but that party refused to participate in the hastily called election, on the grounds that both parties had agreed to reform the electoral system, despite the fact that political opinion was beginning to turn against the JLP because of the influence of the US recession, IMF programmes and other factors which slowed the economy to a crawl. Also, under

Seaga, Jamaica had failed its second consecutive IMF test. This failure meant a period of enforced stringency, and, with an unemployment rate around 30–35 percent, the country was unhappy. But the disturbing political situation in Grenada temporarily reversed the trend beginning to favour the PNP, and, with no opposition, the JLP won all the seats in Parliament.

By 1986, when the long overdue municipal elections were called, public opinion had become overwhelmingly hostile to the Seaga government: so much so that Carl Stone's 1986 political poll predicted that the PNP would get 60 percent of the vote in the municipal elections. It received 57 percent of the votes cast. There was

---

LEFT: Michael Manley, Bob Marley and Edward Seaga at the 1978 "One Love" concert.
RIGHT: Haile Selassie inspired Rastafarians.

to be no comeback. Seaga broke with the IMF, denouncing the institution in terms even harsher than those of the PNP leftists in 1980.

The JLP's economic and social policies had caused enormous resentment among workers and affected Seaga's electability and Jamaica's development overall.

Manley returns

The return of Michael Manley as Prime Minister in 1989 was therefore not unexpected, but this was a new Manley, who accepted the primacy of the market and was content for the private sector to be the driving force in the

economy. The PNP, he said, had learned from its mistakes.

Manley continued Seaga's programme of liberalisation, privatisation and deregulation, but while there were some slight increases in social spending, notably in housing and education, the government was now saddled with the huge foreign debt incurred in the 1980s. The effort required to stabilise the currency caused huge costs, which ultimately resulted in an acceleration in the transfer of wealth from poor to rich as company profits and capital gains rocketed upwards while wages remained stable.

Michael Manley had been diagnosed with prostate cancer in 1988, before he took office,

and by 1993 the work load and the cancer treatment had drained him physically. The athletic, vigorous man of the 1970s was gone. In 1993, the only man to have been elected prime minister of Jamaica three times, he handed over his office to his deputy P.J. Patterson, a lawyer from the right wing of the party. Patterson won the leadership of the PNP, and the succession, against Portia Simpson, a working-class woman.

In the 1997 General Election the PNP won an unprecedented third term, appearing to destroy any prospect of Edward Seaga returning to power, and Michael Manley lost his battle against cancer at the age of 72. In the same year the first in a series of shocks in the financial markets occurred as many of the newly formed and undercapitalised merchant banks went belly-up, precipitating the threat of a collapse in the Jamaican banking sector. This was averted by the government bailing out the banks at enormous cost, slashing all social programmes to the bone and increasing the debt burden on all Jamaicans. In fact, with the cost of mopping up, and the high interest-rate policy to wean speculators from betting against the dollar, Jamaica's domestic and foreign debt repayments in 1999 consumed 63 percent of the country's annual budget

In May 1999 the prospect of an increase in petrol taxes precipitated a three-day rampage by unemployed people, mostly young, which brought Jamaica almost to a standstill. Tourism was affected by the unrest, and Jamaica was once again hitting the headlines because of violence spilling into the streets. The crisis was cooled by the Government's withdrawing part of its proposed taxation measures.

Three-party politics

The JLP has splintered in opposition. A third party has emerged, led by Bruce Golding, once Seaga's second in command and heir apparent. With the opposition ineffective and divided, the PNP appears to be secure, despite the increasing criticism levelled against the prime minister for failing to revitalise the economy and deal with the attendant social problems, including high prices, crime and unemployment. ❏

LEFT: Edward Seaga and cabinet at the tomb of Sir Alexander Bustamante.
RIGHT: law enforcement is a high priority.

BUILDING TO SUIT THE COOLING BREEZES

Modern Jamaica has been influenced by the wooden building design of the Amerindians and the stone of the Spanish and English colonists

When the European colonists arrived on Jamaica they did not encounter any of the stone architecture they were used to at home; instead they discovered cleverly-built wooden structures with thatched conical roofs built by the Amerindians. Both the Spanish and the English had a tradition of building with stone, but the heat and humidity of the Caribbean climate meant that wood was a much more suitable material.

Plantation owners made rich from sugar built grand homes with foundations of rock, while the upper floors were made from wood. Great houses made mainly from stone, such as Rose Hall in the north, are unusual.

NATURAL AIR-CONDITIONING

To take advantage of the cooling breezes, many great houses near the coast were located on hills, where the sea breeze would cool the rooms during the day, and mountain winds would keep the house cool at night. The hills also afforded spectacular views of the countryside. Wooden slatted shutters kept the wind and rain out while allowing the air to circulate. The roofs sheltered wide verandahs which provided places to shelter from the sun, socialise and enjoy a quiet drink. To withstand the battering of hurricanes, roofs were often partitioned with narrow gables. The best examples of this type of construction can be seen in Falmouth in the north of the island.

▷ **DESIGN GRACE**
Harmony Hall east of Ocho Rios was the great house on a pimento farm. It displays graceful 19th-century detail and turrets.

▷ **ROSE HALL**
Restored to its original beauty, this 18th-century great house east of Montego Bay reflects the excesses and luxurious lifestyle of the plantocracy.

△ **SHOWCASE**
The shady verandahs of town houses served as outdoor living rooms. Note the delicate fretwork on the portico of the DeMontevin Lodge in Port Antonio.

△ **MAKING ENDS MEET**
Imaginative rural builders make use of natural materials. This house has a stone base with tree branches as decoration.

▷ **GRAND ENTRANCE**
Stone tiles add style and glamour to the grand entrance of the DeMontevin Lodge. Today tiles are still popular for entrance halls and terraces.

Plantation houses such as Rose Hall Great House near Montego Bay offered every conceivable luxury and comfort, from the extravagant wall decoration of finely woven silk and imported cotton to beautiful furniture made from the finest woods available, including mahogany, blue mahoe and cedar, which could not be surpassed in quality by any European wood of the time. Local Jamaican craftsmen produced chests, cupboards and four-poster beds, often with intricate designs and details. The greatest pride was taken in the production of tables fashioned from one piece of wood. The wider the wood the more expensive the table because it had to be cut from mature trees in remote areas, which made transport laborious and costly. A curiosity which can still be found in some of the island's great houses are chairs with extendable arm rests. Wooden flaps on either side allowed a gentleman to rest his legs so that a servant could easily remove the master's boots.

◁ **COUNTRY COLOUR**
Colourful wooden houses sprinkle the landscape. Originally the roofs were covered with hardy cedar shingles, now replaced by cheaper corrugated iron.

▽ **ORNAMENTAL DESIGN**
Nature inspired the early architects. Birds, flowers, fruit and trees were often used as details in building decoration.

◁ **FOR A LADY'S HAND**
Headquarters House in Kingston was built in 1755 as part of a wager between four men trying to with the hand of a lady.

EMPIRE **WINDRUSH**

LONDON

MIGRATION, EDUCATION AND TRADE

Is tourism a cure-all, or will a move towards Caribbean unity
be the answer to Jamaica's economic struggles?

The past 50-plus years have seen tremendous changes in Jamaica and its people, not least of which has been the astonishing growth of the population. In the 1940s the total population was estimated at just over a million; today there are 2½ million resident Jamaicans, and another estimated 2 million in various countries overseas. To understand modern-day Jamaica and the motivations of its society it is necessary to back-track briefly.

The colonial legacy

By the time of emancipation in 1838 the labour force already outnumbered its white masters, who were responsible for the administration of the country and its businesses. A century later Jamaica was still a British colony, and the structure of society could be compared to a pyramid. At the top were the white administrators, mostly expatriate Britons, while in the middle was a very thin band of middle-class Jamaicans. These were the independent business people, mostly traders of Middle-eastern and Oriental extraction, a sprinkling of professionals of mixed ethnic backgrounds and a few blacks.

The largest wedge at the base of the pyramid was reserved for the largely black population, descendants of the emancipated slaves. They had minimal education and formed a huge pool of unskilled labour and peasant farmers. The colonisers saw to it that the labour force could read, write and do simple arithmetic, but beyond that learning was not encouraged. Cheap labour was still needed for the agrarian-based economy, and too much education would have depleted the ranks of readily available workers.

One result of this attitude was that it bred in the minds of the Jamaican labouring class an association of inferior status and lack of dignity with most forms of manual or menial work. It also bred a determination to beat the system. Despite being free people, they were only free to

LEFT: migration was a route to self-betterment.
RIGHT: raking a path of beans for the local coffee industry.

aspire to whatever their colonial masters allowed. Another result was that every poor Jamaican who was able to struggled to educate his or her children, to enable them to escape from the shackles of this new type of slavery.

Migration was one route to self-betterment, and before the end of the 19th century many

Jamaicans were seeking opportunities abroad: going to Panama to help build the canal, to Costa Rica, Honduras and later Cuba. The largest wave of migrants before World War II (1939–45) went to the United States, primarily to the East Coast cities. It is estimated that today approximately 400,000 people in Boston, New York, Philadelphia and other major Eastern cities are of Jamaican origin.

After the war, when the United States restricted immigration, Jamaicans went to Canada and the mother country, England. Between 1950 and 1960 a quarter of a million migrated to England and subsequently sent for their families to join them. They settled principally in London, Manchester, Liverpool and Birmingham. Eventually the UK was forced to tighten the immigration laws, and for a while the numbers of people migrating declined.

Them and us

Back in Jamaica the middle classes had already achieved a large measure of self determination, and the future of their descendants was more or less assured. Population growth was slower in this group than on the lower rungs of the economic ladder. With the assistance of the churches the middle classes founded schools for their children and saw to it that they were

educated to the highest standards. Those who could afford it sent their children to colleges and universities overseas; if the children were bright enough it was the Ivy League universities of the States or the hallowed halls of Oxford and Cambridge in England.

In general, the middle classes were as patronising and contemptuous of their darker-skinned or less fortunate countrymen as were the ruling white plantocracy, if not more so. In time the mass of impoverished and struggling Jamaicans came to view any Jamaican of lighter skin-tone and greater material wealth as having taken the place of their former colonial masters. Insidious shadism became more pervasive.

With the breakaway from English dominion to full independence in 1962, a surge of renewed hope and a feeling of rejuvenation overtook the population who, for the first time, felt that this was now truly *their* country, and that they had a vested interest in making it work for themselves and their children.

For a long time the only jobs which were considered worth having were the traditional "prestige" professions: medicine, law, banking, engineering and the like. Only a white-collar job would do, and it was a point of pride to be able to say about one's child: "My son the doctor" or "My son the lawyer (or the engineer)" – it didn't matter which as long as it could not be said of him: "Dat wutless bwoy. Him tun labourer!" in tones of utmost disgust.

The emphasis was on educating the sons of the family. It was not widely thought that girls needed to aspire to anything beyond being efficient housekeepers in order to make some lucky man a good wife and mother of his children.

With the dawn of the 1960s the complexion of middle-class Jamaica, particularly in the business place, began to change. Slowly. No longer was it an occasion for comment to see black bank staff and lawyers; it was soon to become the norm. This younger generation of Jamaicans had not had to endure the turbulence of the birth of a new nation. They had enjoyed the first-fruits and led, for the most part, privileged lives. Their attitudes, outlooks and expectations were therefore radically different from those of their parents' generation. These were the baby-boomers who, because of the sacrifices of their families, were able to step into teaching and other professions, or to go into business for themselves.

The country continued to drift further away from an agrarian-based economy towards a more industrial base. Newer and more technology was needed, and an educated workforce became more important. Tourism was a dynamic new growth industry, as was bauxite, both of which were beginning to replace the income-earning potential of the more traditional exports of bananas and sugar. In the 1950s and 1960s Jamaica enjoyed a period of relative prosperity and stability. The Jamaican currency was strong and was trading at US$1.20 to J$1.00. Crime was negligible and was largely confined to pick-pockets and occasional housebreaking in the major towns.

Country comes to town

With prosperity came easier access to radio, television and travel. Television was a somewhat late arrival – in the early 1960s – and as its content was almost 100 percent American it was natural that the population would be influenced by the lifestyles and values of the USA. The desire to escape all reminders of colonial life and attitudes no doubt assisted the enthusiastic embrace of things American. Even Jamaica's folk-music roots began to give way to the influx

CRUISE IN FOR THE DAY

Recent figures reveal that more than 1 million people visit Jamaica every year; 700,000 of them are cruise-ship passengers staying for just one day.

"the good life", or so it seemed to the rural poor. They flocked to the capital city with its burgeoning music and entertainment industry and its promise of a better life. All attempts by the government to persuade the rural population to remain on the farm proved futile. The continuing influx of people from country to city placed unplanned-for demands on essential services and housing. It fell to the government of the day to cope with the needs of the larger mass of people, a task with which it has been struggling ever since.

of American popular music. Sound systems appeared on street corners blaring out the latest hits, with many small Jamaican studios producing mostly cover versions of popular songs.

Kingston in the 1950s and 1960s was a major port of call for cruise ships, and Victoria Pier at the end of King Street was a lively bustling port. The craft market on the pier, a luxury hotel (the Myrtle Bank) and well-stocked shops lining the major thoroughfares were vibrant with

LEFT: a middle-class pursuit – polo at Drax Hall around 1920.
ABOVE: country people come to town to catch up on the news and sell their produce.

In the wake of this migration, disillusion was swift and tragic. There was not enough work for unskilled labour; unemployment grew, as did the incidence of crime. In about 20 years Kingston's population doubled, from 376,000 in 1960 to more than 700,000 in the 1980s. Most gravitated to traditional residential neighbourhoods west and east of the city centre, and these older communities have become sprawling slums of poverty in today's Kingston.

Survival of the fittest

Commerce moved uptown to New Kingston, a cluster of high-rise buildings housing the head offices of banks, embassies and modern shopping plazas. The better-heeled citizens moved north into luxurious suburbs such as Norbrook and Cherry Gardens. The streets remain the preserve of the less prosperous; real city life is played out here, in the main streets of downtown Kingston. The pavements and arcades are the domain of street vendors selling everything from clothing to fruit. The old city seethes with life, and it is clear why the rural folk continue to flock to Kingston. Here they have a chance to earn something.

The struggle to provide education to keep pace with the population growth has been defeated, in part, by the aversion of people in the

lower-income group to any form of birth control. Attempts by successive governments to encourage it were viewed with hostility and interpreted as "a plot to kill black people".

After the debt crisis of the 1970s, government spending on education was drastically cut during the 1980s and 1990s. The result was overcrowded classrooms and a lack, in some cases, of even basic facilities. Poor working conditions and low salaries have forced a considerable proportion of teachers to leave the profession, to emigrate, or to supplement their earnings by working in the private sector.

The distribution of wealth has become increasingly inequitable since independence, with the greatest poverty being in the rural interior and the slum districts of the large towns. Most dwellings in these areas have neither electricity nor running water. Years of self-serving, corrupt and inept government led to problems which were exacerbated by the worldwide oil crisis of the 1970s. While governments flirted with shifting the economy to an industrial base, more cautious voices which suggested building up and maintaining Jamaica's agricultural base were largely ignored.

The IMF approved a policy of retrenchment, beginning in the 1970s. This, coupled with enormous increases in the cost of living ever since, and a continually depreciating currency, has created a barely suppressed anger within all classes of the general population.

Strategies for survival

Many feel the only way out of Jamaica's economic problems is for the country to produce and export more of its goods; the domestic market is too small and impoverished to sustain non-export development. This problem is common to all the Caribbean islands, and attempts are being made to develop regional trade tariffs through Caricom, the Caribbean trading association. As far back as the 1950s the idea of a Federated West Indies was mooted but was defeated at the polls through nationalism and self-interest. With the rest of the world forming powerful trade blocs, the wisdom of a Caribbean trading bloc is belatedly being forced on these island nations.

It is also obvious that, with the dismantling of the Soviet Union, the spread of Communism is no longer a threat. The Caribbean, therefore, is no longer a foreign-policy priority for any US administration, and it would be foolish to base the economy of the region on Washington's continued support. Jamaica, like many of its Caribbean neighbours, is on its own.

In the 21st century the island and its neighbours are again attempting to create an economic union which may turn out to be the only form of protection for their small economies against influential nations as international trade is increasingly liberalised. Caricom is being transformed into a free-trade bloc. It has already created a customs union, and intends to become a single market by the end of 2000. ❏

LEFT: high-rise in New Kingston.
RIGHT: marijuana is a popular crop, providing some people with an invisible income.

THE JAMAICANS

"Out of Many, One People": so goes the national motto which describes
the unique development of the island's people who originate from all over the globe

What is a Jamaican? Jamaicans smile to themselves as they watch the world try to answer the question. They have their own mental images: of "fry fish" and bammy at Hellshire; Buju, Bob and Beenie Man; Tastee patties; Christmas breeze and cricket whites; John Crow vultures over the Blue Mountains; political rivalry; school loyalties. Even as these images and a million more wheel through their heads, they incline them in gracious acknowledgement upon meeting people from other lands and hearing the "Yeah, mon", "Jamaica – no problem!" or "Bob Marley!" cry of recognition that, more often than not, greets them when they say they're from that island.

Whether people think of beach or violence, of gun-toting "yardies" or the colourful antics of the 1998 World Cup football team – the Reggae Boyz – and its fans, of "ganja" (marijuana) or Rastafarianism, the world knows Jamaica. Or thinks it does.

The perpetual adolescent

Jamaica is the perpetual adolescent: opinionated, vocal, loud, proud ("nuff", as they call it on The Rock) – and eternally self conscious. That's not surprising. Historically and contemporarily, 2½ million people have developed and now exist in a space somewhere between an external notion of Jamaican society and their own internal comprehension of themselves.

Jamaicans are a people who have been constantly exposed to external influences. As a largely agricultural economy, Jamaica has always been dependent on an outside market, be it in sugar, bananas, bauxite or slaves. Every Jamaican knows the importance of the tourist sector, and can blithely trip the latest Tourist Board slogan off the tongue. Since the 19th century, Jamaicans have invested many of their hopes in "foreign" (opportunities abroad), trick-

ling out into the Panama Canal for work, seeking out a sentimental dream of ancestral connection with Africa, or boarding any transport for the gold-paved promise of the United States or Mother England. Look up at the hills of Kingston and you will see a chorus of satellite dishes peering down at you like UFOs, evi-

dence of the extent to which people consume American television and the culture, values and attitudes that go with it. At the same time Jamaicans hold in their bones the knowledge of themselves as immigrants to Jamaica. They are not its indigenous people. From the moment the Spanish conquerors, armed with the twin weapons of new disease and old enslavement, saw the last Taino Indian die, people have come to Jamaica from distant lands: from Africa as slaves; from England, Germany, Scotland, Ireland and India as indentured servants; from China to become small businessmen; and from Lebanon, to be christened "Syrian", as all Arab peoples are known in the island.

PRECEDING PAGES: wall art in Rasta colours; waiting for the future to ride by.
LEFT: smile Jamaica.
RIGHT: carrying bananas home.

Perfect harmony

After independence was declared in 1962 it became incumbent on Jamaican people to forge a national identity independent of Commonwealth status. What eventually became active in the national consciousness was the intriguing idea of the land as a country where races lived in perfect harmony. In his 1961 address to the National Press Club in the USA the Jamaican leader and National Hero Norman Manley extolled the virtues of this "non-racialist" haven, presenting receive control of representative government; citizenship rights went next, in 1832, to the "free coloureds" – people of mixed-race heritage who no longer worked as slaves. While both of these groups joined with the black majority to take over government, it was the whites and free coloureds whose influence and social position qualified them to participate in the nominated legislature of the Crown Colony system. Black people had to wait until as recently as 1944 for full political rights.

> ### PASSING FOR WHITE
>
> To stop the practice of "passing for white" among undetectable Octoroons in the 19th century, all free non-whites had to wear a blue cross sewn to their clothing.

Jamaica as a living model for the world, typified in the national motto: Out of Many, One People.

Despite Manley's well-intentioned "blind eye", the die had been cast years before: more than a century after emancipation, Jamaica was yet to lose its grip on the legacy of the past. The social, economic and psychological patterns that resulted from generations steeped in a colonial, plantation-based system remained.

Even today Jamaican society is still affected by its national understanding of "shadism" (as opposed to the less subtle "racism"): the assumption of civic status in the context of racial origin. In the late 17th century white planters were the first group of people to

In the meantime, mixed-race heritage became a kind of calling-card for many, as proportions of "white versus black blood" led to the categories of Quadroon and Octoroon. Everyone in Jamaica knows the socio-economic "advantages" associated with the status of a "browning" or "red" (light-skinned) Jamaican. In the 18th and 19th centuries it was the mixed-race offspring of plantation owners and slaves who were given the relatively easier jobs: taken into the "big house" to serve at table or clean floors, or given the task of overseeing the field slaves. Some were even educated by their wealthy and influential fathers.

Today Jamaicans still understand that

relatively pale skin usually indicates privilege, position, wealth and the kind of virtue associated with Christian imagery, and that blackness is often interchangeable with poverty, manual labour, low status and exclusion.

Black power

Up to the 1950s black pressure-groups demonstrated for the employment of black women in downtown offices and banks and the education of children in what were then prestigious all-white schools. The colour bar was everywhere. Hotels, owned by foreign interests and catering mostly to Americans, were believed to be hung

short of a bishopric, but it was definite progress.

One day the black editor of a news magazine, who had tired of the hypocrisy, dived into a swimming pool at Kingston's exclusive Myrtle Bank Hotel. The splash was heard throughout Jamaica's three counties, and white outrage was only exceeded by mixed-race indignation.

It was this historical reality which created an independent Jamaica that paraded Utopia on the international stage but, by 1964, was forced to admit, in the *Jamaica Report to the United Nations*, that "racial discrimination has yet to be entirely eliminated from the island". In the mid-1980s, when MP Carole Guntley was

up on the issue of colour. In the face of such inequality, embarrassing migrations to other lands – often to work as domestics or in blue-collar jobs, in order to feed the family back home – were dismissed as "love of travel in our people". A black priest never rose above archdeacon, an honourary post usually conferred just before retirement. Rapture engulfed black Jamaicans when a Catholic priest named Gladstone Wilson was elevated to monsignor in 1950. The title fell

appointed Minister of Foreign Affairs, there was some concern that she was too black to represent Jamaica on the international stage, in the company of dignitaries from around the world who would surely look down on the Jamaican nation for choosing a representative of her dark – some might say "inferior" – hue.

There are those who would insist that the spectre of the "browning" is over, and indeed would cite an increase of black people in positions of power and prestige in schools, churches, big business and government as evidence. This progress is true; nevertheless, all one has to do to raise the duppy's (spectre's) head is get involved in one of the country's

LEFT: a resident of Jamaica's German community in Seaford Town holds up family portraits.
ABOVE: Colonel C.L.G. Harris, former leader of the western Maroons.

favourite pastimes: the annual run-up to the Miss Jamaica beauty pageant, which chooses one lucky girl to represent Jamaica's hopes at the international Miss World beauty contest. As semi-finalists become finalists, and the ultimate night of choice draws nearer, murmurs about relative degrees of pigmentation are just as important as – and often more important than – a consideration of physical beauty or the ability (necessary for all finalists) to opine endlessly on the white beaches and be a friend to the people of the country. The contest tends to be dismissed as unfair if the unfortunate winner is deemed too pale, but equally, for many enthusiastic

When the penny needs to be pinched, people move back to, and newly acknowledge, old hurts, divisions and prejudices.

Still, this is a country of people who believe in expressing outrage. Jamaicans, as they say at home, are "never backward in comin' forward", and this is one of their most delightful but potentially confusing features: the unceasing ability to indulge in and enjoy the art of debate in all its forms.

From oral tradition to lyrics

More than the beach, or ganja, Jamaican society can arguably be defined solely in terms of

Jamaicans, she cannot be too dark either. If this delicate balance is not met, Jamaicans are not afraid to express their censure, as many a Miss Jamaica has found to her cost as a barrage of tomatoes and rotten oranges litters her sparkling feet and threatens to bounce off her tiara.

Interestingly enough, there appears to be an intimate, synergistic relationship between colour sensitivity and economic climate. One cultural commentator made the point succinctly: "If in the contemporary USA, racial tension can be said to be a prime reason why poverty has become such a major issue, in Jamaica, poverty has been a major reason why race and colour has become a primary issue."

THE MAROONS

There are two distinct communities of Maroons, although both are descended from African slaves of the Akim, Ashanti, Fanti, Coromantee, Mandingo and Angola tribes.

Accompong is one of the ancient fortress towns in the Cockpit Country. The great Maroon chief Cudjoe harried the English army from here, the land named the "Land of Look Behind" by nervous English soldiers, and other strongholds for 50 years after he left a plantation in 1690.

The Windward Maroons live in the Blue Mountains where the legendary Nanny of the Maroons waged battles against the English colonists. The Maroons are virtually independent, and many still live in the original towns today.

its strong oral tradition and the national need for self-expression. Arrive in Jamaica at any time of the day or night and you will find bars, churches, verandahs and schools alive with talk as people enthusiastically discuss the burning issues of the day.

Radio 'phone-ins were the life blood of Jamaica long before Oprah Winfrey and Jerry Springer established themselves on TV. Up and down the length and breadth of the island the morning begins as radio presenters introduce yet another listener who needs to "add me two cents, sah!" to the contention. Jamaicans are a merrily arguing people, whether cheering for

are the most beautiful woman on the face of the earth and Naomi Campbell can only long for your loveliness – all with a twinkle in his eye – you may even forgive him when you hear the same lyrics delivered to another woman the next day. As they debate, so they sweet-talk, and very few can resist the unnerving combination of confidence, braggadocio and... well, fine form that is a Jamaican man looking to give you a *chups* (kiss) while he *chirps* (lyrics) you into his arms.

Many Jamaicans may have felt irritated when the African-American author Terri McMillan wrote her novel *How Stella Got Her Groove*

the school football team at the Manning Cup or descending in huge numbers on the 1998 World Cup in France, all ablaze in a flurry of black, green and gold flags.

Equally, it is no surprise that Jamaicans have commandeered the word "lyrics" to describe the ritual language of romance. Female tourists may complain that local men are sometimes irritatingly determined, but when a Jamaican man tells you that the pain in his soul is the biggest pain ever known to mankind, that you

Back, a virtual ode to Jamaican toy-boyhood. The book and subsequent film were seen by some as yet another vehicle stereotyping young Jamaican men; nevertheless the internal smile was back – a kind of incipient pride in the face of the fact that yes, Jamaicans had proved irresistible once again.

This island people are amazingly resourceful and creative, and determined to live life to the full. Older Jamaicans will tell you that in the face of misfortune, you must "tun you han' mek fashion" – in a word, improvise. When Hurricane Gilbert decimated the country on 12 September 1988 the population woke to flattened coconut trees, no running water or electric light

LEFT: "ebony and ivory" in the Jamaica Defence Force.
ABOVE: the island has a large Chinese community.
ABOVE RIGHT: family is all-important.

– and several enterprising men walking around with "I Survived Hurricane Gilbert" t-shirts for sale, printed and produced even as the elements raged for hours.

Small children make cheese-pans and ball-bearings into scooters; a cotton reel and a piece of wire can entertain for hours. Don't misunderstand this: it's not that they don't like nice things. In fact, Jamaicans suffer from a quintessential case of "high chest", an appetite for the niceties of life. In the 1970s, when the economy rocked under the weight of oil costs and the resulting increase in import prices, there was great distress when imported cornflakes were

no longer available. Jamaica may well be one of the few places in which a supermarket has literally become a fashionable place to be seen; in Kingston, in the Sovereign supermarket, gossip takes place beside shelves stuffed full of oreo cookies, American apples and strawberries, in a land stuffed abundantly with mangos, pineapples, bananas and papayas.

Celebrities are important, and people trace the Jamaican roots of all international players even if they shock (Grace Jones in her heyday) or make huge, clanging errors (Buju Banton, the dancehall star who caused a furore in the international gay community with his hymn to homophobia, *Boom Bye Bye*). Jamaicans judge the famous, discuss them and endlessly hold them up for admiration – the point is, they are all sons and daughters of the soil. This celebrity watch is national pride in action. After all, what you do as a Jamaican is everybody's business, particularly if you do it in "foreign".

This is a land where every woman tells her children to "study you book"; where checking the *Daily Gleaner* for Common Entrance examination results (the entrance exams for secondary school) is something everybody does – even if they don't have children; where the school that you attended categorises you for life. There is a tale of a British hostess who once introduced two new arrivals from Jamaica during a party, delighted that they should have a chance to meet. The women sized each other up and then exchanged the names of the schools they had attended. The hostess watched in amazement as they – years away from school – turned their noses up at each other and walked away. True story. The two schools had been rivals at a local sports event.

No where nuh better dan "yard"

A nation divided then, you say? Jamaicans would laugh. What's really delightful amid all the noise and passion and opinion and seduction bacchanalia, throughout the shadism, is the bottom line. They are all united in one understanding: "no where nuh better dan yard", (than home). They are a family with all its delicious complexity, dysfunction, old sensitivities and subjectivity. There are disgraceful family members, a drunken uncle or two, a sister who's got herself into trouble, but try to challenge the family and see where it gets you. From the streets of New York to the cool depths of the Blue Hole in Port Antonio, from Iceland and Zimbabwe (yes, they are there too) to the hustle of Montego Bay, Jamaicans will rise and proclaim: *you cyaan come test we. You nuh see seh we big?*

Perhaps the reason Jamaicans are known so well is because they are that beloved adolescent: opinionated and occasionally moody, yet in their hearts, sweet as bougainvillea, changeable as the Caribbean Sea, eagerly looking out into the world for a reflection of themselves. Out of many, one hell of a people.   ❑

LEFT: black, green and gold patriotism at the World Cup in France, 1998.
RIGHT: a Jamaican bushman.

THE VIBRANT SPIRITUAL SPECTRUM

*There's something for everyone within the walls of the island's houses of worship,
from formal high-church Anglicanism to joyful Pentecostalism and Rastafarianism*

I t is Sunday in Jamaica. The opaque sunlight of morning falls upon little girls in bright dresses and white hats as they skip down the mountain roads and village streets of the island. Some hold the hands of their brothers, who look uncomfortable in their suits and ties. Old men in dark double-breasted suits with baggy pants clutch their bibles. Big dark-skinned women dressed in flamboyant satins and laces stumble through stony lanes and fields in their best shoes. Throughout the country, stone churches begin to fill with these people, their fingers tapping out staccato rhythms on tambourines and their voices echoing across the hills.

Here, as in most of the Caribbean, Christianity prevails and thrives. More than 80 percent of the population profess to belong to one form of Christianity or another, the legacy of centuries of European rule and influence. Yet recent years have seen increasing numbers of Jamaicans looking to their ancestral African home for spiritual inspiration, and even within the framework of Christianity the seductive spirits of Africa have reached out across the centuries and the seas.

Zemis and saints

A curious footnote to the Caribbean's reputation as a cradle of Christianity in the New World is found in the name "Jamaica". Historians generally claim that the name comes from the Amerindian word *Xaymaca*, supposed to mean "land of wood and water". But in the time of Josephus, the Jewish historian, there was a district in Palestine called Jamaica, and since Josephus wrote in the lst century AD, it seems reasonable to assume he had not met the Tainos. The theory that the name was chosen for its connection to the Holy Land is plausible, given the piety of the Spaniards who scattered saints' names all over

PRECEDING PAGES: Christians line up for baptism at Gunboat Beach.
LEFT: a Pocomania table deep in the Clarendon parish countryside.
RIGHT: in Mount Zion Church.

their American conquests – including the ultimate Christian appellation, San Salvador.

A scant six years after Columbus left the Caribbean for the last time, the first three abbacies had been created, one of them on Jamaica's north coast near today's resort town of Ocho Rios. From there the Spaniards set about wip-

ing out every other religion and massacring its adherents in the name of God.

The Tainos, like any other careful farming folk, had guardedly scattered their piety among various *zemis* (spirit gods) headed by one Jocuahuma and his wife. But in a fury to plant the "true cross" in every nook and cranny of the New World, the incoming Christians put the Indians to the sword, often en masse, after Absolution had shriven their heathen souls. Those who managed to survive were enslaved and thereafter worked to death.

A Dominican priest named Bartolomé de las Casas, appalled by the unholy scene, led the call for reform. Las Casas was not a member of the Spanish Inquisition. His father had been with Columbus on the earlier voyages; he went to the West Indies as a young man with Nicholas de Ovando, Governor of Hispaniola, in 1502, and in 1523 he was the first priest ordained there. Las Casas's father had taken a Taino back to Spain, and the young Bartolo had taken a liking to him and his people. As a rule, they were gentle – but not when raised. His personal feeling for the Tainos, whom he saw dying off before his eyes, moved him to suggest that, to save those left, the stronger, tougher Africans should be brought in. He knew the black men well. They had lived in Spain for

word for "soul". It is a doctrine that embraces the spirituality of the world's great religions, holding that life comes from a spiritual source, a soul, as distinct from matter. And, like Christianity, it states that life exists everywhere.

White rum and goat's blood

In early Jamaica one manifestation of Animism was *Kumina*. The music and dance of the African *Myal* cult were important components of its ceremonies. Practitioners used potions and entered trances to counteract the influences of *obeah*, the island's peculiar brand of witchcraft and sorcery. Its influence peaked in the

many centuries as both slaves and freed men.

It was of course a Jesuitical solution. After surviving in the tropics for an age, fighting off or staying ahead of the Caribs in their ocean-going canoes, the Amerindians were suddenly (in Fray Bartolo's eyes) incapable of standing the heat and in need of removal from the kitchen. In truth, las Casas was commendably soft on Tainos – but that left him hard on blacks.

The blacks who came to the west from Africa brought their Islamic and animist religions with them. Animism is an intellectually powerful doctrine burdened with a name which at first suggests something akin to animal worship, but which actually comes from *anima*, the Latin

mid-19th century, but it is still practised today.

The *Kumina* ceremony is also practised in modern Jamaica on rare occasions. *Kimbanda* and *kyas* drums beat out hypnotic rhythms. A queen or priestess sprinkles the drums with white rum, then fills her mouth with the liquid and spits sheets of alcohol over the participants. The smell of white rum, cigarettes and sometimes ganja hangs over the scene. The queen calls and sings in quavering shrills mixed with ancient African words. Then a goat is hugged and petted before an executioner severs its head in sacrifice. Blood gushes out of the goat's still trembling body and is mixed with rum and fed to the participants.

For obvious reasons, early *Kumina* rituals somewhat frightened the European conquerors of the island. The British historian Edward Long wrote in 1774: "Some of these execrable wretches in Jamaica introduced what they called the '*myal* dance' and established a kind of society into which they initiated all they could. The lure hung out was that every negro initiated into the *myal* society would be invulnerable to the white man; and, although they might in appearance be slain, the *obeah* man could at his pleasure, restore the body to life."

Forced into an accommodation with Spanish Catholicism, these early forms of African wor-

The marvellously evocative result of this union came to be called Pocomania (from the Spanish *poco* meaning little, *mania* meaning madness). In this hybrid faith the Christian altar has become a *poco* table, its length determined by the size of the congregation. Covered with a piece of white cloth, the African colour for solemnity and mourning, the table is laid with bowls of cooked white rice, white dove-shaped breads and plucked white-feathered chickens. White-turbaned priests sing white Christian hymns, the tunes all but unidentifiable in their *poco* state. Bent, sprung and coiled into wondrously rhythmical shapes, they lift the old

ship found no real difficulty. The incense, chantings, robes and candles were not unlike the formalities of their own priests, the so-called "witch doctors". It seemed that like them, the Christians also conjured up spirits, addressed saints and threatened death as a penalty for disobedience. The plaster statues in the alcoves compared favourably with their own stone and clay *zemis*. It all made for a swinging, rollicking wedlock between both beliefs, with no apparent serious damage to either.

LEFT: Queenie: singer, dancer, and leader of the *Kumina* cult which originated in the Congo.
ABOVE: a typical country church.

OBEAH

The slaves from West Africa not only transplanted but also transformed their traditional religious beliefs and practices, including belief in the supernatural or *obeah*. *Obeah* men (who could also be women) were the equivalent of Christian priests and had great power over their communities. Their powers could be used to help or harm. In modern Jamaica the *obeah* man and belief in the supernatural world still exist in a fairly small way, in spite of the rise in Christianity and other religions. Most often *obeah* men are consulted to curse wrongdoers, but they also claim to be able to help in matters of the heart, such as "tying" an errant lover to his or her partner.

standards into compelling tempi. What emerges is a Rock of Ages that really rocks, *Te Deum* without tedium.

In the ritual of ascent into total purity, Pocomania worshippers exalt God by placating the whole self, body and soul. After being purified by powerful surging, singing and chanting prayers, and a "tromp" or shuffling match around the table, the faithful are capable of entering a state of grace, or trance, that lasts for several hours. As with charismatics, healing and "speaking in tongues" are in the worship.

The Spanish Catholics gave way to the English Protestants in 1655; the Protestants briefly

gave way to the English Catholics before Protestantism was re-established in England in 1688. Since then freedom of worship has long been established in English-speaking Jamaica. The only exceptions were short periods of persecution of Baptists and Jews, the former for being soft on slaves, the latter when they became so rich the gentiles remembered that they had killed Christ.

In the dominant Christian sphere, analysis reveals almost equal percentages of Anglicans, Baptists and members of the Church of God. Other groups include Seventh-Day Adventists, Methodists, the United Church of Christ and Pentecostalists. There is also a healthy smat-

tering of Roman Catholics, mainly among the Chinese, Lebanese and Indian communities whose ancestors arrived in the 19th and early 20th centuries.

The past two decades have marked the rise of the Christian fundamentalists – hand-clapping gospel-shouting sects led by voluble and aggressive preachers. Many are American-oriented, and American-supported, and have made dramatic incursions. There are also members of the Revival Zion sect, cousins of those who shuffle through Pocomania but clinging to belief in Christian dogma.

Nowadays, except for a handful of devotees, "jumping *poco*" is a dwindling religious art form. The drive to identify a cultural origin unentwined with and independent of white Christianity turned the search elsewhere.

It took a while for a solution to the problem to jell. The belief that all things, including man, were an extension of and fused with the God spirit – the principle of the African religion – had been lost under the intentional cultural destruction wrought by the slave system. Ethnic and family dislocation effectively destroyed the historical connections.

But eventually out of this search for a deity whose best works would be in the interests of his followers came the most potent socio-religious political happening since Columbus waded ashore: Rastafarianism.

Marcus Garvey and Ras Tafari

What happened was bizarre, as sudden as it was shocking. A handful of "crazy men" appeared in the 1930s, making absurd claims about the Messiahship of the Emperor of Abyssinia: Ras Tafari, afterwards crowned as Haile Selassie, which translated means "the Power of the Trinity".

At that time few people suspected the profound effect the movement would have on Jamaican society. Rastafarians were long-haired and bearded long before the advent of the hippy fashions of the 1960s. If their interpretations of the Bible were outrageous, nevertheless they quoted with conviction and were ready to suffer for their beliefs.

The movement arrived closely on the heels of another whose impact on the world's blacks was just winding down. Founded and led by a Jamaican, Marcus Mosiah Garvey, the Universal Negro Improvement Association (UNIA) sought to gather ancestral Africans from a diaspora unmatched save by the scattering of the Jews.

Garvey was born at St Ann's Bay on 17 August 1887. He was working as a printer when he founded his little organisation with its grandiose name. The label turned out to be prophetic: Garvey's group did become universal. He soon found the island too small for his ideas, and after visits to some Central American countries he moved to the United States. The UNIA soon became a monolith.

Garvey called for self-reliance among "Africans at home and abroad" and advocated a "back-to-Africa" cause. He awakened a black consciousness and pride that aroused the hostil-

steamship company, the Black Star Line, an understandable corollary to a return of exiles but also a strong plank in his self-reliance platform. His steamship business floundered on what is believed to have been an old-fashioned legal "sting" prepared for awkward uppity blacks in ugliest America.

Garvey's honesty and integrity have never been in doubt, even among his detractors. He died in obscurity in London in 1940, but his body was brought home in pomp and ceremony to his native island for burial in a mausoleum befitting a man who, posthumously, has been made a National Hero.

ity of whites while it stirred the ideas of such young black Africans as Nwamdi "Zik" Azikiwe of Nigeria, Kwame Nkrumah of Ghana and Jomo Kenyatta of Kenya, each of whom would one day lead his country to independence.

In the United States, Marcus Garvey's work led inevitably to the defiant Montgomery bus ride and subsequent widespread bus boycott that signalled the start of the civil rights movement, and to the "canonisation" of Martin Luther King Jr. Garvey also attempted to establish a

LEFT: an interdenominational Eucharist at Kingston Parish Church.
ABOVE: zealously Biblical.

Locks, beards and bibles

Widely powerful overseas as Garvey's UNIA was, its local influence was no match for Rastafarianism. A doctrine that pre-dated the Black Power movement by two decades, it had settled into its rhythm well before the tramp of Black Muslims was heard in Detroit.

Rastafarianism's strength is in the spiritual power it exerts, not only through its teachings but also by asserting a root-continuity of the African race through history. Its adherents are regarded as children of the *Negus*, a title of the Ethiopian kings in their descent from King Solomon and the Queen of Sheba. It is a concept warranted to steady and give hope to any

Ganja: the Sacred Weed

In spite of its contemporary synonymity with Jamaica, *cannabis sativa* – the botanical term for ganja (marijuana) – is not native. Ganja arrived in Jamaica in the satchels of the indentured labourers imported from eastern India in the middle of the 19th Century. Like the Rastas and Coptics of modern-day Jamaica, Hindus of those times revered the so-called "Indian hemp" as a "holy plant".

Sugar-plantation owners soon determined that the use of ganja diminished the productivity of their labourers, so the first legislation introduced in Jamaica to outlaw the use of marijuana stemmed from capitalist concern about productivity and profits.

Still, the use of ganja grew slowly as the numbers of east-coast Indians increased. The birth of the Rastafarian movement in the 1930s provided another boost to its use in Jamaica. But ganja did not become a major influence until the "greening of America" in the 1960s brought the "reefer" out of the ghettos of Harlem and into the mainstream of life in the United States.

Mexico served as the first primary source of supply for the surging American market, but stringent border inspections instituted by US law-enforcement agencies forced American dealers to turn to alternative sources. Jamaica, only two hours' flying time or an easy sail from the Florida peninsula, topped their shopping lists. By 1974 about 70 percent of the ganja grown in Jamaica wound up in the United States.

Most farmers harvest their own crops to maximise profits and eliminate Jamaican middlemen. As one prospering grower explained: "In this business you can spend a year and set your family right. You can build a house, buy a car. You can live a comfortable life. I have seen guys who couldn't change their pants, and since this ganja business they can change dozens of pants now. It has helped a lot of people in Jamaica." Many Jamaicans call ganja "the poor man's friend".

In a country of high unemployment, low wages and a lack of job opportunities for the poorly-educated, the temptation to get rich from ganja is strong. Parliament continues to resist calls to legalise or ease penalties against ganja; but legalisation in Jamaica, in concert with similar moves in the United States, would make ganja just another crop. Its price would plummet and the huge profits would evaporate.

It is virtually impossible to envision a unilateral move by the Jamaican government to lessen or abolish its ganja laws without the blessing of the United States, and this seems very unlikely. Jamaica is in a difficult position. The legal ramifications are many when dealing with a drug that a significant number of the population considers a sacrament, or at least a medicinal godsend, while an equally significant number rely on its cultivation for economic livelihood, albeit illegal.

Visitors to Jamaica can find ganja in ample supply. It's usually available at resort areas, and even deep in the rugged interior where wanderers may be flagged down by youths toting a flour-sack full of it.

But ganja users must bear in mind the official penalties. Jamaica's Dangerous Drugs Act states that, for the possession of ganja, a first offence carries a stiff fine or imprisonment for "a term not exceeding three years or both such fine and imprisonment". The penalties increase with further convictions. ❏

suffering child kidnapped from the Old Country. At the last there is the unshakeable conviction of the Return from Exile – to Ethiopia.

Rastafarianism's contemplative and meditative nature, assisted by sacramental ganja smoking, Bible reading, drumming and chanting, has imbued the best of its followers with an ability to accommodate a religious, abstract-political, non-racist racialism. They have also acquired a capacity to cultivate ideas through music, costume, physical exercises, art, poetry and indigenous "cottage" industries like broom-making.

THE MESSIAH

Rastafarians believe that Haile Selassie, the former Emperor of Ethiopia, is the Messiah. His titles included, King of Kings; Lion of Judah, and Elect of God.

Reggae music developed in the rasta "yards" and produced superstars like the late Bob Marley. Politicians are so conscious of Rasta influence among Jamaica's youthful majority that, as Marley lay dying of cancer in a Miami hospital, he was awarded the Jamaican Order of Merit, equivalent to a peerage in the Commonwealth.

The true Rastafarian trains himself to desire nothing above the essentials in food and materials, to stand fit and feisty, afraid of no loss save his beard and bible. The beard is a sign of his pact with Jah, and the Bible is his source of knowledge, especially the prophecies of the Old Testament which he believes speak of Haile Selassie and Ethiopia. At the core of his faith is an absolute belief in the divinity of Ras Tafari – which underpins a belief in his own divinity as a child of Jah, Jehovah, God. Selassie's physical death did not kill belief in Ras Tafari. The crucifixion at Calvary did not kill Christianity.

I-and-I and Ras Tafar-I

The earliest Rastafarians developed a heroic spiritual strength that withstood ridicule, physical assault, discrimination, and imprisonment for ignoring the "Babylonian Law" against the smoking of the sacramental herb, ganja (marijuana). The appearance of Rastafarianism has been largely attributed to three mystics. Separately and unknown to each other, aided by Holy Writ and working *inwards to the I*, the inner divinity, the id – or, as expressed in Rasta liturgy, the *I-and-I* – these mystics arrived at the conclusion that the King of Ethiopia was

LEFT: the sacred weed.
RIGHT: Bob Marley was a member of the Twelve Tribes of Israel sect of Rastafarians.

the Messiah. His imperial titles included King of Kings, Lion of Judah, Elect of God.

The scriptures refer to Ethiopia and its people more than 40 times. They provided a rich lode of information and interpretation for the Rastas – as they have for the many opposing interpretations that have set believers at each others' throats since the Tower of Babel.

Selassie's visit to Jamaica in 1966 drew larger airport crowds than Queen Elizabeth II's, and incomparably more emotion. An estimated 100,000 followers

braved a downpour. Sceptics of the faith delight in recalling that the Ethiopian Emperor, appalled at the dreadlocked legions that swarmed around his plane, refused to leave the plane until the Jamaican authorities convinced him he would not be harmed. Rastas, in contrast, say Selassie wept at the overwhelming reception.

Selassie's title "Lion of Judah" has inspired Rastafarians to adopt the lion's image as their own. Indeed, the animal's mane has inspired some of the most elaborate of the dreadlock hairstyles. The locks also hark back to Africa, to the hairstyles of Masai and Galla tribesmen, and even to the Biblical story of the power of Samson's hair.

The doctrine has spread worldwide, wherever blacks live, and has attracted a growing minority of young whites. But the movement has also become a cover for opportunist criminals who adopt the distinctive hairstyle of their reggae idols but not the strict moral, social and political philosophies. Rascality is not a Rasta trait. The brethren are too deeply spiritual to doubt that Jah the Father, the inner I, will provide for all needs. That includes the sweetest smoking *sinsemilla* (ganja) this side of Eden.

> ### FUNKY DREADLOCKS
>
> The dreadlock hairstyle of the Rasta is fashionable. While the style gurus' locks flow free, most Rastas cover their heads with hats known as crowns.

> ### ILLEGAL DRUG OR MEDICINAL CURE?
>
> There are stiff penalties imposed on anyone caught selling or cultivating ganja, which can be up to 10 years imprisonment. Offenders prosecuted under the Dangerous Drugs Act includes anyone who manufactures, sells or deals in prepared ganja. It is a criminal offence to possess the weed, or to occupy premises used for preparing, smoking or selling ganja, or carry smoking paraphernalia. Although there is no sign of Jamaica or the international community relaxing drug laws there have been calls to legalise ganja. It has been suggested that it contains untested medicinal properties and has been used cautiously by cancer and multiple sclerosis patients.

The trappings of Rasta

Three major Rastafarian sects have evolved into their own Jamaican subcultures. The older, more traditional communities of the Rasta prophet Prince Emmanuel live in the hills of Bull Bay, east of Kingston. They occasionally can be seen around town, with their hair rolled into turbans, selling brooms and booklets. The Twelve Tribes sect has attracted more of the young political Rastas. Bob Marley, who took the tribal name Joseph, belonged to this group. Its headquarters are near the offices of Marley's Tuff Gong studio in Kingston. And the third sect, the Ethiopian Zion Coptic Church, an entrepreneurial spin-off, has run into problems in the past because of its dealings in ganja.

Indeed, the practice of smoking the sacred ganja sacrament continues to be one of the most controversial aspects of the Rastafarian movement. Not all members use the herb, however. Those who do usually smoke it in a pipe, called a "chalice", made of cow or goat horn or bamboo. The ritual of preparing the chalice with water, mixing the tobacco with "herbs", and lighting it is a sacred one, accompanied by the recitation of prayers, psalms and benedictions.

The Rastafarian religion has established a working code against greed and dishonesty, sexual envy, exploitation and aberration. Yet it has also accommodated the arts and a competitive edge in job efficiency, sports and games – and maintained a strong pride in black history.

The dedication of Rasta men and women has fired the imagination of the young Jamaican. The stylish shoulder-length funky locks or "dreadlocks" fashionably bob about everywhere – at international tennis tournaments, in the national soccer squad, or decently held under a Rasta-knit turban "crown" at important desks in commercial and government offices. The red, green and gold colours of the Ethiopian flag now adorn Jamaican clothes. The "Dread", the true religious Rasta, is a peaceful, careful, preferably self-employed achiever who stays within the law – save for his sacramental smoke. ❏

LEFT: a Rasta usually covers his head with a crown.
RIGHT: the Ethiopian Orthodox Church conducted funeral rites for reggae superstar Bob Marley in 1981.

THE RED-HOT RHYTHMS OF REGGAE

Reggae is synonymous with Jamaica, from ska, roots and rockers

to ragga and Dancehall, but there is a rich tapestry of other music too

What's that music playin' on the radio?
What's that music playin' everywhere I go?
I don't think I've ever heard
A sweeter feelin' in the whole wide world
Than that music playin' in my heart …
　　　　　– Gil Scott-Heron in *Storm Music*

So sings poet-songwriter Gil Scott-Heron in homage to reggae, the hot, raw recipe of rhythm and syncopation that is as synonymous with Jamaica as is jazz with New Orleans, salsa with Puerto Rico, soul with Detroit and blues with Chicago.

In little more than a decade the rugged sound of reggae fought its way up from cheap amplifiers fronting shabby record stores in the slums of Kingston to the sophisticated sound systems of the First, Second and Third World élite. Its influence has been widely felt: reggae has left its mark on the compositions of Paul McCartney, the Rolling Stones, Paul Simon, Eric Clapton, Elton John and Stevie Wonder. And it carried a tough, streetwise kid named Bob Marley from the ghetto to international stardom.

Reggae music has crossed language barriers, broken down race and class lines, patched up political schisms and dissolved religious differences. It has displayed a remarkable ability to drain hostilities and peel away people's prejudices. Its narcotic beat rarely fails to stir the most somnolent of cardiovascular systems.

The universal appeal and acceptance of Jamaica's unique reggae sound have turned the island into what one writer called "The Third World Nashville". Recording studios and record shops abound. Two of the largest studios are Tuff Gong International, a legacy of the late Bob Marley which is now headed by his daughter, Cedella; and Dynamic Sounds, operated by Byron Lee, associated with the

PRECEDING PAGES: music is an important element of Jamaican culture.
LEFT: legendary Burning Spear at Reggae Sunsplash.
RIGHT: Isaac Mendes Belisario's light look at a Jamaican musical combo of the mid-19th century.

legendary Dragonaires. These and dozens of other studios crank out hundreds of new titles each month in an attempt to satisfy the voracious appetite of Jamaica's listening public. New singers, bands and studios appear and disappear almost overnight.

Despite the diversification, reggae music is

the elixir that keeps Jamaica's recording industry healthy, much as country-and-western fuels the studios of Nashville. The story of the evolution of that music is a fascinating journey through Jamaica's colourful musical history.

Origins of reggae

The story starts with a myth that still prevails in some circles – that an import from Trinidad called calypso is Jamaica's music. There are two possible reasons for this.

The first was a talented Jamaican singer named Harry Belafonte. Belafonte recorded folksy commercial tunes like "The Banana Boat Song", "Jamaica Farewell" and "Island in the

Sun". The albums on which these hits appeared also served up a healthy portion of songs with a calypso flavour. The American recording company that turned Belafonte into an international star apparently saw little difference between two tiny islands in the Caribbean, let alone differences in their music or even in their dark-skinned inhabitants.

In reality, Jamaica did have a brand of popular music of its own – mento. Mento came from the music and dance that slaves from Africa used to enliven

> ### MENTO AND CALYPSO
>
> Mento leaned toward playful, almost pornographic lyrics, while calypso embraced amoral themes from the *mauvaise* language of Trinidad and the more genteel, but barbed, traditions of *picong*.

of African/folk culture into the period after Emancipation."

The slaves also took a decidedly African approach to the fashionable Spanish, French and English salon and court dances of the 19th century. Traces of the Parisian Quadrille can still be recognised in contemporary Jamaican folk dances.

At first mento was essentially music that accompanied a dance believed by some to have been sired by the quadrille. It called for a slow, undulating hip

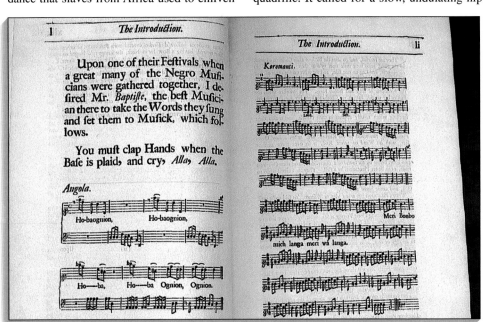

the drudgery of life on Jamaican plantations. Cruel masters often tried to beat the vestiges of African culture out of the souls of their slaves, but some cultural traditions inevitably persisted. Their music survived even after the authorities discovered that rebellious slaves used drumming to communicate with other pockets of dissidents on the island.

The University of the West Indies historian Edward Brathwaite noted in a study of Creole society in Jamaica: "It was this drumming, which the authorities and the missionaries tried unsuccessfully to eradicate by legislation and persuasion, respectively, which retained and transmitted important and distinctive elements

movement and the close body contact below the waist that is commonly called "dubbing". So to assume that mento is merely a Jamaican version of calypso is not accurate. Both forms acted as vehicles for social commentary, and even protest, but calypso embraced amoral and malicious themes that grew out of both the slanderous *mauvaise* language of Trinidad and the more genteel, but barbed, linguistic traditions of *picong*, while mento leaned toward more playful, almost pornographic lyrics.

Mento gained its foothold in rural areas where crowds flocked to lively *brams* dances in pre-radio days. The country bands consisted of a rhumba box (an adaptation of the African thumb piano), bongo drums, guitars and shakers. Even aristocrats sought mento bands to add spice to high-society dances.

But by the early 1950s mento had begun to fade under the assault of popular music transmitted from the United States. The lack of recording facilities in Jamaica at the time, which might otherwise have preserved and popularised mento, hastened its demise. Yet it had already firmly established itself in the island's musical evolution. According to folk-music researcher Marjorie Whylie: "In the context of popular Jamaican music, mento could well be regarded as the matrix."

exciting, danceable beat of rhythm-and-blues. Louis Jordan, Fats Domino, Amos Milburn and Roscoe Gordon became the rage in Jamaica.

Rhythm-and-blues put the stress on the second and fourth beats of the musical measure – the afterbeat – not unlike mento. R&B groups also pioneered the electrification of the guitar and organ, and later the bass. These instruments were to be fundamental in the development of popular Jamaican music.

In addition to its marked similarity to local rhythms, R&B also soared in popularity on the crest of a Jamaican phenomenon called the "sound system", a prototype of the disco.

The dukes of sound

Jamaica's first radio station, an amateur effort called ZQI, turned itself on in 1939. It broadcast live and taped programmes of European classical music and American pop, and smaller servings of Jamaican folk and classical tunes. Radio Jamaica replaced ZQI in 1950 but continued to feed the island a diet heavy in mainstream American music. Meanwhile many islanders had begun tuning in to powerful stations in the southern United States that pumped out the

LEFT: an old musical history shows the African influence on island music.
ABOVE: drumming the beats.

"Sound system men" trucked outsize speakers fed by powerful amplifiers to hired halls and beer gardens in every nook of Jamaica. People packed the halls when "the systems" thundered to the latest rhythm-and-blues recordings from New York and Miami.

Rivalries erupted between the systems men of the 1950s. Two of the greatest were the glittering Duke Reid and Clement Dodd, who discjockeyed under the *nom de guerre* Sir Coxonne. Michael Thomas graphically described Reid's style in an article in *Rolling Stone* magazine: "Reid used to arrive at his dances in flowing ermine, a mighty golden crown on his head, a .45 in a cowboy holster, a shotgun over his shoulder, and a cartridge belt across his chest. He was gorgeous, gold rings on every finger and thumb, the perfect gaudy image-melt of Hollywood gangster and high camp aristocrat. He'd have himself carried through the throng to his turntables, and then he'd let one go, the latest Lloyd Price, a rare old Joe Turner, and while the record played, Duke would get on a mike and start DJing, going 'Wake-it-Up, Wake-it-Up' and 'Good God' and 'Jump shake-a leg'."

The success of Reid and Coxonne spawned more competing systems – Nick's, Tom, the Great Sebastian, each promising systems that challenged the sound barrier and "exclusive" singles. Reid and Coxonne regularly flew to New York to sniff out new music, and Jamaican

artists began to take their cue from American rhythm-and-blues. Early vocalists like Laurel Aitken, Derrick Morgan and Owen Gray cut records strongly influenced by the New Orleans R&B sound. At first intended mainly for the systems market, their recordings found their way into the hands of the public. So Reid and Coxonne exchanged their sound systems for recording studios. By 1959 a record industry weaned on rhythm and blues and a modicum of calypso/mento had begun producing music that wasn't quite either but was very Jamaican.

Local talent

Jamaica's early musicians often developed their skills in military bands. One group at Alpha Boys' School proved particularly fertile ground. Established in the 1890s by the Sisters of Mercy order of Roman Catholic nuns, Alpha

catered to underprivileged youths and orphans. They included trombone players Rico Rodriguez and Don Drummond, tenor sax players Tommy McCook and Roland Alphanso, alto saxman Lester Sterling, trumpeter Johnny Moore, lead guitarists Jah Jerry and Ernest Ranglin, drummer Lloyd Knibbs and Drumbago, bass players Lloyd Brevette and Cluet Johnson and pianists Jackie Mittoo, Gladstone Anderson and Theophilus Beckford. These giants of Jamaican musical history graduated to jobs in dance bands or north-coast hotels until Reid, Coxonne and another systems man-turned-producer named Prince Buster coaxed them into the recording studio.

While this pool of talent was experimenting in the studio, the government's Jamaica Broadcasting Corporation (JBC) took to the airwaves in 1959. Its programmers showed a sensitivity for indigenous music that had been missing on local radio. In fact, the JBC played a milestone tune into prominence.

Beckford's "Easy Snappin'" walked the line between rhythm-and-blues and boogie-woogie, and in the process it stumbled upon a new musical style. Beckford nimbly picked out a steady boogie-woogie riff on his piano on the first and second beat. So did Jah Jerry on guitar, prior to his solo. Cluet Johnson walked his bass on a straight four, while Papa Son's brushwork accented the first and second beat. The horns of Alphanso, Rodriguez and Ossie Scott, meanwhile, lay back behind the beat in the best jazz tradition. Vocalising was kept to a minimum, allowing the musicians more room to play. The cumulative effect proved several degrees cooler than steamy R&B. Beckford had officiated at the birth of ska.

The onomatopoeic sound of the piano – *ska-ska-ska-ska* – gave this newborn musical form its name. The island's musicians suddenly found themselves with a music of their own to play, explore and cultivate.

The rise and fall of the Skatalites

Sir Coxonne succeeded in corralling Alpha's band of iconoclastic musicians; as a result, his Studio One amassed a catalogue that is a veritable encyclopedia of Jamaican music. From its ranks rose the Skatalites, comprised of McCook, Alphanso, Moore, Drummond, Mitto, Jerry, Brevette, Sterling and Knibbs. Although short-lived, the group left Jamaica a lively, largely instrumental musical form that fostered its own peculiar dance movement – a bobbing torso which was seemingly powered by a piston-like arm movement. Dancers grunted – *uh, uh, uh* – virtually echoing the horns and guitar.

Trombonist Drummond dominated ska in much the same way that Bob Marley came to dominate reggae. Drummond developed a highly personal instrumental style that successors have yet to surpass. A significant number of his compositions reflected minor blues melodies, melancholy, and a kind of non-verbal protest, an expression of his own deteriorating mental state.

> ### THE BIRTH OF SKA
>
> The birth of ska gave Jamaicans a music of their very own. It was developed by young local talent influenced by rhythm-and-blues and boogie-woogie.

most eloquent exponent, murdered his sweetheart and was committed to a mental asylum where he died in 1969. The Skatalites disbanded.

Thereafter singers began to encroach upon the music that had once been dominated by instrumentalists, articulating what the horn men had only hinted at. Musicians soon took a back seat to the vocalists. "Rock steady" had arrived.

Renting a tile

Perhaps as a result of the pensive "What do we do now?" period that followed the euphoria of independence, the tempo of Jamaican music

It was this rebelliousness in Drummond's music, and his conversion to the Rastafarian faith, that ultimately had a tremendous impact on the aspiring young musicians of his day.

Rastafarianism, with its spiritual godhead in the Ethiopian Emperor Haile Selassie and its other African cultural inspirations, redefined the folk rhythms of *Kumina* and *Burru*, beginning with the 1959 Folkes Brothers hit "Oh Carolina". That song introduced the legendary drumming of Count Ozzie, a musical guru and an ardent follower of Ras Tafari, who had a major influence on the music of the Skatalites. But ska had peaked in popularity by 1966. Drummond, its

The evolution of contemporary Jamaican music as depicted in album covers: **FAR LEFT**, the legendary Don Drummond; **ABOVE, LEFT AND RIGHT**, the Skatalites and "Toots" Hibbert .

slowed down. More emphasis was put on syncopation. The drop of the drum, characteristic of mento's rhythmic structure, became more pronounced. The guitar strum of rock steady also harked back to mento. The style freed the bass from timekeeping and gave it an infinitely more melodic role, again a possible throwback to the manner in which mento bands used the rhumba box. As the name implies, dance strongly motivated rock steady, but it was slower and more languid than the high-energy exercises sparked by ska. Dancers swayed to Delroy Wilson's "Dancin' Mood" and Alton Ellis' "Rock Steady" as if glued to one spot, keeping all their frustrations in that little space – "renting a tile".

The lyrics of some of these new tunes mirrored the poets' attitudes toward their people's place in Jamaican society. They did not always like what they saw. Consider Bob Andy's "I've Got to Go Back Home":

> *I've got to go back home*
> *This couldn't be my home*
> *It must be somewhere else*
> *Can't get no food to eat*
> *Can't get a job to get bread*
> *That's why I've got to go back home...*

As the lyrics became even angrier, rock steady gave way to reggae. This new emphasis on what songs had to say opened the door for a flood of Jamaican vocalists. Ironically, the best had begun their careers during the heyday of instrument-orientated ska. One of the most suc-

England's swelling population of Jamaicans re-adapted ska and called it "blue-beat". Cliff signed with Island Records in London in 1965 and scored with hits including "Many Rivers to Cross", a brooding ballad about his own hard times and struggles to survive. After winning a Brazilian song contest in 1968, Cliff returned to Jamaica where he immediately cut his first international hit for Leslie Kong, entitled "Wonderful World, Beautiful People".

Cliff's biggest break came when producer-director Perry Henzell cast him in the lead role of a movie, *The Harder They Come*. Cliff portrayed Ivan O Martin, a singing, gun-slinging

cessful was Jimmy Cliff, a skinny teenager with a soothing voice.

Born in Somerton, a small town on the outskirts of Montego Bay, Cliff left home for the lights and lures of Kingston. There he lived in its gaping pits of poverty, singing and recording several rhythm-and-blues-type numbers for sound systems men who balked at playing them. But in 1962 the precocious 14-year-old Cliff persuaded Beverly Records producer and owner Leslie Kong to give him a break. Kong did and never regretted it. Among Cliff's biggest hits for Kong's label was the 1964 story of a storm, "Hurricane Hattie". That same year Cliff emigrated to Great Britain.

tragic hero whose story (to a point) paralleled Jimmy's own life. The film became a cult classic and is credited with properly launching reggae music into the world limelight.

Cliff did not fare quite as well as his music, however. His subsequent conversion from a rebel singer into a clean-cut Muslim apparently lost him many of the fiery young fans looking for anti-establishment heroes. Ironically, these fans turned to another Jamaican singer whom Cliff had introduced to Kong, a man who wore his snaking locks like a crown and claimed the throne of the king of reggae. His name was Robert Nesta Marley.

Cliff has remained original and philosophical

about his unfairly diminished role in the development and popularisation of reggae. "My role has been as the shepherd who opens the gate. Now we're going into a different pasture," he said. With Bob Marley gone, Cliff would probably like another much-deserved crack at the title. His international stature has continued to grow steadily, if not dramatically, and he commands massive international followings.

Whatever happens to Cliff, he has still fared better than the man who apparently gave

ORIGINAL RUDE BWOY

Jimmy Cliff was the original "rude bwoy" and rebel. His role in the film *The Harder They Come* revealed the hardships of many country people living in town.

sellers including "Pain in my Belly". After serving time in prison on charges of dealing in ganja, Toots bounced out in 1966 with a song based on his experience called "5446 Was My Number". He followed it up with the timeless reggae anthem "Pressure Drop".

In Stephen Davis' definitive book *Reggae Bloodlines*, Toots boasted: "I invented reggae. Wrote a song called 'Do the Reggay' in 196- I don't remember when, but I wrote it anyway. It's true. Reggae just mean comin' from the people ... So all our music, our

Jamaica the word reggae, if not the music itself. Frederick "Toots" Hibbert recorded his first single the year before Cliff burst into prominence. Fame eluded Toots despite a powerful voice that he used in the best traditions of American gospel music. His style was inspired by Ray Charles and Otis Redding.

His trio, Toots and the Maytals, survived every twist in popular Jamaican music up until the 1980s. Clement Dodd produced the group's first hit, "Six and Seven Books", in 1962. For Prince Buster's label they produced several top

LEFT: Jimmy Cliff now and then.
ABOVE: Bob Marley on stage.

Jamaican rhythm, comin' from the majority. Everyday t'ing that people use like food; we just put music to it and mek a dance out of it... When you say reggae you mean regular, majority. And when you say reggae it mean poverty, suffering, Ras Tafari, everything. Ghetto. It's music from the rebels, people who don't have what they want."

Regardless of its literary origins, reggae, as the music came to be called about 1968, took the mild protests of the steady poets into the realm of all-out social protest as restlessness increased among Jamaica's poor majority, and rivalries intensified between the two political parties that promised salvation. Many groups even added militant touches to their songs. This marked the era of the "Rude Bwoys", as the word "boys" came out sounding when spoken in emphatic patois.

Birth of the Wailers

In the midst of this rapidly changing music and social scene of the mid-1960s, behind walls of corrugated tin and plywood in West Kingston's tough Trench Town, four youths named Junior Brathwaite, Peter (Tosh) MacIntosh, Bunny (Livingston) Wailer and Bob Marley began rehearsing. When Clement Dodd opened his Jamaica Recording and Publishing studios, in

As the gangs of tough unemployed "Rude Bwoys" began roaming the streets of Jamaica, they protested against their poverty by looting, shooting and defying the police. The music of Bob Marley's group echoed the times. They took the name Wailing Rude Bwoys before shortening it to the Wailers.

Derrick Morgan, the Clarendonians and Desmond Dekker of "Poor Me, Israelites" fame, also took up the tenor of the times, but it was the Wailers who prevailed. With major help from producer Lee Perry they transformed reggae into its best-known form. Others claim to have created the style. Clement Dodd said he

1964, the group was just one of many that came knocking on his door.

"When they first came in, they were like most other groups just starting out – young, inexperienced and willing to learn," Dodd recalled. "I coached them, worked on their songwriting. I had an album from the States by all the top soul artists. Bob Marley liked the Impressions, the Tams and the Moonglows the most. You can hear the influence on some of his early songs." That influence is most apparent in some of the group's slow romantic songs like "It Hurts to Be Alone". Faster ska hits like "Simmer Down" featured superlative backing by the Skatalites.

patented the sound when experimenting with an echo unit when his guitar began strumming the now-familiar *chaka-chaka-chaka* rhythm. But as one writer put it: "Reggae is not just a music, it is more a philosophy, with the advice handed out to a danceable beat."

In an interview with *Rockers* magazine Bunny (Livingston) Wailer offered another description of reggae in perfect patois:

"Well mek me tell you little history about Africa and reggae. Africa a one nickname; Ethiopia is the real name fe the whole a dat place. Reggae means the *Kings* music from the latin *Regis* e.g. like Regal. Now Ethiopia (Africa) is a place with plenty King so they have to be entertained with the King's music. So from you a play reggae with the heavy emphasis pon bass and drums, you a mingle with the spirit of Africa. The rhythm is connected to the heartbeat…"

Bob Marley understood that. His metaphysical imagery, his embrace of Rastafarianism and its inseparable association with the music, made reggae a musical style to be reckoned with.

Stir it up, rub it in

Embittered by the token pay that producers offered Jamaican artists of the times, the Wailers disbanded in 1967. Marley went to live with his mother in Wilmington, Delaware, but after a few months he returned to Jamaica and reorganised the Wailers.

This time the group formed its own label called Wailin' Soul. Despite a string of hits, including "Bend Down Low", "Stir It Up" and "Nice Time", it still failed to turn a profit. To add to the misfortunes, Bunny was jailed for nearly a year on ganja charges.

The restive Marley left Kingston again, this time for the parish of St Ann, where he had been born in the village of Rhoden Hall in 1945. He turned to agriculture and tried planting corn instead of singing. But a black American singer named Johnny Nash came to Jamaica in search of talent. The story has it that when Nash saw Marley performing on television he immediately set out for the country to find him.

The Wailers agreed to record an album for Nash's production company. Nash's own version of Marley's "Stir It Up" climbed into the Top Ten in many countries. Marley also collaborated on a film score with Nash in Sweden and penned the popular "Guava Jelly" with its immortal refrain: "You've got to rub it on my belly like guava jelly."

Meanwhile, Lee Perry had put together one of the great reggae studio bands, the Upsetters, for his new record label of the same name. Led by brothers Aston and Carlton Barrett, the Upsetters released several instrumental hits named for Italian spaghetti westerns, "The Return of Django" and "The Liquidator".

Before these records could fill the void left by Marley's departure, however, he returned

from overseas. The Wailers teamed up with Perry to produce some of their finest work: two classic reggae albums, *Soul Revolution Part Two* and *Soul Rebel*. One featured a song called "Duppy Conqueror" that, with its description of his release from a prison stint, firmly established Marley as a powerful songwriter.

> *Yes me friend*
> *Dem set me free again*
> *Yes me friend*
> *Me dey pon street again.*

Marley's melodies also broke new ground. The timing and the manner in which the importance of the instruments was apportioned just

sounded different. It embraced all the popular musical forms that preceded it, but Marley's brand of rhythm struck original notes that have come to symbolise reggae.

The money finally began trickling in, and the Wailers used it to form their own company, Tuff Gong, in 1970. Late the next year they exploded their biggest hit to that date, "Trench Town Rock".

In 1972 Marley's group joined forces with the Upsetters. Bob did lead vocals and played rhythm guitar, Tosh sang and also strummed guitar, Bunny sang and handled percussion, Eral Wire Lindo controlled the keyboards, Aston "Family Man" Barrett played bass, and

Left: a public invitation.
Right: Tuff Gong record company was started by the Wailers in 1970.

Carlton Barrett pounded drums. The new incarnation of the Wailers rocketed to international fame under the tutelage of a part-Jamaican producing genius named Chris Blackwell.

Blackwell and Marley catch fire

The London-born Blackwell had come to Jamaica as a youth with his Irish father and Jamaican mother. He had a privileged childhood living between a palatial Kingston home, that has since been turned into the Terra Nova Hotel, and a country estate in St Mary.

The versatile Blackwell worked as an aide-de-camp to two British governors of Jamaica,

Sir Hugh Foot and Sir Kenneth Blackburne. He also worked for an estate agent, as a scooter hirer and as a water-ski instructor in Montego Bay before a cousin persuaded him to try his hand at the recording business. Blackwell first hit the top of the charts with his production of Laurel Aitken's "Little Sheila". Pioneer singers Owen Gray and Jackie Edwards also joined his stable of talented artists.

In 1959 Blackwell joined with Leslie Kong and two others to establish Island Records, the label that helped make Jimmy Cliff an international star. It established headquarters in a looming house on Hope Road, Kingston, that subsequently became Tuff Gong's offices.

Rapidly growing sales of Island's records in Britain prompted Blackwell to emigrate there. In 1962 his cover version of Millie Small's "My Boy Lollipop" became the international hit that clinched his reputation as a successful producer of early British rock as well as Jamaican music.

The Blackwell-Marley association spawned the Wailers' first internationally acclaimed album, *Catch A Fire*. Critics in the United States and Great Britain praised it as the advent of a new wave in rock music. Similar applause greeted the release of the follow-up, *Burnin'*.

But the sweetness of success soon soured. Bob Marley's overwhelming stage presence and voice singled him out as the soul of the group. Tosh and Bunny left in 1975 to launch solo careers of their own. Tosh developed his own international following with albums such as *Legalize It* and *Bush Doctor*. Bunny (Livingston) Wailer turned elusively inwards and unpredictable after several stunning efforts, led by *Blackheart Man*.

Acclaim for a musical messiah

Bob Marley became a solo act in essence, too, but beefed up his act with an expanded version of the Wailers and a set of soulful back-up singers called the I-Threes. They consisted of his wife Rita, Marcia Griffiths and Judy Mowatt. With their backing, Marley danced, stomped, sang and shook his shaggy mane to greater success beginning with the release of *Natty Dread* in 1975. Albums like *Rastaman Vibration*, *Exodus* and *Survival* followed. They included such enduring singles as "Natural Mystic", "Jammin'" and "Positive Vibration".

The Third World gave Marley his warmest receptions. He hailed the transformation of Rhodesia into Zimbabwe with a song and a triumphant concert at the Independence Day celebrations in Salisbury on 17 April 1980. The Zimbabweans hailed him as a musical messiah. His own government in Jamaica awarded him the nation's third highest civil honour, the Order of Merit. That made him the Honourable Robert Nesta Marley, O.M. Marley became fabulously wealthy. Still, he never forgot his roots, as he sang in one of his most poignant songs, "No Woman, No Cry":

Said I remember when we used to sit
In the government yard in Trench Town
Observing all the hypocrites

Mingle with the good people we meet...
And then Georgie would make the fire light,
I seh, log would burnin' thru the nights
Then we would cook cornmeal porridge,
Of which I'd share with you...

By 1981 most of the world had acclaimed Marley as an international superstar and a major influence on contemporary music. Only the stubborn, stagnating studios in the United States resisted this man perceived as a Third World upstart. But at the same time they made hits of Marley's compositions recorded by others – like Eric Clapton's version of Marley's "I Shot the Sheriff".

his left. A tam in the red, green and gold colours of the Ethiopian flag covered his head, and his locks were neatly arranged on his shoulders. An estimated 24,000 people filed passed his casket that day, among them the Prime Minister and government officials.

The next day Marley was eulogised at a funeral ceremony conducted by members of the Ethiopian Orthodox Church. His wife, five of his children and his mother celebrated him with some of his own songs. Then his body was driven to a gravesite in the hills of the parish of St Ann near his birthplace. The funeral procession stretched for 89 km (55 miles).

Ironically, it was during a tour that Marley hoped would finally make his mark on America that his meteoric rise to fame suddenly ended. At the age of 36, at the height of his popularity, Marley died of brain cancer in Miami's Cedars of Lebanon Hospital on 11 May 1981.

Jamaica showered its fallen hero with a funeral the likes of which only Jamaicans could stage. Marley lay in state at the National Arena in Kingston from 8am to 7.30pm on 20 May. His body was dressed in a blue denim suit, a Bible propped in his right hand, his guitar in

LEFT: a young reggae fan.
ABOVE: Tuff Gong studios.

Reggae without Marley

Ironically, now that Marley is gone, Americans have finally acknowledged his music. On 19 January 1994 Marley was inducted into the Rock & Roll Hall of Fame before an audience of 1,500 at the Waldorf Astoria Hotel. The posthumous award was accepted by his widow, Rita, his mother Cedella Booker and several of his children. The years since Bob's death have seen the Marley family battling for the rights to the huge fortune left by Bob, who died without making a will.

Four of his children, meanwhile, formed their own successful group, The Melody Makers, led by Ziggy Marley who is backed by his siblings

Sharon, Cedella and Stephen. Reggae is still performed by accomplished groups, such as Third World, who continue to experiment with the genre.

Full circle

From Argentina to Japan, reggae spans the globe. Its influence can be seen in the music of performers such as Paul McCartney, Stevie Wonder, Paul Simon and Eric Clapton, who have borrowed reggae and added their own twist.

The rise of foreign reggae artists and groups

> **REGGAE SUMFEST**
>
> Montego Bay's massive music festival attracts crowds from North America, Europe and Asia. The event includes beach parties and sound system clashes.

on to several other spots on the island. An increasing legion of fans (over 200,000 each year) made the summer pilgrimage to hear the latest sounds of Jamaica. For four days, bands and soloists paraded across the stage from late night to well past dawn. Rastafarian hawkers peddled vegetarian I-tal food and *sinsemilla* (ganja). From time to time, black, brown, white and yellow joined hands in the middle of the night, singing, smiling and swaying in unison. Reggae music had brought them together.

has also paid tribute to the Jamaican music. Among the most successful have been British groups such as Steel Pulse, UB40, Maxi Priest and London-born Shinehead; all are in the vanguard of a new generation of practitioners of reggae. In a return to roots, as it were, from Africa have come Alpha Blondie and Lucky Dube, the latter sounding eerily like Peter Tosh.

From Sunsplash to Sumfest

Jamaica's original annual orgy of music, Reggae Sunsplash, became a sellout event both at home and on tours abroad. 1993 saw the event moved from its traditional home in Montego Bay to a venue in Kingston, and later

Sunsplash began to flounder, and in 1999 there was no event staged in Jamaica, although there were Sunsplash concerts elsewhere, including London, England. Meanwhile Reggae Sumfest filled the void left by Sunsplash, and today it is the biggest annual music festival on the island. Flights and accommodation are booked months in advance as thousands of people converge on Montego Bay.

Still, many wonder whether Jamaica's unique brand of contemporary music is continuing to evolve, or whether it is beginning to stagnate without its most famous practitioner. In the absence of any new direction the local scene has undergone a revival of the "dub" and DJ forms of reggae. This has spawned a new breed of dub poets, notably Mutabaruka, and DJ or Dancehall artists such as Shabba Ranks, Buju Banton and Tiger have shot to international stardom.

Shabba Ranks exploded on to the international music scene in 1989. Since then this Grammy Award winner has brought his own brand of hardcore Dancehall to Europe and the United States. His albums have successfully crossed over into the mainstream charts. Controversial Buju Banton had a record banned from the airwaves before he moved away from the hardcore scene, temporarily, to produce a roots-type album. Today his lyrics remain outspoken.

less succession of DJ artists rules the night and the Dancehall scene.

Jamaica's Dancehall music heralded a new computer dominance with a fast beat. The music is believed to have been born in the dance halls of Kingston, and the popular radio DJ Barry G is credited with creating mass-market appeal when he began playing different records built from the same rhythm track (beat), which were then played in the dance halls. Things snowballed when King Jammy's became its first prominent producer and proponent. Initially the melody was more important as the music evolved from the rock steady and reggae era

Back to basics

What used to be called DJ music has adopted a new name – Dancehall – and created an entirely new craze in fashion and dance. The lyrics of Dancehall music are direct and often controversial; the delivery is harsh and frequently aggressive. Outsize speakers and powerful amplifiers once again hold centre stage in the streets as well as in halls and beer gardens. Unlike the days when a few "sound system" men like Duke Reid and Clement Dodd set the tenor and tone of the music, a seemingly end-

with songs and lyrics from popular figures such as Frankie Paul, Chuck Turner, Sanchez and Pinchers. The emphasis of the genre shifted as it developed; records began to be popularised by the Dancehall fans and not broadcasting. The DJs who delivered the lyrics became the focus of the records which made superstars of Beenie Man, Bounti Killer, Shabba and Buju.

In spite of the music continually developing, realising its commercial appeal and having a high international profile, reggae sales are at an all-time low. There have been calls from within and outside the industry for Jamaican music to return to the reggae with melody, vocals, and conscious and inspirational lyrics.

LEFT: Ziggy, a Marley legacy; and a symbolic album.
ABOVE: shop at the music bus.

Dancehall style

The fashions in hair and dress for patrons of these sessions have likewise undergone radical changes. Men, or "dons", strut their stuff like peacocks in gaudily coloured clothing, bedecked with massive gold chains and jewellery known colloquially as "cargo". Hairstyles with elaborately sculpted patterns are in vogue; very dark sunglasses are obligatory, regardless of the time of day. The women, or "queens", not to be outdone, wear complex hairstyles dyed in multi-colours,

> ### DANCEHALL QUEEN
>
> The exciting and shocking Dancehall lifestyle inspired a Jamaican film about a genuine "Dancehall queen".

gelled to smooth, shiny, hard perfection, or adorn themselves in wigs and elaborate hairpieces. Their clothing ranges from suggestive to downright X-rated; competition for the most attention-grabbing outfit is fierce. In fact, a whole new growth industry devoted exclusively to the designing and making of Dancehall outfits has emerged. The music and the fashions have been successfully exported to the United States and Great Britain.

The undisputed "queen" of the Dancehall scene is Carlene, a girl of middle-class origins who has turned Dancehall into a lucrative business of fashion shows, television advertisements and appearances at home and abroad.

Uptown/downtown

If Dancehall is the vehicle of expression of "downtown", then soca, imported from Trinidad, is the adopted mode of expression of "uptown". This fusion of soul and calypso (hence the name: so-ca) is the essence of Trinidad's annual carnival celebrations. It was brought to Jamaica over 18 years ago by a group of friends who regularly made the annual pilgrimage to Trinidad's carnival, returning with the hits of that year. "Orange Carnival", which they started as a private fête, grew to an annual commercial event for local and overseas fans.

Byron Lee and The Dragonaires, one of Jamaica's most enduringly popular bands, have been regular participants in Trinidad's carnival over the years. It was Byron Lee who took Jamaica carnival to the people, with costumed street parades and invited artists from Trinidad performing together with his own band, The Dragonaires. The carnival scene has since exploded outside the corporate area into resort towns across the island. In the process a number of individual events with fruity names like "Mangerine Carnival" and "Grapefruit Carnival" were born. Back in Kingston, the Oakridge Carnival and Downtown Carnival have joined the burgeoning festivities which take place in Easter week.

Between reggae's offshoot (Dancehall) and the importation of soca there is a void which has been filled by a return to the "golden oldies". A resurgence in popularity of tunes of yesteryear, all the way from the 1940s to the 1980s, is noticeable on the local radio stations and in the frequency of public "Oldies" sessions. Veterans of the music industry, Winston Blake and Bunny Goodison are in great demand both for their knowledge of the music and for their extensive collection of records.

Contemporary artists still maintain the prophetic tradition of reggae music made popular by stars like Bob Marley and Dennis Brown, both now deceased. Luciano is just one such artist producing "nouveau roots" and "culture" music. The evolution of the music into its next phase is still waiting in the wings. ❏

LEFT: soca music and carnival Jamaica-style.
RIGHT: Luciano brings conscious lyrics.

DANCE AND DRAMA: EVERYBODY'S A STAR

The culture of the performing arts is rich and varied: from classical dance to roots theatre and pantomime, from Festival! to Dancehall divas

Jamaicans pride themselves on their sense of rhythm, their love of laughter, their loose-limbed style. It's not peculiarly Jamaican, of course. It's Caribbean. It's African. It's a reflection of the many cultures blended into one unique style, a marriage between the Old World and the New.

In such a society those who entertain on stage must sweep and soar and rise to every occasion to satisfy the demanding audiences. Jamaican audiences can be cruel in their detachment, sitting on their hands until those on stage have earned their approval. But when the performers do gain that respect, the Jamaican audience embraces them.

Regrettably, Jamaica's cultural image has long been linked with contortionist limbo dancers, kerosene-guzzling fire-eaters, and calypso dancers who gyrate to endless repeats of "The Banana Boat Song" and "Island in the Sun." Island tour companies would do well to exploit the sophistication of many modern travellers arriving on the north coast by mounting coach tours to Kingston to showcase what Jamaica really has to offer in the realm of dance and theatre.

Dance to prominence

Even novice travellers would enjoy a performance of the National Dance Theatre Company of Jamaica, popularly known as the NDTC. It vividly embodies the rich tapestry of expression that draws its inspiration from the island's diverse ethnic influences. The company is based in Kingston. Its annual season runs from mid-July to mid-August, but there is also a mini-season in November and December. Special performances include examples of religious works from the company's extensive repertoire, held at the Little Theatre at dawn on Easter

Sunday every year. It's definitely worth rising with the sun to see.

The National Dance Theatre Company is an ensemble of dancers, musicians and singers which started out in 1962 as an offshoot of that

year's Independence celebrations. Two young men, Rex Nettleford and Eddy Thomas, were the catalysts.

The Jamaican company has been acclaimed in concerts from Mexico City to Moscow, from Adelaide to Atlanta and points in between. Elected heads of government and royalty have thrilled to performances of the NDTC. And the dancers have triumphed in spite of the thin air of Mexico City and bouts of jet lag incurred by jaunts from Jamaica to Australia.

They have been cheered by homesick Jamaican immigrants and expatriates in Brooklyn and Toronto, Cardiff and London. Young Muscovites have tried to barter company members

---

PRECEDING PAGES: golden street-carnival performer.
LEFT: a 19th-century John Canoe troupe member.
RIGHT: dance and music work together.

right out of their blue jeans, and Canadian parliamentarians in dinner jackets surprised the Jamaicans by turning up unannounced at an early overseas performance in a small Canadian town.

Dance

The repertoire of Jamaica's dance companies incorporates eclectic dance forms ranging from the indigenous to classical to modern, reflecting the island's decades of exposure to external influences. The Jamaica School of Dance, one of the schools of the Edna Manley College of the Visual and Performing Arts, has helped foster

There is a definite distinction between traditional formal dance and the creative dance developed as part of the vibrant Dancehall music scene. The dancehall diva-dancers have influenced the world of popular music with their outlandish outfits and innovative, acrobatic movements, and the Jamaican film *Dance Hall Queen* explored this scene.

Festival!

Dance is only a small part of the cultural fruits that flourish throughout the island in midsummer each year. The weeks leading up to the annual Independence Day celebrations on 6

the growth and development of dance. In the last 20-odd years other talented dance companies have emerged and gone on to win national and international acclaim. Two such companies are L'Accadco and Tony Wilson's Company.

The Jamaican government has traditionally thrown its support behind the island's artistic movements, a fact that has undoubtedly contributed to Jamaica's pre-eminence in Caribbean-wide artistic and cultural circles. Yet neither the NDTC nor any other performing group has ever received financial aid from any central governmental source. They flourish strictly on the willingness of company members to excel and attract throngs of paying customers.

August have simply been designated "Festival!". Painters, public speakers, singers, woodcarvers, sculptors, musicians, photographers, even chefs roll out their best work and most polished performances in competition for prizes and plaudits.

Festival! merged from old Jamaican community traditions of Christmas morning concerts, "tea-meetings" of songs, dances and recitations, and church fund-raising rallies. It also provides an outlet for the Jamaican flair for "showing off". In the 1950s the Jamaican government began organising this hotchpotch of events into a single massive outpouring of talent. Now a formal Festival! Movement meanders through the countryside each year encouraging competition in various artistic endeavours, village by village and town by town. Finals are held during Independence Week in Kingston, and many are televised nationally.

Obviously, Trinidad's internationally famous Carnival celebrations provided a spark for Jamaica's Festival!. Gate receipts and business sponsorships have added commercialisation to the festivities. But the importance of Festival! shows in the deep involvement of schools throughout the island. They seize the opportunity to motivate their students to maintain and further develop island traditions.

Jamaicans adapted the word to describe a fast-moving musical comedy with plenty of dialogue in the local patois. Far from being a silent show, this delicious concoction produces a potent piece of theatre alive with wisecracks, send-ups of peculiarly local situations and lampoons of historic events. Pantomime "makes sport" of grave matters, and mimics the foibles, the heartbreaks and the joys of Jamaican life. The "pantomime" audience in turn responds with continuous peals of laughter and even joins in repartee with the performers, becoming an integral part of the show itself.

The "pantomime" tradition dates back to the

Pantomime in patois

An old Jamaican phrase advises that "we tek bad sinting mek joke". Roughly translated, this means that the speaker tempers potential tragedy with humour. Nowhere is this Jamaican characteristic more in evidence than in the distinctive 140-year-old tradition called the Pantomime.

Although the word "pantomime" conjures up visions of a performance without words,

FAR LEFT: Independence Day celebrations.
LEFT: celebrating at Accompong.
ABOVE: members of the National Dance Theatre Company in performance.

years when Jamaica's Little Theatre Movement, the Caribbean's oldest theatrical ensemble, staged traditional versions of the British pantomimes that were based on fairy tales. Actors and actresses performed in standard formulas: a Dame, for example, always appeared in a comic, exaggerated manner so that there was no confusion about the actual male identity of the performer. A Principal Boy and a Principal Girl routinely added romantic interest, and a villain provided the conflict in the story line. *Beauty and the Beast*, *Sleeping Beauty* and *Pandora's Box* were among these early favourites.

But, as Jamaicans always do, they soon transformed British tradition into their own thing.

They added characters from Jamaican folklore like Anansi, the West African Spiderman, and his innumerable prodigy – Brer Tacoma, Brer Tiger and others. Soon local playwrights brought in caricatures of public figures like politicians and police chiefs. British music-hall songs gave way to indigenous rhythms, including the drumming frenzies of Pocomania and the beat of Christmastime's John Canoe (Junkanoo) dances. Contemporary rhythms like ska and reggae eventually found their way into pantomime scripts like that of *Johnny Reggae*. *Carib Gold* in 1960 and *Banana Boy* in 1961 saw the introduction of sophisticated dance

movements, ushering in the establishment of the NDTC in 1962.

The island's finest designers of costumes and stage sets, leading composers and musicians, playwrights and directors regard it as an honour to be part of the Pantomime team each year. Major actors, actresses, dancers and singers donate their time and talent. "Miss Lou" (Louise Bennett) and the late Ranny Williams were the stars for many years, and the Pantomime has made household names of performers such as Charles Hyatt, Oliver Samuels, Lois Kelly Miller and Leonie Forbes.

The Pantomime opens its season at 6pm on Boxing Day each year.

Local productions

The national Pantomime, NDTC and Festival! are only the most visible manifestations of Jamaica's rich tapestry of performing arts. Tucked away in unexpected corners of Kingston and even in small villages in the countryside are little theatres where amateurs perform like professionals. One such group is the Montego Bay Little Theatre Movement, formed in 1975, which performs regularly at the city's Fairfield Theatre. Nationally-known playwrights like Basil Dawkins, Ralph Holness, Julie Harris, Aston Cooke, Barry Reckord, Louis Marriott, Sam Hillary and Trevor Rhone unveil new works at these intimate local venues.

Such smaller productions have a built-in advantage: they can be taken on tour through the villages and towns of the island, where they reach an even greater, more appreciative audience. It's not uncommon in Kingston to find as many as six new plays or revivals, and sometimes a dance performance or two, all of them running at the same time.

Since 1976 the Little Theatre Movement has also operated a national School of Drama as part of the Edna Manley College of the Visual and Performing Arts. Some have bemoaned the introduction of "drama education" in an island so full of natural talent. Nevertheless, students are trained in all aspects of the theatre, from acting to light and sound systems. Other drama schools include the Cathi Levy Academy and the Cathi Levy Players, ASHE, and the Area Youth Foundation and Area Youth Crew.

There is also more Jamaican music beyond the beats served up by discos, sound systems and reggae concerts. Music on the island is not just reggae (*see The Red-Hot Rhythms of Reggae, page 107*). The Jamaica Folk Singers, led by Olive Llewin, have earned an international following for performances that weave music and movement into an educational form of entertainment. In addition, the National Chorale and the Carifolk Singers offer folk and classics.

The full spectrum of Jamaica's performing arts – dance, drama and music – adds up to an island that is one vibrant, glowing stage even after the curtain has fallen. ❑

LEFT: Louise Bennett in the Pantomime "Queenie's Daughter".
RIGHT: students perform folk dances at Kingston Parish Church.

JAMAICA ON THE SILVER SCREEN

From Hollywood images of colonial life to comic bobsled escapades and gritty realism from local talent, this island has a rich cinematic history

One of the earliest hit movies which captured the beauty of Jamaica was *Island in the Sun*, filmed in 1957 with a stellar cast of James Mason, Joan Fontaine, Harry Belafonte and Dorothy Dandridge.

The character played by Belafonte reveals much of the politics, and race and class distinction, which permeated every aspect of island life in the 1950s.

However, Hollywood depictions of Jamaica and Jamaicans have concentrated on the beautiful scenery and portrayed the people as having a proclivity towards humour.

It is local film makers and writers who tend to deal with the unpalatable aspects of island life, as seen in *The Harder They Come*, *Dancehall Queen*, *The Lunatic* and *Third World Cop*.

SWEET REGGAE MUSIC

No self-respecting film made in or about Jamaica could be produced without a pumping reggae soundtrack, and often the music is more popular than the movie.

The soundtrack to Perry Henzell's 1973 cult classic *The Harder They Come* included reggae hits like "You Can Get It If You Really Want It", "Many Rivers To Cross" and "Pressure Drop". And *Dancehall Queen* featured the music of Beenie Man, Third World and Bounti Killer, and the outlandish hairstyles and fashion of Dancehall culture *(see page 120)*.

▷ **RUDE BWOYS RULE**
The Harder They Come showed the harsh realities of Kingston; directed by Perry Henzell, it made a screen star of Jimmy Cliff.

△ **PAPILLON**
In *Papillon*, made with film extras from Seaford Town, Steve McQueen played a French thief who escaped from Devil's Island prison.

△ **DANCEHALL QUEEN**
The Kingston ghetto and the outrageous Dancehall music scene featured prominently in this rags to riches tale.

◁ **CLUB PARADISE**
Jamaican beach life was the backdrop for the movie starring Robin Williams, Twiggy and Jimmy Cliff.

ART IMITATES LIFE: COOL RUNNINGS

In 1988 Jamaica fielded a team in the four-man bobsled event at the Winter Olympic Games in Canada: this from a Caribbean island famous for its blazing sun, beaches and blue sea, but no snow. From practice runs in a pushcart on the hills of Jamaica to coping with freezing conditions in Calgary, the 1993 Disney film *Cool Runnings*, based on the team's experiences, reveals a determination to triumph over adversity. Although the real bobsled team didn't win a medal in 1988, finishing 29th overall, it earned the admiration of Olympic fans, and Jamaica entered a team in the Winter Games in 1992, and at Lillehammer in 1994 finished 14th, the best position yet (*see Sport* page 154).

◁ THE MIGHTY QUINN
Two American actors, Denzel Washington and Robert Townsend, starred in the comedy-thriller set in Jamaica.

▽ BOND COUNTRY
Novelist Ian Fleming created his James Bond character in Jamaica. The film of the book *Dr No* was shot on the north-coast.

◁ COCKTAIL
Tom Cruise tends bar from New York City to a white-sand beach in Jamaica. The tropical location is in fact Dragon Bay in Port Antonio on the east coast.

▷ WINTER SPORTS
The Jamaican bobsled team which competed in the 1988 Olympics inspired a film starring Leon Robinson.

TALES FROM "BACK 'A' YARD"

Jamaicans may not be avid readers, but an oral tradition that goes back to the days of slavery has given birth to a vibrant literary scene

orget sugar, bauxite or bananas: Jamaica's biggest export over the last 50 years has been culture. Reggae, of course, but a lot more besides. In a part of the world famed for its artistic flair, the island has developed an enviable reputation for producing world-class painters, sculptors, opera singers, dancers and writers. It was a Jamaican, Claude McKay, who was the first black author in literary history to write a bestseller – *Home to Harlem* (1928). In his footsteps has followed an impressive line-up of poets, novelists and dramatists, who have written about everything from Kingston's slums to the lost innocence of village life.

Literary achievements have not gone un-recognised. When independence arrived, in 1962, the young Edward Seaga – then in the Ministry of Development – commissioned an anthology of Jamaican writing. Jamaican authors have won international prizes and are studied in American and European universities. The press reviews the latest literary offerings, and a handful of local publishers offer the best in home-grown talent. Understandably enough, Jamaica is proud of its writers.

Simple diversions

And yet few Jamaicans are avid consumers of literature. If the island is a literate society (an esti-mated 95 percent of adults can read), it is by no means a literary haven. Most Jamaicans' acquain-tance with poetry or fiction ends when they leave school. "I had to read the classics when I was at school," says a young law graduate, "and I haven't been near a novel since." One Jamaican publisher ruefully admits that he knows by name most of the people who buy his books. On closer inspection, the bookstores – most towns have at least one, and Kingston has several – hardly go out of their way to promote local authors. Their books are often lumped together in a "West

Indian" section, hidden behind American paper-back blockbusters and accountancy textbooks.

Part of the problem is the easy availability of other media: satellite TV, videos, radio. Another is price, since books can be expensive in rela-tion to income. But perhaps the biggest obsta-cle to Jamaican literature is language itself.

Standard or patois?

Most Jamaicans can read and speak "standard" English, the language in which they are taught at school. But few, not even the most educated, view this as their first language. This is instead Creole – also called patois or "Jamaica Talk" *(see Pardon my Patois, pages 167–168)*. It is in Creole that the majority of Jamaican families and friends converse, and it is this language which most directly and spontaneously expresses the entire range of ideas and emotions.

In fact, to be Jamaican is to be more or less bilingual, but standard English, the language of the law, officialdom and authority, is still a more alien, less comfortable means of expression than

PRECEDING PAGES: folk stories for all.
LEFT: education brings literacy.
RIGHT: the National Library is home to Jamaican clas-sics in both patois and English.

Creole. Newspapers and American television mostly come in the standard form, but the most popular forms of self-expression – music, drama, rap and performance poetry – are more likely to take the form of Creole.

The history of Jamaican literature is to a large extent built around the tension between two languages: on the one hand, the language of the old colonial system, the élite, the educated minority, a mostly written language; on the other, that of the majority, the language of the urban street and the rural village, a spoken language. Since Jamaicans began writing they have been aware of this contradiction. Increas-

ingly, poets, playwrights and novelists have tried to bridge the linguistic gulf, to bring Jamaica Talk into their work as a way of expressing and responding to the experiences of ordinary Jamaicans.

Followers of fashion

Literature from, as opposed to about, Jamaica was slow in coming, as the colonial period, with its slavery-based plantation system, did little to encourage aesthetic activity among the vast majority of people. What writing there was came from white clergymen or leisured professionals, and tended to copy the conventions of whatever was currently in fashion in London.

One interesting exception was Francis Williams, an 18th-century black Jamaican who was sent by his master to Cambridge to prove that "a negro given the right circumstances could acquit himself as creditably as a white man". Williams wrote odes in Latin and penned this revealing advice to himself: "Nor let it be a source of shame to you that you bear a white body in a black skin." The few novels published at that time were mostly sentimental and didactic tracts on the inhumanity of slavery.

It was not until the end of the 19th century and the consolidation of a post-abolition society that the island began to witness the arrival of local literature. A key figure at this time was the Jamaica-born white writer Thomas Henry MacDermot (1870–1933), who reversed his last name to give the pseudonym Tom Redcam. A journalist and publisher, Redcam launched the "All Jamaica Library" of cheap fiction by island authors. Alas, it was a flop, but Redcam's own *Becky's Buckra Baby* (1904) was an early attempt to inject Caribbean dialogue into a novel. He also included elements of dialect in his poetry, but most of it followed the ornate fashion of the day:

A Little Green Island, in far away seas!
Now the swift Tropic shadows stride over thy leas;
The evening's Elf-bugles call over the land,
And ocean's low lapping falls soft on the strand.

New days, new beginnings

One of the writers published by Redcam has been hailed as one of Jamaica's finest, and was also the first of many to seek success overseas. Claude McKay was born in 1890, the son of

EXPATRIATE WRITERS

Sunny Jamaica seemed a million miles away from cold post-war London, and in the 1940s and 1950s the island was home to two expatriate British writers.

Noël Coward bought a house near Ocho Rios and wrote in 1949: "The house is entrancing. I can't believe it's mine... we had one more martini and sat on the verandah on rockers, looking out over the fabulous view, and almost burst into tears of sheer pleasure."

Ian Fleming entertained such literati as Graham Greene and Evelyn Waugh at his Goldeneye home, also on the north coast. He named the hero of his books after the author of a book on the birds of Jamaica.

poor black farmers in Clarendon parish. His precocious talent was soon recognised by Redcam and others, and in 1912 he emigrated to New York where he became an integral part of the Harlem Renaissance, the literary movement that brought black writers such as Langston Hughes to international attention. Much of McKay's prose and poetry dealt with American themes, but his *Banana Bottom* (1933) is a classic evocation of Jamaican village life; in it the foreign-educated heroine, Bita, finally rediscovers her rural community and identity. McKay was never to return to Jamaica, but his work reveals an enduring nostalgia for the island's landscapes and people.

The 1930s and 1940s were tough times for Jamaica, and the literature which appeared after World War II reflected a new social realism as well as a thirst for positive change. New political parties had emerged from the strife of the 1930s, including the nationalist People's National Party (PNP), which attracted writers and intellectuals. The landmark novel of the post-war period was V.S. Reid's *New Day*, (1949) which celebrated the coming of a new constitution and universal suffrage in 1944. But it also looked back to the violence and trauma of the 1865 Morant Bay uprising, making an explicit connection between Jamaica's divided past and brightly nationalist future. Writing in a much-modified form of Creole, Reid, a PNP stalwart, sought to capture the voices and aspirations of a people on the move.

Yard rhythms

The dirty and dangerous slums that had mushroomed around Kingston also entered Jamaican literature, most dramatically in the work of Roger Mais, another PNP supporter. Far from McKay's rural idyll, the world evoked in *The Hills Were Joyful Together* (1953) was one of inner-city squalor, poverty and police brutality. Mais quite clearly wanted to shock his readership with a novel of tragic inevitability, where the good and bad alike are dragged down by their corrupting shanty-town surroundings. In his next novel, *Brother Man* (1954), the degrading slum tenement or "yard" is again the set-

LEFT: Sean Connery with Noël Coward at Blue Harbour, his home in Ocho Rios.
RIGHT: Roger Mais and Orlando Patterson wrote about Ras Tafari and life in the tenement yards.

ting, but here a glimmer of hope appears in the Christ-like shape of John Power, the Rastafarian whose healing and peace-bringing qualities were foreshadowed in the previous novel's ganja-smoking character, Ras.

Dungle fever

Rastafarianism was to receive fuller treatment in another "yard" epic, *The Children of Sisyphus* (1964) by Orlando Patterson. This powerful and poetic depiction of Kingston's notorious Dungle slum showed why the lure of millenarian cults and the mirage of a promised African homeland were so strong among the

urban underclass. Like Mais, Patterson inserts elements of spoken patois into his dialogue and narrative, as when the fatalistic Miss Rachael reflects that she will never escape the Dungle: "Massah God know why 'Im put we down ya. 'Im say is ya we mus' stay. Wha' de use yu try an' run?"

Perry Henzell's film *The Harder They Come* (1973) was the ultimate tribute to one of Jamaica's more disreputable folk-hero types, the country boy turned ghetto gangster. Based on a real 1940s gunman, and with a classic Jimmy Cliff soundtrack, Jamaica's first feature film followed the rise and fall of one Ivanhoe "Rhygin" Martin, a romantic but criminal outsider at odds with the police. Capitalising on the film's cult success, Michael Thelwell wrote a fictional version of the "rude boy" story which was surprisingly good. Thelwell injected splashes of Creole into the dialogue to recreate on paper the violent atmosphere that Cliff's songs immortalised. After Rhygin's death he is remembered as a hero by the ghetto kids:

> "Bram, Bram, Bram!" he leapt from cover, guns blazing.
> The posse returned fire. "You dead!" the sheriff shouted. "Cho man, you dead!"
> "Me ah Rhygin!" the boy shouted back. "Me can' dead!"

Dub poetry lives on

The advent of "dub poetry" in the 1970s and 1980s further strengthened the link between reggae, yard culture and literature. Blending chanted lyrics with the rhythmic intensity of bass and drums, this socially conscious brand of performance poetry included practitioners such as Mutabaruka and Linton Kwesi Johnson, the latter based in London. This was as near to "downtown" literature as anything before or since, emphasising the spoken over the written, Jamaica Talk over standard English.

Like reggae DJs or rap artists, the dub poets (most rejected this categorisation) articulated the grievances and passions of inner-city hot-spots like Trenchtown. According to Oku Onuora, dub poetry involved "dubbing out the little pentameter and the little highfalutin' business and dubbing in the rootsical, yard, basic rhythm that I-an-I know". One of the most promising of this generation, Michael Smith, the author of *It a Come* (1986), died at the age of 29, a victim of Kingston's culture of political violence.

Miss Lou – a gentle poet

A far gentler form of spoken poetry is to be found in the work of Louise Bennett (known universally as "Miss Lou"), who for several decades has championed patois in her work as a popular entertainer and folklorist. Her themes are the trials and tribulations of everyday life, but these are explored with humour and a verbal ingenuity often missing in the more strident dub poets.

Although Miss Lou's poetry is published, it is in her live readings and recordings that it most directly comes to life. Some of her most celebrated poems deal with migration, such as

THE CUNNING SPIDER

Apart from the African linguistic ingredients in Jamaican patois, the form in which the island's people most directly maintain links with their pre-slavery heritage is folk culture, which ranges from herbal medicine and religious beliefs to story-telling. In the dark days of slavery, folk tales were a vital way of maintaining some sort of cultural contact with the lost homeland and passing down wisdom and knowledge to succeeding generations.

Through the oral tradition, characters and stories survived and developed over the centuries to take on more modern forms. One such character is Anansi, the cunning spider who is still the subject of countless morality tales in

Jamaica, the wider Caribbean and his birthplace, Ghana.

Several Jamaican writers, including Miss Lou and Salkey, have adapted traditional Anansi stories for a contemporary readership. While the theme of these tales is usually similar (Anansi is physically weak, but clever enough to fool the stronger Tiger, Monkey or Dog), the setting and the moral of the stories can be varied. Almost invariably, though, the "trickster" Anansi triumphs over the slow-witted personifications of power and authority.

It is hard not to see in these stories a reflection of Jamaicans' respect and affection for the clever individual who gets the better of those at the top.

Colonization in Reverse, a wry look at the exodus of Jamaicans to Britain in the 1950s and 1960s. But she has come in for criticism among those who think that patois and poetry don't mix. At an early performance, she relates, an indignant voice was raised in protest: "A dat yah modder sen yuh a school fa?"

Following in Miss Lou's footsteps, a number of female poets and novelists have earned a following at home and also further afield. Olive Senior, for instance, won acclaim and the Commonwealth Writers' Prize for her short stories *Summer Lightning* (1987), which recreate a range of standard and patois registers inside

fat when she leave Jamaica and get worse fat since she go to America, what was this woman doing dressed like this?... See ya Jesus! Bella no done yet, she had dyed her hair with red oxide and Jherry curls it till it shine like it grease and spray."

No Jamaican family has been unaffected by emigration during the last century, and the experience of separation and return looms large in the island's writing. In cases such as Bella's the treatment is comic, while in others the emphasis is much more on the poignant. Along with the money, emigration has also brought disillusionment and homesickness. In his poem

sharply observed vignettes of rural Jamaica. Other successful women writers include Velma Pollard, Pamela Mordecai and Lorna Goodison.

Going foreign

In her short story *Bella Makes Life* (1990) Goodison describes the return from New York of Bella, transformed by her period of exile: "Bella dressed in some clothes which make her look like a chequer cab. What in God's name was a big forty-odd-year-old woman who was

---

LEFT: rural Jamaica is a recurring image in local writing.
ABOVE: everyone knows someone who has left the island and "gone 'a' foreign".

The Lament of the Banana Man Evan Jones gives voice to the ex-farmer who is now a bored ticket collector in the London Underground:

> *Gal, I'm tellin' you, I'm tired fo true,*
> *Tired of Englan, tired o you.*
> *But I can't go back to Jamaica now.*

For many Jamaican writers, emigration to Britain, the US or Canada has been the only way of winning wider recognition and making a living from their work – only V. S. Reid spent his entire career on the island. Their dilemma is concisely expressed by Andrew Salkey: "Yes, I am one of those who left the island; but I am also one of those few who remained behind; I never left." ❏

ART, FROM GHETTO TO GALLERY

There is art on every street corner, from murals to mahogany carvings to sculpture, installations and paintings from the intuitives, surrealists and modernists

Tivoli Gardens grows from the rubble of West Kingston. The street pavement is cracked and potholed; the vacant lots are indiscriminately littered. Poverty glares at the people of Tivoli Gardens. But it has not blinded their visual appreciation or stripped them of their self-esteem.

In defiance of the destitution that surrounds them, these people have transformed block-house architecture into an artistic wonderland. Tivoli Gardens' residents have painted the walls of their flats – not just in solid shocks of colour, but with individualised works of art. There are red, green and gold tributes to former Ethiopian Emperor Haile Selassie, who is revered by the country's Rastafarians. There are pastel, pop-style pastiches that have now been made famous by reggae record-album covers. A flowery paean tells visitors: "Welcome to our New City."

Mostly, there are pristine landscapes and florals that remind residents of the natural beauty that lies only a few minutes away from the ghettos of West Kingston. A mother and daughter, arm in arm, look out at a lake while father romps with a dog. These images are bold statements proving that rampant poverty has not robbed the Jamaican spirit of its richness. The walls of Tivoli constitute only one example of the island's colourful tradition of "yard art".

Surprising strokes from painters' brushes decorate the island – from cliffside villages in the Blue Mountains to makeshift cafés in Negril. Even the execution, symmetry and poetry of the reams of political graffiti scrawled on every inch of unadorned island space in the run-up to general elections underline the Jamaicans' drive to express themselves, to create.

Unfortunately, honest, unpretentious "yard art" has inevitably "inspired" rows of banal woodcarvings, baskets, beads and paintings that

PRECEDING PAGES: bold and bright: painting at Ocho Rios craft market.
LEFT: "Homage to Beethoven", a painting from the palette of National Gallery Director David Boxer.
ABOVE: the late artist Edna Manley relaxes at home.

gather dust on the shelves of the souvenir stands. This commercialisation of genuine artistic values, mass-produced with little care or pride, is aimed at earning an easy buck from the indifferent visitor bent on bringing home a sample of "native art" – bought at the airport on the way home – to wave under the nostrils of

envious neighbours, and to fill the gap on the mantelpiece between the Niagara Falls souvenir plate and the bowling trophies.

More satisfying – and worthy of the praise, attention and higher prices it commands – has been the work of the self-taught intuitive artists who have emerged from the masses of yard artists. Many actually hailed from the Tivoli Gardens and the "Trench Towns" of Jamaica.

John Dunkley, for instance, was a humble Kingston barber. Born in 1881, Dunkley had limited schooling, but he followed many other young Jamaican men of that time and went to Central America to seek his fortune. Dunkley returned in the 1930s and set up his barber shop in a poor neighbourhood of downtown Kingston. Although he had no formal training in art, he covered his shop and even the barber's chair with colourful patterns, flowers and motifs. He also began painting on canvas, dark, almost morbid images: stunted tree trunks, embryonic rabbit holes and mesmerising shapes and symbols that sometimes seem subtly Freudian.

Dunkley did not sell many of his paintings during his lifetime because they were so unusual, so non-European and so different. Today his works are almost impossible to purchase and command the highest prices paid for Jamaican art.

Those who followed him captured untrained,

in isolation from each other and from foreign influences, each of these artists developed a technique totally unique in style and theme. Kapo's paintings and woodcarvings include lush landscapes and "Garden of Eden" images. The Browns produce bright paintings that mesh with the colourful essence of their Rastafarian themes and motifs. McLaren brings the human side of Jamaican life to the canvas in detailed landscapes and cityscapes.

The early artists

Art lovers attending new exhibitions often buy the best of the works and spirit them away to

untempered visions of Jamaican life at the grassroots with honesty and clarity. Gaston Tabois, the late Mallica Reynolds (who painted under the pseudonym "Kapo"), Everald and Sam Brown, Albert Artwell, Allan Zion and Sydney McLaren comprise the vanguard of the artists who are Jamaican originals. They draw their inspiration from the country's colourful and complex traditions and not from the dictates of outside influences.

Compared with the older and more internationally known works of the self-taught artists of neighbouring Haiti, the works of the Jamaican school are less homogeneous and stylised and, consequently, often more interesting. Working

private collections. In this way, Jamaicans celebrate an artistic tradition that dates back even before the Europeans set foot in the Americas. The island's first inhabitants, the Tainos, used cave walls instead of canvas. The drawings have been compared to prehistoric African art and resemble ancient Hawaiian petroglyphs. Figures of birds, and humans carrying spears and wearing headmasks, have been discovered in Mountain River Cave north-west of Spanish Town.

The Tainos, in turn, may have inspired the figures found at Sevilla la Nueva, Jamaica's first capital, in architectural friezes which were created by equally anonymous Spanish artists who accompanied Christopher Columbus on his voyages. These pieces are on display at the Institute of Jamaica in Kingston.

The earliest published works of note were the so-called Spillsbury prints, executed by an unknown English artist and printed by "Mrs Spillsbury of London"; they depicted the harbours of late-18th-century Jamaica. William Beckford, a wealthy property owner, brought two artists to Jamaica in 1773: Philip Wickstead painted portraits of the island's plantocratic families; George Robertson did landscapes.

AWARD-WINNING ART

Ceramicist Gene Pearson was awarded the Musgrave Bronze Medal in 1993. His artwork in clay, earthenware, stoneware and raku is influenced by nature.

parade in grotesque costumes still celebrated during the Christmas and New Year holidays.

Joseph Bartholomew Kidd, a Scottish painter, produced a series of sensitive sketches of Jamaican estates and Kingston.

Another interesting artistic development was the commissioning and importation of some of history's finest works of religious Neoclassical sculpture to trim the island's Anglican churches, tombs and monuments. Two famous pieces that still stand are the Rodney Memorial Statue in Spanish Town,

More famous itinerant artists followed and succeeded in capturing for posterity the essence of 19th-century Jamaica. James Hakewill's watercolours were transformed into aquatints and bound in one volume. Isaac Mendes Belisario, an Italian Jew born in England, arrived in 1830 and set up a studio in downtown Kingston where he produced portraits. He is best known for 12 sketches of the slave custom of Junkanoo, or John Canoe, a lively musical

LEFT: the surreal flights of fancy of artist Colin Garland show in his painting of "Mr and Mrs Goose".
ABOVE: one of the paintings that have decorated the walls of Kingston's downtrodden Tivoli Gardens.

sculpted by John Bacon Sr, and the monument to Simon Clarke in the 18th-century Anglican Church in Lucea, executed by John Flaxman.

But these early Jamaican works reflected a colonial society, and virtually ignored the heritages of the African slaves and smaller pockets of indentured labourers from other countries. All that changed in the 20th century with the emergence of nationalism in Jamaica and other British colonies.

The 1930s spawned traumatic events which prompted the island's black majority to join labour unions and political parties in a political awakening aimed at improving their lot in spite of continuing British control. The nationalistic feelings also surged through the veins of Jamaica's artists. A group of middle-class artists began to probe the Jamaican psyche, utilising indigenous subjects and themes. European styles continued to influence their approach to brush and chisel, but their changing directions formed the nucleus of Jamaica's modern-art movement.

In the colonial social structure, some of these artists actually lived at the top. They were the privileged bourgeoisie of Jamaica. Among their leaders, in fact, was Edna Manley, the wife of one of the founding fathers of independent Jamaica, Norman Manley, and mother of the former prime minister, the late Michael Manley.

ourselves from the domination of English aesthetics," said Manley in an interview before her death. "It came out in the poetry. You had the poets in those days writing about the daffodils, snow and bitter winds they had never experienced. I told them, 'Why don't you describe the drought, when the sun gets up in the morning and is king of the world all day, and everything is parched? You can smell the seymour grass, and the sun goes down in a blaze of glory only to come up again tomorrow. The drought is on.' That is a very Jamaican and artistic and poetic theme. And we had the most terrific arguments over this."

Edna Manley mothered the infant art movement, helping to organise art classes at the Institute of Jamaica, and inspiring others to meet and exchange ideas and opinions.

The personalities in Edna Manley's circle included the poet George Campbell, artist Albert Huie, interior decorator and furniture designer Burnett Webster, photographer Dennis Gick, sculptor Alvin Marriott and novelist Roger Mais. These dynamic talents held provocative meetings where they would show each other the work they had been doing, which generated extended critiques and heated arguments.

"The great thing was to be able to see ourselves as Jamaicans in Jamaica and try to free

The Jamaican establishment at that time, Manley added, "thought we were bonkers". Differences in attitudes towards the arts exploded in 1939 when a group of 40 liberals stormed the annual general meeting of the Institute of Jamaica. The Institute had been created "for the encouragement of arts, science and culture in Jamaica", but the board of directors was perpetuating a colonial interpretation of arts and culture.

"Our leader was a lawyer, Robert Braithwaite," said Edna Manley. "He pointed to the portraits of the English governors on the wall and said, 'Gentlemen! We have come to tell you to tear down these pictures and let the

Jamaican paintings take their place.' There was pandemonium. But we knew they could not ignore us any more."

The incident at the Institute meeting sparked prompt action. Manley and some volunteers began to give art classes. That mushroomed into larger, more formal training courses until, in 1950, the Jamaica School of Art was finally established. The school has since trained most of the country's established artists.

During his directorship in the 1970s, Karl Craig expanded the school and opened its doors to a wider segment of Jamaican society. Its success, particularly in obtaining international funding, led to the establishment in 1976 of a Cultural Training Centre in Kingston. Now renamed the Edna Manley College of the Visual and Performing Arts, the college houses the schools of Art, Music, Dance and Drama.

The National Gallery

The Institute also transformed a small collection of local art into a major establishment, the National Gallery. The paintings, sculptures, sketches and woodwork of most of the island's leading artists were initially housed in Devon House, itself a fine example of Jamaican architectural art; the elegant white wooden structure stands back from a wrought-iron gate on Hope Road in New Kingston. The National Gallery has since moved to more secure premises in the Roy West building on Kingston's waterfront.

The Gallery's current curator, a noted artist in his own right, is Jamaican David Boxer, an art historian educated at Cornell and Johns Hopkins universities. Boxer has nurtured the young collection of works and helped it to blossom into a major collection. The Gallery, in cooperation with the Smithsonian Institute, sent a representative group of Jamaican works on a North American tour in 1983.

By the 1960s and 70s many young Jamaicans had been sent abroad to study and had returned home with new ideas and strong styles. They applied their nationalistic themes to their external experiences in Cubism, Modern Abstract, Nordic Expressionism, Surrealism and other

INTUITIVE ART

The gallery at Harmony Hall in St Mary is the only place on the island which has a room dedicated to Intuitive Art.

contemporary techniques. Their work added another dimension to the island's art.

Leading names in the National Gallery's collection include Carl Abrahams, Karl Parboosingh, Ralph Campbell, David Pottinger, Cecil Baugh, Edna Manley, Barrington Watson, Colin Garland and Christopher Gonzalez. Gonzalez trained at the Jamaica School of Art, where he later taught, and at the California College of Arts and Crafts in Oakland. His work as a sculptor earned him a commission from the Jamaican government to

fashion a statue of the late reggae superstar Bob Marley. This impressive work now stands in the Gallery.

Noting that US artists look on his work as old-fashioned and romantic compared with their experiments in super realism and the abstract, Gonzalez said: "American art is less people-oriented than ours. In Jamaica, we still deal with people as human beings. Maybe they will say that Jamaica is a more primitive place, but the human element is much stronger. The artist reflects this in his work." For the visitor to the island who has thrilled to the colourful spectrum of life in Jamaica, the focus on humanity makes Jamaican art that much more rewarding. ❑

LEFT: David Pottinger adds the finishing touches.
RIGHT: a portrait of the late Michael Manley exhibited at the National Gallery.

SPORT

This small island claims as sons and daughters international stars in the fields of athletics, boxing, cricket, football, basketball, netball and dominoes

To excel at sport in Jamaica has been seen by many as the ticket to a university education, travel, fame and wealth. A sports scholarship can provide a wonderful opportunity. Until the late 1990s the arena was dominated by cricket, athletics, boxing and basketball, all sports which offer poorer youngsters the chance to use their talent as professional sportsmen and women. Dominoes also features prominently within the culture, and though that considered a more sedate sport the Caribbean version tends to be loud, requiring real skill and nerves of steel.

Since Jamaica qualified for the 1998 World Cup finals the spotlight has begun to shine more brightly on football, transforming it from a previously under-resourced and amateur sport.

Football

Early one afternoon in June 1998 the streets of Kingston, usually choked with traffic, were deserted. There were very few criminal incidents, the police reported later. For two hours Jamaicans sat transfixed in front of their televisions while the Reggae Boyz, the national football team, were playing their first match ever in the World Cup finals in France, the third Caribbean country, after Cuba and Haiti, to reach this level of the competition.

That the team failed to make it to the second round was a disappointment to all Jamaicans, but in the end it did not matter. The team was beaten by Croatia and Argentina but defeated Japan, and many took solace from the fact that very few "first-timers" managed to score any goals, and even fewer won any matches.

The effects of the island's rise to the élite group in world football went beyond the field of play. The team's success was a source of unprecedented displays of national unity, with

PRECEDING PAGES: playing a few holes of golf at the Half Moon Club.
LEFT: the legendary cricketer George Headley shows the form that made bowlers tremble in the 1930s.
RIGHT: Ricardo Gardener plays in World Cup 1998.

the qualifying matches at the island's national stadium watched both by spectators draped in the national colours and by politicians from opposing parties sitting together and shaking hands with each goal and each win – a far cry from the traditionally antagonistic nature of the island's party politics.

The success of the football team has elevated the sport to the same level as high-profile track and field athletics and cricket, the two sports which have traditionally dominated the island. Inevitably, it also inspired a debate between fans of cricket and football about which sport is the more popular. The debate has been inconclusive, but the Reggae Boyz' performance has given a fillip to previously slow moves to reorganise football in Jamaica.

The sport is well managed within the school system, with matches attracting large crowds, but there has been no infrastructure for football to grow after the players leave school. While athletics and cricket offer chances for a professional career, there has been no such opportunity for footballers. However, several Jamaican players have professional contracts overseas.

Most have been to the United States to play in the Major League and the "A" League, while some still have contracts in Britain. The connection between British football and the game in Jamaica is strong. Several British players from the professional league, born of Jamaican parentage, opted to play for Jamaica during the World Cup in 1998. They provided the professional support for an otherwise amateur and inexperienced team. Such is the promise of Jamaican football that each January talent

scouts from US universities descend on the island looking for players for their schools from the national under-20 competition.

The success of the Reggae Boyz was also aided by more foreign input: in the shape of René Simoés, a diminutive Brazilian football lecturer and coach of Brazilian junior teams. He brought to Jamaican football an exciting element of samba which, combined with reggae, produced a heady mixture.

After he had watched the team play he was quoted as saying: "When I came to Jamaica and looked at the football team at play, I found 11 talented seals who could balance the

THE DOMINANCE OF DOMINOES

Dominoes is the island's most popular pastime. The game is played by two, three or four people, using small tiles traditionally carved from ivory or bone with small round pips of inset ebony.

To the casual observer it would appear that the aim of the game is to match tiles; in fact it is a sophisticated game of strategy, with players "reading" the game – as one does in poker – to determine how many and which tiles or numbers are outstanding and should be played.

Dominoes originated in China, and made its way to Europe in the 18th century. Over the years the game has developed. It changed to its current form when it was

transported by Europeans across the Atlantic to the Americas, including the Caribbean islands.

In Jamaica dominoes is played by young and old, it can be played anywhere and anytime; for high stakes or just for fun. The game is often a popular event at informal dinner parties and community-centre and social-club gatherings. Many domino teams, affiliated to clubs, have in the past competed for a national title, and against other Caribbean island teams. The game has now gone international with players from the USA, Canada and the UK. In June 1999 Jamaica hosted a tournament which included competitors from the United Kingdom and the Cayman Islands.

ball on their noses for a long time, but who could not pass it to each other. We had to loosen them up by teaching them that playing football was like dancing, much as you do to my samba and their reggae."

His approach is uncomplicated: "I tell the players that there is a philosophy they should adopt. They should enjoy the game. They should think of it as if they are going to a party. And at the party, the ball is their girlfriend. So you do not allow the other guy to take your girlfriend and dance with her. You must keep her."

There are plans to set up a professional league, but although Jamaica did reach the

from the record-breaking male quartet of Arthur Wint, George Rhoden, Les Laing and Herb McKenley, which individually and collectively dominated the 440 yards and mile relay races in the late 1940s, to Mel Spence, Donald Quarrie, Grace Jackson Small and the indefatigable sprinter Merlene Ottey, who vowed to continue to win medals even at the age of 40.

Explanations vary: one suggestion, that children in deep rural areas can get to school on time only if they run, is accepted with some cynicism. However, a more plausible explanation is that the sport is well organised in schools. The annual school track and field

World Cup finals it will be some time before it can become as significant an international force in football as it is in athletics and cricket.

Athletics on track

There are many ways of assessing Jamaica's wealth in track athletes. While no figures exist, it is believed that, for an island of 2½ million people, Jamaica has the highest per capita volume of Olympic medals in the world.

There is some mystery as to why the island has produced so many world-class sprinters,

LEFT: don't be fooled: dominoes is a game of skill.
ABOVE: the indefatigable Olympian Merlene Ottey.

championships, held over four days at the island's national stadium, produces budding champions who often go on to win scholarships to prestigious US colleges and universities.

Netball

Jamaica has also made its mark internationally in netball, a game played mainly by women and similar in many respects to basketball. It is played mainly by countries of the British Commonwealth, and Jamaica's team has ranked over the past five years between two and four in the world. Again, this sport has benefited from a well organised school league. Because of the similarities to basketball, some members of Jamaica's national team have graduated to playing professional basketball overseas and are vying for lucrative contracts with increasingly popular teams in the Women's NBA (National Basketball Association) in the US.

The Jamaica connection

In addition to producing their own athletes, Jamaicans are eager to claim as their own any leading sports personalities who have a connection – even the most tenuous – with the island. Having produced world boxing champions, such as Michael McCallum, Trevor Berbick and Simon Brown, Jamaicans also embrace

those who were born in the island but left at an early age, and those who were born elsewhere of Jamaican parents, including Lennox Lewis, Donovan Ruddock and Lloyd Honeygan.

If Jamaica could recruit members for a basketball team with a connection to the island, the squad would include Patrick Ewing of the New York Knickerbockers. The island also claims to have contributed more than a few cricketers to the England squad, including Devon Malcolm and Dean Headley, grandson of the great George Headley. There are also first-class footballers like John Barnes and Robbie Earle, and athletes such as Linford Christie. Jamaica's sporting prowess is also being

shown in less traditional fields. There is no record of snow having fallen in Jamaica, but the efforts of the competitive bobsled team at the 1988 Winter Olympics in Lake Placid, initially met with derision, were subsequently treated with respect, and a team has been fielded ever since. The trials of the first-ever bobsled team were the subject of a Disney film, *Cool Runnings*. By 1999 the sport was being carried along by a new momentum. Jamaica hosted the annual meeting of the International Bobsled Federation, and the local association announced it had recruited one of Norway's leading coaches for the national team.

Beneath the veneer of the island's international success in major sports there is a gnawing concern among administrators that standards could fall and that sports could be affected by the demands of the modern game and pressure from technology. Except for cricket, and more recently track athletics, Jamaican sport has been slow in making the leap into professionalism, and most of the island's professional sportsmen and women take their skills abroad.

There has been little interest in or financial resources aimed at establishing professional leagues in any of the major sports, but this is changing. The government has set up the Sports Ministry and the Sports Development Foundation, and the success of the national football team in the World Cup has resulted in business elements taking a greater interest in sport.

The US influence through the ubiquitous satellite dish means that basketball, with its associated glamour and excitement, is becoming more popular, a development which some administrators think will turn youngsters off traditional sports such as cricket, football and track athletics.

The island has also had success, albeit moderate, in tennis, badminton, swimming, cycling, polo and hockey. Strangely enough, some might say that the most popular of all Jamaican sports is not an Olympic event. In the evenings, at weekends and on holidays, from rural villages to the most affluent neighbourhoods, there is the persistent and loud crack of bone on wood, punctuated by an occasional shout. A domino game is under way. ❑

Left: basketball reflects the US influence, the promise of college scholarships and financial security.

Cricket

To the uninformed, cricket comes across as an utterly preposterous game played by a faintly ludicrous group of men who should know better. To the knowledgeable it is nothing of the sort. Not in Jamaica, and particularly not in Kingston's Sabina Park, where the staging of a "test" match (an international lasting five days) or a "limited overs" game (lasting one day) ignites as much excitement as a World Cup football match or a heavyweight boxing championship.

In test matches both teams wear white uniforms, while in modern one-day matches they wear coloured ones. Jamaica plays in regional competitions against other Caribbean countries. But the ultimate in cricket are the test matches in which the West Indies team, drawn from the islands and Guyana, plays against the national teams of Australia, England, New Zealand, Pakistan, India, Zimbabwe, Sri Lanka and South Africa.

Rules of the game

A "bowler", like a pitcher in baseball, throws the ball to the batsman, who attempts to hit it into the field, out of the reach of the opposing team's fielders. When the ball has been hit the batsman then attempts to run between the "stumps" (three wooden sticks stuck into the ground) at either end of the 20-metre (22-yard) "pitch".

Hitting the batsman's stumps with the ball, or having the ball caught off the bat by a fielder, are the more straightforward ways of getting the batsman out. When 10 of the 11 members of a team are out it is the turn of the other team to bat in an attempt to get as many runs as possible.

In test matches each team bats twice, and the runs from each of these "innings" are combined. The team with most runs wins, although if time runs out and there is no conclusion, the game is deemed a draw. In one-day matches, the teams are limited to a specific number of balls bowled to their batsmen. The team scoring the most runs wins the match.

Cricket is played across the island, especially at weekends. School playing fields, parks or any flat, open areas are frequently used for the game by village, parish and county teams. The sport is played in all schools, and, increasingly by women.

RIGHT: record-breaking Courtney Walsh with the West Indies cricket captain Brian Lara.

This is a far cry from the cricket introduced to the region by the English in the late 19th century. Then the games were a social affair, with locals serving tea, and retrieving balls from the bush, rather than playing. But today some of the most intensely passionate test matches are those played between the West Indies and England.

Jamaica has contributed some of the greatest players to the game and to the West Indies team. George Headley, who established himself as the world's greatest batsman, is to cricket what his contemporary Babe Ruth is to baseball. Other great Jamaican batsmen include Lawrence Rowe, J.K. Holt Sr and J.K. Holt Jr, and O.G. "Collie" Smith, one

of the best all-rounders. There have also been talented bowlers such as Alfred Valentine, a left-arm spin bowler (who makes the ball veer at different angles when it hits the pitch). He and his Trinidadian colleague Sonny Ramadhim were immortalised in a calypso tune for their performance in a West Indies versus England match in 1950.

More recently the island has contributed two of the world's great pacers – fast bowlers who hurl the ball at the batsman at close to 160 kph (100 mph). The first of these is Michael Holding, once the fastest in the world, now retired. The other is Courtney Walsh, who has taken the third-highest number of test wickets in cricket history and seems destined to become the number-one wicket-taker. ❏

DISCOVERING NYAM

Originating from Africa, nyam *means "eat" in Jamaica, and once you discover this island's delicious food you won't want to* nyam *anything else*

Spicy and pungent, aromatic and enticing, greasy and filling, mouth-watering and hot: a blend of African, Chinese, Indian and European cuisines, yet individualistic in its appeal – this is Jamaican food. Unfortunately, the visitor who sticks to resort-hotel restaurants will never be exposed to the incomparable taste of Jamaican cuisine or to the great variety of seasonal fruit.

From jerk pork to ackee and salt fish, rundown to callaloo, "curry goat" to mannish water, Jamaican cooking is still a little-known delight, although it has been slowly gaining international attention since the 1980s. And while some hotels are becoming more adventurous, adding ackee quiche and staple soups like pepperpot and red pea to their menus, these tend to be pale imitations of authentic Jamaican cuisine, which is best experienced in home cooking. A close second are the wayside food stalls, many of which are located on tourist routes and are characterised by quaint shelters with equally quaint names.

Ackee – a national delicacy

The delicacy which arouses most curiosity in visitors is ackee, one of the main ingredients in the national dish. This red-skinned fruit with a taste all its own is treated like a vegetable, and can only be eaten after the pod opens; unripe and unopened ackee is poisonous. Inside the pod are three yellow lobes with black seeds. The seeds are discarded, and the lobes are carefully cleaned of a thin red membrane before being boiled. The cooked and drained lobes are then reheated gently (they disintegrate easily when cooked) with cooked onions, peppers and salted cod imported from Canada.

As a Sunday breakfast special, ackee and salt fish is often served with a choice of roasted breadfruit, boiled green bananas, fried plantains, johnny cakes (fried flour dumplings from

PRECEDING PAGES: Jamaican dinner table at Jake's.
LEFT: fresh fruit abounds.
RIGHT: rural children sell a stick of fresh ackee.

the English "journey cakes") or bammies (flat round breads made from cassava flour).

Weekend extravaganzas

The weekend is the time when Jamaicans can indulge themselves in cooking meals which require a certain amount of lengthy preparation.

Saturday's main meal is traditionally a hearty soup – red or gungo pea, pepperpot or beef simmered with salt beef or pickled pig's tail, yams, dumplings, sweet potatoes and vegetables in season and accompanied by thick slabs of harddough bread.

Another popular dish is mackerel run-down ("run-dung" in patois). Whole salted mackerel is soaked to rid it of excess salt, boned and then cooked to a meltingly tasty stew in coconut milk, tomatoes, onions, scallion, thyme and hot country peppers. Traditional accompaniments for mackerel run-down are boiled green bananas, yams and boiled dumplings.

The main course for Sunday lunch may be a

roast of beef, pork or chicken, usually accompanied by steaming mounds of rice and peas, an assortment of white or yellow yams, sweet potatoes or pumpkin (collectively referred to in local parlance as "ground provisions" or "food"), carrots steamed with the squash-like cho-cho, fried or boiled ripe plantains and a simple salad of lettuce and sliced tomatoes. A feast fit for a king – or a gourmand.

Gourmet treats

Seafood is exquisite, as is the bounty of the rivers and streams. A popular method of preparing freshly caught fish is called escoveitch (es-

ko-veech). The fish is cleaned and left whole, highly seasoned with salt and black pepper, then fried and left to marinate in vinegar, thinly sliced onions, cho-cho, carrots and hot peppers for hours, preferably overnight. It is eaten hot or cold. Peppered shrimps are a speciality of the Black River area. You can purchase a paper bag of these dried, exceedingly peppery tiny shrimps from wayside vendors. Elsewhere you may be offered janga, or jonga, soup made from small river crayfish.

At times of celebration there is the inescapable goat's head soup, or mannish water, which is an important part of any festive menu, especially at country weddings. This is usually followed by "curry goat" and rice. Another gourmet treat is fresh oysters with a blend of vinegar and pepper.

Jerk cooking

Matthew Lewis, in his *Journal of a West India Proprietor*, was one of the first to describe the Jamaican eating experience. "We had at dinner a land tortoise and a barbecued pig, two of the richest dishes that I ever tasted, the latter in particular, which was dressed in the true Maroon fashion… I have eaten several other good Jamaica dishes, but none so excellent as this…"

Lewis didn't know it, but he was describing what is rather unflatteringly known as jerk cooking. No article on food and drink in Jamaica would be complete without a word about this latest food craze from Jamaica to hit the international market – jerk just as the Maroons used to do it.

The term refers to the special spices used to season the meat as well as the method by which

---

SPECIALITIES OF THE ISLAND

The variety of Jamaican foods and fruit is too numerous to list in detail, but some of the more unusual ones include:

● **Bammy**, a round flat bread made from cassava (a tuberous root vegetable) flour. It is fried, grilled or steamed.

● **Breadfruit**, a round green starchy fruit that is a dietary staple. It can be baked, boiled, roasted, fried, made into chips, flour or substituted for potatoes in salads.

● **Callaloo**, a leafy spinach-like vegetable.

● **Cho-cho**, also known as christophene or chayote. A pear-shaped prickly-skinned vegetable, light-green or white in colour, with a delicate flavour similar to squash.

● **Festival**, a sausage-shaped, deep-fried cornmeal

dumpling, served with fried fish, jerk pork or chicken.

● **Guinep**, a small green fruit, borne in clusters like grapes. The leathery outer skin covers a soft orange-coloured pulp, somewhat similar in taste to lychee. Large central seed.

● **June plum**, also called Jew plum. A tart fruit with a large spiky seed. Can be eaten fresh or stewed, or juiced.

● **Naseberry**, also known as sapodilla. Small round brown fruit with a thin edible skin and sweet pale-brown pulp.

● **Star apple**, an orange-sized fruit with shiny purple or green skin, whose pale purple pulp forms a star pattern when it is halved. In a dessert called Matrimony, the pulp is blended with orange segments sweetened with condensed milk.

it is cooked. The traditional method is on a barbecue of pimento wood over a pit dug in the ground in which a fire smoulders, a technique rather similar to Maori cooking in New Zealand.

The Maroons adopted the Amerindian method of cooking meat over a *barbacoa* (from which comes the word "barbecue"), but it is their special seasoning of lime juice, crushed pimento berries, hot peppers and other spices that gives jerked meat its distinctive flavour. Around 400 years ago they used this method to cook wild pigs in the mountain fastnesses of Portland, and it is still done this way in Boston, Portland, where you can find the most flavoursome and

Roadside stalls

Driving through the streets of Kingston in the evenings, particularly at weekends, you will encounter several of these roadside jerk stands, filling the air with the pungent smoke of jerk chicken, the cheapest and most easily available meat. Sometimes it may be fish or pork.

There are few, if any, wild pigs left in the hills around Portland, and demand far outstrips the supply of farm-bred pigs. But so popular has jerk cooking become that many restaurants and bars offer it on their menus, and it is also available in restaurants around the world. Several jerk cookery books have been published, too.

authentic jerk pork and chicken on the island.

The two-hour drive to Portland for jerk pork, along the winding, rugged coastline or over the equally winding mountain road, is too time-consuming for most Kingstonians. No problem! Ever-inventive Jamaican entrepreneurs have devised a portable barbecue, made of oil drums sawn in half and fitted together with hinges and a funnel on top to allow smoke to escape. A fire is built in the bottom half, the seasoned meat is rested on a grill, and the whole contraption stands on a metal frame.

LEFT: a street chef serves up crab claws.
ABOVE: a spicy jerk-chicken stand at Boston Bay.

When your mouth waters for the taste of something spicy, and your stomach longs for something filling, a paper-wrapped portion of jerk pork or chicken, with some slices of hard-dough bread, does the trick every time. Topped off with a cold Red Stripe beer, it is the Jamaican answer to the Englishman's fish-and-chips with a pint of best bitter.

Drinks all round

Drinking is an intrinsic part of the country's social pattern. When Jamaicans get together to relax, the question "What would you like to drink?" does not refer to coffee or tea, although you may have that if it's your preference. It is usually an offer of beer, rum, or any of the other locally available spirits, mixed with a chaser or on the rocks, but always served ice cold.

No matter where you go on the island, you are likely to find a busy bar. What's more, almost every corner grocery sells and serves beer and stout, as do many of the fast-food outlets. Most Jamaicans, from the rural villager to the city sophisticate, have their favourite drinking spots. Indeed, the quickest way for a visitor to penetrate the local lifestyle is to drop into one

> **RED STRIPE**
>
> An award-winning beer, Red Stripe is also known as "The Policeman" because of the red stripe on the uniforms of the island's police force.

of the popular neighbourhood bars or rum shop.

Locally available drink runs the gamut from imported whiskies, wines and champagnes to white rum, beer and stout, accompanied by the continuous "bang" of dominoes in a back room. In rural areas, you may be confused by a patron's order: "Serve me a 'ot 'ops" (hot hops: beer which has not been chilled). It's quite popular. The brewers of the award-winning Jamaican beer Red Stripe, Desnoes & Geddes, also bottle Dragon Stout and Guinness.

There are a number of liqueurs native to Jamaica, of which the most widely known is Tia Maria (coffee liqueur), offered in better bars throughout the world. Other fine coffee and fruit

liqueurs are produced by Sangster's, under the label "Old Jamaica", at their World's End factory in the Blue Mountains above Gordon Town. Unusual fruit flavours have been blended with selected aged Jamaican rums, and have been winning international gold medals for several years. But as the world knows, it is rum that is synonymous with fine drinking in Jamaica.

A rum with a punch

Today Jamaica produces a full range of rums, from light to dark, of which the best known brand is Appleton, made by J. Wray & Nephew. Appleton rum is exported to 64 countries, and there are two principal blends: Appleton White is light, smooth and mellow; Appleton Special is a blend of aged Jamaican dark rum, with a distinctive taste of its own.

Something to remember when ordering in a country bar: if you want, say, an Appleton Special with ginger ale, be specific, otherwise you will be served white, 100 percent overproof rum chased with ginger beer – powerful stuff which could leave you gasping for breath.

If you visit Jamaica during the "winter" season you may see bundles or plastic bags of spiky-looking dark-red leaves on sale. This is sorrel, and it is used to make a traditional drink at Christmas time. The leaves are covered with water to which a piece of ginger root, or a few pimento (allspice) berries, even a handful of cloves, has been added. It is left to steep, then strained and sweetened with sugar. A dash of rum may be added to give it an extra "kick".

For those not inclined to alcoholic drink, the island's array of fruit produces some of the most refreshing, delicious and unusual juices. Not to be forgotten is the perennial favourite, coconut water, and the succulent "jelly" or meat inside the nut. "Ting" is an exotic bottled grapefruit-based drink; or try a fizzy tamarind juice, Irish Moss (made from seaweed), or a fresh-fruit punch made from bananas and a variety of fruit in season. Jamaican fruit juices have won several international contests.

Whatever your fancy, it's "cheers!". ❏

LEFT: roadside vendors can sate your hunger and quench your thirst.
RIGHT: the traditional way to carry a fruit basket.

PARDON MY PATOIS

Jamaican patois is colourful and complex, but listen carefully and you will hear no end of humorous turns of phrase within this developing language

English-speaking visitors to Jamaica often wonder what language is spoken on the island, especially after they encounter their first Rastaman espousing the glories of "Jah", or a good-natured beachboy who inquires: "Everyt'ing kool, mon? Everyt'ing *irie?"* The newcomers soon think their tour guide lied in telling them that everyone here speaks English. This is an understandable reaction – except to Jamaicans, who are under the impression that it is the Americans, British and Canadians who speak in their own unintelligible dialects. Indeed, Jamaicans do speak English, but some of it is so ancient that even the British have abandoned it. William Shakespeare and his contemporaries might understand, though.

For instance, Jamaicans use the word "up" as an intensifier. A car that is "smash up" is in worse shape than one that has merely been in a smash. You "slip up" when you trip, you "soak up" when you make a mess of a job, and you get "beat up" when you suffer a serious mugging.

Compare this to the words of the character Jacques in Shakespeare's *As You Like It.* He tells of hunters who haunt the Forest of Arden and "shoot the deer and kill them up". Jacques later uses the word "physic" to connote the act of purging. Jamaican country children all know that when their parents threaten to "physic" them it means castor oil or Epsom salts ("salt physic") next morning.

Biblical influence

African slaves, brought to Jamaica centuries ago, adopted the speech mannerisms of their British masters. In their new home, Jacobean phraseology and the language of the King James Bible of 1611 (still a fixture in the homes of both Christians and Rastafarians) crept into the distinctive patois. So on parting, a mere

PRECEDING PAGES: a country way with words: the "1 Stop" fish shop in Black River.
LEFT AND RIGHT: "cuss-cuss never bore hole in skin" is the Jamaican way of saying "hard words break no bones".

"goodbye" seems inadequate when one can say: "Peradventure I wi' see you tomorrow."

Some of the most colourful of Jamaican expressions can be traced back to the languages of West African countries like Ghana. Early arrivals from these lands found it difficult to pronounce barbaric linguistic usages like *th*, so

"the" became "de", "them" became "dem" and "that" became "dat" – a speech pattern that conformed with those of Africa and which persists here today. *Th* at the end of a word proved particularly tricky. If a Jamaican man says his girlfriend has beautiful "teet", rest assured he is complimenting her dental appearance, not her bustline!

To simplify further the Africans' transition to life in colonial Jamaica and its strange tongue, the peculiarities of English grammar were often simplified or totally abandoned. Both case and gender were ignored in favour of simply "him" – for men, for women, for "you" or "I" alike. A young girl or woman became "gal", but the plural became "de gal dem". In fact, the plural "dem" applies to almost everything – cars, people, dogs, even children.

Vowel games

Jamaicans play speech games with vowels, especially the letter *a*. A garden can become either a "gyarden" or a "gorden", depending on the gentility of the speaker.

The influence of Africa is also found in the way that Jamaicans shift syllables and rearrange the stress to suit their purposes. A mattress becomes a "mat-rass". A tomato

becomes either "tomatis" or "salad" depending on its size. The ubiquitous surname Smith becomes unrecognisable to the visitor as "Simmit". Words with African roots that linger in contemporary patois include *putta-putta* for mud, *duckanoo* for a particular kind of pudding, and "*Anansi* story" for fairy tale. (In the Akan language of Ghana, *Anansesem* means "words about the spider".)

More recent years have found yet another form of African influence creeping into patois – the language of the Rastafarians. Central to their speech is the emphasis on the singular "I" or the plural "I and I" to underline the importance of the individual. Thus, "divine" becomes "I-vine", "Ethiopian" is "I-thiopian" and all right has become *I-rie*.

Jamaicans regard time and distance as subservient to the individual, so the often misunderstood phrase "soon come" should be interpreted to mean that the speaker will turn up sooner … or later. Another source of confusion is the use of measurements unknown elsewhere. In measuring land, the old English unit "chains" is still employed. The original measuring chains used by surveyors consisted of heavy wire links, so that the chain could be conveniently folded and carried in a bag. One hundred links equalled a chain of precisely 20 metres (22 yards), the length of a cricket pitch. If a Jamaican tells you that your destination is "a few chains from here", it is not far away. If it is "a stone's throw", on the other hand, it may be anywhere. Travelling time is a flexible thing.

Terms of endearment

The ultimate key to Jamaican speech is the word *rass*. Originally it meant backside, bum, derrière, and it still retains that meaning in Jamaica, but as Humpty Dumpty told Alice it also "means what I intend it to mean". Thus a man who is a *tiefin rass* is a dishonest thief. On the other hand, "Come here, you ole *rass*, mek I buy you a drink!" may be used when men greet their friends. Jamaicans may even say to each other with envy: "Dat is a rass house."

Or a man who spots an attractive woman walking past may lean over to his friend and smile: "Dat gal pretty to rass" – about which no further comment is necessary. ❑

JAMAICA TALK

● A "carry go bring come" is an incorrigible gossip.

● To be put "under manners" is a term usually used to refer to a man or woman who is placed under a regime of discipline by his or her partner following a misdemeanour.

● The term "hard ears" is used to describe a stubborn person, and many youngsters grow up hearing the phrase "him nuh hear will feel" – he who doesn't listen will learn a painful lesson.

● When things go wrong the "eye water" (tears) will fall.

● To be "facety" is to be cheeky, and a much more serious offence is to "diss" – to disrespect, or slight, someone.

LEFT: "soon come" could mean a long wait.
RIGHT: Jamaicans love to talk.

PLACES

*A detailed guide to the entire island, with principal sites
clearly cross-referenced by number to the maps*

> *Get it together in Jamaica,*
> *Soulful town, soulful people,*
> *I see you're having fun.*
> *Dancing to the reggae rhythm,*
> *Oh, island in the sun! Come on and*
> *Smile, you're in Jamaica!*
> – Bob Marley, from *Smile Jamaica*

The island of Jamaica provides a steady stream of surprises, fairly constant in mood and cadence yet seductive and hypnotic in the way they brand themselves on your brain. Even the standard tour-bus stops – Dunn's River Falls, Bamboo Avenue, Rose Hall Great House, the Blue Hole, the Rio Grande River rafting trip – provide an astonishingly wide variety of experiences. Greater rewards await the traveller who dares to take the turning down an unpaved country road and lose himself in the Cockpit Country, who puts on his or her hiking shoes and scales the Blue Mountains, who heads down to the Treasure Beach to relax, or who saunters into a Darliston restaurant to order "curry goat", rice and breadfruit.

The travel section that follows gives a taste of both worlds: out-of-the-way coves and crannies as well as the well-trodden trails. For the usual routes you need only check with travel agencies or hotel tour desks for a list of guided tours. For the less-travelled byways you will need to hire, beg or borrow a sturdy car, or join the Jamaican people on their full-to-capacity buses and mini-vans.

This section has been divided into 10 chapters. From a detailed look at Jamaica's business and governmental nerve centre, the Kingston-lower St Andrew corporate area, you go on to a tour of the Blue Mountains and a glance at historic Port Antonio and its beautiful surrounding east-coast countryside, all within the County of Surrey.

The north-coast tourist centre of Ocho Rios is a good base from which to explore Jamaica's heartland and the County of Middlesex. You will travel the north coast, then head south through the hills.

Next you travel west through the County of Cornwall to Jamaica's tourist capital – Montego Bay (or "MoBay") – and its coastal resort neighbours. There's also a brief dip into the mysterious Cockpit Country southeast of MoBay. Then on to Negril, Jamaica's funkiest tourist development. Finally you head for the undeveloped south coast and then south Middlesex, where the two main areas of interest are Spanish Town and Mandeville. As in any country, it's the human landscape that really counts, and, most Jamaicans will enjoy meeting you as much as you will enjoy meeting them. ❏

PRECEDING PAGES: climbing into the Blue Mountains; cycling through Bamboo Avenue, Lacovia; local country-music club.
LEFT: Treasure Beach on the south coast is still one of Jamaica's best kept secrets.

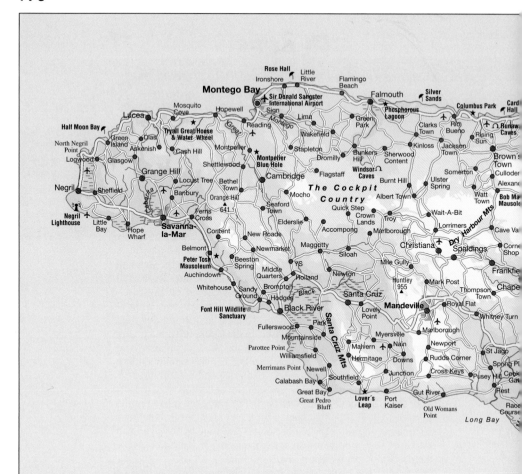

Rose Hall
Little River
Ironshore
Flamingo Beach
Montego Bay
Silver Sands
Sir Donald Sangster International Airport
Falmouth
Columbus Park
Card Hall
Mosquito Cove
Hopewell
Lima
Phosphorous Lagoon
Lucea
Sign
Reading
Green Park
Clarks Town
Rio Bueno
Runaw Caves
Half Moon Bay
Diaz
Green Island
Tryall Great House & Water Wheel
Wakefield
Rising Sun
North Negril Point
Askenish
Cash Hill
Montpelier
Stapleton
Kinloss
Jackson Town
Brown's Town
Logwood
Glasgow
Shettlewood
Montpelier Blue Hole
Dromilly
Bunkers Hill
Sherwood Content
Somerton
Culloder
Grange Hill
Cambridge
Flagstaff
Windsor Caves
Burnt Hill
Ulster Spring
Alexand
Negril
Locust Tree
Bethel Town
Mocho
The Cockpit Country
Albert Town
Watt Town
Bob Ma Mausole
Sheffield
Banbury
Orange Hill
Seaford Town
Quick Step
Crown Lands
Troy
Wait-A-Bit
Negril Lighthouse
Little Bay
Ferns Cross
641
Elderslie
Accompong
Marlborough
Lorrimers
Cave Va
Savanna-la-Mar
Content
New Roads
YS
Siloah
Mile Gully
Christiana
Spaldings
Corne Shop
Hope Wharf
Belmont
Newmarket
Maggotty
Newton
Huntley 955
Mark Post
Frankfie
Peter Tosh Mausoleum
Beeston Spring
Middle Quarters
Holland
Thompson Town
Chape
Auchindown
Brompton
Black
Santa Cruz
Royal Flat
Whitehouse
Sandy Ground
Hodges
Lovely Point
Mandeville
Whitney Turn
Font Hill Wildlife Sanctuary
Black River
Fullerswood
Park
Myersville
Marlborough
Mountainside
Malvern
Nain
Newport
St Jago
Parottee Point
Williamsfield
Hermitage
Downs
Rudds Corner
Spring Pl
Cook Gat
Merrimans Point
Newell
Junction
Cross Keys
Pusey Hill
Rest
Calabash Bay
Southfield
Gut River
Race Course
Great Bay
Great Pedro Bluff
Lover's Leap
Port Kaiser
Old Womans Point
Long Bay

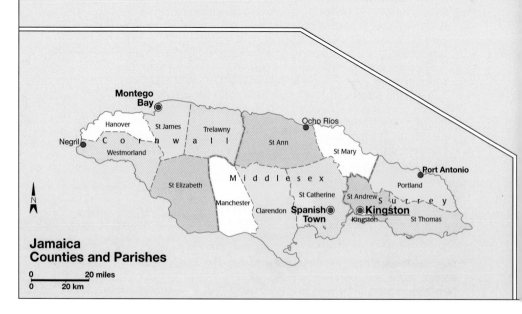

Montego Bay
Ocho Rios
Hanover
St James
Trelawny
Negril
C o r n w a l l
St Ann
St Mary
Port Antonio
Westmorland
Portland
M i d d l e s e x
S u r r e y
St Elizabeth
Manchester
St Catherine
St Andrew
Clarendon
Spanish Town
Kingston
St Thomas
Kingston

N

**Jamaica
Counties and Parishes**

0 ———— 20 miles
0 ———— 20 km

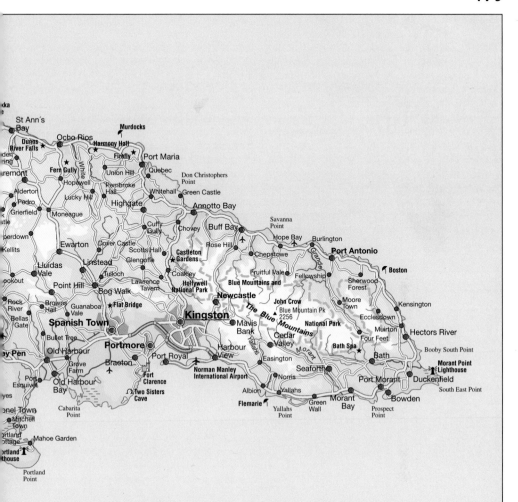

St Ann's
Bay
Ocho Rios
Murdocks
Dunns
River Falls
Harmony Hall
Firefly
Port Maria
Fern Gully
Union Hill
Quebec
Hopewell
Don Christophers
Point
Pembroke
Whitehall
Green Castle
Hall
Alderton
Lucky Hill
Pedro
Highgate
Annotto Bay
Grierfield
Moneague
Savanna
Point
Cuffy
Gully
Chovey
Buff Bay
Ewarton
Dover Castle
Hope Bay
Burlington
Scotts Hall
Rose Hill
Chepstowe
Port Antonio
Lluidas
Linstead
Castleton
Vale
Glengoffe
Gardens
Boston
Coakley
Fruitful Vale
Fellowship
Point Hill
Tulloch
Sherwood
Lawrence
Hollywell
Blue Mountains and
Forest
Tavern
National Park
Newcastle
Moore
Bog Walk
Flat Bridge
John Crow
Town
Browns
Guanaboa
Kensington
Rock
Hall
Vale
Blue Mountain Pk
River
2256
National Park
Ecclesdown
Bellas
Spanish Town
Kingston
Muirton
Gate
Bullet Tree
Mavis
Cedar
Four Feet
Hectors River
Bank
Valley
Bath Spa
Portmore
Harbour
Old Harbour
View
Easington
Bath
Booby South Point
Grove
Port Royal
Braeton
Farm
Seaforth
Morant Point
Lighthouse
Old Harbour
Norman Manley
Norris
Port Morant
Duckenfield
Port
Fort
International Airport
Bay
Esquivel
Clarence
Albion
Yallahs
Bowden
South East Point
Two Sisters
Morant
Cave
Flemarie
Green
Bay
Cabarita
Yallahs
Wall
Prospect
Mitchell
Point
Point
Town
Town
Mahoe Garden
Portland
Point
Portland
Point

CARIBBEAN

SEA

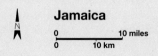

N

Jamaica

0   10 miles
0   10 km

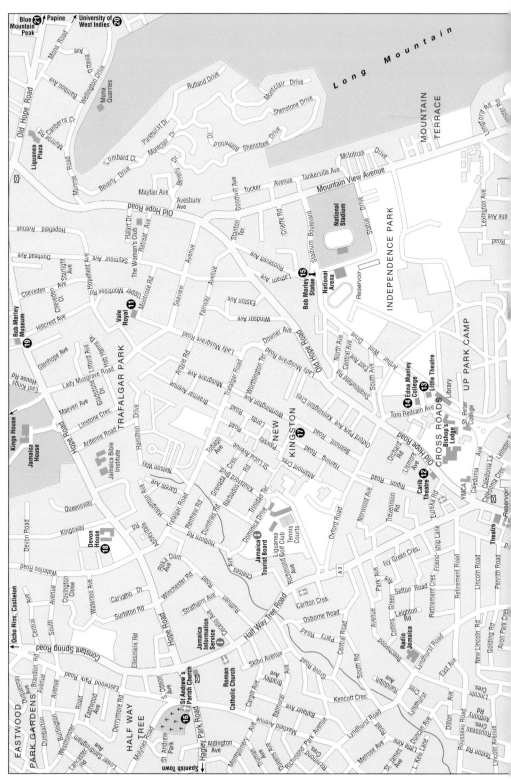

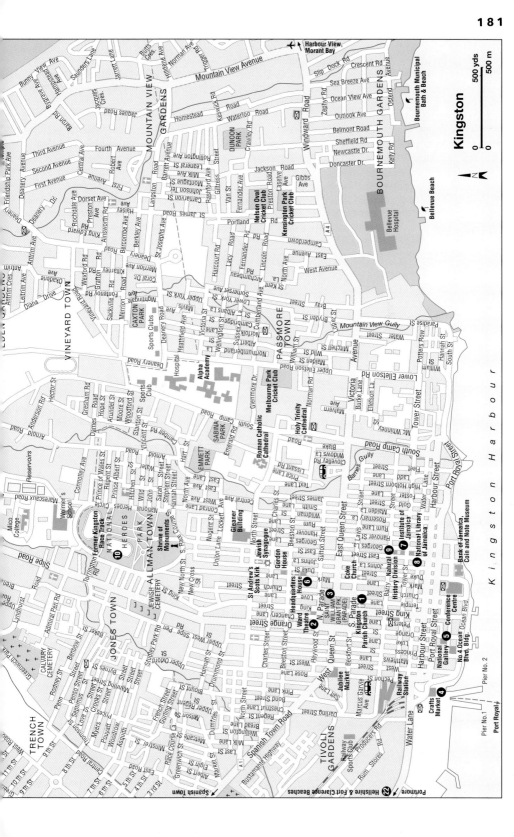

Kingston

0 500 yds
0 500 m

KINGSTON AND ENVIRONS

Map on page 180–81

The capital is fast and furious compared with rural Jamaica. Here in the shadow of the Blue Mountains is the commercial and cultural centre, with theatres, museums, galleries and great places to eat out

Kingston

I f the expression "urban sprawl" had not existed, the city of Kingston would have invented it. Established in 1693, it makes up for its lack of elegance and graciousness with the exuberance and gusto of the perpetual adolescent. Kingston is a capital city which has defied all the efforts of its city fathers and planners to curb, tame or confine it, or to discipline its citizens.

From every street corner, reggae music blares. Bars and betting shops jostle with churches as the most ubiquitous non-residential buildings in the city. Obsolescent narrow streets challenge drivers' nervous systems. Pound laws notwithstanding, animals wander at will. Street signs are usually absent. Amidst this endless chaos, Kingstonians have an inbred natural radar of direction and survival. They find meaning or pattern in what outsiders consider disorder.

This is a city that has never caught up with itself, for it has never stopped growing. Its population is swelled daily by starry-eyed youths from the mountains who dream of hitting it big in the city. They inflate the numbers of "yard" or tenement dwellers, and their dreams and hopes burgeon into the city's headaches: outgrown water supplies, public transportation, sanitation services, schools, jobs and housing.

To make ends meet, many people have turned Kingston into a city of hustlers. Hawkers (known as higglers), their bargains purchased overseas, return to set up their wares on the sidewalks, competing with merchants who display goods indoors. The hustle on the sidewalk is known as "Ben Dung Plaza" – you have to bend down (*ben dung*) to buy.

Kingston began as a well-designed seaside town on the edge of a magnificent natural harbour, but it has voraciously gobbled up all of the Liguanea (pronounced *Li-ga-nee*) Plains and mounted the surrounding mountains. In the last ten years, encouraged by a causeway across the western end of the harbour, Kingston has also embraced part of the promontory known as the Hellshire Hills which separates the harbour from the rest of the south coast.

A city of views

What redeems Kingston – and makes up for the noise, the squalour, the inconveniences and the sometimes oppressive heat – is the city's splendid setting. The readily accessible panoramic views make this evident. From Hellshire Beach, at Naggo Head, the city unfolds, framed by the mountains. And from the hills – Beverly Drive (in Beverly Hills), Skyline Drive (on Jack's Hill) and the spectacular crest of Red Hills Road – are incomparable views of the city, plains, mountains and sea.

From its sweeping harbour Kingston sprawls along

LEFT: Kingston Synagogue is the island's only Jewish house of worship.
BELOW: carnival in Kingston.

A mango tree – fruit trees grow all over the island

the fan-shaped plain, rising imperceptibly for 13 km (8 miles) into the foothills which surround it. Another 16 km (10 miles) inland the hills give way to the spectacular Blue Mountain Range and culminate in Blue Mountain Peak (2,257 metres/7,402 ft).

You can orientate yourself by facing the mountains, your back to Kingston Harbour. On the east, to your right, is a rocky low-lying hill near the coast. This is **Long Mountain**, whose northern flanks are covered with the **Beverly Hills** mansions of the nouveau riche. Halfway up the slope is the **Martello Tower**, built of stone in 1803 to guard against French invasion. Beyond is a higher limestone hill, **Wareika** (said to be an Arawak name), and behind that is **Dallas Mountain**, which takes its name from a family whose descendants emigrated to the United States and achieved great prominence. One of them, George Milfin Dallas, became America's vice-president (1845–48) and gave his name to the Texan city-cum-TV soap.

As you look westwards, the land drops slightly at the Hope River gorge and then rises sharply again in **Jack's Hill**. Skyline Drive is perched along its spine. Another dip in the landscape occurs where the residential suburb of **Stony Hill** and a major highway which leads to the north coast are located. Then the land rises again to the heights and residential areas of **Red Hills**.

"Under the clock"

BELOW: the Parade of yesteryear.
RIGHT: Kingston Parish Church.

Kingston is the Americas' largest English-speaking city south of Miami. Its population, estimated at just over 1 million, seems to grow daily.

Old-timers will proudly claim that the only true Kingstonians are those "born under the clock" – that is, the clock of the **Kingston Parish Church ❶**. This

Map on page 180–81

downtown landmark at the corner of King Street and South Parade dates from the late 17th or early 18th century; the oldest tombstone in its cemetery is dated 1699. Throughout Jamaica, during the time (before 1872) that the Church of England, or Anglican form of Christianity, prevailed as the sole official creed, the parish church was always one of the first public buildings erected in a settlement. The original Kingston Parish Church was destroyed in the 1907 earthquake; the current structure, based on the same design, was erected in 1911.

The square clock tower on the west side of the church was erected in memory of those who died in World War I, 1914–18; its bell is older, having been cast in 1715. But it is centuries since all of Kingston fell within this area. The original section of the city (bounded roughly by today's North, East and West streets and the harbour) was laid out over 300 years ago to house survivors of the earthquake which destroyed Port Royal in 1692.

Across the harbour, the new city was laid out in a rectangular grid pattern. In the north is an open square known as **The Parade**, the upper limit of which is marked by the **Ward Theatre ❷**. Today the theatre, across the street from **St (Saint) William Grant Park ❸**, looks over a monstrous confusion of street markets, hustlers, idlers, traffic of all sorts – a typical Third World mixture of urban decay and cacophonous energy.

The Ward occupies a site which has been used as a theatre for centuries. The original stage on this site attracted many well-known English and American touring companies. The theatre was a gift to the city from Colonel Ward, nephew and partner in the famous rum firm of J. Wray and Nephew Limited. In 1825 John Wray, a wheelwright, started a business as a liquor dealer in the Shakespeare Tavern next door to the theatre (now gone) and eventually entered into

Methodism today is one of the largest organised Christian denominations in Jamaica.

BELOW: the Ward Theatre.

rum-making, perfecting a superior blend. "Superior Jamaican" remains one of Jamaica's best, but internationally least-appreciated rums.

Theatrical activity of every description is at home in the Ward. Most popular is the annual Pantomime – staged for over 50 years – which opens on Boxing Day (26 December) and runs for several months.

Back to The Parade. It was here in colonial times that the English Redcoats, shining with spit and polish, drilled for the edification and delight of the Jamaicans. They were often joined by the Militia, an island-wide force of callow clerks and bookkeepers, paunchy merchants and dyspeptic planters, led by doddering colonels and major generals. Militia duty was compulsory for all who qualified – usually freed men between 16 and 20 – and officer status, which gave social advantage, was eagerly sought and bought.

The Parade also served as a promenade for the local folk, and a venue for public events such as the hanging of prisoners or putting them in the stocks. When the island worked itself into a state of hysteria over a threatened French invasion in 1694, a fort was temporarily erected on The Parade with guns pointing down King Street.

When the British troops and Militia took their parades to **Up Park Camp** The Parade lost much of its splendour. In 1870 the garden was laid out, and in 1914 it was officially named Victoria Park in honour of the queen whose statue – once a prominent landmark – looked down King Street and out across the seas ruled by Britannia.

The north and south sections of the park are dominated by statues, two of them, of the 20th-century Jamaican leaders Sir Alexander Bustamante and Norman Washington Manley, executed by the Jamaican sculptor Alvin Marriott. Edna Manley's statue *Negro Aroused* also overlooks The Parade.

In the mid-1970s the park was officially renamed St William Grant Park, after the labour leader of the 1930s. Like most politicians and orators of the time, Grant used the steps of the Coke Church on the eastern side of the park as his main platform.

The present **Coke Church** is on the site of the first Methodist chapel erected in Jamaica. It is named for the Reverend Dr Coke, a Wesleyan missionary who came in 1789 to establish a mission. Coke Chapel was opened in 1790 but was soon closed when a grand jury found it "injurious to the general peace and quiet of the inhabitants". Missionaries were frowned upon because of their activities among the slaves.

On the waterfront

Urban activity in Kingston has shifted. People have increasingly deserted the downtown area, and the heart of the old city has been left to decay – the old 18th-century town houses have been turned into tenement yards for those too poor to move upwards.

However, urban restoration of the waterfront area is planned. Since the 1960s there have been attempts to regenerate downtown to its former glory, and efforts have come in sporadic outbursts of enthusiasm. The Kingston Restoration Company, a public-private sector organisation, is responsible for the most recent

The statue of the British monarch placed in Victoria Park (now called St William Grant Park), facing King Street, is said to have turned around on its pedestal to face the opposite direction during the 1907 earthquake.

BELOW: *Negro Aroused by Edna Manley.*

work. Time will tell if urban renewal here will set an example for the rest of the decaying city.

Until the 1960s, finger piers jutting into the sea were characteristic of Kingston's waterfront. But when the redevelopment company was established to undertake the renewal, a commercial and shipping area called **Newport West** was built from reclaimed lands on the west side of the harbour. This modern port complex, known as **Port Bustamante,** has the capacity to handle millions of tons of cargo annually. It includes a free zone and a trans-shipment port.

Modern Ocean Boulevard embraces a complex of high-rise buildings: apartments, offices and shops, collectively known as the **Kingston Waterfront.** The Central Bank (Bank of Jamaica) and the Jamaica Conference Centre built homes here in the 1970s, hoping that the area would be selected as the site for the International Seabed Authority. Both buildings are landmarks to the first phase of an ambitious and much-delayed programme aimed at transforming the area.

Further along is the **Crafts Market ❹**. Although it has not benefited from its location it continues to offer straw goods, carvings and embroidered goods, along with more esoteric objects like dried calabashes.

The original 19th-century Victoria Crafts Market, at the foot of King Street, was one of the casualties of progress. In centuries past this site was the location of a Sunday Market which attracted thousands of slaves, free people and white hucksters from surrounding parishes. When slavery ended, the market's character changed. It became known as the Christmas Grand-market, a special attraction for children who came to buy paper hats, balloons, *fee-fees* (whistles) and toys.

In front of the market was the Victoria Pier, landing place for nearly all famous visitors including kings, queens and other heads of state.

Map on page 180–81

The Crafts Market in Kingston can be a treasure chest. Look out for yo-yos made from cacoon, one of the largest seeds in the world. It grows on vines along the river valleys, and its pods can grow up to 1 metre (3 ft) in length.

BELOW: straw baskets on sale at the Crafts Market.

The Roy West Building on the corner of Orange Street and Ocean Boulevard houses part of the Institute of Jamaica, including the **National Gallery ❺** (open Mon–Thur 11am–4.30pm, Fri 11am–4pm). The development of a national art movement dates only to the 1930s but has escalated since then. The National Gallery has a fine collection of work by some of the most popular and talented Jamaican artists, including Kapo, John Dunkley, Edna Manley, David Boxer and Dawn Scott, and many of their pieces are on permanent display here. Unfortunately weekday opening hours are very restrictive, and it's closed at the weekend.

Jamaican dollars.

The National is also home to the original symbolic statue of Bob Marley by Christopher Gonzalez; it is of a messianic Marley, semi-tree, semi-rootsman, rising from the earth singing songs of freedom. It was planned to stand on Arthur Wint Drive, opposite the National Arena, but upon unveiling it caused such an outcry that it was promptly withdrawn and replaced with a more traditional statue.

Another waterfront attraction is the **Coin and Note Museum** in the Bank of Jamaica Building. Although Jamaica switched to dollars and cents in 1967, before independence the pre-decimal British coinage of pounds, shillings and pence was in use. The folk names for these old coins were popularised in song and story: "*Carry me ackee go a Linstead Market, not a quattie wut sell.*" Quatties may be seen in the museum, along with souvenir coin sets, tokens, tallies, pirate pieces of eight and other fascinating fragments of the past. Tallies, incidentally, were substitutes for coins given to task workers such as banana loaders.

BELOW: see the works of art at the National Gallery.
RIGHT: craft on display.

The decay of the downtown area was hastened by the city's spread northwards. In the 1960s, a commercial revolution created North American-style shopping centres all over the city. Commerce became diffused, and small shops or boutiques

sprang up everywhere. The main shopping areas are located along Constant Spring and Red Hills Roads, and in Liguanea, Cross Roads and Manor Park.

King Street, the downtown area's main thoroughfare, is a sorry spectacle. In 1909, when the public buildings flanking King Street were built, they were regarded as the last word in modernity and were featured in every photograph of Jamaican "progress". They were constructed of reinforced concrete, then a relatively new material, following the destruction of most of the old wood or mortar buildings in the earthquake and fire of 1907. The public buildings house the Treasury, Law Courts and offices, often in a sorry state of repair.

Of the downtown areas, it is probably only lower **Duke Street** which retains some of its original flavour as a business and commercial centre. Once the address of the best law firms, Duke Street is still full of lawyers' offices, but chambers there are no longer regarded as essential to success and prestige. However, lower Duke Street and Harbour Street have benefited from some restoration projects, and, although the bustle of a modern centre is absent from these streets, there is still a fairly large and loyal population of shop and office workers downtown, notably employees of the Bank of Jamaica, the Stock Exchange, and Grace, Kennedy and Company, one of Jamaica's oldest firms.

Duke Street is home to some interesting buildings, among them **St Andrew's Scots Kirk**. This octagonal church was built in 1814 when Scots were prominent in the island's commercial life. Jamaica's first Presbyterian church, it was damaged in the 1907 earthquake and thereafter reduced in size.

Further up Duke Street is **Gordon House**, where Parliament meets. Its name honours the patriot and martyr George William Gordon, a noted legislator branded as one of the "villains" of the 1865 Morant Bay Rebellion.

Map on page 180–81

The grandmother of all Jamaican markets is loud and chaotic Coronation market in Kingston. It is not for the faint-hearted, and is best visited in the company of a local. Arrive between 5.30am and 6am.

BELOW:
Coronation market.

Headquarters House has stood the test of time.

Directly across from Gordon House, facing Beeston Street, is one of Jamaica's most historic buildings. **Headquarters House** 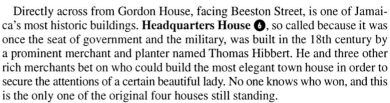, so called because it was once the seat of government and the military, was built in the 18th century by a prominent merchant and planter named Thomas Hibbert. He and three other rich merchants bet on who could build the most elegant town house in order to secure the attentions of a certain beautiful lady. No one knows who won, and this is the only one of the original four houses still standing.

Also on Duke Street is the **Synagogue** (at the corner of Charles Street); it is the island's only Jewish house of worship. The United Congregation of Israelites represents an amalgamation in 1921 of two separate Jewish congregations – the Sephardic or Portuguese Jews and the European Ashkenazi from England and Germany.

On East Street (No. 12) are the main buildings of the **Institute of Jamaica** ❼, (tel: 922 0620). Founded in 1879 for the encouragement of literature, science and art, it has since functioned as a kind of mini-Smithsonian Institution. Divisions include the National Gallery, the Edna Manley College of the Visual and Performing Arts (in which are located the national schools of Art, Dance, Drama and Music), a Junior Centre (in the building opposite the headquarters), a Museums Division, an **African Caribbean Institute** (engaged in research on African traditions in Jamaica and the Caribbean) and Publications.

Housed at the East Street site are the two major collections of the Institute – the **National Library of Jamaica** ❽ (formerly the West India Reference Library), containing the largest collection of West Indian material in the world, and the **Natural History Division** ❾ (open Mon–Thurs 9am–4.30pm, Fri 9am–4pm), which includes a small **museum** and a large herbarium. Exhibits include a marine-life display, and there are also summer workshops for children.

The **Gleaner Building** on North Street is the home of Jamaica's oldest newspaper, the *Daily Gleaner*. It was founded in 1834 by Joshua and Jacob de Cordova. Jacob, a civil engineer, later emigrated to Texas, where he laid out the town of Waco and served in the state legislature.

Further along North Street the dome of **Holy Trinity Cathedral** marks the focal point of Roman Catholicism. The island's largest Catholic church was once a landmark for those who arrived by sea. Introduced by the Spanish, Catholicism received a fresh impetus in the late 18th century with an influx of French Catholics from nearby Haiti. In true Jesuit tradition, the Catholics pioneered educational institutions throughout the island, including St George's Boys' School which adjoins the cathedral.

East and West reunite around reggae

As Kingston expanded, polarities developed between "uptown" and "downtown" as two distinct residential areas, both economically and psychologically. The stereotypical "uptowners" were wealthy folk who aspired to the middle-class norms of North America and Europe. They went downtown to work or shop, but left for uptown suburbs in the evenings. The "downtowners" were ghetto-dwellers who lived in the decaying tenements and shacks. And as has happened elsewhere, in *shebeens* or *favelas*, it was in West Kingston's ghettos that Jamaica's most significant cultural products were spawned: reggae and Rastafarianism.

The first songs of bondage and redemption came from an infamous settlement known as Back O'Wall. In the 1960s this was converted into a model community, **Tivoli Gardens**. It became the centrepiece of the political constituency of the then prime minister, Edward Seaga, who first envisaged it while serving as minister of finance in the 1960s. Tivoli Gardens, with its carefully planned pattern, modern buildings, community spirit and lovingly painted murals, was an oasis of hope in an area of decay.

Trench Town and other similar areas are referred to in Kingston as the "West" and used as a metaphor for the birthplace of reggae music. Visitors who feel the pull of the West are advised not to go to it without a reliable and trusted guide from the area; it can be rough. The Trench Town Development Foundation has launched an ambitious plan to develop a Bob Marley Culture Yard here.

From horses to heroes

Horse-racing was probably the most popular sport in Jamaica in colonial days. There were well-patronised racecourses in each parish, and race days were occasions for social splendour. The first race on Kingston Race Track was run in 1816, and racing continued until the outbreak of World War II in 1939. In 1953 racing was moved to **Knutsford Park**, and soon thereafter to the modern **Caymanas Park** just across the county boundary in St Catherine.

Kingston Race Track later became George VI Memorial Park. After independence in 1962 it was laid out as a shrine to the National Heroes and renamed **National**

Map on page 180–81

The tenement yards in Trench Town popularised by Bob Marley were built in the 1920s and 30s to relieve the housing problem caused by urban drift. By the '70s and '80s Trench Town symbolised the heart of the ghetto.

BELOW: Caymanas Park is now the only racetrack on the island.

Norman Manley commemorated.

Heroes Park . Former prime ministers and National Heroes are buried here, including Marcus Garvey, Norman Manley, Alexander Bustamante, Donald Sangster and, most recently, Michael Manley. Today their monuments can be viewed in the park.

Outside the park, in front of the Ministry of Education, is another monument to a Latin American revolutionary: **Simón Bolívar**, "The Liberator". Bolívar spent seven months in Jamaica in 1817 while leading the fight to free the Latin American colonies from Spanish rule. While here he wrote the famous "Jamaica Letter" – regarded as one of the greatest documents of his career – and survived an assassination attempt at the boarding house at the northwest corner of Princess and Tower streets where he lived. The monument is a gift from Venezuela.

Streets of schools

Immediately north of National Heroes Circle, **Wolmer's School** marks the northern boundary of Kingston proper. It was founded over 300 years ago with proceeds from the estate of John Wolmer, a wealthy Kingston goldsmith. It started out strictly as a boys' school; the girls' school was founded later.

Mico College, next door to Wolmer's, is one of the oldest teacher-training institutions in the world. It indirectly owes its establishment to a London gentleman who refused to marry any of his aunt's six nieces, desspite a £1,000 dowry being involved. The strings-attached inheritance which the wealthy Lady Mico had left him in her will was invested instead, and the income was later used to rescue Christians captured by Barbary pirates.

When piracy was stamped out the Lady Mico Trust lay dormant for 200 years, growing to an enormous sum. It was used by English philanthropists to start

Mico Schools throughout the West Indies to educate the soon-to-be freed slave population. The Kingston college, established in 1834, is the only Mico institution still existing. Now co-educational, it was originally a boys' school. It has produced many of Jamaica's outstanding citizens, including the first native governor-general, Sir Clifford Campbell. At one time Mico also trained missionaries for service in West Africa. The college was moved to its present location in 1896; the main building dates from 1909.

The street on which these schools are located – **Marescaux Road** – sometimes offers an excellent opportunity to see Jamaica's national flower. The *lignum vitae* is a small tree whose branches might go unnoticed until they begin flowering around mid-July. At first there is a light dusting of purple on the leaves; eventually the tiny purple blossoms with their bright yellow stamens entirely cover the boughs. The plant fascinates a certain white butterfly (*Kricogonia lyside*), and in some seasons the blossoms can hardly be seen for the thousands of these creatures which set each tree shimmering.

Lignum vitae's name is Latin for "wood of life". As a medicine, its gum is reputed to be a cure for venereal disease and many other ailments. Its wood is so heavy – it will sink in water – that it is ideal for specialised purposes such as ships' propeller-shaft bearings, mortars, mallets, pulleys and policemen's batons; being attractive it is also used to make furniture and curios.

Refuge in the "pens"

By the 18th century, Kingston's rich merchants were discovering that it was much cooler and healthier to live in the foothills, and they moved to more expansive new homes surrounded by a great deal of land. These were known as

Map on page 180–81

BELOW: the *lignum vitae* (*Guiacum officinale*) tree grows throughout the island.

The Cuban hero of independence, General Antoneo Maceo, found sanctuary on the island. As a thank-you Jamaica was presented with a bust of him in 1952; it can be seen in National Heroes Park.

BELOW: Vale Royal.

"pens", for there was now space for their horses and other livestock, and enough acreage to grow their own grass.

One of the oldest and most splendid of these pen residences was built in 1694 and has been in continuous use ever since. Known as **Vale Royal** ⓫, it is now the prime minister's official home. Although no prime minister in recent years has lived there, it is well-maintained and used for official entertaining. It is located on Montrose Road off Lady Musgrave Road; one of its most notable features is its striking façade with a rooftop lookout tower, typical of early Kingston houses. This would have had a spyglass for keeping an eye on doings in the harbour. Vale Royal was built by Simon Taylor, one of the richest men of his time.

Beyond the area of pen residences, sugar estates once covered the Liguanea Plains. The estates gave their names to many Kingston locations, including Hope, Liguanea, Constant Spring, Mona and Barbican.

Urban expansion northwards led to the creation of several important cross-roads, one of which still retains that prosaic name. **Cross Roads** is a busy junction poised between uptown and downtown. It had been known as Montgomery's Corner, after a lieutenant who was thrown from his horse here, but it was officially renamed early in the 20th century. The clock tower, erected in memory of the Jamaican servicemen who died in World War II (1939–45), and the white **Carib Theatre** ⓬ have been Cross Roads landmarks for decades. In the tradition of grand theatres of the 1930s and '40s, the Carib served as the city's main concert hall for generations. Destroyed by fire in late 1996, it was speedily restored and is now a five-screen cineplex.

Not far to the east of Cross Roads is **Up Park Camp** on South Camp Road. Best known simply as "Camp", it was established in 1784 as the home of British

regiments stationed in Jamaica and is now the headquarters of the Jamaica Defence Force. Duppy Gate, the southern entrance, recalls the legend of an officer of the old West India Regiment whose ghost regularly called out the guard there for inspection.

Map on page 180–81

Kingston's cultural core

South Camp Road leads to **Tom Redcam Avenue**, Jamaica's "cultural" street, named for a former poet laureate of Jamaica. Here are located the public library service, the Little Theatre and the headquarters of the Anglican Church.

The library system, established in the 1950s, is highly regarded. An island-wide system of main parish libraries, branch libraries, a school library service and a mobile library service is administered from here.

The **Little Theatre** ⓭ was built in 1961 through the untiring efforts of Henry and Greta Fowler, who founded the Little Theatre Movement in 1942. The movement, which established the Jamaica School of Drama (now incorporated into the Edna Manley College of the Visual and Performing Arts), also sponsors the annual Pantomime. The Little Theatre is used by theatrical groups throughout the year, many of which hold annual seasons here. In fact the demand is so great that the small rehearsal room attached to the theatre has itself been converted into the **Little Little Theatre**, which is also booked up all year.

Memorial to a poet laureate of Jamaica.

The architecturally exciting **Edna Manley College of the Visual and Performing Arts** ⓮, formerly known as the Cultural Training Centre, on Arthur Wint Drive, just around the corner from Tom Redcam Avenue, houses the national schools of Dance, Drama, Art and Music. The College instructs performers and practitioners, and also trains Jamaican and Caribbean teachers

BELOW:
Dance Theatre
Co. rehearsal.

The Marley memorial welcomes people into the National Arena.

as art educators. Placing all the schools in close proximity is expected to develop cross-fertilisation in the arts. Students are encouraged to explore other forms outside their own disciplines.

Arthur Wint Drive continues around the northern end of Camp to the **National Stadium**. The stadium was built for the independence celebrations in 1962 and has been the venue of major sporting events ever since. The **National Arena** next door hosts other sports and more diverse activities, including a two-day National Flower Show in July and a biennial trade exposition. At the entrance to the stadium is a statue by the sculptor Alvin Marriott, which symbolises Jamaican athletic prowess. **Arthur Wint Drive** is named after a famed Jamaican athlete who won a gold medal in the 400 metres at the 1948 London Olympics, bringing international fame to his tiny island home. Wint was also a member of Jamaica's gold medal-winning 4x400-metre relay team at the 1952 Olympics in Helsinki.

Another famous Marriott, the **Bob Marley statue ⓕ**, commissioned to replace the more symbolic one created by Christopher Gonzalez, stands in a small area – which may be developed into a park – across the Drive from the the entrance to the National Arena. At Marley's funeral it was announced that a memorial park would be established, dedicated to famous sons and daughters of Jamaica who have won international recognition and brought honour to the nation. The park has still not come to fruition.

Half Way Tree

BELOW: Half Way Tree around 1890.

From Cross Roads, busy Half Way Tree Road leads north to Constant Spring, Kingston's northern gateway. Here you will find the city's golf club and its 18-

hole course. Dominating the skyline is a luxury hotel, the city's pink elephant, the Crowne Plaza Hotel.

Map on page 180–81

The name **Half Way Tree** was in use as early as 1696: a reference to the giant *kapok* (silk-cotton) tree which once threw its huge buttresses in all directions here. Before the tree died of old age in the 1870s it was a resting-place for market women travelling from the hills to town with their wares. Roads west to Spanish Town, north to the coast via Stony Hill, and east to the mountains via Papine all join here.

A few yards south of Half Way Tree's main intersection is **St Andrew's Parish Church** ⓰, the island's oldest church. Its registers date back to 1666; the first building was raised here in 1692. The foundation of the present structure was laid in 1700, though it has undergone many renovations since then.

The community of Half Way Tree is the centre of government for the parish of St Andrew, and parish law courts sit here. East of Half Way Tree, via Hope and Trafalgar roads, **New Kingston** ⓱, built on what was once the Knutsford Park Race Track, accommodates many leading hotels, including Le Meridian Jamaica Pegasus, the Kingston Hilton, the Courtleigh and the homely colonial-style Liguanea Club, a modest hotel and tennis club.

Hope Road itself leads to scenic drives in the mountains to the northeast. It contains several places of interest en route, including the stately Devon House at the junction of Trafalgar Road. **Devon House** ⓲ (open daily; entrance fee) was built in 1881 by a black Jamaican, George Stiebel, who made his fortune in South America, some say as a gold miner. Stiebel was also a builder, so his house was harmoniously constructed. It is regarded today as the best preserved example of Jamaican classical architecture.

The national flag was first used on 6 August 1962 – Independence Day.

BELOW: Devon House in oils.

Bob Marley 50th-anniversary stamp.

BELOW: the Bob
Marley Museum.

The government bought and restored the house in the 1960s and opened it to the public. Former stables surrounding the building were converted to craft shops, and a popular bar and restaurant known as the Grog Shoppe was opened. There is an ice-cream shop with delicious ice-cream, a bakery and Norma's on the Terrace, a verandah restaurant operated by celebrated chef Norma Shirley. For a time Devon House was the home of the National Gallery but with the removal of the gallery to downtown Kingston, it has reverted to its original concept.

The modern **Jamaica House**, further north, was built in the 1960s as the residence of the prime minister. It served that purpose only for a short time, and was soon converted into the prime minister's office instead.

At the traffic lights by East King's House Road and Hope Road is **King's House** (open Mon–Fri by appointment; tel: 927 6424/6143), the official residence of the governor-general. Originally the residence of the Bishop of Jamaica, the building was wrecked in the earthquake of 1907 and rebuilt to a design by Sir Charles Nicholson. Visitors may also see the attractive 80-hectare (200-acre) grounds.

The **Bob Marley Museum** 🕙 (open daily; entrance fee; tel: 927 9152) is unmistakable just beyond the Lady Musgrave intersection. A plaque of the reggae star graces the gates which lead into the house and gardens which he once called home. There are guided tours around the house, a film show and a shop offering Marley memorabilia. Snacks and drinks are also available on site.

The busy intersection further north is known as **Matilda's Corner**, probably after a French Haitian refugee who settled here. The official name for the wider area is Liguanea, a name which may derive from the iguana, the large lizard which was much esteemed by the native Tainos.

Hope Road leads to **Hope Gardens** (open daily) and the campus of the

ROBERT NESTA MARLEY

On his deathbed, in May 1981, Bob Marley was awarded the nation's third highest civil honour, the Order of Merit (OM), which entitled him to the title The Hon. Robert Nesta Marley. The then prime minister, Edward Seaga, who delivered the eulogy at Marley's state funeral in the National Arena, reported that when the honour was offered to him Bob replied: "Big man, if you can do it, do it."

To the large crowd at the funeral Bob's widow, Rita Marley, declared: "Bob lives." And indeed Bob Marley in death has outstripped the fame and success of Bob Marley in life. But long, bitter battles over his estate leave some issues unresolved; the production of a film about the reggae star's life continues to be stalled, and regular calls to name him a National Hero have raised questions about his ganja smoking and the paternity of several children outside his marriage. What is unquestionable is that, almost 20 years after his death, his name is synonymous with Jamaica, and his museum and statue are "must sees" for visitors. The first statue commissioned by the government was executed by Christopher Gonzalez. The symbolic sculpture was so unpopular that it was replaced by a more realistic representation, and the original is on display at the National Gallery.

University of the West Indies. Major Richard Hope, who came here with the conquering British Army in 1655, gave his name to this area. Hope's land grant, which extended from the hills at Newcastle to the harbour, was one of the most progressive estates on the island. By 1758 his descendants had built stone aqueducts to carry water from the Hope River to turn the estate mills. The city's first public water supply came from this source, and sections of the aqueduct are still in use in the vicinity of Hope Gardens and Mona Heights.

Hope Gardens have been a favourite sanctuary for sweethearts and amateur photographers since they were built over a century ago. The gardens were laid out in 1881 on 80 hectares (200 acres) acquired by the government from the Hope Estate, and were officially designated the **Royal Botanical Gardens** in 1953, on the occasion of a visit by Queen Elizabeth II. The gardens have been somewhat neglected and much diminished in recent years, but efforts are being made to revitalise the complex, which includes a small **zoo** (open daily; entrance fee).

The University of the West Indies

The lovely campus of the **University of the West Indies** (UWI) **20**, known locally as "You-wee", is wedged in the hills between Long Mountain and Dallas Mountain. From small beginnings in 1948, with just 33 medical students, the university has grown to embrace three campuses – in Jamaica, Barbados and Trinidad – and university centres in the other Caribbean territories which support it. This is a regional institution, and the crests of all its member states can be seen inside the Chapel.

Located near the main entrance, the Chapel is the foremost visitor attraction on campus. The old cutstone building of classically simple lines was formerly

Map on page 201

Aqueducts which flank Half Way Tree Road were built in the 1770s; the water carried sugar to what was then a vast estate.

BELOW: mobile sound system in downtown Kingston.

The Strawberry Hill Hotel (tel: 944 8400) in Irish Town is a popular, but not inexpensive, Sunday brunch stop. Wealthy Kingstonians brave the rough roads to reach the mountain area and enjoy the wonderful view.

the sugar warehouse of Gales Valley estate in Trelawny; it was pulled down and reassembled here stone by stone, as directed by its last owner. The original owner and the date of construction –"Edward Morant Gale: 1799" – are written at the top of the pediment, just under the roof. This is by no means the university's only connection with sugar. The campus embraces parts of the old Mona and Papine estates, and there are ruined aqueducts and sugar works throughout the grounds. The **Philip Sherlock Centre**, formerly the Creative Arts Centre, has been renamed for the "grand old man of letters" and former vice-chancellor. The UWI is an important cultural space.

The **University of Technology, Jamaica** was granted university status in 1995. (It was formerly the College of Arts, Science and Technology, popularly known as CAST.) Its campus is within throwing distance of UWI, nestled in the foothills of the Blue Mountains at Papine. The university caters for 7,000 students and incorporates the region's only architectural school, the Caribbean School of Architecture. The School of Hospitality's teaching restaurant, **Lillians**, is housed in a charming Georgian-style building and offers a good and modestly-priced lunch.

The Gordon Town Road beyond Papine travels along the gorge of the Hope River for some miles, climbing to the **Blue Mountain Inn** – a very romantic dining place. Established in 1754 as a plantation coffee house, it is set at the foot of waterfalls where the Mammee River joins the Hope.

A left turn above the inn leads to **Irish Town**, home to the exclusive and architecturally exquisite **Strawberry Hill Hotel**, and eventually to **Newcastle**; a right turn goes to **Gordon Town**, Mavis Bank and other hill villages, and ultimately to the **Blue Mountain Peak ㉑** walking trail.

BELOW: playing soccer in the street.

The Hope gained fame at the turn of the 20th century as the "Healing Stream" of the self-proclaimed Prophet Bedward, who attracted thousands of followers to his church at **August Town**, below the university. Bedward's much-publicised announcement that he would fly to heaven on a certain day was not fulfilled, but that did not dampen his followers' ardour. Support did fall off, however, when the authorities decided to confine him to an insane asylum.

Map on page below

The Hellshire Hills

Southwest of Kingston, off Marcus Garvey Drive and across the causeway on the west side of the harbour, are the city's dormitory communities and some of its favourite beaches.

In a few short years the Hellshire area has been transformed from an un-inhabited headland to urban extension of Kingston. **Portmore**, at the entrance to the region, which extends to the Hellshire Hills, is now home to an estimated 250,000 people; the population has more than doubled in 10 years. Long-term

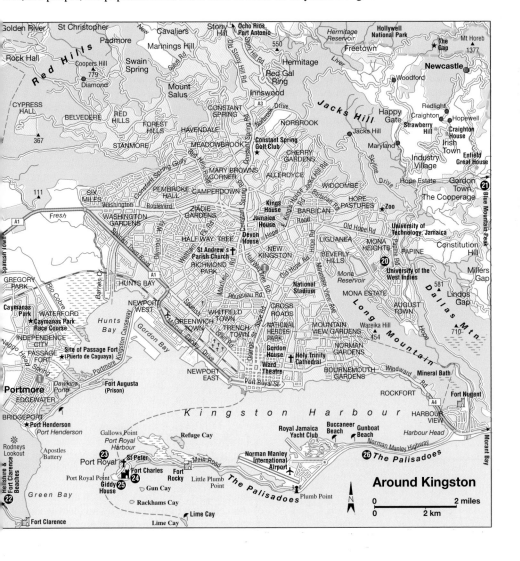

Around Kingston

Map
on page
201

BELOW: Twin
Sisters' Cave near
Hellshire Beach.
RIGHT: a luxury
yacht in
Kingston Harbour.

plans for the 117-sq. km (45-sq. mile) promontory include provisions for natural areas and forest parks, but much of its original character is disappearing beneath the demands of a burgeoning population. Portmore is also home to **Jamworld**, created by private developers as an 34-hectare (85-acre) entertainment park; now taken over by the government, it is to be transformed into a national park with sports, camping, recreational and entertainment facilities.

Although Portmore is actually in the parish of St Catherine, it is indubitably an essential part of the greater Kingston Metropolitan Area. There have been frequent "improvements" and upgrades of the road system here, in an effort to accommodate the expanding community, resulting in a maze for the uninitiated. So confusing is the area that all the communities "Across the Water" (Garveymeade, Edgewater, Independence City, Braeton, Bridgeport, Portmore and Greater Portmore) are referred to by the generic term "Portmore". Directional signs may help if you already have a clue about where you are going, but signposting is a new discipline for Jamaicans, and one not yet mastered.

As you drive across the causeway from Kingston proper, look to the west toward Caymanas Park and an area called **Passage Fort**. Formerly on the mouth of the Rio Cobre (which has since shifted course), Passage Fort was the island's principal shipping port in Spanish Town's early years as the country's capital, before the development of Kingston Harbour. It was here that a British fleet landed in 1655, later marching 10 km (6 miles) inland to capture Spanish Town and end Spanish rule in Jamaica. The imposing structure on the left is **Fort Augusta** prison; it was originally constructed in the mid-18th century as the major fortification on the western side of the harbour.

Where the road forks, proceed left, bypassing on the sea side a series of short-stay hotels, such as **Moments**, and a string of ramshackle eating-places, which at night serve as romantic trysting spots and are popular for a Friday-evening fish dinner. At the end of this stretch are the remains of the charming 18th-century village of **Port Henderson**. Six of the original buildings have been restored by the Jamaica National Trust, among them **Rodney's Arms**, a bar and restaurant. A stone's throw further on from Rodney's Arms is a sort of T-junction. Near the junction, on a slip road running parallel to the main road, is the famous Greater Kingston nightspot **Cactus**, the original club owned by the creators of **Asylum** (on the Knutsford Boulevard strip in the heart of New Kingston).

Kingston's beaches

You are now on the way to the most popular of Kingston's beaches, **Hellshire** and **Fort Clarence 22**. Fort Clarence, in spite of its lifeguards and toilet facilities (there are none at Hellshire), has not managed to develop the ambience of Hellshire. Or, as Jamaicans would say: "It don't have the vibes."

The other popular beach strip is on the road to St Thomas in the area called **Cable Hut**. The beach has hot black sand, strong waves, and a dangerous undertow. To reach it from Kingston take the A4 out of the centre and go past the roundabout leading to the airport, heading in the direction of St Thomas. ❏

Map on page 201

PORT ROYAL: LAIR OF THE BUCCANEERS

Little remains of the pirate past except for the artefacts displayed in the Maritime and Archaeological museums, but there are plans to turn this historic village into a heritage attraction

Kingston

Port Royal

BELOW: cannon salute at Fort Charles.

T he quiet, gritty fishing village of **Port Royal** ㉓, resting at the tip of the 7-mile-long (11-km) Palisadoes spit, sleeps on a turbulent past. Famed as the principal port of the pirates of the Caribbean in the late 17th century, it was also once the regional headquarters for the British Royal Navy – at a time when seapower controlled the world.

Today little remains of Port Royal's glorious past, but a massive restoration is planned to make the town one of the significant historical attractions of the Americas, with underwater viewspots, restaurants, museums, re-enactments depicting crucial periods in its history, and eco-tours through the mangroves and bird sanctuary nearby.

The name "Port Royal" evokes tales and legends of fabulous wealth beneath the ocean waves – "the El Dorado of the Caribbean". The sea floor 9 metres (30 ft) below this sultry town is where most of the town ended up when it was destroyed by a devastating earthquake and tidal wave in 1692. Underwater searches have revealed little treasure but have produced some fascinating and historically valuable artefacts, which can be seen at the **Archaeological Museum** (open daily; tel: 922 1287) located in the former naval hospital (built in 1819).

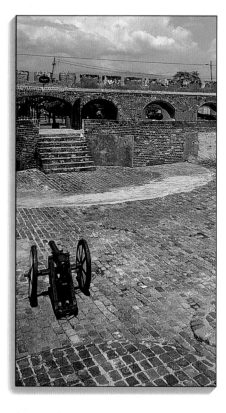

Port Royal's booty was the gift of the buccaneers, who carried it here from every city they sacked and every ship they robbed on the high seas. These "Brethren of the Coast" had the longstanding approval of the English authorities since they were acting against England's deadly enemies, the Spaniards.

The buccaneers themselves hardly ever got rich. There were too many temptations in Port Royal, including women, rum shops and up to 40 taverns. Port Royal soon gained a reputation as "the wickedest city in the world". Christian moralists said it could not go unpunished, and pointed to the ruinous 1692 'quake as retribution.

But the town refused to die. Some of the survivors returned to rebuild their houses, and, though Port Royal could never be the same again, it achieved a different character as a naval port.

The great British admiral Horatio Nelson once trod the streets of Port Royal, and visitors can still follow in his footsteps at **Fort Charles** ㉔ (open daily 9.30am–4.30pm, closed pub hols; entrance fee; tel: 967 8438). As a 20-year-old officer in the Royal Navy, Nelson was left in charge of the fort's batteries in 1779 when a French invasion was feared. The attack never came, probably because the fort's 104-gun complement was the strongest in the British Caribbean, but

Nelson spent many anxious hours pacing the verandah-like deck. Today the platform is known as **Nelson's Quarterdeck**.

Fort Charles was Port Royal's original structure, its foundations laid by the English shortly after their capture of Jamaica in 1655. Today it houses a small **Maritime Museum**.

Another attraction in Port Royal is the **Giddy House** , so-called because it leans at an impossible angle. An old artillery store, it was tilted by the 1907 'quake; it is now due for restoration, and there is little to see inside.

A fascinating reminder of the 1692 'quake is found in the epitaph on **Galdy's Tomb** in St Peter's Churchyard. Mr Galdy was swallowed up by the earth during the tremor, but there must have been something unappetising about him – he was spewed out again, living to a ripe old age to tell and retell the tale.

The Norman Manley Highway from Kingston to Port Royal skims across **The Palisadoes** , an alluvial strip created by centuries of sand, gravel and debris deposits from mountain streams. The alluvium joined a string of small islets, of which Port Royal was one. The spit encloses Kingston Harbour and acts as a breakwater.

The road was built in 1936, and prior to that a ferry – still operating from the foot of King Street – was the only form of transportation between Kingston and Port Royal. The highway cuts through what was once a flourishing coconut plantation; it has now reverted to its indigenous vegetation, including many native species of cactus and mangrove.

The broadest part of the Palisadoes is today occupied by the **Norman Manley International Airport**, which began as a supplementary landing-strip during World War II (1939–45) for seaplanes which set down in Kingston Harbour. ❑

IN THIS PLACE
DWELT
HORATIO NELSON,
You who tread his footprints
remember his glory.

A tribute to the admiral stationed here.

BELOW: Giddy House stands at an impossible angle.

PIRATE PRINCESSES

Although the notorious cutthroat buccaneer Sir Henry Morgan and pirates such as "Calico Jack" Rackham – so called because of his love of calico underwear – and the brutal and fearsome "Blackbeard" achieved the greatest infamy during Port Royal's heady days of the 17th and 18th centuries, two women earned their own special place in the history of piracy in the West Indies.

The true identities of Anne Bonney and Mary Read, who dressed as men and were "two of Rackham's toughest crew members", was only discovered at Rackham's trial, where it became clear that Rackham alone knew of their identities after being enlightened by his lover Anne Bonney as to the nature of her friendship with the "fierce and courageous" Mary Read. Life on the high seas must have been very rough, and they did well to conceal their true identities and earn fearsome reputations that any pirate – male or otherwise – would have been proud of.

Both women were convicted of piracy on 28 November 1720 and condemned to death (which was usually by hanging at a place called Gallows Point on the Palisadoes). However, Anne appears to have escaped punishment, and Mary later died of fever in prison at Port Royal before the sentence could be carried out.

HIGH IN THE BLUE MOUNTAINS

The Caribbean's highest mountain range affords views across the island and as far as Cuba. This is coffee country, rich with colourful flora and fauna, trees and a rainforest

Map on page 212

Kingston

The majestic **Blue Mountains** range from Kingston's northern suburbs to the north coast. They encompass the tallest mountain on the island, a high-altitude botanical garden, a national park and bird sanctuary, old plantations, great houses and magnificent hill walks.

At least three days should be devoted to exploring the Blue Mountains, and a sturdy, preferably four-wheel-drive vehicle is recommended for covering the rugged roads. Those from Kingston to Mavis Bank, via Guava Ridge, and Kingston to Hardwar Gap are paved: potholed but passable in all weather. But unpaved roads connecting Content Gap and Section and the Yallahs Crossing can be difficult during or immediately after heavy rains. Route B1 follows Hope Road from Half Way Tree to Papine. Your last chance to fill up is at the Papine Service Station. At Papine the B1 passes left round the little park and becomes Gordon Town Road. It follows the Hope River Valley past the **Blue Mountain Inn ❶**, a restaurant that was formerly the "Great House" of a coffee plantation. The coffee produced was shipped in wooden casks, made up the road at **The Cooperage** by imported Irish coopers, who were quartered farther up the Mammee River Road at the village still called **Irish Town**.

At Cooperage the road forks. Continue straight ahead to a village called **Industry** – a slightly incongruous name in view of the normal level of activity there. Five kilometres (3 miles) from Papine, 366 metres (1,200 ft) up the valley, stands **Gordon Town ❷**, a metropolis by Blue Mountain standards. It has a police station, a courthouse, a post office, two schools, a clinic and its share of bars.

Gordon Town was the site of Jamaica's first botanical garden, established by Hinton East in 1770 at **Spring Garden**. East introduced hundreds of foreign plant species from places as diverse as China and Sweden. Many of his imports – including hibiscus, azalea, cassia, magnolia, oleander, croton and jasmine – permanently altered the Jamaican scene. Nothing survives of the original garden except the profusion of attractive plants around Gordon Town.

Higglers and hairpins

The road to **Guava Ridge** leaves the town square from the police station, crosses a narrow bridge over the Hope River, and climbs above the town along the side of the river valley. As the road twists and turns in and out of a succession of valleys, the red roofs of the Newcastle army camp, 1,220 metres (4,000 ft) up across the valley, constantly appear, then recede from view, straggling down the mountainside. From here Newcastle looks like some lost Inca city in the Andes, especially in low-hanging clouds.

A succession of tiny houses dots this route. Some

PRECEDING PAGES: mountain mist near Hardwar Gap. **LEFT:** Blue Mountain man. **BELOW:** the Blue Mountain Inn is an exclusive hideaway.

Sangster's World's End factory (tel: 926 8888) is located 760 metres (2,500 ft) up in the mountains.

BELOW:
mountain-bike
tours go downhill.

cling precariously to the hillside, a small patch of banana, coffee and vegetables around them, and many more can be seen scattered over the valley floor down below the road. Such smallholdings supply most of Kingston's vegetable and fruit needs. As the weekend approaches, the road fills up with brightly painted market trucks carrying unbelievable loads of higglers with their baskets of produce to sell to city markets. This was the free land settled by the newly emancipated slaves in 1834, and the pattern of their agricultural life has not changed significantly since then.

Two hairpin bends straddle the 18-km (11-mile) post as the road climbs steadily around the sides of the mountains. Shortly before the 21-km (13-mile) post, on the left-hand side, is **World's End ❸** (open Mon–Fri 10am–4pm; guided tours; tel: 926 8888). Here some of Jamaica's most famous liqueurs and rums are produced under the **Sangster's "Old Jamaica"** label. Dr Ian Sangster, originally from Scotland, began production in 1973. This attractive little factory straddles several levels as it descends the side of the valley to a visitors' terrace commanding a fine view of Newcastle. Tours (including product sampling and purchasing) are available.

At the junction beside the bus shelter beyond World's End, at an elevation of 914 metres (3,000 ft), take the right fork through the scattered township of Guava Ridge and descend via Mavis Bank to the Yallahs River at 519 metres (1,700 ft).

Shortly before Mavis Bank, where the main road bears left over a bridge, a dirt road leads to **Mavis Bank Coffee Factory**, where the preparation and roasting of Blue Mountain coffee-beans may be seen. The factory processes about 12,000 bushels annually; the beans are purchased from 4,000 surrounding farms.

CYCLING AND HIKING

The best way for nature lovers, and the adventurous visitor, to explore Jamaica is on foot or by bike. At least half a dozen organisations now offer a variety of walking tours: from a half-day hike from Jack's Hill in Kingston to Hollywell Park (1,542 metres/5,060 ft) above sea level) by way of the Fairy Glade Trail, with a qualified guide and snack included, to the more strenuous 2-day guided trip up to the Blue Mountain Peak, at 2,256 metres (7,402 ft) the highest point in the Caribbean's highest mountain range, with a visit to Mavis Bank Coffee Factory and World's End distillery (Sangster's Liquors), and an evening meal and stopover at the simple but charming Whitfield Hall or Wildflower Lodge in nearby Abbey Green.

Cyclists can choose almost anything: from a half-day tour on the coast road to the popular downhill tour (from Hardwar Gap, at about 1,524 metres/5,000 ft) which takes in coffee, banana, spice and cocoa plantations, pine and rainforest as well as waterfalls, streams and pools – food and riding gear are provided.

Also on offer are more extensive 2- and 3-day customised mountain-bike tours through the scenic but demanding central highlands. The best time to go is during the December-to-April dry winter season.

The most prized coffee is a form called "rat-cut": rats eat the ripe berries and excrete the beans; the resultant seedlings are extremely sturdy and produce superior berry-bearing plants. The factory was established in the 1920s by Victor C. Munn; the original pulpery was destroyed by fire in 1955 but rebuilt, and still operates today. In spite of the coffee production this is still a small township, but it has both a police station and a post office.

Map on page 212

A place in the pines

Backtrack to the junction near World's End and the fork in the road to Guava Ridge. The left fork ascends after a mile to the gates of **Pine Grove Guest House** (tel: 922 8705). Besides panoramic views over Kingston and around the mountains, the hotel offers chalet accommodation and typical Jamaican food. Pine Grove is the best central point from which to explore the Blue Mountains. And you can sit here in the evening with the mountains all around, while the sky changes from blue through turquoise to pink and the lights of the capital gradually come to life far below.

After Pine Grove, the road passes **Valda** at 1,145 metres (3,758 ft), then drops steadily to **Content Gap**, a village connected by footpath to Gordon Town, 550 metres (1,800 ft) below and a 6-km (4-mile) walk. At the round water-tank the left-hand track offers an easy one-mile walk up to **Charlottenburg House ❹** (tours by appointment Tues, Thur and Sat; tel: 994 9265), a well-preserved great house furnished with antique Jamaican furniture. Former slave quarters, dating from coffee-plantation days, still stand adjacent to the house. The durable and attractive hardwood used in the construction is local cedar, cut from the plantation when it was cleared for coffee.

BELOW: view of Newcastle.

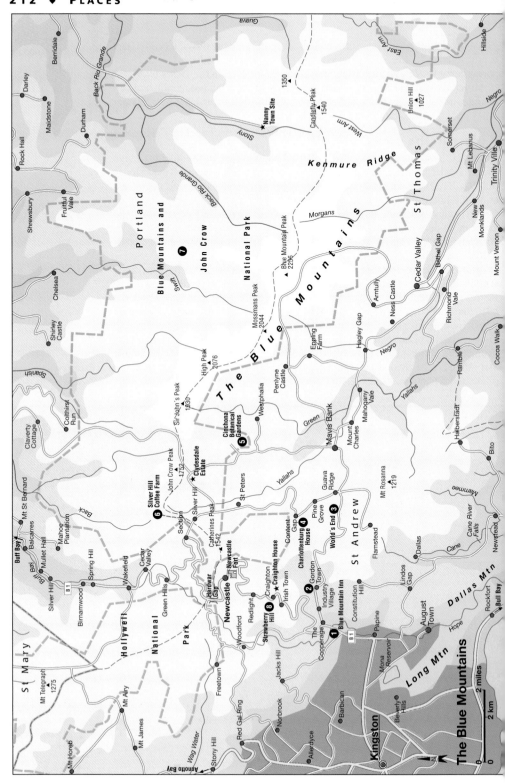

The Blue Mountains

Past **St Peters** there is a junction with the road to **Clydesdale**, a picturesque forestry station on the River Clyde, 2.5 km (1½ miles) up a bumpy little road. Also once a coffee plantation, it still has coffee-drying barbecues and an old water wheel. The Forestry Department rents out the two-bedroomed main house at Clydesdale (currently closed for repairs, but the grounds are suitable for campers. However, obtain permission to camp from the Forestry Department in Kingston beforehand; tel: 924 2667). Linen, towels and essentials are not provided. The house looks down on Clydesdale town above thousands of tiny conifer seedlings standing in serried ranks. The entrance road is to the left of the seedling beds.

Map on page 212

A flowery high

A worthwhile side-trip from Clydesdale takes you to the Cinchona Botanical Gardens. Follow the descending road on the right which passes below the old wooden coffee-mill house. About 100 yards later the dirt road divides. The branch on the right leads 3 km (2 miles) up to **Top Mountain**, where a rough Jeep road on the left side (if you reach some houses of the Yallahs Valley Land Authority, you've gone too far) leads demandingly, if scenically, up to **Cinchona**. If you don't have a four-wheel drive vehicle, park at Top Mountain for a breathtaking if strenuous walk of more than 300 metres (1,000 ft). The "main" road at Top Mountain junction leads on to **Westphalia**; from here a bridle road beside the water tanks leads 1.5 km (1 mile) up to the lower end of Cinchona. The left-hand fork from Clydesdale passes a picnic rondel on the left en route. This is quite steep, but is by far the easiest route.

Bougainvillea blossoms in island gardens.

The **Cinchona Botanical Gardens** ❺ cling to a magnificent stretch of ridge

BELOW: view of Hollywell Park, located above Newcastle.

which is 1,371–1,677 metres (4,500–5,500 ft) above the valleys of the Yallahs, Clyde and Green rivers. Cinchona may have the most inspiring site of any botanical garden in the world. It was founded in 1868 as a centre for the cultivation of Assam tea and cinchona trees, whose bark was in great demand as a source of quinine for the treatment of malaria.

The cinchona is a native of the high Andes; its medicinal properties were passed to the Spaniards by the Quechua, descendants of the Incas. An experimental few hundred acres were planted around Cinchona and proved initially profitable. Later, however, large-scale production in India proved to be cheaper, and the Jamaican plantations of both cinchona and tea failed. The plantation shrank to an expatriate's dream, a "European Garden" established by an English gardener to supply Kingston with flowers and vegetables. As a result of its success, the trade remains an important source of income for local people.

Look out for the exclusive and expensive Blue Mountain Coffee, or alternatively try the high mountain variety.

Cinchona affords views in all directions, with John Crow Peak and St John's Peak to the north, the main ridge of the Blue Mountains stretching east (and viewed spectacularly from the **Panorama Walk** on the east side of the gardens), and Kingston and the sea shimmering away to the hot south.

The uninhabited Great House was formerly the home of Jamaica's Superintendent of Gardens. Well-tended lawns bordered by a profusion of flowers front the house, and around the lawns is a veritable labyrinth of paths and walks that lead through the loosely arranged trees. These include many imported types: some huge specimens of eucalyptus, easily recognisable by their spear-shaped leaves and peeling whitish barks; juniper; cork oak, whose bark is in fact cork; Chinese cypress; ferns and tree ferns; rubber trees, whose leaves when plucked emit a white latex; and some fine examples of Blue Mountain yacca, a tall

BELOW: Blue Mountain coffee-beans on the bush.

COFFEE

Currently in administrative disarray, Jamaica's Blue Mountain Coffee still rates as one of the world's finest coffees and its most expensive. But – and it is a very big but – the Coffee Industry Board, which controls the quality and purchase price of beans from the coffee farmers, is insolvent, with liabilities exceeding assets by around $1 billion in 1999. In fact the volume of coffee-beans delivered to the processing plants in 1997–98 fell to 16,727 tonnes, or 10 percent less than in 1996–97. The volume of exports declined by 54.8 percent, to 882 tonnes.

However, the government and the Coffee Board recognise that coffee is still a valuable asset to the nation, generating both agricultural employment (particularly in Portland) and vital foreign exchange, and are setting in place a strategy for raising exports to 75 percent of production and improving production by 20 percent. But how to achieve that, while still meeting its debts, without raising prices has so far challenged the industry without success. A high percentage of the coffee produced in Jamaica is shipped straight to Asia; however, the collapse of that market in 1997 precipitated the decline in exports and threatened many livelihoods. Some producers are now discovering the potential of exporting worldwide by selling online.

tree with tiny dagger-shaped leaves and reddish marks on its smooth trunk.

Follow the main route half a mile after the Clydesdale detour to a small road on the right leading to **Silver Hill Coffee Farm ❻**, which was once a coffee factory. Between September and February you can see workers picking the red coffee berries. They remove the outer pulp from the two inner green beans to prepare them for drying, husking and roasting.

In the Blue Mountains, optimum soil and climatic condition combine to produce coffee of exceptionally fine flavour, believed to be the most expensive and sought-after in the world. After the introduction of coffee, in 1728, its cultivation spread throughout the Blue Mountains. Most of the Great Houses here were plantation homes built during the halcyon years 1800–1840, when coffee exports rose to 17,000 tonnes per year. After emancipation the large plantations declined and were split up among small farmers, but that system has never produced more than a fraction of the earlier tonnages. Silver Hill is just one of numerous small coffee farms in the Blue Mountains.

Misty roads and militiamen

At **Section** the road joins route B1, which connects Kingston to the north coast at **Buff Bay**. Turn right and the partially paved road on the right drops north through the mountains, via villages with engaging names like **Birnamwood** and **Tranquility**, to Buff Bay. But bear left to **Hardwar Gap**. The undulating hills around the Gap constitute the **Blue Mountain and John Crow National Park ❼** and **Conservation Area**, a fine example of montane mist forest. The area has an annual rainfall of more than 250 cm (100 inches), with wet clinging mists occurring daily.

Map on page 212

JAMAICA
$25

The giant swallowtail butterfly can grow to 15 cms (6 inches), but it is rare; it can occasionaly be spotted in the John Crow Mountains.

BELOW: blue hut in the mountains.

Map on page 212

Blue Mountain coffee ranks among the best in the world.

BELOW: a mountain man and his mule.

In the almost constant moisture the flora is quite distinct even from that of Newcastle, only 3 km (2 miles) away. Pine trees predominate among the many tree types, while a striking feature is the profusion of a wide selection of Jamaica's 550 types of fern, including the high tree ferns, *Cyathea arborea*. Some of the trees grow to over 9 metres (30 ft) tall, and many support climbing plants and even orchids. The bird songs that fill the forest include the harsh cry of the redheaded Jamaican woodpecker and the hauntingly plaintive call of the solitaire thrush. Delightful walks and picnic areas with views of Kingston speckle the hillside in Hollywell Park. The Forestry Department rents out log cabins at reasonable rates, and maintains the trails within the 120-hectare (300-acre) forest, rich with ferns and vibrant carpets of flowers.

There are numerous well-trodden walking and hiking trails criss-crossing the Park, which can take anything from under one hour to a whole day. For most of them a local guide is not just recommended: it is essential, because it is so easy to lose your way in the dense forest. The climb up to Catherine's Peak at 1,542 metres (5,060 ft) affords wonderful views over Kingston if the sky is clear of mist. The Fairy Glade trail is also popular because of the beautiful views and flora and fauna to be seen along the way.

From **Hardwar Gap** follow route B1 to **Newcastle** along the contours of **Mount Horeb**, with views over the Mammee River valley. Newcastle is a military camp, occupied by the Jamaica Defence Force, built between 1,067 metres (3,500 ft) and 1,372 metres (4,500 ft). The road passes right through the parade ground, and you may find yourself in the middle of a military drill. General Sir William Gomm established the camp in 1841 in an attempt to reduce the high death rate from yellow fever at lower altitudes. Visitors may use the facilities of the Sergeants' Mess, located in the building above the parade ground.

The Japanese connection

From Newcastle the road drops steadily to the few houses of **Irish Town**, passing the signposted entrance drive leading up to **Craighton Great House** and estate (view by appointment; tel: 929 8490). This old property was purchased in 1981 by the UCC Coffee Company of Japan to expand production of Blue Mountain coffee for the Japanese market, which absorbs virtually all of Jamaica's production.

On a hill above Irish Town lies the elegant **Strawberry Hill Hotel ❽**, opened in 1995, which has won architectural awards for its use of traditional Jamaican construction methods and 19th-century Georgian vernacular. This hotel has become a favourite Sunday brunch stop for wealthy Kingstonians, who head for the cool mountains at the weekend.

At the 21-km (13-mile) marker a signposted road leads to **Bamboo Lodge**. Once an attractive small hotel and now a private house, it was formerly a British Naval Hospital claiming associations with Admiral Nelson, commander of Port Royal in 1799. Below Bamboo Lodge is **Belancita**, home of the late Sir Alexander Bustamante. The road continues down the mountainside to the Mammee River, whose course it then follows back to the Blue Mountain Inn at Cooperage Junction. ❑

Scaling the Blue Mountain Peak

The most popular approach to the Blue Mountain Peak itself begins from Guava Ridge. The road descends through pinewoods along the broad valley of the Falls River to Mavis Bank. After one of the bends a panoramic view of the Grand Ridge, including the Blue Mountain Peak at 2,256 metres (7,402 ft), suddenly unfolds. The Peak is a rather rounded hump amid a series of others almost equally high. The Blue Mountain range is about 45 km (28 miles) long and is believed to be 19 km (12 miles) wide at its widest point. The forest proper begins at about 610 metres (2,000 ft) on the northern slopes, while in the more heavily populated and farmed southern area the trees have been pushed up to between 914 and 1,220 metres (3,000–4,000 ft). Most of the mountainside is now a protected area called the Blue Mountain and John Crow National Park, which was established to prevent further reduction of the woodland.

Shortly before you reach Mavis Bank, where the main road bears left over a bridge, a dirt road leads into the Mavis Bank Coffee Factory. A broad dirt track continues straight through the Yallahs River at Mahogany Vale, then climbs steeply to Hagley Gap, the nearest village to the Peak. Here, at the tiny square in front of the village store, take the dirt road to the left. Climb for 1.5 km (1 mile) to Farm Hill, bear right and continue for half a mile to Whitfield Hall, 8 km (5 miles) and 975 metres (3,200 ft) below the Peak. The house is clean and homey, if somewhat ascetic, and resembles a European youth hostel. Start your hike from here.

Only the hardy will succeed in reaching the summit of the Blue Mountain Peak, a three-hour scramble up a rough track. The climb begins in a montane mist forest, a rare remnant of Jamaica's original forests. Its name derives from the characteristic mist which often lies on the peaks between 10am and 4pm. This reduces the incidental sunlight greatly, which affects the flora.

The Elfin Woodland starts at about 1,677 metres (5,500 ft), petering out in windswept scrub on the summit. It is an open and eerie woodland, consisting mainly of short, twisted, gnarled trees, often laden with lichens, mosses and ferns. A dwarf species of orchid grows here in the swirling mist. Other flowers which grow well are honeysuckle, rhododendron, ginger lilies and the lesser-known merianias (called "Jamaica Rose"), whose hanging rose-like blossoms appear to be lit from within when bathed in sunlight.

Once you are on the Peak there is an incredible view over most of Jamaica. In clear weather you can see as far north as Cuba. Temperatures drop quite low here, and it can become cold, so take a sweater.

The best time to explore the Peak and the surrounding area is during the dry winter months between December and April. There are many specialist guided hiking, cycling and four-wheel-drive tours available. Contact: Blue Mountain Tours in Ocho Rios, tel: 974 7075, or the Jamaica Tourist Board, tel: 929 9200 or 974 2570, for more information.   ❏

RIGHT: view of the John Crow Mountains.

PORT ANTONIO

In the county of Surrey, surrounded by wildlife and a rich landscape, lies a small fishing village, steeped in history, an ideal place for rest and relaxation, and the choice of the rich and famous

Nor th of the Blue Mountains, Jamaica slopes gently back to the Caribbean. Surrey's coastline, carved out by volcanic activity, has the most ruggedly beautiful scenery on the island – and the wettest parish. With its thick, lush undergrowth, secluded coves, turquoise seas and omnipresent Blue Mountains, the area around Port Antonio has a staggering beauty ready to be explored on foot, horseback, raft or bike. This is "Country", as Jamaicans call any region that lies outside Kingston.

Route A4 winds through local fishing villages and hidden coves of jagged rock and secret sandpits. The seas swell in on northern fronts, and currents crash against cliff and sand in some of the island's biggest breakers. From the county of Surrey's western boundary, below Annotto Bay, east around the coast, through Port Antonio, Morant Bay and Yallahs, and back to Kingston, the discriminating visitor will discover some of the Caribbean's most breathtaking vistas.

The heart of this region is **Port Antonio ❶**, once the cradle of Jamaica's tourist trade. In the 1890s visitors arriving by ship marvelled at the little town perched above the twin harbours. The poet Ella Wheeler Wilcox called it "the most exquisite harbour on earth".

Most first-time visitors who don't arrive by cruise ship come by car from the north-coast resorts or from Kingston. The popular, sight-saturated approach from Kingston is via Route A3, usually just called the Junction.

To follow this route you should take Constant Spring Road north out of Kingston. Bear right into Long Lane after negotiating the Manor Park roundabout. The road will swing north again to become Stony Hill Road, Route A3. A right-hand detour on Gibson Road, past the red, slate-roofed **Stony Hill Hotel**, provides majestic views of Kingston and an insight into the lives of Jamaica's élite, who live in the hillcrest mansions behind barred entrance gates guarded by security dogs.

The A3 main road takes you through the bustling centre of **Stony Hill** and smaller towns like **Golden Spring**. Drivers should take care around the increasingly hairpin corners and on the narrowing and deteriorating potholed roads. Buses and trucks rarely slow down on them.

Castleton Botanical Gardens ❷ (open daily; tel: 927 1257), on the boundary of Surrey and Middlesex counties, demands a visit. Established in 1862, it has blossomed into a showcase of exotic Jamaican flora. The highway bisects its 6 hectares (15 acres). Huge trees provide shade and cool resting spots in the upper half. The lower part runs along the bank of the **Wag Water River**, with which the road plays tag from this point on. There is convenient roadside parking, and

PRECEDING PAGES: Trident Castle, Portland. **LEFT:** the Junction road to Portland. **BELOW:** exotic plant, Castleton.

The dye taken from annotto seeds was the main ingredient in the Tainos' body paint.

plenty of riverside spots for picnicking and bathing. For a tip, guides willingly introduce you to fascinating plants like the *strychnos* – from which strychnine poisons and medicine are derived. Further on, inviting bamboo lines the river, usually a mere trickle that exposes enormous, water-worn boulders.

The views become more spectacular beyond the gardens. Look out for a graceful suspension bridge at boulder-crested **Mahoe Hill**. The road eventually winds down out of the Wag Water ravine into broad plains of sugar cane and banana plantations.

Turn east when the road dead-ends at the Caribbean Sea. **Annotto Bay** takes its name from an orange dye made from a Central American tree that once grew in the area. The town, like most in north-coast Surrey, has a weather-beaten **station** that hasn't been used since Hurricane Allen shredded Portland's railway tracks in 1980. There's also an imaginatively-structured **Baptist chapel**, built in 1894, beyond the market square.

You cross back into Surrey and the parish of Portland at **Windsor Castle**. Further east at **Buff Bay** is the junction with the sensational but tortuous back route from Kingston. This road climbs up through Newcastle, then plummets 1,372 metres (4,500 ft) from Hardwar Gap to the Buff Bay River gorge.

Of rats and rafts

The road winds east, turning inland into thick, wet foliage, beyond **Spring Garden**. William Bancroft Espeut lived on an estate here, where he introduced the mongoose in 1872. Plagued by rats that annually damaged some £45,000 worth of his sugar crop, Espeut imported nine mongooses from India. Though they ate the rats, they also preyed on birds, crabs, lizards, domestic stock and

Map on page 236

fruit, and became as much of a pest as the rats. Wildlife experts blame the mongoose for endangering the dwindling populations of coney and Jamaican iguana.

The only evidence of recent volcanic activity on the island is a low ridge about 183 metres (600 ft) high just beyond **Orange Bay**. It was formed by lava believed to have poured from a fissure in the earth.

Take a dip in the cool cascading waters of **Somerset Falls** near **Hope Bay**. There's a small admission charge here, as well as a snack bar, gardens and changing facilities. Swim, or take a boat, beyond the small trickles at the top of the stair for a look at bigger, more secluded waterfalls in a blue-green grotto.

Another road swings inland at Hope Bay, which provides spectacular views of the Blue Mountains before rejoining the coast road at **St Margaret's Bay**. Here, on the old **Burlington Estate** grounds, a tree exemplifies the region's fertility by growing out of the factory chimney.

A bridge crosses the **Rio Grande ❸**, the island's largest river. Maroons and other residents once floated bananas down the stream on long rafts; now they do the same journeys with tourists. In the 1940s, Port Antonio's most notorious resident, movie idol Errol Flynn, arrived and began organising raft races. The Earl of Mansfield later built the landing site, shops and restaurant at **Rafters' Rest**.

A relaxed ride on a 9-metre (30-ft)-long raft is still one of Jamaica's major tourist attractions. Licensed raftsmen, some of whom have spent up to 10 years as apprentices, guide your craft through gentle rapids with long poles. The 2–3 hour trip begins at **Berridale** (or 3 hours from Grant's Level), south of Port Antonio off Red Hassel Road. About 150 rafts work the river, but it rarely appears crowded. The sight of mothers washing children or clothes, or kids swinging from vines along the banks, makes the trip an exotic adventure for most visitors.

If you have a hired car and want to enjoy the one-way raft ride, drive to Berridale where an authorised driver will take your vehicle to the river mouth so that it will be waiting for you at the end of the ride.

BELOW: cruising the Rio Grande.

RIVER RAFTING

Once used to transport bananas and fruit from the interior to the coast and the wharf in Port Antonio, the Rio Grande now has one of Jamaica's most popular forms of ecotourism: river rafting.

Safe for all ages, the two-seater bamboo rafts set off from Berridale and glide gently and quietly downriver, past towering bamboo arches and fern-shrouded groves, over rippling shallow shoals and through a narrow passageway of moss-covered stone known as Lovers' Rock. Take a hat to shade you from the tropical sun on the one-way trip. Relax and admire the scenery, or stop for a picnic and a swim before completing the journey to Rafters' Rest – which also has a restaurant, bookstore and gift shop – by the bridge where the river meets the Caribbean Sea.

If you fancy doing the trip by candle- or moonlight, just ask. Once all the rage, evening raft trips are now discouraged, but they could make a return if a reliable insurance package can be agreed. Buy your tickets through Rio Grande Attractions (tel: 993 2778; charges are per raft) located at Rafters' Rest, through your tour operator or at your hotel. Avoid negotiating your own price directly with the rafters, because it will probaby cost you more than the official price in the end.

The land around Port Antonio is fertile and rich, with colourful flora.

The Rio Grande rises nearly 900 metres (3,000 ft) up into the mountainous interior of Portland, and torrential rainfalls often swell it beyond its banks. Portland's wet reputation results from the meeting of the moist northeast trade winds with the Blue Mountains. The winds, forced to rise, mix with ever-cooler air and form pregnant clouds; they drop most of their load here, leaving leeward areas such as Kingston parched. As much as 762 cm (300 inches) of rain falls annually in parts of inland Portland.

Twin harbours

Portland's rugged terrain long deterred settlement of this part of the island. Nature was so unbridled here that early settlers probably felt threatened by its very presence. Even the Taino Indians seem to have shunned Portland, as no signs of their presence have been found here.

The first Europeans here were the Spaniards. They named the Rio Grande and the twin harbours just east of it – Puerto San Francisco and Puerto Antón, from which Portland's principal city got its name. They are now known rather prosaically as **West Harbour** and **East Harbour**.

The Spaniards carved a few *hatos* (cattle ranches) out of the jungle, but made no serious strides towards settlement. Portland remained virtually unknown territory long after the British settled the rest of the island.

The British created the parish of Portland in 1723; 50 years later Port Antonio had no more than 20 houses. The government offered free land and slaves to prospective settlers, as well as seven years' freedom from land taxes, arrests or prosecutions. Two barrels of beef and one of flour would be given to everyone until they reaped their first crops. But only the most desperate of settlers took

BELOW: Port Antonio gateway.

Map on page 225

up the challenge, discouraged as they were by heavy tropical downpours, the dense jungles and the swampy, mosquito-infested coastline. Raids by the feared mountain-dwelling Maroons also deterred pioneers.

To combat invasions from Maroons or Spaniards, in 1729 the British began to build **Fort George Ⓐ** on the peninsular bluff that juts into the harbours. Its 3-metre (10-ft) -thick masoned walls had spaces for 22 guns. The old barracks have been turned into classrooms, and the parade grounds form a playing field for the **Titchfield School** compound. The existing cannons date from a later period but are mounted on the original gun emplacements.

The small island to the north, with a secluded beach, wonderful snorkelling and short-stay chalets, all just a five-minute boat ride from the harbour, was originally intended to be the town's site; it was also acquired by the British military. The navy established a formidable installation there, but only the name **Navy Island Ⓑ** lingers. The island became more famous when it was purchased in the 1940s by lusty Errol Flynn, whom Jamaicans fondly recall as having staged wild Hollywood parties there. The likes of Clara Bow, Bette Davis and Ginger Rogers became part of the swinging Port Antonio scene.

Flynn is long gone, and Port Antonio has settled back into its serene role as a resort for visitors wanting to get away from the commercial tourist scenes at Ocho Rios and Montego Bay. Just south of Titchfield School on the peninsula is one of adventurous visitors' favourite haunts, **DeMontevin Lodge Ⓒ** (tel: 993 2604), built about 1898 at the corner of Fort George Street and Musgrave. If you don't intend to stay, at least sample an authentic Jamaican meal of suckling pig, codfish and ackee, or lobster. This is by arrangement only: you must phone in your order before you are ready to eat.

Guided tours of Navy Island are available. Call: 993 2667 for details.

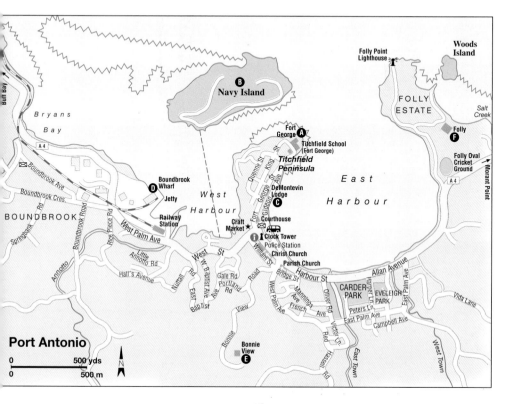

Although Titchfield Hill is but a shadow of its former self, there have been proposals made to restore and preserve some of the once beautiful Georgian architecture in Port Antonio.

DeMontevin Lodge sits on "**The Hill**", once an exclusive residential area restricted by race, class and wealth. The British named the town Titchfield after the English estate of the Duke of Portland. The Hill became Upper Titchfield, and the common people lived in Lower Titchfield along the seashore.

After the signing of a treaty with the Maroons in 1739, Titchfield grew more rapidly with the steadily increasing influx of sugar-cane money. By the end of the 18th century Portland had 38 large estates and more than 100 smaller ones. But while sugar grew readily in most of Jamaica's soil and climate, heavy rain took its toll here. By 1854 only four estates remained; all had vanished by the turn of the century.

But another green crop saved Port Antonio from economic ruin. As the large estates dwindled, Jamaicans carved them into smaller plots where peasants began to grow yams and other "ground provisions", as root crops are called. They also began to grow bananas.

The banana business

The empty wharves and vacant warehouses of modern Port Antonio provide little evidence that this town was once the world's banana capital, the very stereotype of Harry Belafonte's "Banana Boat" song, where men and women carried heavy banana bunches on their heads as they swayed and sang "Day-O".

If you time your trip right, you may still see green bananas being loaded at **Boundbrook Wharf ❺**, near the railroad crossing, when you drive into town from the west. Packaged elsewhere, they are loaded into the ships mechanically.

The Spanish brought the banana to the West Indies from the Canary Islands in 1516. The trade was later founded on a large, sweet, creamy fruit called the

BELOW:
pretty fretwork
revealed on
DeMontevin Lodge.

EVERYONE'S GONE BANANAS

Following a World Trade Organisation (WTO) ruling – precipitated by the US – that the current EU banana policy, which grants preferential market access to former colonies, breaks free-trade rules, Jamaica (particularly Portland) and fellow West Indian banana producers stand to lose out to the giant and more efficient US-owned Central American producers like Chiquita.

For over 80 years it has been known that the climatic and soil conditions of the Central American countries are more productive than Jamaica's, but Jamaica has not been able to increase its yield per acre (0.4 hectares) average of 7 tonnes, compared to the Latin American average of 15 tonnes per acre (0.4 hectares). Although Jamaican bananas are tastier and sweeter than Chiquita's, they also have a shorter ripening time during ocean shipment and a shorter shelf-life in the supermarket. In addition, Chiquita bananas look more attractive, offer better value and are bigger, with yellower skins.

Although banana exports to Britain for 1999 are estimated at 65,000 tonnes, with a value of US$40 million, this is expected to fall dramatically as the Jamaican banana industry is forced to explore other markets and processes such as canning.

Gros Michel (and pronounced "Gross Mitchell" by Jamaicans), which was initially wiped out by Panama disease. The *Gros Michel* can sometimes be bought in the markets or on the roadside, but no longer exists in large enough quantities to be exported.

For the first 350 years after it arrived the banana was disparaged as animal food. But canny 19th-century Yankee sea captains loaded them green, watched them ripen on board ship, and found they could sell them for a profit on the eastern seaboard of the United States.

Captain George Busch carried the first bunch of bananas from Port Maria, west of Port Antonio, in 1869. Captain Lorenzo Dow Baker turned bananas into an industry in 1871 when he sold 1,450 stems in Boston at a US$2,000 profit. Baker organised planting, collection and marketing systems among the peasants in Portland's interior. His efforts grew into the Boston Fruit Company, later acquired by the giant United Fruit conglomerate.

With fleets of empty banana boats traveling to Jamaica to pick up their cargos, the enterprising Baker filled them with tourists seeking refuge from harsh winters, simultaneously touching off Port Antonio's tourist trade. He built the first Titchfield Hotel on "The Hill" in 1905.

Bananas became big business in Port Antonio. In the town's heyday, weekly sailings of banana boats were said to exceed weekly departures from the big British port of Liverpool. The arrival of a ship in those days was signalled by the blowing of a conch shell. All hands rushed to the fields to cut down mature fruit with machetes; then they wrapped it in banana "trash", or dried leaves, for its short journey to the docks.

The banana plant is a tree with a succulent stem (sometimes used as animal

Map on page 225

BELOW:
unripe bananas
ready for market.

fodder) formed by overlapping leaf bases. The mature plant sends out a purple bud which reveals rows of tiny flowers when it opens. The flowers develop into small "fingers", and each grows into a banana. A cluster of fingers forms a "hand", and several hands make up a bunch.

When bananas were unloaded from trucks, two checkers would take a "stem count" of each bunch. Nine hands or more were considered a "bunch"; eight hands were a three-quarter bunch; anything less was rejected. "Six hand, seven hand, eight hand, bunch!" as the song says. When a carrier walked the line, he received a metal disc showing the bunch count, to be redeemed later. Another long human chain, this one mainly female, carried the bunches aboard the truck. Here the famed "tallyman" of Belafonte's song gave each carrier a "tally" to be redeemed.

Bananas grow up to meet the sun.

The plaintive songs of banana workers were very real reflections of their lives. "Mi back dis a bruck with the bare exhaustion," they sang as they carried heavy loads from dawn to dusk, earning only 25 to 70 cents per day. Portland-born Evan Jones, screenwriter of *Funeral in Berlin* and other movies, wrote in his poem "Song of the Banana Man":

> *Thank God and this big right hand.*
> *I will live and die a banana man.*

Devastating hurricanes and Panama disease eventually crippled the banana industry. The trade passed temporarily into the hands of large operators who had the resources to control the disease; today it is back in the hands of small-to-medium-sized growers. The government controls marketing and shipping. Bananas continue to be an important crop, but the days of the tallyman have gone.

BELOW: façades mark Fort George Street mall.

Many varieties of the banana, and its fat cousin the plantain, can be sampled at the **Town Market** in West Street. All you have to do to locate it is follow your nose and the crowds of clutter and colour opposite the cenotaph. Port Antonio's best food-market days are Thursday and Saturday. Also on West Street is **Gallery Ambokile** (tel: 993 3162) which is run by artist Philip Henry; it exhibits and sells ceramics, paintings and sculptures.

The town centre, with its faded and, in parts, neglected architecture is still worth strolling around. The **clocktower** is a useful landmark. One of Port Antonio's most recent curios is in Fort George Street – a shopping mall hidden behind a series of stunning façades reminiscent of European architecture at the time of Columbus. Sadly, the mall is half empty, but the contrasting European styles placed in a colonial Caribbean setting is an arresting sight.

Bonnie views

From ground level, particularly around the market, Port Antonio displays a dingy, dusty, lived-in look. But a drive up to **Mocking Bird Hotel** (on the eastern edge of town), which is also home to the **Gallery Carriacou** (tel: 993 7267), or up Richmond Hill changes all that. Built in 1943 as a honeymoon retreat, **Bonnie View Hotel ⓔ** has always had its spectacular view as its chief attraction. Here, the noise of the town vanishes in the hill air, and gives way to sweeping panoramas of Port Antonio, its twin harbours, Navy Island and Portland parish.

Some consider it charming, others annoying, that Port Antonio lacks a cohesive infrastructure to stimulate its tourist trade. For many visitors, however, the town represents seclusion – for now. Port Antonio has thrived as a hideaway for the "rich and famous", including, in the early days, Bette Davis, Ginger Rogers, J.P. Morgan and Errol Flynn, but the development of the North Coast Highway will bring the town within easy reach of day trippers from Ocho Rios, Montego Bay and Kingston.

Patrice Flynn, Errol Flynn's widow, balked at the idea of allowing her husband's remains to be buried in Port Antonio as he had wished; to the dismay of Jamaicans – who still delight in relating tales about the star – he was buried instead in Forest Lawn cemetery in Hollywood.

But Mrs Flynn later returned to the area and has lived ever since at the Flynn ranch. Situated on Priestman's River near Boston Bay, it is surrounded by fields of coconuts, pineapples, pimentos, bananas and about 2,000 head of cattle.

A rich man's Folly

Brooding **Christ Church** on Harbour Street is an Anglican Church built in 1840 in neo-Romanesque style by the English architect Annesley Voysey. The Boston Fruit Company donated the lectern in 1900.

East of East Harbour, outside Port Antonio proper and close to the red-and-white lighthouse, rises another fascinating bit of Parthenon-type architecture now simply called **Folly** ❻. It is the subject of a favourite romantic legend. As the story goes, a rich man built the mansion for his bride. He stocked its gardens with flowers, birds and animals – all of them white – then brought his lady to Jamaica for the honeymoon. Just as he carried her over the threshold the

Among the numerous endemic flying species of animal in Jamaica is the endangered Giant Swallowtail butterfly, which can be found in the forests of the Rio Grande Valley. With a wingspan of 15 cms (6 inches), it is the largest butterfly in the Americas.

BELOW: Folly.

concrete that had foolishly been mixed with sea water began to crumble. So did the rich man's dreams. His bride burst into tears at the omen and fled, never to return to him or his mansion.

In reality, a Connecticut jeweller named Alfred Mitchell built the mansion in 1905 and lived there occasionally with his family until his death in 1912. His wife, one of the Tiffanys of New York, was already a grandmother when they moved in. The building began to fall apart in the 1930s. Salt air rusted the steel reinforcement rods, and the roof caved in.

Just east of Port Antonio is a castle-like mansion begun several years ago by a European baroness, who reportedly encountered some financial problems. It is now the private residence of Earl Levy, owner of the Trident hotel.

The Maroons of Moore Town

One worthwhile side trip from Port Antonio takes you to **Moore Town** ❹, the capital of the Windward Maroons' community. Before you go, try to contact the leader of this proud, secretive people through the local office of the Tourist Board, or get in touch with **Valley Hikes** (tel: 993 3881), which organises walks in Maroon land with Maroon guides. The scenery around Port Antonio is breathtaking and can really be appreciated on a hike or a mountain-bike ride through the Rio Grande Valley and neighbouring mountain range. Visitors can learn about the butterflies, birds, herbs and vegetation from experienced tour guides, some trained in herbal medicine.

If you get the chance to visit Moore Town and learn about its people's fabled history, prepare for a rocky, 16-km (10-mile) ride up a steep, winding dirt road into the John Crow Mountains. Take Sommers Town Road behind Port Antonio,

Valley Hikes organise trail walks off the beaten track in the Rio Grande Valley, and also a one-day downhill cycling tour of the Blue Mountains, from Port Antonio or Ocho Rios. The starting point of the descent is near Hollywell Park.

BELOW:
Monkey Island,
San San Bay.

Map on page 236

and turn left at the town of **Fellowship**. Through **Newington** and **Windsor** you will be struck by the wild blends of river, vegetation and mountains. Turn left again at **Seaman's Valley**. The last small dirt road leads to Moore Town. As you enter, on your left there's an **Anglican Church** fronted by a serene graveyard. The church, one of seven in Moore Town, is the community's oldest building.

A bridge crosses the **Wildcane (Negro) River**. Moore Town's school is the low rambling set of buildings on your left. More than a century old, it has an enrolment of about 300 children aged from 6 to 15 years. **Bump Grave** is across from the school, a simple stone monument wherein lies the body of National Hero Nanny, the founder of the town and legendary chieftainess of the Windward Maroons. Here, the flagpole flies the Maroon flag next to the Jamaican flag. **Cornwall Barracks**, another Maroon settlement, lies just across the river.

Maroons from throughout the region – from Comfort Castle, Ginger House and Seaman's Valley – travel to Moore Town annually, on National Heroes' Day, to celebrate Nanny's canonisation as a National Hero in 1975. The *abeng* horns and Coromantee drums call them here. *Kumina* African-origin ancestral dances last deep into the night, and stories of old are told. High up on the Blue Mountain Ridge to the northwest is a trapezoid-shaped bump, believed to be the site of the legendary **Nanny Town**.

The Maroon communities in Portland became known as the Windward Maroons because of the position of their settlements which lay in the path of the trade winds.

The price of paradise

East of Port Antonio, several high-priced hotels have been cloaked in some of Jamaica's most splendid scenery. You will first pass the **Trident hotel** ❺, an elaborate reincarnation of a regional favourite that succumbed first to Hurricane Allen and then to Hurricane Gilbert. Set on 7 hectares (17 acres) of coastline,

BELOW: exclusive villas overlook the Blue Hole.

Map
on page
236

*Conch shells washed
up on the beach.*

RIGHT: cannon at
Frenchman's Cove.
BELOW: diving boat
in the waters
around Dragon Bay.

this hotel sprawls along the rocky, volcanic coast, offering luxurious suites and villas and a four-room château.

In 1956, the Canadian biscuit heir Garfield Weston opened a resort that further enhanced this area's élite aura. **Frenchman's Cove ❻**, tucked back from the road in a magnificent setting on the lava-rock cliff, is a cottage-style colony. In its glory days the rent of the luxury cottages was £1,000 (US$1,600) a week, a small fortune in the 1950s. For that price, everything a vacationer could possibly want – and then some – was included: personal servants, all food and drink, sports equipment and activities, a golf cart for zipping around the expansive grounds, caviar flown in from Russia, French champagne, and free flights up and down the coast.

The author V.S. Naipaul spent several days here in 1962 and wrote in *The Middle Passage*: "Within 24 hours my interest in food and drink disappeared. Everything was at the end of the telephone, and it was my duty to have exactly what I wanted. But how could I be sure what I wanted best?"

The glory didn't last, and Frenchman's Cove eventually went bankrupt. But this delightful beach with a freshwater river is open to the public; a small entrance fee is charged.

As you round a bend along the water beyond Frenchman's Cove, you will see the kind of picturesque island you thought existed only in Hollywood movies. **Monkey Island**, also called Pellew Island, no longer has any monkeys. You can swim or boat to it across the unimaginably blue waters of **San San Bay ❼**, but beware of sea urchins, which can leave a nasty sting in an unsuspecting swimmer's foot.

Just half a mile further, bear left past palatial private villas (also for renting) to the **Blue Hole ❽**, otherwise known as Blue Lagoon. Its intense natural colour is a result of the depth of the lagoon, estimated by realists at 64 metres (210 ft) and by romanticists as bottomless. The area is good for swimming, snorkelling or picnicking. There is also a good, but pricey, watering-hole which serves cocktails and food. The Lagoon and surrounding properties are lit up at night, a pretty sight if you approach by boat. Fine hotels here include **Dragon Bay**, with its lily ponds, almond trees, dragon fountain and small private beach, and **Goblin Hill villas**, back from the beach but with a glorious clifftop view.

Cavers can wander up into the hills beyond **Sherwood Forest** to the **Nonsuch Caves ❾** (open daily 10am–4pm; entrance fee). They are dry, subtly lit, have helpful handrails, and can easily be negotiated with the aid of local guides. Tours can take anything from 30 minutes to 1½ hours, depending on the pace and your interest in the surroundings. The caves are believed to have been formed more than a million years ago and are 92 metres (100 yards) long. No-one really knows how deep they are; mud removed from them is estimated to be more than 6,000 years old. The road leading to the caves is poor and hard to negotiate, making the journey slow, but they are worth seeing although the surrounding gardens, once an attraction, have gone into decline because of serious damage caused by hurricanes Allen and Gilbert. ❑

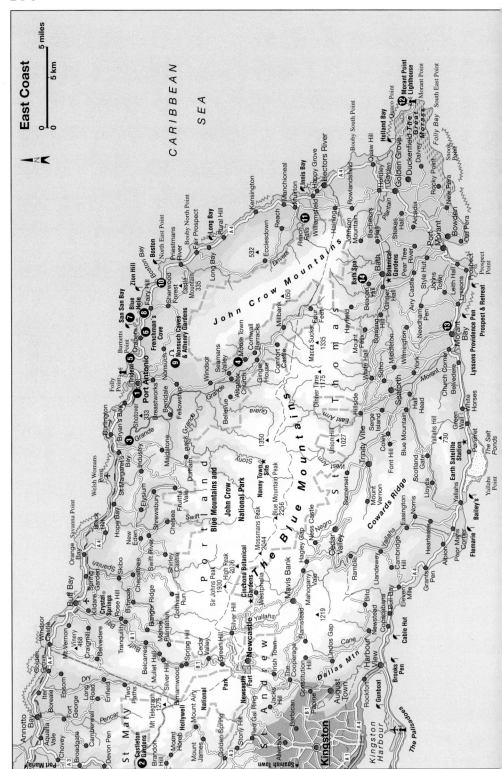

East Coast

N

0   5 km
0   5 miles

C A R I B B E A N

S E A

John Crow Mountains

The Blue Mountains

Port Antonio

Kingston

Blue Mountains and
John Crow
National Park

THE EAST COAST

With its varied landscape of mountains and cattle pastures, this
coast has a few good beaches, is great for surfing, has
a mineral spa and is home to a truly Jamaican culinary speciality

Map
on page
236

From Port Antonio round the east coast to Kingston, Jamaica offers a rich collage of contrasts to the explorer. This is not tourist country, being less accessible and less populated than the better known northern areas, yet it is fascinating, with an "undiscovered" feeling to it. It is simultaneously flat by the coast and mountainous inland, with both the Blue Mountains and the more eastern John Crow Mountains; wet to the north in Portland and dry to the south in St Thomas; with few beaches to the south, and a variety of bays, coves and stretches of sand to the east and north. Yet drive north to Serge Island through Seaforth and you could easily be forgiven for thinking you are in the UK, in rural Wales with its rich green cattle pastures.

Boston Bay ⑩, beyond Fairy Hill, is a necessary stop for gourmands of uniquely Jamaican cuisine. Here the local people make what is reputed to be the island's best jerk pork. This delicacy was the creation of Maroons, who seasoned wild pig with herbs and pimento (or allspice) and pit-barbecued it on pimento wood. Jerking takes several hours (to season and cook slowly), so you probably won't be able to buy any before mid-morning. And most will have been eaten by mid-afternoon. Alternatively, try jerk chicken or lobster, cooked to order.

Patrice Flynn, the widow of Hollywood legend Errol Flynn, owns the **Priest-man's River Plantation**, which lies a few miles east of Boston Bay. From here the road winds around rocky cliffs slapped by waves, through small villages and past outcroppings of dense rainforest, all reminiscent of Maui's Hana Coast in Hawaii. Enjoy the scenery until you reach **Manchioneal**.

When the United Nations drew up a "national physical plan" for Jamaica in 1970, the committee members found the Manchioneal area so magnificent that they recommended setting up a coastal wilderness area here.

From here you can also get to **Reach Falls** ⑪ (open daily; entrance fee). Take the turnoff just before the Driver's River bridge, then continue on a rough road, that in places resembles a one-vehicle dirt track, for a mile or two inland until you come to a fork in the rocky road. A hand-scrawled sign directs you to the spot. It's a tricky walk down stone steps carved into a cliff to the bottom. Few tourists venture to this out-of-the-way spot, so except for the local guides or a free-lance mento drummer you should have the lovely cool water and falls all to yourself. Climb up into the caves under the falls themselves for a look. The guides will take visitors on a tour through the cave network, which was probably used by runaway slaves. Places such as nearby Mandingo Cave are hard to reach and require a flashlight, but are worth the trek; Mandingo is a quarter of a mile long and has a whirlpool.

PRECEDING PAGES: enjoying a quiet moment by the coast. **BELOW:** rugged Portland coast near Manchioneal.

Quakers and Africans

On top of the hill east of Manchioneal is the **Happy Grove School**, founded by Quakers in 1898 for sugar workers from eastern India. Soon after that you leave the parish of Portland and cross into St Thomas, and the scenery begins to change. The plains at the island's eastern tip are laden with palm and sugar cane, an impressive view of which is available as the road winds down **Quaw Hill**.

Turn off at **Golden Grove** onto a long road that leads to the **Morant Point Lighthouse ⑫**. Built in 1841, the 30-metre (100-ft) high cast-iron structure is listed by the Jamaica National Trust as a historic monument. Its engineer, George Grove, is better known to musicians as the author of *Grove's Dictionary of Music and Musicians.*

Jamaicans today regard St Thomas as one of the parishes where the African heritage is strongest; the ancestor-worship cult of *Kumina* flourishes here. Among St Thomas's many historical relics are the overgrown ruins of the oldest house in Jamaica – **Stokes Hall**, slightly off the highway near Golden Grove. In 1656, the governor, Luke Stokes, seeking colonists, attracted 1,000 settlers from the Leeward Islands of Nevis and St Kitts. Less than three months later Stokes and his wife died, along with two-thirds of the other pioneers. The disease-ridden Morant swamps had taken their toll. But Stokes's three sons survived, and, although all were under 15 years of age at the time, they apparently prospered; one is believed to have erected Stokes Hall. Like many plantation houses, it was built with loopholes in the walls through which guns could be fired in case of attack, a grim reminder of those hard times.

Continue on the A4 to **Bowden** and **Port Morant**, both of which were busy harbours in the days of sugar and bananas. Port Morant was guarded by **Fort**

GOATS ENTERING PREMISES WILL BE ●CURRIED●

"Curry goat" is another Jamaican culinary speciality, served with plain white rice.

BELOW: try jerk pork or chicken from a roadside vendor.

BOSTON JERK

Variously attributed to Henry Morgan, the legendary Port Royal buccaneer, and his rowdy band of men, who roasted meat using greensticks, and the Maroons, who caught wild boar in the hills of Portland, seasoned the meat with a sauce made from the fiery Scotch Bonnet pepper and roasted it over pimento-wood fires, jerk pork is a great tasty experience for any visitor.

The area around Boston Beach (also a good place for surfing), on the beach side of the A4 main road, shortly after Dragon Bay, is its culinary home. The jerk vendors cook up a storm on a fragrant pimento-wood open fire. Weekends and lunchtimes are busiest, when you will find locals and visitors alike sitting outside at the specially installed tables and benches. Open the paper wrapper and eat the flavoursome meat by hand. Try it with harddough bread or "festival" for a filling meal. Watch out for the heat though. Even if you've had jerk pork, chicken or fish elsewhere, take care, as Boston jerk is high octane and requires at least one Red Stripe Beer or cool coconut water, drunk directly from the shell, to quell the flame. Extra fire can be added to taste by applying hot pepper sauce, which can also be purchased in bottles to help recreate the experience in the comfort of your own home.

Lindsay (now in ruins) on Morant Point and **Fort William** on the other side. Bowden, on the eastern end of the harbour, gave its name to the **Bowden Formation**, which has yielded extensive fossil remains from the late Miocene geological period. Several hundred species of marine shell have been discovered in this formation.

Map on page 236

The legacy of Morant Bay

At Port Morant beaches like **Lyssons** and **Roselle** you can mingle with the people of St Thomas. The shores swing toward Kingston in soft undulating curves quite different from the jagged beauty of the Portland coast.

The parish capital of **Morant Bay** ⓭ was the site of the famous rebellion of 1865. The bloody reprisals in which National Heroes Paul Bogle and George William Gordon were executed, with hundreds of other residents, live on in a dramatic **Statue of Bogle** that dominates the town square. Created by Edna Manley, the sculpture depicts a defiant Bogle clutching a machete.

The statue stands in front of the **court house**, a reconstruction of the one burnt out during that rebellion. Gordon and 18 others were hanged from a boom in front of the court house, while Bogle and his brother were hanged from the centre arch of the gutted building. Seventy-nine skeletons were found behind the wall of the old **Morant Bay Fort**, behind the court house, during excavations in 1965. A mass grave and a monument have been installed under the fort cannons. The fort dates to 1773, but the three cannons were installed early in the 19th century. The **Parish Church** nearby was built in 1881.

Today Morant Bay has forgotten its melodramatic past and evolved into a quiet town with unusual street names like Soul Street and Debtor's Lane.

BELOW: the former Holland Estate in St Thomas, near Morant Point, in the 19th century.

Map on page 236

Bright pink bougainvillea.

BELOW: liquid refreshment.
RIGHT: Reach Falls.

Water of life

For a pleasant side trip into inland St Thomas, take the road from Morant Ba through Airy Castle to the **Bath Spa ⑭** and **Bath Botanical Gardens**. Th mineral bath opened in 1699 after a runaway slave discovered its waters an claimed it had cured chronic ulcers on his legs. The government bought th spring and 526 hectares (1,300 acres) of surrounding land, and examples c cures immediately began to be recorded. A certain Mr Watson had a "dry belly ache eased by the first draught of the water", and a Mr Gordon was cured c "lowness of spirit and a depraved appetite".

The mineral baths do have considerable therapeutic value for treatin rheumatic ailments and skin diseases. Hot water reaching 53°C (128°F) an "cold" water at 46°C (115°F) miraculously pour from the same igneous rock above the Sulphur River, and are mixed in the baths to a proper bathing ten perature. They contain high (but safe) concentrations of lime and sulphur. Li tle of the early splendour of the original spa, once known as the Bath of S Thomas the Apostle, remains today, but the spring continues to attract healt addicts from around the world.

Nearby (south of the town centre) is the Western Hemisphere's second olde botanical garden, established in 1779. The breadfruit trees growing in one corne are offsprings of those brought from Tahiti in 1793 by Captain William Blig of *Bounty* fame.

From Morant Bay the highway traverses Jamaica's longest span, **Bustaman Bridge**, across the Morant River. The arid district of **Yallahs** provides a dust change of scenery. The huge **Yallahs Ponds**, south of the highway, are separate from the sea by an arm of land. With twice the salinity of sea water, they pro vided ample salt supplies for early settlers.

The **Yallahs River** is usually a dry riverbed fille with enormous boulders, but it can become a ragin torrent during the rainy season, since its source lie 1,372 metres (4,500 ft) up in the Blue Mountains. A huge landslip upriver occurred when a mountain fe into the valley during the 1692 earthquake. A 300-metr (1,000-ft) escarpment left behind is called **Judgemen Cliff** because the rubble buried a plantation belongin to a wicked Dutchman – or so say the locals. The bes view of the cliff is from **Easington**.

The road soon bends back into beautiful valley: the foothills of the Blue Mountains. At the hamlet c **Eleven Miles** keep a watch for the roadside marke commemorating Three-fingered Jack. This Jamaica equivalent of Robin Hood was an escaped slave wh was courtly to ladies and the poor, but cruel to mal travellers and British soldiers. He pillaged until hi death at the hands of the Maroons in 1781.

Evening light falls upon these mountain roads lik a sprinkle of dew. The road bottoms out at **Bull Ba** home to a community of fervent Rastafarians. A roa from the settlement leads up to the small but lovel **Cane River Falls**.

Wickie Wackie and **Copacabana Beach** are disap pointing dirt slivers, despite their alluring name: Harbour View's popular drive-in cinema and Kingstc lie just beyond.

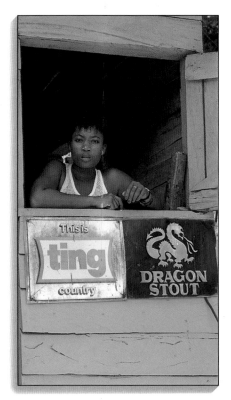

This is **ting** country

DRAGON STOUT

OCHO RIOS AND ENVIRONS

This north-coast beach resort is a popular tourist destination
for travellers seeking fun in the sun and lively
nightlife, but within the country towns are important historical sites

Map on page 253

Ocho Rios
Kingston

The northern region of the county of Middlesex reflects two sides of Jamaica. There is the beach-fringed coast, where fishing villages huddle between the major tourist resorts and modern hotels, and there is the interior: tourist-free small towns and hamlets, where Jamaicans earn a simple, but seemingly adequate, living from the soil.

Both sides of this intriguing heartland can be explored on solid roads. Routes A1 and A3 skirt the coast, and Route B11 winds inland almost parallel to it. A tangle of criss-crossing roads connects the routes, so you can drive by any portion without having to double back. Along the coast you will find many popular tourist meccas and Columbus country, as well as the town where Ian Fleming's James Bond, Agent 007, was born, while the inland route offers glimpses into typical Jamaican lifestyles and scenic hills.

At the core of this part of the county lies one of Jamaica's premier travel destinations, **Ocho Rios ❶**. You may wish to make your "base camp" in one of its plush hotels or villas, or perhaps in more modest accommodation, as you wander into other parts of northern Middlesex on jaunts of a day or two.

The most popular route to Ocho Rios from Kingston follows the A1 through Spanish Town, along the lovely Rio Cobre river, through Linstead and Ewarton, with its massive Alcan bauxite complex, then up **Mount Diablo** and down into the parish of St Ann. At the crest of the mountain you can look into an enormous sea of red earth, one of the most unfortunate legacies of a bauxite-mining industry that has otherwise brought a measure of prosperity to many Jamaican communities. Just before that, you will come to a wide-open tract that is a popular spot to stop, stretch your legs and fill your belly with saltfish, yams, corn and fresh fruit from roadside vendors.

Past **Moneague**, where Route A1 forks west to an inland route covered later in this chapter, you follow the A3 into **Walkers' Wood ❷**. This area lives up to its name with a dense, pastoral, Tolkienesque setting of rounded hills, pastures and valleys criss-crossed by stone walls. The English countryside couldn't look more English. A worthwhile stop in Walkers' Wood is the **Artbeat** craft gallery (open daily; tel: 917 2154). Located directly in front of the post office, it displays a dazzling array of decorative functional art, such as handpainted place-mats and bags, and mirrors framed with drift wood.

Take the road to **Friendship Farm**, which offers a farm tour, and also incomparable views of the storybook scenery from its handsome great house and swimming pool. Along the Friendship Farm road, through the small villages of Labyrinth and Cascade, is the **Wilderness Resort ❸** (open Tues–Sun,

PRECEDING PAGES: Dunn's River Falls. **LEFT:** jet-skiing in action-packed Ochi'. **BELOW:** there are lots of places to visit in St Ann.

Fern Gully was once home to 60 species of fern.

BELOW: the Fern Gully canopy pleases the senses.

10am–5pm; entrance fee; tel: 974 5189). The Resort is actually a commercial fish farm set in 193 hectares (477 acres) of land dotted with orange groves and coconut palms. It is accessible only by a winding, rough road, so the best advice is to take your time getting there and maybe stay for a half or a whole day. It is a good spot for a relaxing day with the family, but if you want more action you can book an All Terrain Vehicle (ATV) tour of the surrounding landscape; also available are a Valley Tour and a two hour Country Tour. Alternatively you can take a look around the plantation on horseback, ride quad bikes, hike along the nature trails or fish in any of the property's 37 fish ponds. If you get a bite the resort staff will, if asked, prepare the fish any way you wish – for a price.

Two miles past the farm on Route A3 you suddenly plunge from daylight into semi-darkness down the roller-coaster ride of **Fern Gully** ❹, once a river bed. Dense growths of ferns and trees blanket the road and block the sun. Don't allow the surreal surroundings to distract you from the tricky drive. The road is often slippery, and its corners are sharp, so low gear is recommended. The fern population has diminished somewhat – there used to be more than 60 species here – probably through a combination of vandals, hurricane damage, fire and pollution (including car exhaust fumes), but Fern Gully still pleases the senses. At the bottom of Fern Gully is a road on the right leading to **Golden Pond**, and less than 2 km (1 mile) inland is the **Wassi Art** pottery factory (open daily 9am–4.30pm; tel: 974 5044) established in 1990. Behind its doors lies a stunning display of some of Jamaica's most beautiful and collectable pottery; accessories, functional ware and souvenirs. The handmade pottery is fashioned from Castleton clay by more than 20 young artists and traditional potters, and the factory tour offers visitors a chance to see the potters at work.

Scaling the falls

The main attraction of Ocho Rios drops 180 metres (600 ft) to the seacoast in a series of cascades 3 km (2 miles) west of the town centre. **Dunn's River Falls ❺** (open daily 9am–5pm; entrance fee) have been delighting visitors since Spanish times. They are the most spectacular of a series of waterfalls that gush from lushly, wooded limestone cliffs along this ridge. A large park, full of snack bars, souvenir stands and woodcarvers' shops, has grown up at the entrance to these falls. But the tradition at Dunn's River Falls is to climb them.

Stairs lead downhill through a tunnel under Route A1 to a beach where you can leave your clothes and valuables in a locker. You must purchase a ticket; this entitles you to climb with (or without) an official guide. If you do choose to employ a guide to help you up the Falls he will expect a tip. It's a common sight to see a guide, his dreadlocks dangling among the dozens of cameras strung around his neck, leading a daisy-chain of tourists in bathing suits up the rocks and through the falls to the top. Take the climb slowly and check your footing. The rocks are slippery in spots, and the torrents are powerful enough to knock you over. There are several spots along the way to exit back to dry land if the climb becomes too nerve-racking.

Dunn's River Falls are one of the island's most famous attractions and as such can be crowded, but the Falls and the sandy beach below are worth a visit. Beware of unwanted attention from unofficial guides and insistent vendors.

A smaller, less crowded spot for showering in a waterfall is located less than a kilometre (1 mile) west of Dunn's River, by the hydroelectric station. The best section of **Roaring River** falls on a private property called **Laughing Waters**, where scenes for the first of the James Bond films, *Dr No*, were shot.

Walkers' Wood spices take their name from the woods south of Ocho Rios.

LEFT: sailing on Mallards Bay.
BELOW: scaling Dunn's River Falls.

Ocho Rios, cruise capital

Hoardings announcing the American hotel chains and Kentucky Fried Chicken fast-food franchises bring you out of Fern Gully and back to 20th-century reality. You have entered Ocho Rios, the centre of island tourism. Ocho Rios is hardly a town: it is more like a village mugged by tourist development. Its hotels, houses and shops are haphazardly strung out along the coastal strip.

Ocho Rios' name is not what it purports to be. There are not eight rivers in the town, although a translation from Spanish might suggest that. Its original name in *español* was *Las Chorreras*, "the waterfalls", obviously a reference to the magnificent Dunn's River cascades just west of town. Apparently English settlers heard it wrongly, and it's been called Ocho Rios ever since.

Ocho Rios's only historical claim to fame is as the lair of the pirate John Davis. Rich local planters were said to have subsidised Davis' enterprising rape-and-plunder expeditions, which included sacking the city of St Augustine in Florida. The only reminders of those days are the walls and cannon of an old fort, buried in dust from the Reynolds bauxite terminal next to them.

The town's growth as a magnet for tourists began in the 1950s, and its reputation has accelerated in recent years; Ocho Rios has now surpassed Montego Bay and Port Antonio to become Jamaica's top cruise-ship destination. It's an attraction in itself to rise early in the morning to watch the enormous luxury liners inching into berths at the wharf near the bauxite terminal.

Passengers are usually greeted in "Love Boat" style by an old-style mento or calypso band and dancers. Two of the monstrous ships often moor in Ocho Rios Bay at the same time, and their arrival turns Ocho Rios into an anthill of activity. Higglers, craftsmen, taxi drivers and mini-van operators all jockey for

BELOW: Ocho Rios is Jamaica's cruise-ship capital.

good positions from which to be the first to offer their wares or services to free-spending cruise passengers.

Rum and resorts

For a John Crow's (bird's-eye) view of Ocho Rios, try **Shaw Park Botanical Gardens** Ⓐ (open daily 8am–5pm; entrance fee; tel: 974 2723), up the hill to the west of the A3 as you enter the town from Fern Gully. These landscaped grounds were once the setting for the Shaw Park Hotel; although the hotel was demolished in 1959 the original swimming pool and dance floor remain. There are also a variety of flowers and trees, including a banyan tree planted in 1920, royal palms, hibiscus and begonias, a rushing stream and waterfalls in the gardens.

Further up the road is the lush **Coyaba River Garden and Museum** Ⓑ, (open daily 8.30am–5pm; entrance fee; tel: 974 6235). The 2-hectare (5-acre) gardens surround a small archaeological museum with rare artefacts of Taino culture and a brief but impressive tour of Jamaica's history. Visitors can also tour the tropical gardens along a river that meanders through the property, which is also a site for musical events and weddings.

Other prime draws in Ocho Rios are its strands of fine white sands, **Turtle Beach** Ⓒ and **Mallards Beach** Ⓓ. At night you can reggae with Jamaicans in the Jamaican Grande hotel's disco, or try the romantic setting of The Ruins night-club, where music plays against the background of a waterfall.

Route A3 twists and turns east through Ocho Rios's most pleasant area. Here, hotels like the Plantation Inn, Carib Ocho Rios and Sans Souci Lido nestle amid the trees and nudge the rocky coast. One of the grandest old lodgings is the **Jamaica Inn**, perched on a cliff above a secluded slice of beach. Time has

Map
on page
249

A zemi image.

BELOW:
waterfall at Shaw
Park Gardens.

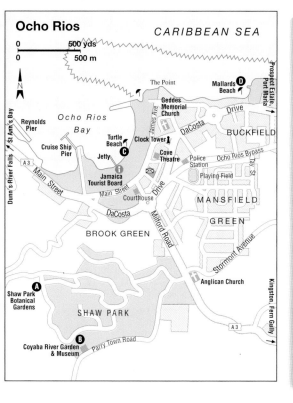

If you are in Jamaica in the month of June you can catch the Ocho Rios Jazz Festival, which attracts a host of international musicians. The main venues in Ocho Rios are the Jamaica Grande Hotel and the Almond Tree Gardens. There are also events in Montego Bay and Kingston. Call: 927 3544.

stopped here: waiters in white coats serve you rum punches, and trade winds cool the beautifully furnished verandahs adjoining each room.

Continue east to the **White River**, once lined with tall, handsome Jamaica palms; the mysterious Lethal Yellowing disease has taken its toll, and only the trunks of the trees remain. They are being replaced with the sturdier, but less attractive, Malayan Dwarf. Dead stumps are processed into parquet flooring.

Exotic torches will burn along the bank for "A Night on the White River". Guests at this event have a romantic cruise down the stream to a forest clearing for dinner, drinks, a show and dancing.

A signposted road near the river leads inland for less than 2 km (1 mile) to the grounds of **Prospect Estate** ❻ (open Mon–Sat; tel: 974 2058; entrance fee). It offers tours of the plantation, the White River gorge, **Sir Harold's Viewpoint** over the coast, and a lane of memorial trees planted by such eminent and varied notables as Winston Churchill, Noël Coward, Charlie Chaplin and the former Canadian prime minister Pierre Trudeau. A scheme at Prospect Estate trains young men from poor backgrounds as "cadets" who live and work on the estate while learning skills. Nearby **Reggae Vibes Beach** (open daily; tel: 974 2433) was once part of Prospect Plantation. The beautiful crescent of mile-long white-sand beach has facilities including changing rooms, toilets, showers and beach games. The beach also has one of the best chefs around when it comes to authentic Jamaican meals.

East of White River, Annabella and Peter Proudlock have handsomely restored **Harmony Hall** Great House ❼ (open daily; tel: 975 4222), which was a Methodist Manse built in the mid 1800s and subsequently became a small pimento estate. Upstairs is an art gallery and a craft shop. The gallery exhibits work from leading artists such as Graham Davis, Susan Shirley and Gene Pearson.

BELOW: the gallery at Harmony Hall.

AN ARTISTS' PARADISE

The parishes of St Ann and St Mary have drawn in an eclectic circle of Jamaican and foreign artists. Among them is Juliet Thorburn, a young Jamaican watercolour artist who is drawn to St Ann by the space, light, natural beauty and lushness of the parish, inspirations for her treasure-chest of paintings.

Laura Facey, a Jamaican sculptor, loves the quiet places and long lush walks of her Orange Hall Estate. She creates images of ritual and healing, and uses cedar, mahogany, clay jippy jappa and feathers.

Australian-born Colin Garland lives and works in Oracabessa, St Mary; he is attracted to the area by the allure of the sea, Ian Fleming's home down the road, and Oracabessa Bay. Colin's work has been described as surrealistic, dreamlike and fantasy filled.

Graham Davis lives in St Ann; he moved to Jamaica from England in 1970. He attributes his passion for the area and its influence on his work to feeling at home in a beautiful part of the world.

Rita Genet, originally from Connecticut, moved to the island in 1988. Her inspiration comes from Jamaica's landscape and historical architecture, which is almost always the subject of her whimsical, naïve work.

Map on page 253

Harmony Hall is the only gallery in Jamaica that has a room dedicated to Intuitive Art and houses work from notables such as Allan Zion, Ras Dizzy, Deloris Anglin and Brother Brown. Downstairs visitors may dine at **Toscanini** (tel: 975 4785), an authentic Italian restaurant, open for lunch and dinner.

Couples, for couples

Further east and across the road, commanding another pretty beach on the turquoise waters of the Caribbean, rises **Couples**, formerly the Tower Isle Hotel, where, unlike its Negril affiliate, Hedonism II, only couples are permitted. A marriage certificate is not necessary, and wedding services can be arranged as part of its package for those who impulsively decide to tie the knot. Ceremonies are performed on the tiny offshore island with the tower – after suntanning hours. During the day the island is strictly reserved for those who prefer to swim and sunbathe in the nude. Couples earned a flurry of publicity when it opened with its advertising poster of two lions, one a well-endowed female, mating.

From Couples, Route A3 continues down the increasingly scenic coast. **Rio Nuevo** ❽ is the spot where Great Britain finalised its claim on the island of Jamaica in June 1658 by routing the displaced Spanish governor Ysasi and his men from a stockade above the river mouth. A small monument marks the site of the last battle.

A side road that leads south from here, Route B13, provides a picturesque tour past banana plantations up the Rio Nuevo valley to **Retreat**, where a suspension footbridge straddles the river. The beautiful old **Holy Trinity Church** and an abandoned sugar mill lie further on. The road climbs to Gayle and Guy's Hill, where there's a junction with a road to **Highgate**.

Visitors can marry 24 hours after landing in Jamaica. Apply for a marriage licence before leaving home, or contact the Ministry of Security in Kingston, tel: 922 0089, upon arrival.

BELOW: the view from Noël Coward's room at Firefly.

Look out for Special Agent 007 on the beach named for Ian Fleming's most famous fictional character.

BELOW: relaxing on Port Maria's monument to Tacky.

James Bond, bird-watcher

East of Rio Nuevo, Route A3 enters Jamaica's most lovely coastal country. The gorgeous seascapes extend all the way to Manchioneal at the eastern end of the island. The first point of interest is in **Oracabessa** ❾, "Golden Head" – from the Spanish words *oro* for gold and *cabeza* for head.

Opposite the Esso gas station north of the main road is a small lane leading to **James Bond Beach** (open daily 9am–5pm, closed Mon except pub. hols; entrance fee; tel: 975 3663). Three magnificent white-sand beaches hug this private peninsula just 20 minutes from Ocho Rios. Visitors can enjoy a range of watersports facilities, and the restaurant serves delicious fresh seafood and other dishes. Live reggae bands perform on certain days.

Nearby is a well-protected private residence called **Goldeneye** ❿. Only just visible from the road, the property is owned by Chris Blackwell. Goldeneye was built by Ian Fleming, author of the 13 James Bond novels that have sold more than 18 million copies in 23 languages. Fleming wintered here from 1946 until his death in 1964. Ironically, he borrowed the name for his secret agent from a most unlikely source.

In *Ian Fleming Introduces Jamaica* he explained: "I was looking for a name for my hero – nothing like Peregrine Carruthers or Standfast Maltravers – and I found it, on the cover of one of my Jamaican bibles. *Birds of the West Indies* by James Bond, an ornithological classic." Fleming goes on to add: "Would these books have been born if I had not been living in the gorgeous vacuum of a Jamaican holiday? I doubt it."

The literary juices of another famous author, this one also a playwright, flowed just down the coast from Oracabessa, near the town of Port Maria. Watch

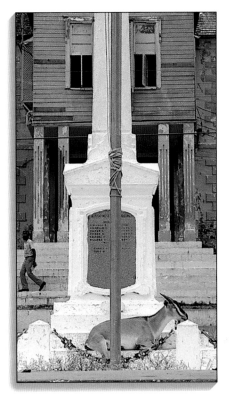

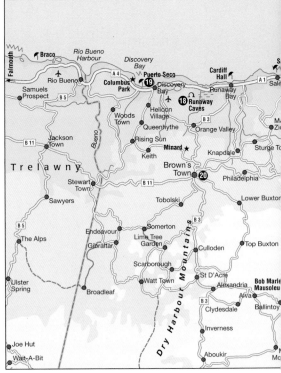

for the sign that directs you off the A3 and up a rutted dirt road to **Firefly**
(open Mon–Thur, Sat 8.30am–5pm; tel: 994 0920). Here the actor and master of
waspish British wit Sir Noël Coward spent many of the last 23 years of his life.
He died here on 26 March 1973 and is buried in a simple grave in an idyllic
spot on the lawns in front of the house. The house is now a protected property
under the auspices of the National Heritage Foundation Trust (NHFT).

During his years at Firefly, Coward entertained the likes of the Queen Mother
and Princess Margaret. The property has been leased from the NHFT by Chris
Blackwell, himself a native of St Mary. He has painstakingly restored the buildings and grounds to convey, as accurately as possible, the way they were when
Coward was alive. There is a guided tour of the property, and also a regular
programme of entertainment.

On the coast road below Firefly, lying in a narrow bend, is the charming **Blue
Harbour Hotel** (tel: 994 0289), Noël Coward's first house in Jamaica, where
he welcomed guests such as movie stars Marlene Dietrich and Sean Connery.
Blue Harbour has three one- and two-bedroom villas, a swimming pool and a
small beach from which guests may snorkel and kayak.

East of Firefly, **Port Maria** springs up after you round a rocky cliff. It has
the standard town trappings – a court house built in 1820 and a church that
dates from 1861. A bridge joins a noisy shopping section to a quiet residential
area. A sign at the church gates points you to the **Tacky Monument** that com-
memorates the leader of the slave rebellion of Easter 1760.

One side trip from Port Maria leads up Route B13 to **Brimmer Hall**. You can
ride a wagon through fields of banana, coconut, pimento and other crops, tour
the great house, have an authentic Jamaican lunch, and take a swim in the pool.

*The sunroom at
Firefly was thought
to have been the
inspiration for the
song "A Room with a
View", but in fact
Coward moved to
Jamaica years after
he wrote it.*

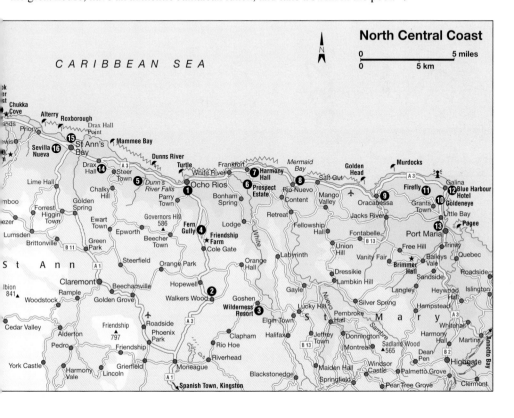

BELOW: Port Maria as it looked in about 1830.

Beyond Port Maria, the A3 curves back inland through thick rainforests. Look for the shop near **Whitehall** where a Rastaman sells solid cast-iron pots. Just before reaching Annotto Bay you can take the Junction road that goes off to Kingston, or you can continue east to Portland and Port Antonio.

The road west from Ocho Rios passes Dunn's River Falls and Roaring River. Take Route A3 west past Sandals Dunn's River Hotel and then by **Drax Hall** ⓮, a polo field. Polo was, of course, imported by the British colonial élite. Now the game is open to any sport-minded Jamaican who has a horse.

Prior to reaching **St Ann's Bay** ⓯ the road goes through plantations of elegant coconut palms that have thus far managed to resist the blight of the Lethal Yellowing disease. These palms mark the approaches to **Sevilla la Nueva** ⓰, the first Spanish settlement in Jamaica. You are now entering Columbus Country. In fact, foreign research scientists are working with the Jamaican Government to find the hulks of the last two caravels abandoned here by Columbus in 1504. The government plans to rebuild the ruins of the Spanish town with an archaeological park at the Seville Estate.

The modern history of Jamaica began near present-day St Ann's Bay, just north of the junction of routes A1 and A3. The town has been bypassed by the new trunk road (the A.G.R. Byfield Highway), but leaving the bypass makes a worthwhile detour to this pleasant parish capital.

The court house on the main street, next to the parish church, was built in 1866. Beyond the town on the landward side of the road is a **Statue of Columbus**, cast in his native town of Genoa, Italy, and behind the statue is a **Catholic Church**. It was built in 1939 of stones from a variety of local sources, including those from the ruins of the original Spanish Church of Peter Martyr,

which stood slightly west of the present church. Peter Martyr of Anghiera was a 16th-century soldier-turned-priest who wrote a book about the New World – but never set foot in Jamaica.

A more fitting island tribute is the **Marcus Garvey Monument** fronting the town library. Garvey was born in St Ann's Bay in 1887, and has been elevated to National Hero status owing to his work in developing among black people a sense of pride and identity in their African heritage.

Route A1 swings south into the mountains from St Ann's Bay to **Claremont**, a bauxite centre once called Finger Post, and then proceeds to Moneague, where roads connect to Kingston and Ocho Rios.

A detour from Claremont leads some 8 km (5 miles) to the village of **Pedro**, where Jamaica's most macabre ruin stands. In the hill tower of **Edinburgh Castle** lived Lewis Hutchinson, a sadistic red-haired Scotsman. In the 1760s this ex-medical student murdered more than 40 travellers by shooting them from the slit windows of his tower. The bodies were robbed and decapitated; they are thought to have been thrown down a nearby sinkhole.

Hutchinson was captured while trying to board a ship offshore; he was unrepentant. Before being hanged he left £100 for the erection of a monument to himself, with the requested inscription to read: "Their sentence, pride and malice I defy. Despise their power, and like a Roman I die." The monument was not erected.

The ruins of the first Spanish settlement in Jamaica, at Sevilla Nueva, lie just west of St Ann's Bay. After crossing the river, take the dirt road behind the gate that crosses the seaward side of the main road. Castle ruins have been discovered to the right of the road, while the remains of a Spanish sugar mill, surely the island's first, are strewn to the left of it. These buildings are believed to have been

Map on page 253

Monument to Marcus Mosiah Garvey.

BELOW: polo was the sport of gentlemen.

Bright heliconias can be found in tropical gardens large and small.

BELOW: anthuriums are grown commercially.

some of the few structures constructed in the settlement before the Spanish decided to pack up and relocate their capital at Villa de la Vega, the modern-day Spanish Town. The **Seville Great House and Heritage Park** (open daily 9am–5pm; entrance fee; tel: 972 2191) is a real historic gem. It lies on what was the Sevilla la Nueva Estate. For a small fee, visitors can enjoy a guided tour of the small museum and the ruins of the great house and its environs. It was here that the Tainos, Jamaica's first inhabitants, established their largest town, and it was here too that Christopher Columbus landed and lived for over a year. In 1655 the British arrived, capturing the island from the Spanish. Building on the remains of the estate, the British established a large sugar plantation, which is still referred to as Sevilla today. On the tour you'll discover the site of the Spanish **Church of Peter Martyr**, the ruins of the Spanish fortified castle (Governor's House) and the base of the Spanish Sugar Mill.

Beyond this cradle of modern Jamaican history, Route A1 continues through the sugar-cane country of Priory and the Llandovery Central Factory to the charmingly-named **Laughlands**.

The colourful and peaceful **Cranbrook Flower Forest** ⑰ (open daily; entrance fee; tel: 995 3097) is located here, and on the left-hand side of the road is a carved wooden sign indicating the entrance. The guided tour passes through only part of the 53-hectare (130-acre) gardens, which have many varieties of trees and plants, including a forest of ferns and bamboo. Visitors may swim in the rivers and streams, explore the **Orchid and Anthurium House**, enjoy a picnic, or linger in the shade of the trees that dot the property with the sound of the water in the background (music is not encouraged). Just beyond Laughlands are the Chukka Cove playing fields, the north coast's polo centre.

Runaway Bay, so called because the last Spaniards allegedly left Jamaica from here after their final defeat by the British, is a booming tourist area. On entering you'll find a settlement of small conical habitations, like a Hottentot housing scheme. This is Club Caribbean, tourist accommodation with individual cottages arranged around a central clubhouse that contains a restaurant and bar.

Next is the Jamaica, Jamaica! hotel, one of the most expensive in the area. It has an 18-hole golf course on the opposite side of the road. The Franklyn D. Resort, or FDR, is next, one of only two all-inclusive hotels here that cater for families. Accommodation is condominium style. A string of smaller hotels and guesthouses follows. **Eaton Hall** is notable for being built on the foundations of an old English fort, complete with an underground passage that leads to the cliffs.

Beaches and hotels are Runaway Bay's claim to fame; as a town it is non-existent. Much of it consists of **Cardiff Hall**, a vast estate of privately owned houses. A short detour up the road by the Shell Service Station leads to the Runaway Bay HEART Academy, the main training centre for the hospitality trade.

Well signposted beyond are the **Runaway Caves ⑱** and **Green Grotto**, the most accessible of Jamaica's large limestone caves. Guided tours take in 2 km (1½ miles) of the caverns, and can include a sail across an eerie grotto 37 metres (120 ft) below the earth's surface. Discreet lighting brings out the grotesque beauty of the stalactites and stalagmites. A fascinating property of some formations is that they are hollow; by cunningly striking them with a stick the guide coaxes music from them. Outside the caves is a 49-metre (160-ft) -deep lagoon.

Discovery Bay ⑲, 8 km (5 miles) further on, is slowly developing under the stimulus of the Kaiser bauxite operation, but many tourists are put off by the presence of the great, dusty Port Rhodes bauxite shipping terminal in the middle of the

Map
on page
253

BELOW: cycling through sugar-cane country near Ocho Rios.

Map on page 253

There is a pilgrimage to Bob Marley's tomb every February.

BELOW: view of the Kaiser bauxite works from Columbus Park.
RIGHT: rural St Ann.

bay. Guided tours of the mine and plant are combined with a stop at **Armadale Approved School**, where you can listen to performances of traditional songs.

Beyond the bauxite terminal, with its huge green storage dome, is **Columbus Park**, which despite its name is a pleasant open-air museum on the cliff with a panoramic view over the bay. Cannons and sugar-mill fragments (including a water wheel and the old cast-iron pans used for boiling juice down to sugar) are on display. You will also find a stone crest of the Clan Campbell of Argyll dated 1774, taken from Knapdale in St Ann parish.

Discovery Bay's name originates from the claim that Columbus first landed here in 1494, calling it *Puerto Seco*, "dry harbour", because of its lack of water. Today **Puerto Seco** beach is open to the public. Opposite is **Columbus Plaza**, containing modern amenities. The road crosses the Rio Bueno river by the **Bengal Bridge** – a stylish stone structure of 1798 which serves as a boundary marker between St Ann and Trelawny parishes. It is an interesting combination of both bridge and hill: its eastern end is much higher than its western end.

Rio Bueno, in a bay at the mouth of the river of the same name, also has claims to being Columbus's landing site. It is an unspoiled fishing village, the main street of which has some old stone houses. **Gallery Jo James**, with its little jetty behind, serves light though expensive meals. **St Mark's Church** at the water's edge, fronted by its walled churchyard, is photogenic, and inside, a J.B. Kidd print shows how Rio Bueno looked in the 1830s. At the far end of the town was Fort Dundas, built in 1778 to command both sea and bay.

From Brown's Town to Marley's tomb

Route B3 from Runaway Bay, and a smaller road from Puerto Seco, both lead south into the main structures on the enormous **Orange Valley Estate**. If you can arrange a tour of this private estate you will see a sugar-works factory that looks much as it did centuries ago.

Another lovely estate that looks like a slice of the English countryside is **Minard**, behind imposing gateposts south of Orange Valley. Minard's first owner was a man named Brown, and it is for him that the next community on this route, **Brown's Town ⑳**, is named. A quaint and picturesque country town, it is built up and down the sides of hills and valleys.

Facing the central market is **St Mark's Church**, an arresting example of 19th-century Gothic architecture. It was completed in 1895. The main street also features a twin post office and police station, each with stone arches, balconies and tiled roofs that give them a distinctly Spanish look. Above these two structures is a Georgian court house, well built in cut stone with a pillared portico. The many-tiered layout gives Brown's Town a Mediterranean flavour that is good for photo buffs but hard on the legs. At the fork in the middle of the town you can proceed south on the B3 through splendid hills and dales to **Alexandria**. Stop here for the **mausoleum ㉑** of Jamaica's international superstar Bob Marley, who was born near the village of Nine Mile. Fans and reggae stars make a pilgrimage to this site on Marley's birthday in February, when they play his music long into the night. ❑

JAMAICA'S NATURAL EXTRAVAGANCE

The variety of flora and fauna inspires images of the Garden of Eden, rich in fragrance and colour, and abundant in tropical fruits, food and wildlife

This beautiful island has a kaleidoscope of natural diversity from the balmy shores of the Caribbean Sea to the windswept ridges of the Blue Mountains, which peak at 2,225 metres (7,400ft), rising to meet the rain clouds from the south coast.

The lushness of the vegetation on the north-eastern coast around Port Antonio is typical of the tropics. The gentle coconut palms and banana trees, just like breadfruit and citrus, are not indigenous to the island; they were brought by the early settlers. Cultivation and the clearing of the once dense forest area for sugar cane have greatly reduced Jamaica's woodland to a dwindling 7 percent of the original area, while modern housing and tourist development along the coast have proven lethal to the ecologically precious and sensitive mangroves.

GARDEN OF EDEN

The region's exotic flowers and fruit trees can make an ordinary garden extraordinary, inspiring thoughts of Eden.

The wildlife here is as varied as the landscape, from the harmless yellow snake and iguana to the pesky mongoose. There are 26 species of endemic bird, including the hummingbird and the spectacular red-billed streamertail, the national bird known as the Doctor Bird.

▷ **HIBISCUS**
This flowering bush is a native of Asia. Its blossom comes in shades from white to crimson pink.

▷ **ACROBATS**
Hummingbirds have the rare ability to hover in the air when collecting nectar from flowers. The birds play an important role in the pollination of plants.

△ **CACTI**
The *xerophytic* plant endures the extreme heat and drought characteristic of the dry south and the Hellshire Hills. Some species bear edible fruit.

△ **VIBRANT FLORA**
Bougainvillea is named for an 18th-century French botanist who first saw it in Brazil. Flowers grow in tropical gardens.

▷ **BANANA FLOWERS**
The fruit and the dark odd-looking flower grow together on one branch. The fruit grows upwards towards the sun.

THE QUEEN OF FLOWERS

The big business of floral decoration has brought much needed revenue to Jamaica's economy. The warm climate provides ideal conditions for growing orchids and other tropical plants such as red, pink and white anthuriums, red ginger, heliconias and strelitzias, also known as "bird of paradise".

The flowers of the pale-pink torch ginger look man-made and have been likened to porcelain, which is why the French refer to it as "fleur de porcelaine".

On the north coast, close to Montego Bay and Ocho Rios, there are expansive fields of flowers, and commercial greenhouses packed with beautiful flowers awaiting transport to the island's hotels and flights to the USA, where they grace American homes and provide exotic displays in prominent places.

△ **BUTTERFLIES**
Modern insecticides and pesticides are endangering many species of tropical butterfly because their herbivorous caterpillars feed on local plant life.

△ **GREEN PARAKEETS**
The Green Parakeet can be best seen, and its loud calls heard, in the wooded areas throughout the island. The colourful birds feed on seeds and fruit.

▷ **QUALITY COFFEE**
Coffee bushes thrive in the cool mountains 600–1500 metres (2,000–4,920ft) up. Altitude affects the quality of the beans, called "lowland" or "highland".

MONTEGO BAY

Jamaica's second city offers much to the visitor who ventures outside the all-inclusive compounds, from lively nightlife to country hamlets and the striking architecture of the great houses

Maps:
Town 266
Area 272

In many ways Montego Bay and its north-coast suburbs are the least Jamaican part of Jamaica – an "Independent Republic of Montego Bay" built almost exclusively around the annual invasion of hundreds of thousands of international sun worshippers.

The phenomenon has resulted in a riotous clash of cultures, where young men with their hair in dreadlocks walk arm-in-arm with visiting co-eds; where foreign businessmen chat up bikini-clad Jamaican girls; where retired couples chase goats off the golf greens before putting; where waistcoated waiters serve champagne and caviar in plush hilltop restaurants overlooking valleys of wooden shacks and poverty. It's all relatively new, and still growing, but nevertheless suitably off-beat and thus typically Jamaican.

Apart from Kingston, Montego Bay is Jamaica's only city, a helter-skelter development without distinct boundaries that has slowly swallowed up the coastline as far east as Rose Hall, as far west as the Tryall Club, and as far north into the Caribbean as sailboats, windsurfers and jet-skis will take you.

This is all tourist territory, and beyond it, Jamaica itself slowly resurfaces in such historic places as Falmouth and Lucea, and in typical small towns like Green Island, Anchovy and Duncans. So visitors can spend the daytime hours exploring Jamaica – and return home to the "independent republic" of Montego Bay at night.

PRECEDING PAGES: Rose Hall Great House. **LEFT:** in the shade of a coconut palm. **BELOW:** life's a beach in MoBay.

Bay of butter

To modern visitors **Montego Bay ❶** means soft beaches, transparent waters, exotic living. To the first European visitors it meant lard. Historians believe the word "montego" evolved from *manteca,* Spanish for lard or butter. Early Spanish occupants used the bay for shipping fat from wild and domesticated pigs and cattle. Now most people simply call it MoBay.

Christopher Columbus anchored in the bay, a crescent of beach that rolls into gentle hills, during his first visit to Jamaica in 1494. He found Taino villages already onshore; stories claim that he recruited one of the Indians as a crew member. But the Spanish did not establish a settlement here until about 1655.

Ten years after that the British established the parish of St James, but settlers trickled in slowly during the latter part of the 17th century and the early part of the18th. Potential residents feared the bay's vulnerability to attacks from pirates and from Maroons living in the nearby Cockpit Country. But by 1773 Montego Bay had the island's only newspaper outside Kingston, the *Cornwall Chronicle*, and even had a regular theatrical season, making it a respectable centre for the north coast's aristocracy.

Fires destroyed chunks of the town in 1795 and

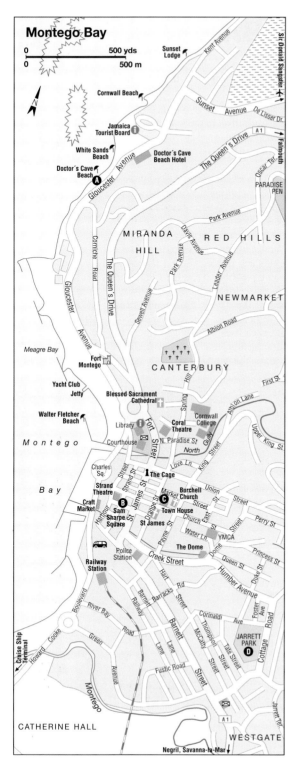

Montego Bay

0   500 yds
0   500 m

1811. Sam "Daddy" Sharpe led the area's slaves in revolt during the winter of 1831–32; the British authorities reacted by hanging him in The Parade on 23 May 1832, and by killing an estimated 500 of his followers. Then MoBay lapsed into a period of decline until the seeds of its tourist industry were planted around the turn of the 20th century.

The feature that made Montego Bay's future, **Doctor's Cave Beach** , still draws the tourists of today. The beach took its name from Dr Alexander McCatty, who owned it and turned it into a semi-public bathing club in 1906. A small nearby cave no longer exists. Another doctor, British osteopath Sir Herbert Baker, further heightened the allure of the beach in the 1920s by claiming its waters could cure a variety of ailments. You will be asked to pay a small fee for use of the beach and its facilities.

The later development of a series of hotels along Kent and Gloucester avenues has created MoBay's **Strip**, now called the "Hip Strip", a scaled-down version of Waikiki or Miami Beach.

Arriving in MoBay

Most travellers get their first look at Montego Bay from the window of an aeroplane, and many never see much more of the island than this. **Sir Donald Sangster International Airport** has connections with airports in the United States, Europe and the rest of the Caribbean, as well as with Kingston's Norman Manley International Airport. The loveliest drive into MoBay is west up **Queen's Drive**, which skirts the cliff above the beach strip.

Queen's Drive bends back down **Miranda Hill** past the remnants of **Fort Montego**. Three of its 17 original cannons remain pointed seawards, and its massive powder magazine lies landwards. No one is sure when the fort was built, but historians first described it in 1752.

Fort Montego's contribution to the struggle for power in the Caribbean was negligible. It only fired its guns twice: once to celebrate the surrender of Havana (a defective cannon exploded and killed a gunner), and the second time in 1795,

Map on page 266

when local soldiers fired at what they believed to be a French privateer entering the harbour. They missed, fortunately. The privateer turned out to be a British ship.

At the roundabout you can swing back north along Gloucester Avenue to the Strip beaches. To the south the roads converge into **St James Street**, the main thoroughfare through the town. It leads to the inevitable town square; formerly known as Charles Square and The Parade, it is now called **Sam Sharpe Square ❸**.

The square is a miniature version of The Parade in Kingston, a jumble of tacky new buildings and crumbling old structures, dusted by fumes from cars and buses. In its northwest corner is an attractive little building called **The Cage**. As its name implies, it was once used for imprisoning runaway slaves, and (in those bad old days) any black people found on the streets after 3pm were considered runaways. The Cage dates to 1806.

At the corner of Union and East streets is another reminder of that grim era: **The Slave Ring**, a decaying stone amphitheatre believed once to have been used as a slave market, and later the scene of cockfights.

Church Street, which crosses St James Street west of the square, has a fine old plantation house, slightly obscured by foliage; it is now the **Town House ❹** Restaurant at No. 16. **St James Parish Church** rises opposite it on Church and St Claver streets. Built from limestone, the church is a fine example of modified Georgian architecture. Its foundation stone was laid in 1775. Artist James Hakewill described it as "the handsomest church in the island" at that period.

The elegant monuments inside include a tribute to Rosa Palmer sculpted by Britain's John Bacon, who also executed the Rodney Memorial in Spanish Town. The lady draped over the urn has faint purple markings in the marble

Sam Sharpe was believed to be the son of an overseer, and although he was a slave he is thought to have been able to travel freely among the area's plantations.

BELOW: the Sam Sharpe memorial.

The sea around the north-coast resorts is ideal for watersports. Note that the Walter Fletcher Beach, opposite Fort Street Craft Market, is now the Aquasol Theme Park.

BELOW: welcome signs abound in Montego Bay.

around her neck and nostrils which support the theory that Rosa Palmer may actually have been the legendary, and probably fictional "White Witch of Rose Hall" who murdered many husbands and lovers until she was strangled by one of her slaves.

Poverty and elegance

For a good view of Montego Bay, and a startling look at the gap between its affluent visitors and poor residents, take Church Street back to Union Street and then head east up the steep hill to the **Richmond Hill Hotel**.

To see a rather different style of life, look down into the valley called **Canterbury** which is not very well hidden by the stone wall in the car park. Thousands of small wooden dwellings cling precariously to a hillside devoid of paved streets and other modern amenities. Here live many of the poorly-paid personnel who wait on you in hotels and restaurants and try to sell you souvenirs along the streets of MoBay. Their ramshackle homes are made from plywood, cardboard, corrugated tin, concrete and any other building materials that the residents can lay their hands on. The steady din of life hovers above the whole surreal scene. Yet you're only steps away from the comfort and old-world elegance of the Richmond Hill Hotel, formerly the 18th-century Spanish-style residence of a local plantation owner.

Back down Union Street, take Dome Street to its junction with Creek Street. The small, unimportant-looking structure in the intersection is called **The Dome**. In the 18th century it controlled the distribution of the small river called **The Creek**, once the main source of water for MoBay. Its architectural style might be called "Greek Orthodox", after the white domes that litter the far-off Greek islands.

Map on page 266

Continue east on Humber Avenue and round the corner into Cottage Park Road. Behind the wall west of the road lies **Jarrett Park ⓓ**, once the original home of the world's biggest reggae music festival, Reggae Sunsplash, and a sports ground. Before its demise Sunsplash was a magnet drawing people to a week-long celebration of Jamaican life and rhythms; today **Reggae Sumfest** has taken over as the foremost annual music event. In August thousands of music lovers from North America, Europe and Asia head for Montego Bay and its various Sumfest venues. The main events are held at Catherine Hall Entertainment Centre, in the west of the city near the harbour.

MoBay offers a variety of day and nightlife. When you've finished parasailing above coral waters, dance to the latest reggae and funk at **Disco Inferno** (in the shopping centre across from the Holiday Inn) or at the **Hurricane Disco** in the Breezes Hotel on Gloucester Avenue. Here you can also enjoy a beautiful view over Doctor's Cave Beach. Further along is **Margueritaville** sports bar which has a lively atmosphere and is a good place to watch the sunset, as is its restaurant. **Mobay UnderSea Tours** (tel: 940 4465) run semi-submersible trips around the Marine Park from the pier behind Margueritaville. Book at the office a few doors away and then pass through the sports bar to reach the pier.

Haggling with higglers

Harbour Street's wharves still hum with activity when the fishermen come ashore with their daily catch, and MoBay still ships its share of fruit, produce and other goods from the port area.

The local **Crafts Market** is located along Harbour Street, where you can haggle over prices for souvenirs, Bob Marley T-shirts or fruit from a higgler's

If you plan to visit Jamaica for Reggae Sumfest it would be a good idea to book your flight and accommodation as much as four months in advance.

BELOW: the craft markets are good for basketware and souvenirs.

head-basket, and even have your hair turned into a mass of African-style braids and beads.

To experience a genuine Jamaican market, however, head for the **Fustic Street Market** off Barnett Street, where women higglers reign supreme. The practice dates back to early colonial times when slaves brought their sales practices from West Africa. Here, as in Africa, the "Market Mammy" is an important person.

Markets first bloomed on the sugar estates or at busy crossroads where slaves and free persons alike met to trade and barter. Each slave received a plot of land for cultivation, and what he didn't eat he traded. Some also crafted baskets or *bankras,* clay bowls called *yabbas,* and "jackass rope," tobacco twisted and rolled into long ropes to make it easier to carry while travelling.

The men usually did the cultivating and manufacturing, and the women became salespeople. They controlled the money. Often the peasant women walked as far as 32 km (20 miles) loaded with goods to sell at the market. Today higglers remain the queens of the trade. The young ones dress in contemporary fashions, but the older women cling to the age-old uniform of a large apron with huge pockets worn over a dress. They wear head-ties, and keep their money buried in their bosoms in cloth "threadbags".

It's a tough life, and higglers have developed a reputation for being loud and quarrelsome, but approach them with a smile and a query and you will find that most warm up to you quickly. They are certainly not shy.

Route A1 east of Montego Bay follows Queen's Drive past another shanty village and an airport runway. The junction turns left to **Tropical Beach**, a favourite spot for musical events or a quiet day on a sandy beach (there is a small entrance fee), and to **Sandals Montego Bay Hotel**, one of many popular all-

Reggae Sunsplash is on hold. There was no event in 1999, and, although there are plans to reschedule the festival to January or February, the future of Jamaica's Sunsplash is uncertain.

BELOW: selling fruit by the sea.

REGGAE SUMFEST

The theme of Reggae Sumfest, Jamaica's annual reggae music festival held in Montego Bay, is: "music: the universal force". In August thousands of people flock to the resort from all over the world just to take in the party vibes and enjoy the loud roots and Dancehall reggae music. At this time of year Jamaica's second city is bursting at the seams with music lovers, boosting visitor arrivals by up to 25 percent. This is most apparent when one stands in the centre of the revellers and watches over 10,000 people from Jamaica, the USA, the UK, Germany, Japan and other countries paying homage to the island's influential music at venues all over the city.

The one-week festival kicks off with a wild beach party; then comes a sound system clash (play-offs), and the festival ends with a three- or four-night stint at Catherine Hall featuring local and international artists such as Chaka Demus and Pliers, Buju Banton and Beenie Man. Here, eager reggae lovers can be found gyrating – horizontally or vertically – to the music or sleeping on a "reggae mat". Such is the stuff of an event sometimes described as the "greatest reggae festival on earth".

If you want to join the Sumfest revellers, book your accommodation well in advance.

inclusive complexes where one price buys all accommodation, entertainment, food and beverages. Only couples are allowed into Sandals. Further east lie more hotels, from the inevitable **Holiday Inn** to the plush **Half Moon Club**. Considered to be one of the island's top three hotels, the Half Moon takes its name from the shape of its perfect beach. It has 146 hectares (360 acres) of gardens and manicured lawns, its own championship golf course which was designed by Robert Trent Jones, tennis courts, horse-riding and prices to match. Next door is the expensive and upmarket Half Moon Shopping Village, with a medical centre. Within the plaza is a shop called the **Bob Marley Experience**, which has a large collection of T-shirts and souvenirs relating to the reggae super-star and regularly shows a short but interesting film about the man and his music.

The White Witch of Rose Hall

Looming mightily on a ridge just east of the Half Moon is one of Jamaica's premier attractions, **Rose Hall Great House ❷**. Drive up the road and pay the stiff admission charge for a look at this plantation house built about 1770 by John Palmer, when he served as the *custos* (queen's representative) of the parish of St James. It was restored by the American millionaire John Rollins, who was a former governor of Delaware.

In Rose Hall, Rollins and his wife Michelle have attempted to recreate the typical grandeur of an 18th-century plantation house. Its antiques and art treasures are museum-quality pieces dating to the 17th century.

Nevertheless, Rose Hall's trappings and restoration remain overshadowed by its famous legend. One of the many versions says that its "heroine", Annie, was an Englishwoman tutored in the black arts of voodoo by a Haitian priestess.

Map on pages 272–73

The Rose Hall Beach Club (open daily), next to the Wyndham Rose Hall Hotel, is a good place to spend the day. The entrance fee covers all beach and watersports facilities.

LEFT: Rose Hall, home to the "White Witch" who became a legend. **BELOW:** fishing near Cornwall Beach.

*Seashells on
the coast.*

She came to Jamaica and supposedly, at the age of 18, married John Palmer. Three years later Palmer died, reportedly poisoned by the petite and pretty but sadistic Annie. She later stabbed a second husband to death and strangled a third. The legend also says that she took slaves as lovers and murdered them when she got bored. Finally the slaves rebelled and murdered Annie in her bed in 1833.

Naturally, Rose Hall is now said to be haunted by the ghost of the "White Witch", Annie Palmer.

The legend makes a great story – probably more fiction than fact. There *was* an Annie Palmer at Rose Hall, but she wasn't English, had only one husband, and died a respected citizen in 1846. Rosa Palmer of Rose Hall *did* have Irish connections and four husbands, but she kept the last one for 23 years; in fact it was he who buried her, aged 72, in the Montego Bay churchyard.

A side road leads from the main road past the right corner of Rose Hall to the walled burial ground of the Moulton Barrett family, 180 metres (200 yards) below the 19th-century great house. The Barrett family, which produced the poetess Elizabeth Barrett Browning, lived in the **Cinnamon Hill Great House** further up the road, which has been modernised, restored and purchased by the American country-and-western star Johnny Cash as his private residence. He has become a valued patron of the Montego Bay SOS Children's Village, which provides family-type homes for destitute and abandoned children.

Route A1 continues east, past souvenir stands which are chock-a-block with conch shells, to reach yet another mansion. **Greenwood Great House** was also built by the Barrett family between 1780 and 1800. Its antiques include the largest collection of rare musical instruments in the western hemisphere.

A worthwhile detour from Montego Bay is **Barnett Estate Great House**,

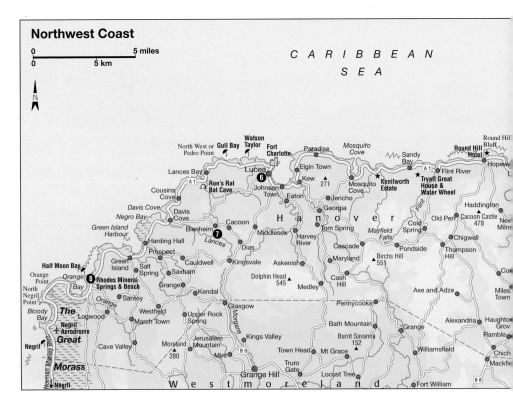

Northwest Coast

0 —————————— 5 miles
0 —————————— 5 km

N

CARIBBEAN SEA

which lies 5 km (3 miles) south east of the city. Built in 1655 by Colonel Nicholas Jarrett, the house and surrounding grounds were once part of a large estate encompassing the land of the Rose Hall and Greenwood estates. Barnett reveals something of the luxurious life of wealthy 18th-century settlers. An old sugar mill on the property has been converted into a restaurant, **Belfield 1794**, a lovely place to stop for a bite to eat after a tour of the estate.

The next major town, **Falmouth ❸**, virtually dates *in toto* from the time the famous Barrett family of Cinnamon Hill roamed Jamaica. It was developed as a sugar port during a period of wealth and good taste – the end of the 18th century. The taste is shown in its broad streets and well-built stone and wooden houses; the Georgian heritage here is better preserved than elsewhere on the island. The greatest concentration of Georgian buildings is on **Market Street**, west of the central **Water Square** with its small ornamental fountain.

The **Post Office** has a well-balanced pattern of upper windows that sit boldly on a support of semicircular arches. At the bottom of the street is the **Methodist Manse**, built in 1799 by the Barretts, a stone-and-wood house with elegant wrought-iron balconies and fine Adam-style doorways and friezes.

Adjacent to Water Square is the 1815-era **court house**, one of the finest Georgian buildings in Jamaica despite a poor restoration attempt after a fire in 1926. A double exterior staircase leads up to a portico with a pediment supported by four doric columns. The building now houses the offices of the town council. On leaving the town via Upper Harbour Street you pass by the 1801 **Phoenix Foundry**, one of Jamaica's earliest ironworks.

Like Port Antonio in the east, Falmouth has its rafting river, the **Martha Brae**. There's a **Rafters' Village ❹** a mile upriver, at the neck of an oxbow in

Map
on pages
272–73

Scenes from the film Papillon, *starring* Steve McQueen *and* Dustin Hoffman, *were filmed in* Falmouth, *close to the court house, in 1972.*

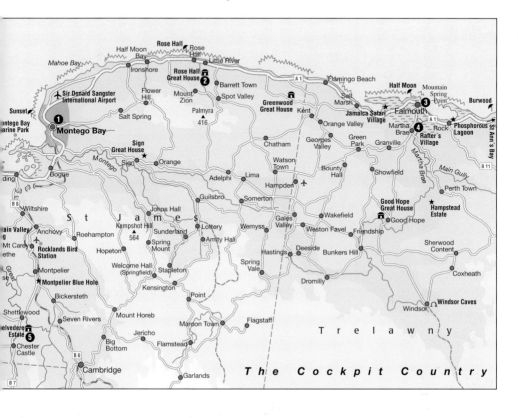

the stream. It has a restaurant, a bar and boutiques. The trip downriver takes 1½ hours; you will be driven back to the village afterwards.

Half an hour's drive from Falmouth lies the beautiful 18th-century **Good Hope Great House**, surrounded by citrus orchards and rolling hills where the owners breed horses. Part of the imposing plantation house, as well as the old coach-house, has been converted into cosy rooms for visitors.

East of Falmouth on Route A1 there is a phosphorescent lagoon at **Rock**. At night microscopic organisms glisten when the water is agitated with a stick or a stone. **Glistening Waters** seafood restaurant in front of the lagoon serves good fresh food at reasonable prices. You can charter deep-sea fishing boats here, to try your luck at catching marlin, kingfish, wahoo or barracuda, or take the diving boat and explore the offshore reefs.

An impressive ruin, **Stewart Castle**, can be reached a mile up a dirt road from the main highway past Rock. The structure appears to be a large home that was fortified with thick stone walls perforated with musket and cannon firing slits, and seems to date from the early 18th century, when large landowners constructed such dwellings to protect themselves from attacks by Maroons, slaves or pirates. Designated a national monument, Stewart Castle is earmarked for renovation.

At **Silver Sands**, an excellent beach-cottage colony, you can head south up Route B10 for a look at the **Long Pond Sugar Factory and Distillery**, where Jamaica's famous Gold Label Rum is manufactured. Then head back west at **Clark's Town** on Route B11, or continue south to Duanvale and Sherwood Content, on the fringes of the almost inaccessible **Cockpit Country**, and Windsor Cave, discussed in detail in *Conquering the Cockpit Country* (page 281).

Time 'n' Place beach-cottage colony, east of Falmouth, is worth a stop for lunch or a light snack. (tel: 954 4371).

BELOW: a motor-cycle police patrol.

West of MoBay

West of MoBay a spur road off A1 leads to a shopping complex designed to cater for passengers who spill out of passing cruise ships. Its products are in-bond (duty free) as well as out-of-bond. Beyond are the twin towers of the **Sunset Beach Hotel** (formerly the Seawind Hotel) complex and a yacht marina.

West of **Reading** is a junction with a road that jogs across the island to Savanna-la-Mar on the south coast. The road climbs up **Long Hill**, providing views over town and coast. About 3 km (2 miles) up, a signpost indicates the route to Rock Pleasant. A bird reserve owned by Lisa Salmon is less than 1 km (½ mile) along this route. Bird-watchers carrying their bird-society cards are welcome at **Rocklands** all day, but for the general public the feeding of the birds starts daily at 3pm. Rocklands is a "bird-feeding station", as opposed to a sanctuary, and many of the feathered visitors are known by name. Even the skittish Doctor Birds are so tame they feed from your hand here. The station was established in 1958.

Close to Rocklands, in Lethe, is **Mountain Valley Rafting and Rhea's World** (tel: 912 0020; entrance fee). Take a leisurely journey down Great River, or explore the gardens nearby where orchids are grown for export.

The road continues to **Anchovy**, then to the town of **Montpelier**, centre of the local dairy and beef cattle industry. The road's right-hand fork proceeds to Savanna-la-Mar via Ramble.

West on the A1 beyond Reading the scene is graced by some large and elegant homes, many owned by wealthy winter visitors. Shortly after you cross the parish boundary into **Hanover** at **Great River**, round, beehive-like gate-posts on the right, seaward side indicate the location of **Round Hill Hotel**, one of the

Map on pages 272–73

A hummingbird gathers nectar.

BELOW:
Montego Bay has excellent beaches.

Pineapple images were used in early Caribbean architecture to represent prosperity.

most exclusive and expensive in Jamaica. It is also one of the most beautiful, enjoying an incomparable setting on its own private beach. A list of guest names over the years resembles *Who's Who* and includes the rock star Paul McCartney and US Senator Edward Kennedy. The fashion designer Ralph Lauren, of "Polo" fame, owns the estate west of Round Hill.

Further south, about 30 minutes' drive from Montego Bay centre, is the **Belvedere Estate ❺** (tel: 952 6001; open Mon–Sat; entrance fee), southwest of Rocklands. This working plantation has orange groves, coconut palms and pineapples and an excellent tour with knowledgeable guides. It was the home of Sam Sharpe, whose 1831 slave rebellion was based here. He was publicly executed in Montego Bay and is now a National Hero.

Sharpe was believed to move between Belvedere and a nearby plantation which is now **Croydon in the Mountains** (open Tue–Wed and Fri 10.30am–3pm; entrance fee; tel: 979 8267), a pineapple and coffee plantation at the foot of the mountains at Catadupa. The road leading to Croydon is rough, but persevere for spectacular panoramic views of the surrounding countryside, and a tour.

Sugar and golf at Tryall

Seven kilometres (4 miles) further on the left is the magnificent **Tryall Water Wheel** and ruins. The wheel is still turned by water carried via aqueduct from the **Flint River**. Its brick chimney was rebuilt in 1834 after the old sugar works were destroyed during Sharpe's rebellion of 1831. The water wheel turned the single three-roll crushing mill. In the old days the mill could also be turned by means of wind power (the island is dotted with old sugar towers which carried sails), animal power or even human power. On the right is the picturesque Tryall

BELOW:
Tryall Water Wheel.

championship golf course, and above on the hill is the small and exclusive Tryall Hotel.

Beyond **Sandy Bay** are perhaps the finest sugar-estate ruins in Jamaica, **Kenilworth Estate**. The sugar-factory buildings, which are located a mile south of the main road, were built on a far grander scale and more durably than the adjacent great house. The first block is the sugar mill, with long, deep, rectangular housing for the water wheel (which probably looked like the one at Tryall). The two-storey building is beautifully constructed of limestone in two different shades, with oval Palladian windows trimmed in light stone and an arched front doorway reached by a semicircular flight of steps.

The second block, the sugar-boiling house and distillery, is in the form of a long central room with two wings, while the sloped hillside accommodates the furnaces on a lower level.

About 48 km (30 miles) beyond Montego Bay is the quiet little town of **Lucea ❻**, the administrative centre of Hanover parish. It was once a busy port for the shipment of sugar; its economy now is based around bananas and molasses. Pimento, ginger and yams grown in the surrounding districts are also important products. The town centre was dedicated by Queen Elizabeth II during her 1966 visit to Jamaica. Lucea's 19th-century **court house** is an attractive but slightly neglected stone-and-wood structure with a clock tower.

Fort Charlotte, behind the school and the Public Works Department, is another Jamaican fort which never actually fired a cannonball in anger. Named after George III's queen, this octagonal structure had ports for 20 guns; only three remain. The former constabulary and prison close by now house the well-arranged **Hanover Museum**.

Backtrack to the main road, which continues west in and out of little nooks like **Cousins Cove**, **Davis Cove** and **Negro Bay**. A paved road from Davis Cove leads 3 km (2 miles) inland to **Blenheim ❼**, birthplace of Alexander Bustamante, National Hero and Jamaica's first prime minister, , who came from relatively humble origins. Bustamante's father, Robert Clarke, was the overseer on the Blenheim Estate, and his famous son was born in the overseer's home there. The house has been reconstructed on its original site as both a national monument and an excellent and well-maintained museum.

The next town on the main road is misleadingly named **Green Island**, with a fishing-village flavour and an old Presbyterian chapel. There are several important transport junctions here, with roads that spider's-web up into the hills toward Savanna-la-Mar. But before you head back stop off at the **Rhodes Mineral Springs and Beach ❽** (entrance fee). Boat tours such as the catamaran *It's A Wild Thing* stop off here so that revellers can party on the beach. The spring water is considered pure enough to drink and is good for bathing too. There are fishing and scuba diving, and horse-riding tours in the mountains. Go back to the main road now; Route A1 cuts a steady course down the coast to Jamaica's centre of hedonism, **Negril**, which is dealt with in the chapter *Negril and the South* (page 291). ❏

Map on pages 272–73

Lucea was once home to a flourishing and influential Jewish merchant community.

BELOW: damp scamper in the rural north.

CONQUERING THE COCKPIT COUNTRY

Much of this almost impenetrable land remains unspoilt; nature lovers head for these hills where rare species of flora and fauna survive as well as stories of Maroon wars and slave rebellions

Map on page 282

Kingston

Most people know the story of Columbus crumpling up a sheet of paper to simulate the topography of his latest discovery – Jamaica – for his patrons, Ferdinand and Isabella, monarchs of Aragon and Castile. The story is attached to many other islands in the Caribbean, all mountainous. Jamaica can probably lay claim to being most rugged of all.

More than half Jamaica's countryside is 500 metres (1,640 ft) or more above sea level; the island basically consists of a central ridge of mountains surrounded by a narrow coastal plain not more than 20 km (12 miles) wide. But there is another part of Jamaica which is largely a blank space on the map, just as it was when Columbus arrived in 1494. It is immediately noticeable from the air, because from above the Cockpit Country seems to be a stupefying succession of wooded hills stretching mile after uninhabited mile.

PRECEDING PAGES: country girl carrying water. **LEFT:** the 1846 grave of a British soldier near Maroon Town. **BELOW:** Accompong celebrations.

The Land of Look Behind

The **Cockpit Country** is near impenetrable, and as such is almost as mysterious today as it was 500 years ago. That it isn't still *quite* as mysterious as then is due to the fact that it formed a perfect theatre for guerilla warfare during the Maroon Wars. The region provided refuge for the Tainos (once mislabelled Arawaks), who were the gentle Amerindians Columbus found in possession when he first arrived. The few who had escaped Spanish enslavement and European disease welcomed into their communities other runaway slaves fleeing the Spaniards. To this day there is a village called **Refuge** on the northern edge of the Cockpit Country. Later the area became the operations base of the Maroons – descendants of runaway African slaves – in revolt against the British colonists. The British dread of the place is perfectly suggested in the sinister nickname of a part of it: The Land of Look Behind.

Although Columbus found thriving populations of Amerindians in the Caribbean, within thirty years the indigenous populations had almost gone. Many Tainos died under Spanish occupation and oppression. Diseases such as influenza and smallpox devastated the people, but killed less Europeans than Amerindians because they had some immunity to the illnesses.

One Spanish historian, Toribio Motolina, said that in most provinces of Mexico "more than one half the [native] population died, in others the proportion was a little less; they died in heaps, like bedbugs", and a German missionary wrote in 1699 that the Indians "die so easily that the bare sight and smell of a Spaniard causes them to give up the ghost".

The destruction of the indigenous peoples and cultures has meant an incalculable loss to human ethnic and cultural diversity. It was the Amerindians who brought to the English language words like hammock, hurricane, canoe and barbecue and, indirectly, buccaneer – *boucanier* from *boucan*: seasoned smoke-dried meat, the lineal ancestor of Jamaica's now famous jerked pork.

All South Trelawny Environmental Association (STEA) tours originate in Albert Town, which is easily reached by public transport. The route from the north of the island is through Duncans and Jackson Town.

The Maroons

The imported African slaves who replaced the Amerindians – who were dying out – in the 16th century began to run away from their Spanish masters almost as soon as they came off the slave ships. They became known as Maroons and lived in the mountains. By the time the English took the island from the Spanish in 1655, it was the Maroons under Juan Lubola (also known as Juan de Bolas) who made English settlement unsafe in Jamaica for several years.

By the early 18th century the Maroons had established themselves in several independent settlements, in **Nanny Town** and **Moore Town** in the Blue Mountains to the East, in **Scott's Hall** in central Jamaica, and in Accompong and Trelawny Town in the West. The Maroons' running fights with the British exploded in 1733 into what the British named the First Maroon War. At the end of that struggle, probably the world's first modern guerilla war, the Maroons wrested from the British a grant of land and a non-aggression pact, which guaranteed them freedom from official interference but committed them to turning in runaway slaves and suppressing rebellion. The slaves, considering themselves abandoned by the Maroons, continued their struggle, led by the indomitable Coromantee people of the Gold Coast, one of whom, Tacky, had several important victories in the north-east of the island until he was killed in 1760.

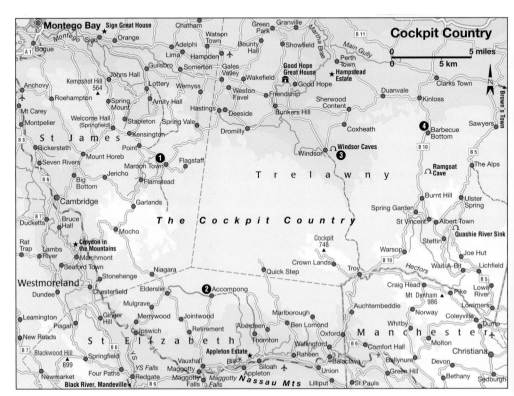

Maroon Town ❶, on the northwestern edge of the Cockpit Country, is a good place to begin a brief four-wheel-drive tour of the surroundings. Maroons settled here a long time ago, but they no longer live in the village. A side road off the main track slices through banana plantations to **Flagstaff**, formerly a Maroon settlement called Trelawny Town.

You must backtrack to the main road from here, then head south past **Elderslie** where a sign will point to the Maroon capital of the region, **Accompong ❷**. The village can be reached from the south by way of Maggotty and Retirement, and is a settlement of scattered rural houses around a small square flanked by shops, a church and a school. The town is governed by a council headed by a "colonel", the successor to Cudjoe, the fierce leader of the First Maroon War, but these days he is an elected official. **Cudjoe's Day** is celebrated, with great ceremony, on 6 January every year.

Backtrack again to the main road, which dead-ends in the town of **Quick Step**, in the district of **Look Behind**. You can swing back west again on Route B11 to **Sherwood Content**, where a side road at Sherwood darts back into the Cockpits, to **Windsor Cave ❸**. The cave's first two chambers can be easily negotiated, but step carefully through the layers of "rat bat" manure. More advanced cavers will find that the cave plunges to uncharted depths.

The area is a classic example of Karst topography, in which, over aeons, water has dissolved limestone into sinkholes and caves, leaving the harder rocks in majestic isolation. Minerals colour the rocks in strange hues in some areas, and in places like **Barbecue Bottom ❹** the road is on the edge of a perpendicular precipice above an enchanted green glade hundreds of metres below.

The sinkholes lead to deep and sometimes extensive caverns and underground

Map on page 282

The Cockpit Country Adventure Tours are conducted by guides from the surrounding communities, who are carefully selected and trained by the STEA with assistance from the Jamaica Red Cross and the Tourist Board. All guides are certified.

BELOW: sheltering from the rain.

Map
on page
282

Jamaica
90c

YELLOW-BILLED PARROT   *Amazona collaria*

Yellow-billed and
black-billed parrots
live in the Cockpit.

BELOW: village
laundry.
RIGHT: view of the
Cockpit Country
landscape.

lakes. Windsor Cave is reputedly 11 km (7 miles) long, but most of the systems have never been fully explored. They make the Cockpit Country into a huge sponge, soaking up and storing rainwater, producing springs which turn into some of Jamaica's most dependable rivers: the **Dornoch** (Rio Bueno), the **Martha Brae**, and the **Black River**, Jamaica's longest. The Cockpit Country system is also believed to be the source of the intermittent **Moneague Lake** 16 km (10 miles) or so to the east, and of the springs in the verdant and paradisiacal **Queen of Spain's Valley** to the West.

Beyond Sherwood Content and Windsor Cave, much of the Cockpit Country is said to remain unexplored, but if you can find a reliable guide it is worth trying to negotiate the area, which is steeped in history.

Two roads, one on the east, the other on the west, were driven along the edges of the main Cockpit Country. The Burnt Hill Road, to the west, is now overgrown but still provides spectacular views for the intrepid hiker. The Jackson Town Road, less scenic, is a romantic adventure through an imposing landscape.

The Cockpit Country's relative inaccessibility and unusual properties make it Jamaica's most important refuge for endemic plants and animals. At least 101 endemic species of plant can be found here, some restricted to a single hillock. There are over 500 species of fern, more than in any other rainforest in the tropics. The yellow-billed and black-billed parrots are among the 79 species of bird, including all the species endemic to Jamaica, which live in the wilderness. This is also home to the endangered Giant Swallowtail butterfly, the largest in the Americas and second largest in the world. There are 16 species of amphibian and 22 species of reptile, with new species being discovered. The entire area has been proposed as a National Park and a UNESCO World Heritage Site.

Environmentalists, led by the South Trelawny Environmental Association (STEA), have been campaigning for the region to be designated a protected area in order to preserve the wilderness, which is one of the last wet limestone forests in the Western hemisphere to be in more or less the same condition as when Columbus came to Jamaica five centuries ago. The Jamaican government, local groups and international agencies including UNESCO are working on a plan for the sustainable development of the area, now threatened by unlawful logging, charcoal burning and illegal marijuana (ganja) plantations. One proposal is to provide hiking, caving and historical tours of the area. Since the Cockpit Country is just an hour's drive from the north-coast tourist areas, getting here is simple.

Bed and breakfast is provided by local people under the auspices of STEA. Three main guided tours are offered: the Barbecue Bottom Natural History Tour along the Burnt Hill Road is great for birdwatchers and students of natural history; the more demanding Rock Spring Cave and River Adventure takes visitors through a maze-like cave, with fantastic rock formations, and an underground river with waterfalls. At **Quashie Sink** visitors can explore a sinkhole and cave, descending steep ladders into the bowels of the earth, traversing underground waterfalls and viewing fossils and rare formations. There are also hiking tours of varying duration and levels of difficulty.   ❑

BLUE MOUNTAINS AND MANGROVE SWAMPS

Like its Caribbean sisters, Jamaica has a fragile ecosystem to protect – an ecological treasure trove of mountains, wetlands, beaches and coral reefs

Tropical nature surrounds us, we enjoy it during our holiday, but what do we know about it, except that there are more mosquitoes than at home, and the plants we try to grow in pots reach tree size in the wild? Over the decades this ignorance has come close to destroying the very asset that attracts people to Jamaica. However, since the 1990s the creation of the Natural Resources Conservation Authority (NRCA) has increased public awareness of environmental matters and is in the forefront of the drive for sustainable tourism – balancing short-term economic needs while at the same time ensuring their long-term (ecological) supply – or ecotourism. On these lines, three national parks have been established: Montego Bay Marine Park, The Blue Mountain and John Crow National Park, and the Negril Watershed, and there are similar plans for the Hellshire Hills, Cockpit Country and Black River. But there is still much to be done.

PLANTATION TOURS

Many of the old estates, such as the Georgian Good Hope Great House (above), have been preserved and are still active. Tours round the plantation houses and their fields reveal an island life intertwined with nature – for example the use of plants to cure headaches, stomach troubles and broken hearts. Some have preserved stretches of land where man's impact has been small, keeping them as "showcases" of the genuine island.

▷ **BLUE MOUNTAINS**
Ambitious hikers or cyclists will find themselves immersed in nature in this eco-friendly and enlightening National Park.

▷ **BLACK RIVER**
In 1851 naturalist Philip Gosse watched the now endangered manatees (sea cows) playing in the river after his breakfast of manatee steaks.

△ **HELLSHIRE HILLS**
The dry forest grows on the limestone hills and supports palms, blue-flowered *lignum vitae*, tiny white orchids, cacti and wild pineapples.

△ **CROCODILES**
The tangled and dense mangroves on the south coast are perfect places for protected species, such as the crocodile, to make their home.

▷ **NEGRIL'S PALMS**
The Swamp Cabbage Palm, or Royal Palm, has been saved from the loggers in a small reserve in the Great Morass wetlands.

REAPPEARANCE OF THE DRAGON

Once the food of the Amerindians, who named the dragon-like lizard *iwana*, the Jamaican iguana (*Cyclura collei*) was considered extinct for half a century – until in 1990 a hog hunter encountered one caught by his dog in the mainly untouched dry forest of the Hellshire Hills southwest of Portmore.

He informed Kingston Zoo that he had caught a "dragon", and what zoologists thought to be a joke turned out to be the sensation of the century. The Jamaican iguana's fascinating limestone habitat is to become a national park, which will prevent the local charcoal-burners from felling the trees for their kilns.

Another enemy of the iguana is the mongoose, introduced to the island in the 19th century to eliminate rats. But rats are nocturnal creatures, and the mongoose operates by day – they got rid of the snakes, and now the iguanas are regrouping…For more details: Iguana Conservation, tel: 927 1660.

◁ **MANGROVES**
The dense mangroves at Black River and Milk River protect the land against gnawing waves.

△ **UNDERWATER**
The warm Caribbean sea offers a rich marine life. In Negril there is a conservation project aimed at preserving the coral reef.

◁ **WILD FLOWERS**
A trip through the Blue Mountains will reveal thick colourful carpets of wild flowers.

JAMAICA GROUND IGUANA

NUFF RESPECT DUE
TO JAMAICA'S LARGEST LAND REPTILE.
THE JAMAICAN GROUND IGUANA,IT CAN
REACH A LENGTH OF FIVE FEET. FOUND
ONLY IN JAMAICA A SMALL POPULATION
SURVIVES IN THE LIMESTONE FOREST OF
HELLSHIRE HILLS.

NEGRIL AND THE SOUTH

The beach scene and all-inclusive hotels dominate, but head south and inland to discover cane country, crocodiles at Black River and the tranquillity of Jamaica's south coast not yet affected by tourism

Map on page 292

Beaches and sugar: these are the main calling-cards of southern Cornwall county. But lest the visitor be misled, the county offers much more. The parishes of Westmoreland and St Elizabeth also feature mountains, swamps, the island's longest river, an avenue lined with bamboo, major agricultural and industrial areas and important historical sites.

The chances are you'll start your wanderings at Negril's famous 11-km (7-mile) beach, Jamaica's westernmost escape – a home for hedonism and bacchanalia, a nook for nude bathing, sun and sin.

Negril ❶ is no longer known only for swinging singles and wild nights but has been transformed into a mecca for health-spa goers, families looking for laid-back fun, and exhausted executives who need to "cool out" on the pristine beach. Negril was originally "founded" by the hippies and "flower children" of the 1960s and 1970s, and its flavour remains carefree and unhurried. No building can be built taller than a coconut palm, so even the most modern sprawling hotels are tucked away in an effort to retain a small village atmosphere.

It is precisely this relaxed attitude that attracts the "Spring-breakers" to this part of the island. During the Spring-break holiday hundreds of mainly US university students descend on the area to spend up to a fortnight on the beach and in the bars of Negril, enjoying discount accommodation and drinks. Some of the most popular places are **Hedonism II**, the all-inclusive, anything goes hotel, and the **Risky Business** and **Compulsion** bar/discos. Parties on the beach are almost an everyday event here, but for even more music and partying Montego Bay is the Spring-break capital.

More than in any other resort area in Jamaica, accommodation here ranges over all levels of price and quality. Hotels stretch along the full length of the lovely beach, interspersed with local homes, fishermen's huts, patches of indigenous flora, stretches of coconut trees and even some deserted sand. Local residents mix with the tourist population in a manner not commonplace elsewhere.

Food shops are almost infinite in number and variety, ranging from small "supper shops" selling hot pepper-fried fish and harddough bread to high-class seafood restaurants. Clothing varies as well, from none at all (on Booby Cay and at Hedonism II) to colourful locally made sarongs to sophisticated dress in the resort's better hotels and restaurants.

There are many fascinating places to dine and sleep, especially along **West End Road** ❷; although here they don't usually have access to the white-sand beaches that make the area famous, they have superb sea views. The **Rock House** consists of a series of thatch-roofed clifftop bungalows with a bird's-eye

PRECEDING PAGES: diving near Negril. **LEFT:** getting married on the beach at Negril. **BELOW:** fun on the beach.

*Negril Lighthouse
sits on Jamaica's
most westerly point.*

view of waves crashing against the rugged shoreline. At **Rick's Café** ❸ diners come not only for the seafood but also for spectacular sunsets and to see local youths (and brave visitors) diving 30 metres (100 ft) from the clifftop into the crystal water below. Dive at your own risk, or simply enjoy the lively atmosphere. Once the sun sets Rick's empties out pretty quickly. Beyond is the **Negril Lighthouse** ❹, built in 1894; the white-and-blue-painted structure, still in operation, overlooks the rocky coastline on West End Road. At the garden entrance to the lighthouse are two ancient cotton trees; the tough wood was traditionally used for canoes by early Jamaicans. Further still is a relaxing holistic spa, **Jackie's on the Reef**. The spa and retreat is an ideal place to unwind in simple surroundings; it offers yoga, meditation, Tai chi, drumming and African dance. West of here is nothing but 970 km (600 miles) of ocean to Yucatán.

Continue along West End Road, and Negril Hills comes into view although this is mainly a residential district, with small villages and farmland, there are still places to explore. The **Negril Hills Golf Club** (tel: 957 4638; entrance fee), on the Negril to Savanna-la-Mar and Sheffield road, has 18- and 9-hole courses.

Among Negril's popular all-inclusive luxury hotels with white-sand beaches are places like **Swept Away**, **Poinciana Beach Resort** (managed by Sandals), **Negril Gardens**, **Sandals** and **Beaches**. Scuba diving and snorkelling, sailing and parasailing, windsurfing and waterskiing are just some of the daily activities available to guests.

Hedonism II is located on a 9-hectare (22-acre) resort fronting **Long Bay** ❺. Next to it is the luxurious up-market **Grand Lido**, on **Bloody Bay**, where pirate "Calico Jack" Rackham and his colleagues Anne Bonney and Mary Read were captured in 1720. Bloody Bay was not named for the pirates, though. It got its

BELOW:
clifftop diving
at Rick's Café.

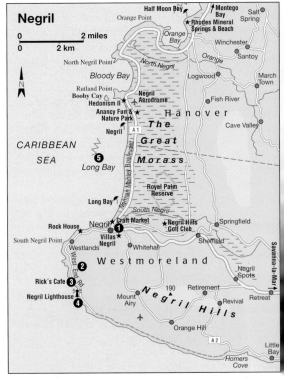

name from passing whalers who disembowelled their catch here, leaving the waters red with blood.

Back towards the main centre on Norman Manley Boulevard, across the road from the Poinciana Beach Resort, is the **Anancy Fun and Nature Park** (open daily; entrance fee; tel: 957 5572), a fun spot for families. Here visitors will find a wide range of facilities including go-karts, mini-golf, a nature trail, fishing and a snack bar.

Map on page 292

One of the best ways to see Negril's waters is by Polynesian catamaran. The 12-metre (40-ft) *Reggae II* leaves the harbour daily at 4pm for a sunset-party cruise along Long Bay's beautiful cliffs, or you can take a ride on the *Jolly Mermaid,* run by Sandals, for a view of the coral reef. At the northern end of the bay is **Booby Cay**, a small island used for filming scenes in Disney's 1954 screen version of Jules Verne's *20,000 Leagues Under the Sea.* The awkward booby, a species of gannet, flies to these cays to breed.

On the east side of the Negril Beach road is the **Great Morass** of Westmoreland, the habitat of an interesting variety of rare birds and plants. Explore it by airboat: the *Swamp Dragon* skims across the bog between 9am and 5pm daily. The southern part of the Morass, near the town of Sheffield, is given over to the **Negril Royal Palm Reserve** (daily 10am–6pm; entrance fee; tel: 816 9150), 160 hectares (400 acres) of palm trees with colourful and sometimes rare wildlife.

Fun for children of all ages.

Through canefields to Savanna-la-Mar

The highway east from Negril crosses several miles of swampland before emerging onto the vast Westmoreland Plain with its canefields and pastureland.

At **New Hope Estate** note the fanciful 1920s Oriental gateways. Then

BELOW: cruising along Long Bay.

SAVING THE REEF

Negril's 11-km (7-mile) white-sand beach, and in particular the coral reef at the western end, is a diver's dream. It used to be one of Jamaica's best kept secrets, but environmental threats from pollution, ships' anchors, overfishing and global warming have gone unchecked for so long that there is a real risk of losing this paradise. The reef is a marine forest which not only serves as a habitat to a variety of tropical fish and other animals which are essential to Jamaica's ecosystems but also protects the beach. Therefore reef damage means that Negril's beautiful beach is slowly being eroded.

The Negril Coral Reef Preservation Society (tel: 957 4626), a non-profit-making organisation, was formed in 1990 by a small group of locals concerned about the degradation of Negril's beautiful coral reef. The Society has had real success in preventing further damage to the best reef in Jamaica. The NCRPS has installed more than 40 mooring buoys; it trains rangers, runs workshops and provides information about the reef. The Society is also exploring alternative ways of earning a living for local fishermen. To date, damage to the reef has been reduced, and there is evidence of new coral growth which will ultimately protect the beach against further erosion.

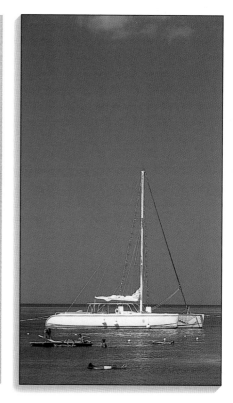

The Negril Royal Palm Reserve was set up to preserve the Swamp Cabbage Palm, previously mislabelled the Royal Palm. The reserve, near Sheffield, can be explored by foot trails; it is good for birdwatching and has a picnic area.

continue to **Little London**, which is nothing like its British namesake. In fact many feel it would be best renamed "Little Southall" (an Asian-dominated area of west London) for the large numbers of Indians who make it their home. Descendants of the indentured labourers who were transported from the east coast of India to Jamaica following the abolition of slavery in the mid-19th century, many of these Indians still work in the sugar industry.

The capital and chief city of Westmoreland parish is **Savanna-la-Mar ❻**, best known as "Sav-la-Mar" or just "Sav", meaning literally "the plain by the sea". That plain has not always been kind to the town, which since its establishment in 1703 has been devastated by hurricanes in 1748 and 1912, and by a tidal wave in 1780. The 1912 storm left a schooner stranded in the middle of **Great George Street** – with the crew still aboard.

Great George Street is the longest city street in Jamaica. At its seaward end is the **Old Fort**, the surviving stone walls of which form a swimming pool for locals. Further up the same street is the **court house**, with its ornate cast-iron drinking fountain dating from the 19th century. Note the admonition on all four sides of the fountain to "keep the pavement dry".

Savanna-la-Mar was established as a sugar port, and that is still its most important function. The bustling wharf is near the end of Great George Street, next to the Old Fort. Watch as raw brown sugar is loaded onto ships to be transported to refineries abroad.

Most of the sugar comes from factories around **Frome**, 10 km (6 miles) north of Sav-la-Mar towards Lucea. The **Frome Central Sugar Factory ❼** processes cane from estates throughout Westmoreland and Hanover and is the largest sugar factory on the island.

BELOW: you can shop outdoors on Long Bay.

NEGRIL AND THE SOUTH ♦ 295

Sugar-coated riots

Sugar cane is in fact a type of grass that grows to 3 metres (10 ft) or more in height. Inside the hard rind of its stalk is a soft sugary fibre. Between mid-November and June this cane is harvested and transported by road or rail to the mill. Here a double series of rollers crushes out the juice, containing about 13 percent pure sugar. At first a cloudy green in colour, this cane juice is then clarified, evaporated and separated in centrifugal machines into golden sugar crystals and cane molasses. One of the eventual end products of the molasses, of course, is Jamaica's famed rum.

In 1938 Frome was the site of riots which led to the rise of Alexander Bustamante as a national labour leader. The sugar mill, then the largest West Indies Sugar Company plant in the country, had just been built. Thousands of unemployed Jamaicans converged on Frome hoping to find work, but were turned away. Police were called in to quell the property destruction and cane-field burning that ensued. The disorder spread to other parts of Jamaica, and led to the formation of the island's first lasting unions and the political parties linked with them.

Not far from Frome, at the Shrewsbury Estate, is the source of the **Roaring River**. Seemingly from nowhere, the river emerges in a **blue hole ❸** from a subterranean course – it actually only makes a noise resembling a "roar" after the month of May. Don't be put off by the terrible roads leading to the **Roaring River Park** (open daily 8.30am–5pm; entrance fee; tel: 979 7987) near Petersfield. Visitors can enjoy the park grounds with a picnic and a guided tour through the dripstone cave with its magic pool and beautiful surroundings.

If you drive through the village of Roaring River and up the hill, you'll find a tiny welcoming *ital* restaurant opposite the **Blue Hole Garden Resort** where

Map on page 296

Some Jamaican rums are so strong that they are referred to as "fire water".

LEFT: hanging out at Sandals.
BELOW: sugar is still an important crop.

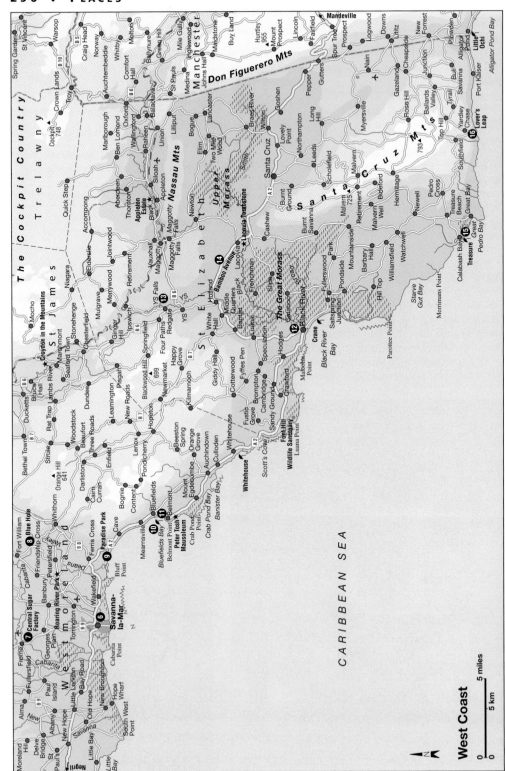

you can swim in a blue hole and sleep in well-kept cabins. Don't miss the Ital Herbs and Spices Farm next door with delightful cottages for rent, camping and swimming. About 8 km (5 miles) east of Sav-la-Mar, at **Ferris Cross**, is **Paradise Park ❾**, a 800-hectare (2,000-acre) 18th-century plantation. Book in advance, and take a tour on horseback through the cattle ranch, tropical farm and bird-rich woodland to the ravishing turquoise-coloured Bluefields Bay.

Map on page 296

The inland route

Ferris Cross is the junction of Route B8 to Montego Bay and also the starting point for an interesting inland tour. At the hamlet of **Whithorn** turn right (east) toward **Darliston**. The winding 8-km (5-mile) climb up **Frame Hill** offers grand views across the sugar plains. Darliston itself is a tobacco-growing centre where cheap local cigars are a popular purchase.

At **Struie** is a roadside landmark called the **Soldier Stone**. The inscription is almost illegible, but local folklore tells of an infantryman named Obediah Bell Chambers who rode out on muleback to do battle with rebellious slaves and had his head severed. Struie residents returning from market at night often claim to hear the clash of steel as they pass the Soldier Stone.

After passing through another village, with the unlikely name of **Rat Trap**, you'll enter **Seaford Town**, the island's best-known community of people of German descent. In fact, although many of the residents have fair skin, blue eyes and German surnames, they have disappointingly preserved virtually no other traces of their European language or culture. Instead, this is a sadly inbred group. Seaford Town was founded in 1835 by peasant farmers from northern Germany. Its economy depended at first on sugar cultivation, and later on

BELOW: Seaford Town inhabitants.

bananas. As late as the 1960s the population was close to 500; today it is nearer 200, and many have emigrated to Canada. East of Seaford Town, Route B6 runs north to Montego Bay.

Buccaneers and fishermen

The tour now returns to Ferris Cross and follows Route A2 down the south coast to **Bluefields Bay ⑩**. It was from this wide curving bay, today popular as a swimming area, that Henry Morgan sailed in 1670 to sack Panama. No remains have been found, but this is believed to have been the site of the early Spanish settlement of Oristano. Captain Bligh may have anchored his *Providence* in the bay in 1793. At **Bluefields House**, near the Bluefields police station, naturalist Philip Henry Gosse gathered materials for two classic reference books: *Birds of Jamaica* and *A Naturalist's Sojourn in Jamaica*. He lived here for 18 months in 1844 and 1845. A breadfruit tree on the lawn of the house is reputed to be the oldest in Jamaica.

In the hills above Bluefields – with the most breathtaking views of sunsets in the bay – stands **Shafston Great House**, a guesthouse run by Frank Lohmann.

Belmont ⑪ is a small hamlet where only a few tourists stop to visit the grave of Peter Tosh (Peter MacIntosh), close to the house which was his childhood home. Tosh (1944-1987), an acclaimed reggae musician, had a successful career with Bob Marley and the Wailers; he also produced several landmark solo albums. The area is also a good place to buy fresh fish, which is sold by roadside vendors here and further south, in Scott's Cove at the border with St Elizabeth; their speciality is "fry fish and bammy".

Auchindown Farm has its entrance on Route A2 just above Banister Bay. A

Reggae fans gather on 19 October to honour the birthday of Peter Tosh.

BELOW: the Parish Church of St John the Evangelist, Black River.

CROCS AND 'GATORS

Whether the Taino Indians had a crocodile god like the old Egyptians we do not know, but from the rock paintings and pre-Spanish clay figures unearthed today we know that the now near-extinct creatures were a common feature in the life of the early Jamaicans. They were hunted for their tasty meat in colonial times, and later slaughtered because of fear and superstition.

Village names like Alligator Pond or Alligator Hole are, however, misleading, because it was the crocodile and not the alligator which was once widespread in the estuaries and coastal mangrove swamps all around the island. It is the protruding fourth tooth of the lower jaw visible when the mouth is closed that distinguishes the native American Crocodile from the alligator.

Crocodiles can grow to an enormous size – animals more than 4 metres (13 ft) long have been spotted – and hunt for food at night in the form of fish and small animals. The largest colony of crocodiles (*crocodylus acutus*, also *c. americanus*) survives in the Black River Great Morass, with rare sightings at the mouth of the Milk River or at the Font Hill Reserve near Whitehouse. The best time to see an ancient crocodile is in the morning hours when, out of the water, they bask in the sun.

working pimento property, its grounds include a ruined castle which rumour says was built to house the deposed Emperor Napoleon. That claim is disputed. The castle was certainly built early in the 19th century by Archibald Campbell, a descendant of the noted Scottish Clan Campbell of Argyll. An underground passage running to Orange Grove may have been used by smugglers.

The main road passes through **Whitehouse** village, where most of the north-coast hotels get their supplies of seafood. Every morning, weather permitting, local fishermen sell their previous night's catch on the beach.

At **Black River ⓬** you enter the first sizeable town since Savanna-la-Mar. The capital of St Elizabeth, it is nevertheless a sleepy settlement strung along the shore of Black River Bay at the river's mouth. Many Georgian-style buildings remain from days long past when logwood and fustic – both dye-producing trees – and the ubiquitous sugar gave a strong base to the local economy. Among the architectural remnants are **Invercauld** Great House and **Waterloo Guest House**. The typical wooden structure and delicate fretwork are well maintained.

Around the turn of the 20th century Black River was a bustling port. In 1893 it became the first community on the island to have electric light, generated and sold by two local merchants, the Leyden brothers, and in 1903 there were already motor cars being driven on its streets. The **Parish Church of St John the Evangelist** was founded in 1837.

The Black River itself is the longest river in Jamaica, following a winding course of 71 km (44 miles) from the mountains of southern Trelawny parish. There is good fishing for both freshwater and sea fish on a stretch of water about a mile from the river mouth. Much of the Black River's lower course takes it through the Great Morass, a huge freshwater swamp that constitutes

Map on page 296

Waterloo Guest House claims to be the first house in Jamaica to have had electricity installed.

BELOW: "gingerbread" architecture in Black River.

the largest remaining crocodile refuge in Jamaica. Slaughter by sportsmen and farmers has reduced the crocodile population to a fraction of what it once was. Some of the crocodiles still living in the river are estimated to be about 150 years old; they can grow up to 4 metres (13 ft) long, but don't appear so ferocious when you discover that they have names like George, Margaret and Keisha. Several boat companies, including **Black River Safari** (daily from 9am; tel: 965 2513), offer 1½–2-hour guided tours of the river and its flora and fauna.

At the upper end of the Morass, 13 km (8 miles) from Black River, is the little village of **Middle Quarters**. If you stop your vehicle here you'll be set upon by women vendors urging you to try the savoury local shrimp. Hot and peppery, these morsels should be taken with some harddough bread and a bottle of beer lest the unsuspecting visitor's throat be set on fire.

Close to where Route A2 crosses the oddly labelled **YS River** (whose name may have been adapted from the Welsh word *wyess*, "winding"), the **Holland Estate** and sugar factory stand just off the roadside. This small mill, no longer in operation, was once owned by John Gladstone, the father of the famous Victorian prime minister of the United Kingdom who made his fortune in the colonies, trading out of Liverpool. At Holland a dirt road on the left leads to the starting-point of a bumpy tractor-drawn jitney (open carriage) ride to the spectacular **YS Falls** ⓭ (open Tues–Sun; entrance fee; tel: 997 6055). There are landscaped picnic grounds, a giant treehouse and stairs cut into the path leading to several levels of the falls. Lifeguards, who will help guide you onto the rocks and onto a rope for swinging out over the water, are stationed at all the swimming holes. The falls are on a 9,000-hectare (23,000-acre) working farm, where beef cattle and race-horses are raised along with pumpkins and other crops.

A 5-km (3-mile) stretch of road between the Holland Estate and Lacovia is known as **Bamboo Avenue** ⓮ and is one of the most-photographed locations in Jamaica. It is easy to see why it is so well known and loved. Entering the avenue is like walking into a giant cathedral whose nave disappears in the distance. Bamboo was planted on both sides of the road in the 19th century by local landowners who appreciated the shade as they travelled the road. The Hope Royal Botanical Gardens now maintain the bamboo, assisted by local people who are swift to raise the alarm if anyone is discovered interfering with the plants.

At the eastern end of Bamboo Avenue is **Lacovia**, one of the longest villages in Jamaica. Divided into West Lacovia, East Lacovia and Lacovia Tombstone, it sprawls along Route A2 for some 2 miles (3 km) on either side of the Black River bridge. Originally a Jewish settlement, it was an inland port for the shipping downriver of sugar, logwood and fustic .

Logwood and fustic dyes were so important in the days before the development of synthetic dyes that even the ermine robes of British peers were stained in logwood. Although Jamaica's dye factories closed down in the 1950s, recent discoveries indicate that natural dyes are in fact brighter and longer lasting than synthetic ones. Today Lacovia is a centre for growing cashew nuts.

Lacovia Tombstone is so named for two tombs in

Try the spicy, peppery shrimp before you buy from roadside vendors in Middle Quarters.

BELOW:
spectacular YS Falls.

the middle of the road. Beneath are the bones of two young men, one of them just 15, who died following a tavern brawl in 1723.

A short detour south of Lacovia as you travel away from Bamboo Avenue is the **Cashoo Ostrich Park** (open Tues–Sun 10am–4.30pm; entrance fee; tel: 961 1960). This working ostrich farm has guided tours by jitney and includes a nature walk through a tropical fruit orchard and a herb garden. Discover herbal remedies said to cure a host of modern ailments.

Return to Lacovia Tombstone, which is the junction for a road leading inland to **Maggotty**, where it connects with Route B6. Cecil Baugh, one of Jamaica's leading pottery artisans, maintains his workshop in Maggotty, a 11-km (7-mile) excursion. Just further along, in Siloah, try Apple Valley Nature Park for fishing, hiking, canoeing and camping.

Reynolds Jamaica Mines established its **Revere Works** bauxite operation – now closed – a short distance north of Maggotty. From there is a road heading north to the Maroon village of Accompong in the Cockpit Country. Route B6 heads west to Seaford Town and east through Appleton and Siloah to Mandeville.

Rum and ganja

Appleton is best known as the home of Wray and Nephew, Jamaica's famous and popular rum. The **Appleton Sugar Factory and Distillery** is picturesquely located alongside the Black River in a lovely green valley, surrounded by canefields and framed by mountains. It was founded in the 19th century by a former St Ann wheelwright named John Wray, who acquired his plantation after perfecting his blend of rum in a small shop on a site next to Kingston's Ward Theatre.

Route A2, meanwhile, proceeds through Lacovia to **Santa Cruz**, St Elizabeth's

Map on page 296

Cashoo Ostrich Park has a petting area for young visitors which includes goats and young ostriches.

BELOW: riding down Bamboo Avenue.

Map on page 296

Authentic Jamaican cuisine on the south coast.

BELOW:
storm clouds over Lovers' Leap.
RIGHT: stop by Middle Quarters for peppered shrimp.

bustling market centre. Traditionally an area of horses and livestock, Santa Cruz once provided mules for all the British Army's garrison troops as well as for parish councils and public works departments throughout the island. **Gilnock Hall**, just outside the town, still has a polo field in use. Next to the hall is **St Andrew's Church**, an Anglican house of worship built in the 1840s by Duncan Robertson, chief of the Scottish Clan Robertson of Struan.

The **Braes River**, **Elim** and **Barton Isles** districts northeast of Santa Cruz are noted for their prolific ganja farms. Rice and cattle farming, for beef and for dairy products, are more legitimate economic mainstays.

It is another 11 km (7 miles) on Route A2 from Wilton to Gutters at the Middlesex county line, and another 22 km (14 miles) into Mandeville. At **Goshen** the Ministry of Agriculture has established a **Dairy Industry Training Centre**. In addition to dairy cattle, a special ovine breed known as the St Elizabeth Sheep has been developed here. It lambs twice a year, and its coat is too hairy to be called wool and too woolly to be hair.

South-coast paradise

The south coast of the island has retained a relaxed, undiscovered atmosphere with its rambling main road, side tracks to beach and bay, and plethora of cottages to rent, perfect for backpackers, coastal walkers and families. It is precisely this unspoilt quality that attracts visitors, and those looking for something special would be strongly advised to head for **Treasure Beach ⓫** (a generic name for the area) with its rustic fishing bays – **Great Bay**, **Calabash Bay**, **Frenchman's Bay** – unspoilt beaches, magnificent landscape and charming people, some of German origin. Explore the coast by sea – the fishermen are keen to earn extra cash and offer a variety of long or short trips. Swimming can be dangerous owing to localised sea currents, so take care: there are no lifeguards.

A great place to stop for an authentic meal or spend a few quiet days is **Jake's**, run by Jason and Sally Henzell. The rooms are beautiful, all individually designed, charming and relaxing – no satellite TV here. **Treasure Beach Hotel** offers the more conventional comforts of a holiday hotel on the beach, without watersports or evening entertainment.

This out-of-the-way area is a great spot for a relaxed holiday, quite a contrast to the approach of the all-inclusives of the north coast. Approach either from Black River via the coastal road or from the north – the route from Santa Cruz is an extremely picturesque one. It first winds uphill to **Malvern**, an old resort town which sits 730 metres (2,400 ft) up in the Santa Cruz Mountains. The climate is cool – seldom exceeding 27°C (80°F) – and dry. Today it is a quiet village whose continued existence is due largely to the three fine schools located within a few kilometres of one another along the ridge.

About 16 km (10 miles) to the south of Malvern is **Lovers' Leap ⓬**. This beautiful viewpoint – with a lighthouse – is a 490-metre (1,600-ft) cliff that drops dramatically to the sea. Legend has it that two lovers jumped to their deaths from here rather than face continued slavery and separation. ❏

SPANISH TOWN AND THE SOUTHWEST

*From the historical first capital of the Spanish colonists,
to the cool mountainous south-western interior,
to the land splashed red from bauxite and rich with agriculture*

The southern half of Middlesex County is a land of enormous variety. Sites of great historical importance – including Spanish Town, Jamaica's original capital, and caves once inhabited by the Taino Indians (previously called Arawaks) – are part of a landscape that encompasses bauxite-filled plateau country, rolling green "English" hills and undeveloped coastal grasslands.

Most visitors are introduced to the region at **Spanish Town ❶**, 23 km (14 miles) west of Kingston on Route A1. The approach leads across the **Ferry River**, which until the early 20th century was still important as the last staging-post for horses and carriages travelling from Kingston to the west of the island. Planned by a son of Christopher Columbus, Spanish Town was the colonial capital from the early 1520s to 1872.

Five kilometres (3 miles) outside Spanish Town is the **Taino Museum** (formerly the White Marl Arawak Museum; closed for refurbishment). Located on the site of a large Taino village, the building is said to be a replica of a Taino hut. Important archaeological finds were made here. Further on the main highway passes **Iron Bridge ❷**, regarded as a national monument. Indeed, this span over the Rio Cobre, while no longer in use, is the oldest surviving cast-iron bridge in this hemisphere. There are plans to restore it.

From the time of its founding by the Spanish, in 1523, until the British moved the capital to Kingston in 1872, Spanish Town was the seat of Jamaican government. The Spaniards called it Villa de la Vega, "the town on the plain", and also St Jago, in honour of St James of Compostela, the patron saint of Spain. The English (after their 1655 conquest) kept the name St Jago for a while, but gradually people simply began to call it Spanish Town, even though all its Spanish buildings had disappeared by the 18th century.

In the centre of Spanish Town is the **Square**, surrounded on all sides by Georgian-style buildings constructed during the heyday of sugar. Many of the once wonderful buildings have fallen into disrepair, and there is little else to see here, so if you do pass this way it is worth only a brief stop. On the east side is the **Parish Council Office**, formerly the House of Assembly. Built in 1762, it is notable for the superb brickwork of its long, shady colonnade and the pillared wooden balcony above. Opposite, on the west side of the square, are the remains of **King's House**, also dating from 1762. Slave emancipation was proclaimed from the steps of the building, which was gutted by fire in 1925; only the grand portico and façade remain. There is also an archaeological museum.

PRECEDING PAGES: a quiet south-coast beach. **LEFT:** the Rodney Memorial, Spanish Town. **BELOW:** Iron Bridge.

Admiral George Rodney.

Also in the King's House building is the **Jamaican People's Museum of Craft and Technology** (closed for refurbishment), which is located in the adjacent former stables. Its collection features relics from years past – everything from home furnishings to a village store.

On the south side of the square stand the ruins of the **old court house**. Built in 1819, it attracted a vociferous throng of defendants, witnesses and onlookers outside its doors when court was in session. The upper floors contained the **Town Hall**, where concerts, plays and other public entertainments were held.

The **Rodney Memorial**, at the north end of the square, was sculpted in Italian marble by the noted English artist John Bacon. It was erected in the late 18th century as a token of gratitude to Admiral George Rodney for saving the West Indies from French domination with his famous victory at sea over the Comte de Grasse in 1782. Rodney is depicted in the dress of a Roman emperor, which was the artistic convention of the day. The statue is missing a hand and has a few chips, the result of a feud between the residents of Spanish Town and Kingston. When it was removed to Kingston along with the island's administration, the Spanish Town citizens were outraged and went to reclaim the statue. It has remained in Spanish Town ever since.

Behind Rodney's statue is the **Archives Office**, where many historical documents are kept, and the **Records Office**, where legal records for the entire nation are stored, from birth certificates and wills to title-deeds. Among the old records still on hand is the last will and testament of Sir Henry Morgan, the 17th-century buccaneer-turned-governor. Under the auspices of the Institute of Jamaica Museums Division, the Rodney Memorial buildings will also house a **Museum of Spanish Town**.

BELOW: Rio Cobre, circa 1800.

A short five-block walk back in the direction of Kingston on White Church Street will take you to the **Cathedral Church of St James**, also known as the Cathedral of St Jago de la Vega. Constructed in 1523, this small house of worship was the first cathedral to be built in the New World. The British replaced it in 1666, and the current structure was raised in 1714 after a hurricane destroyed the original.

The cathedral church is built of brick, in the form of a cross, and the wooden steeple was added in 1831. In and around it are tombs and memorials to 17th-century settlers and notables of later centuries. Since 1843 it has been the Cathedral of the Jamaica Diocese of the Church of England.

Further on from the Cathedral is St Catherine district prison, a grim, grey-walled high-security facility. Although there are several penal institutions on the island, this is the only one to hold prisoners on death row, and it is where executions are carried out.

A worthwhile detour from Spanish Town is to the **Mountain Valley Cave ❸** (known locally as Cudjoe Cave). The cave and its contents were discovered in 1897. It is a tricky place to find; it is about 13 km (8 miles) northwest of town, and is a good place to see some rare and ancient Taino rock and cave drawings. Take a left turn off the Spanish Town bypass and follow the signs to Friendship on the western ringroad; continue on towards **Kitson Town** and pass **Guanaboa Vale**, where you should turn left at the village and travel up **Cudjoe's Hill** for about half a mile.

From Spanish Town to Bog Walk the road follows the Rio Cobre river to **Flat Bridge**, a Spanish relic set just a few feet above water level between towering vertical walls of limestone. Heavy rains frequently make this bridge impassable.

Map on page 310

Stained glass at the Cathedral.

BELOW: majestic organ pipes in the Cathedral Church of St James.

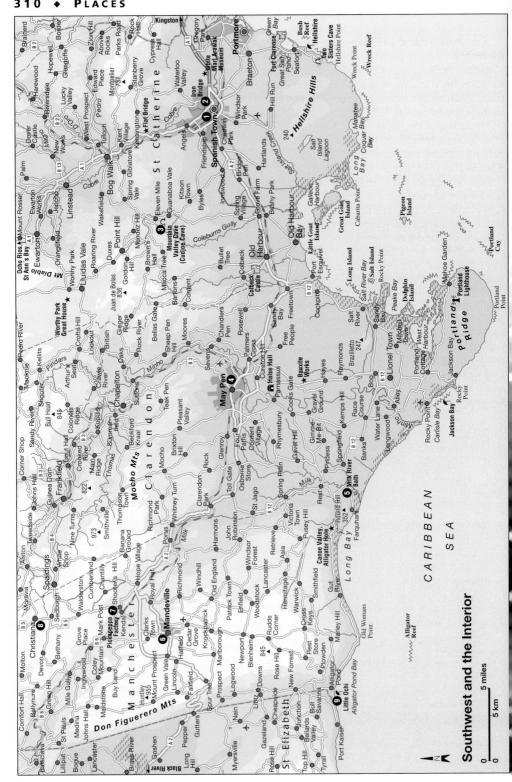

Southwest and the Interior

A high-water mark of 1933 is indicated on the rock face, 8 metres (25 ft) above the bridge.

At the roundabout the left fork leads to **Bog Walk**, on the main A1 highway between Spanish Town and St Ann's Bay. Bog Walk is one of the oldest settlements in Jamaica; it was a rest-stop for cattle wagons carrying hogsheads of sugar from nearby estates to ships waiting at Passage Fort. Today, Bog Walk is a railway junction and the site of a milk-condensing plant, sugar factory and citrus-packing plant.

North of Bog Walk, the A1 continues through the town of **Linstead**, whose market (beneath the little square clock tower) is the subject of a famous folk song (*see page 188*). Eleven kilometres (7 miles) further on is **Ewarton**. Alcan has a major alumina factory here; bauxite is supplied by ropeway from a mining area 10 km (6 miles) north, processed, then shipped to Port Esquivel.

Route A2 begins in Spanish Town and continues west through Mandeville to Savanna-la-Mar. Nineteen kilometres (12 miles) from Spanish Town down this route is **Old Harbour**, best known for its iron Victorian clock tower. Such towers can be found all over the island, having been constructed mainly between 1890 and 1930. This one is unusual: it has been maintained in excellent condition, and usually keeps accurate time.

Colbeck Castle is located 3 km (2 miles) north of Old Harbour on a side road. Once perhaps the largest building in the Caribbean, it is generally thought to have been built in the late 17th century by an English settler named Colonel John Colbeck, as protection against Maroon attacks and possible invasion by the French. The main walls of this huge brick mansion are still erect, although the roof and floors are gone. Beam slots in the higher walls give an idea of the size

Map on page 310

For a close look at the Taino cave drawings at the Mountain Valley Cave you will need to contact one of the guides who live in the houses near the cave sign at the top of Cudjoe's Hill. The cave entrance is protected by bars and a door, and the guides have a key.

BELOW: the ruin of Colbeck Castle.

Goats are a common sight in rural Jamaica.

of the timbers which were used in construction. Four underground slave quarters can be seen at each corner of the castle. The building is in the midst of what is now a large tobacco farm.

A short distance west of Old Harbour on the A2 is the **Bodles Agricultural Station**, where some of Jamaica's finest dairy cattle are bred. The Jamaica Hope, the world's first tropically adapted dairy cow, was developed here by Dr T. P. Lecky as a cross between the Jersey and Brahmin breeds. It is particularly hardy and heat-tolerant. Crosses of Holstein and Friesian breeds have also been successful.

Opposite Bodles, beside a railway crossing, is the entrance road to **Port Esquivel**, a deepwater port of the Alcan Jamaican Company. From here, alumina is shipped to smelters in British Columbia and Scandinavia. You can visit the port by calling the firm's Kingston office in advance; they will arrange to have a pass waiting for you at the gate.

In Old Harbour Bay, beyond Port Esquivel, lie the two **Goat Islands**. Great Goat Island was an American naval base during World War II (1939–45). Some of the old fortifications, barracks and ammunition stores can still be seen here, although now the island is used only by occasional fishermen. Further down the coast, in Vere, is the site of another former US base, Fort Symonds, now known as **Vernam Field**.

Crocodiles and sugar

At **Freetown**, Route B12 branches south towards Lionel Town and Milk River. The road first passes through mangrove swamps, once a refuge for Jamaica's crocodile population, then enters **Salt River**. This was once a major port for shipping sugar, despite its lack of deep-water facilities. The estates on the

BELOW: dangerous territory for goats.

GOATS
WILL BE SHOT
BY ORDER
THE MANAGEMENT.

MOUNTAIN VALLEY CAVE

Among all the Antillean caves, no other is believed to have so many Taino drawings; 150 cover the walls and ceiling of the small cave northwest of Spanish Town, locally known as Cudjoe Cave, discovered in 1897. Archaeologists estimate the age of the paintings to be between 500 and 1,300 years.

The Tainos used ground charcoal mixed with animal fat to depict turtles, iguanas, crocodiles, frogs and waterfowl in a style likened to the modern abstract artists. There are also drawings of people hunting with spears, and ornaments like spirals decorating the cave high above the lush valley. The cave is quite a distance from the known pre-Hispanic Indian settlements which dotted the shores of the sea and banks of estuaries, and it has been suggested that this secluded place might have been a ritual gathering-place where *caciques* or hunters worshipped a god with sacrifices. There are no indications that the area was used as a burial ground.

The cave is not easy to reach, but with perseverance the trip may prove worthwhile. Local guides live in the houses near the sign directing visitors to the cave. They are usually happy, when asked, to open the cave entrance, which is protected by bars and a door.

surrounding plains of Vere can still be seen, although many have amalgamated under the influence of Tate and Lyle and its Jamaican subsidiary, the West Indies Sugar Company (Wisco).

A small road leads south to **Rocky Point**, a scattered fishing village on a quiet part of the coast. North of this hamlet is the town of **Alley**, with its sugar factory windmill-turned-library and its 18th-century St Peter's Church, surrounded by old tombstones and huge *kapok* (silk-cotton) trees.

May Pen ❹, the halfway point between Spanish Town and Mandeville, is the market centre for Clarendon, Jamaica's largest parish. Friday and Saturday are market days; May Pen's downtown area becomes colourful, crowded and chaotic. The Clarendon capital, along with the parish church and hospital, is actually at Chapelton, north of here, but May Pen is really far more active commercially. The famous Trout Hall citrus products are canned here, under the direction of the Sharpe family, developers of the *ugli* fruit.

A visit to **Trout Hall** and its surrounding citrus orchards, north of Chapelton, is very rewarding. Let the Sharpes know of your planned visit by telephoning the May Pen or Kingston office of the Citrus Company of Jamaica, then head north on B3 out of May Pen. After passing through the old sugar capital of **Chapelton**, now notable chiefly for its war-memorial clock tower, parish church and hospital, you'll travel up the Rio Minho valley. The citrus plantation is located at the junction of routes B3 and B4.

From Trout Hall you can continue north to Runaway Bay and its hotel resort strip, passing en route through **Cave Valley**, site of a Saturday-morning donkey, mule and horse market, or you can proceed west through Frankfield and Guinea Corn to the town of **Spaldings**.

Map on page 310

TIP

Some parts of the route from Freetown through Lionel Town to Rocky Point can be unsavoury and unsafe at times, so be alert if you choose to travel this stretch unaccompanied.

BELOW: Milk River.

On the boundary of Clarendon and Manchester parishes, Spaldings is famous for its co-educational **Knox College**, founded in 1947 by the Church of Scotland and the Presbyterian Church of Jamaica. Based on the progressive concept that education must extend beyond the classroom, this boarding school offers a wide curriculum of academic subjects; a printing works, a farm and a meat-processing plant make it almost self-sufficient.

Spaldings sits at about 900 metres (3,000 ft) elevation, so it has a cool climate year-round. The ginger grown in this region is said to be the best in the world.

Back on Route A2, a few miles west of May Pen are the **Denbigh Agricultural Show Grounds**. The island's biggest show is held here annually over the long Independence Day weekend in early August. Just south of May Pen is the **Halse Hall** alumina plant, owned by Alcoa Minerals of Jamaica. It takes its name from the Halse Hall Great House, the focal point of the company's operations, and the house has been beautifully restored. Contact Alcoa's Kingston office ahead of time if you wish to visit.

At Toll Gate, 13 km (8 miles) west of May Pen, Route B12 branches south toward Milk River. **Milk River Bath** ❺, not far from the river's mouth, is the island's leading spa. The spring waters here, known since the 17th century, are the most radioactive on earth: three times more than Karlovy Vary (Karlsbad) in the Czech Republic, and 50 times more than Vichy in France. The minerals in the water are said to have curative powers for those suffering from gout, sciatica, lumbago, rheumatism, neuralgia, eczema, and liver and kidney complaints. The baths at the Milk River Bath Hotel can also be used by non-residents, and this is an ideal way to spend a day.

Beyond Toll Gate, Route A2 crosses the Manchester parish line and enters

BELOW: the water at Milk River Bath is said to have curative powers.

Porus, a thriving market town for citrus, coffee and other cash crops of the region. Leave this mini-metropolis via **Melrose Hill**, which climbs more than 600 metres (2,000 ft) in 8 km (5 miles); you can stop to admire the view from roadside shops which sell delicious roast corn and yams to weary travellers.

Map on page 310

Jamaica's "Last Resort"

A new highway winds into clean, cool **Mandeville ❻** town, cradled in a hollow at about 610 metres (2,000 ft) elevation. Often called "the most English town in Jamaica", it has a resident population heavy in North Americans employed in the bauxite industry, and also Jamaicans returning from abroad. It is a busy and bustling place with lots of shops, street vendors and traffic congestion. The roads in and out of the town link the east and west of the island and Kingston with the north coast, so the bus terminus here is always buzzing with activity.

Mandeville is the capital of the parish of Manchester, created in 1814 from pieces of other parishes. The parish was named after the Jamaican governor, the Duke of Manchester, and the town after the duke's heir, the Earl of Mandeville. Mandeville's pleasant climate (around 20°C/70°F in the summer, 16°C/60°F in the winter) appealed to many English colonialists, who came to think of it as their "last resort". But while some retired here, many more stayed only long enough to make their fortunes in coffee and pimento before heading home.

There are few points of particular interest in Mandeville itself. The Georgian court house and stone parish church were built around the central green soon after the town was founded. The oldest golf course on the island, the nine-hole **Manchester Club**, is half a mile from the town centre. The major hotels include the Mandeville, built on the site of the 18th-century British garrison's hillstation

BELOW: the peaceful south coast.

THE RETURNEES

In the 1950s the first substantial exodus of Jamaicans from the island since the Panama Canal project occurred. They left in search of work and a better life. Most migrants left for the UK, Canada and the USA, intending to stay only a few years, but in fact they stayed much longer and actually ended up living longer off than on the island.

Even after 30 or 40 years away some migrants still dream of returning "home". The Jamaican government estimates that more than 10,000 people have returned to settle permanently since 1993; some are retirement age, but others are younger and bring with them skills and valuable foreign currency.

Returning residents, as they are known, tend to make their home in the places where they grew up and have family ties, or in the quiet country areas. The cooler mountain temperature of Mandeville and the surrounding hill areas in the parish of Manchester have made it an attractive place to settle for those who are no longer accustomed to the heat after decades in North America or Europe. Today the largest numbers of migrants are returning from the UK; in 1996–98 Jamaica welcomed 5,882 from the UK, 5,232 from the USA, 1,650 from Canada and 770 from the rest of the world.

barracks, and the Hotel Astra. Nearby is **Marshall's Pen**, an 18th-century great house set on a 120-hectare (300-acre) working cattle farm. Visitors are not encouraged, although a handful of ardent birdwatchers are sometimes accommodated. There are no signposts to guide you, and access to the land is by a private single-track road only.

The countryside around Mandeville is rich in citrus fruits, particularly oranges and tangerines, grown on small farms by independent cultivators. An odd but tasty fruit called the "ortanique", a unique natural cross of the orange and tangerine, was discovered here and propagated by Charles Jackson.

The mining of bauxite

Jamaica is the world's largest producer of bauxite, and a visit to a mining operation and alumina factory should be included on any itinerary. Most hotels can arrange tours, or permission can be obtained from head offices in major towns.

Perhaps the most easily reached operation is Alcan's **Kirkvine Works**, just off the new highway on the northeast approach to Mandeville. You can't miss its red bauxite "lake" at the foot of Shooter's Hill. This was Jamaica's first alumina plant (completed in 1957, although mining began in 1952) and is still the country's largest.

Alcan (more properly, the Canadian Aluminum Corporation) is the largest of four multinational firms in Jamaica. The other three are American: Alcoa, Kaiser and Reynolds. Between them they claim well over 10 million tonnes of bauxite annually from Jamaican soil.

Bauxite is an iron-rich mineral containing approximately 50 percent aluminium oxide. Commercially exploitable bauxite lies close to the earth's surface,

Marshall's Pen was the home of Robert L. Sutton, a noted ornithologist and co-author of Birds of Jamaica: A Photographic Field Guide. *His family still live in the great house.*

BELOW: bulldozing the bauxite-rich soil near Mandeville.

Map on page 310

so it is mined in open pits. The ore is then transported to a processing plant, where it is crushed, washed, kiln-dried, powdered, and shipped to another factory for refining into alumina. This product is ultimately smelted into aluminium. Four to six tonnes of bauxite ore will yield a single tonne of aluminium.

Most of the valley northeast of Mandeville belongs to Alcan and bears the scars of the industry. It includes **Shooter's Hill**; at its peak is the tomb of Alexander Woodburn Heron, the original owner of the property. Heron's tomb and an adjacent lookout are preserved by Alcan. On clear days the Blue Mountain Peak, 100 km (60 miles) to the east, is easily seen.

Another attraction at the base of Shooter's Hill is of more interest to gourmets. At the crossroads where routes B4, B5 and B6 converge is the famous **Pickapeppa Factory** ❼ (tel: 962 2928; tours by appointment only). This sauce, made from a secret recipe, is sold throughout the world, and is similar to Worcestershire Sauce. Jamaicans insist it is much tastier, and on a short factory tour you can see the mixing procedure for the tomato, onion and spice sauce with its extra-special ingredient. The sauce is not made anywhere else, but you will see it sold in shops and served in many eating-places throughout the island.

As you proceed north on Route B5 the road passes through **Walderston**, founded by a Moravian missionary who bought the land and sold it in parcels to free slaves. None of his descendants remains in the village. The road continues through lovely mountain vegetation to **Christiana** ❽, a trading centre for ginger, bananas, Irish potatoes and other hill-country crops. It is known as "cool, cool Christiana" because the temperature is a welcome relief from the heat of lower ground. The **Villa Bella**, which sits atop the hill, is the only hotel here. It is a simple, peaceful place with good food. When the railway was still in operation the

Pickapeppa Sauce has a secret ingredient.

BELOW: weighing the catch at Alligator Pond.

Map on page 310

The land near Long Bay with its rocks and cacti is reminiscent of Africa.

BELOW: carrying fruit to market.
RIGHT: enjoy the tropical waters.

train used to struggle up the hill, and passengers are reported to have been able to hop on and off and still beat the train to the top. You can return to Mandeville via **Mile Gully**, notable for its lovely early 19th-century church, and **Grove Place**, site of the island's largest livestock-breeding research station.

South to the coast

From Mandeville there is easy access to Jamaica's south coast. Start to the west, via Route A2. At the top of the steep descent of **Spur Tree Hill**, turn into the Alpart (Aluminum Partners of Jamaica) Farm's parking lot and gaze across a 610-metre (2,000-ft) drop into eastern St Elizabeth parish. Directly in front of you are the Malvern Hills. To your right, or north, lie the peat-rich swamps of the Black River, the ganja-rich plains of Elim and the rum-rich Appleton Estate. To your left, or south, is the world's largest open-field bauxite mine, at Nain. While it is an eyesore in the daytime, it turns into a veritable fairyland of lights at night.

The steep descent to appropriately named **Gutters** has seemingly endless hairpin bends, but tiny cookshops selling "curry goat" line the route, providing energy to continue. Turn south at Gutters and proceed through Downs to **Alligator Pond** on the south coast. (Another route from Mandeville winds through Newport, Rudds Corner and Plowden Hill to Alligator Pond.)

Alligator Pond is a quiet fishing village outside the influence of the tourist industry. The early-morning fish market attracts mainly local people, and the proliferation of bars caters primarily for fishermen. Accommodation is limited to a few small cottages. One big plus in the area is **Little Ochi ❾**, a tiny golden-sand beach area with seating and shade. It comes alive at the weekend and is popular with picnickers and day-trippers. A snack shack on the beach has fresh seafood, cooked while you wait, but expect a long wait if it's busy. The water here is clear and refreshing.

A 29-km (18-mile) dirt road follows the Long Bay coastline through Gut River to Milk River. The final portion of the route is almost impassable without a four-wheel-drive vehicle. Vegetation along the rutted road changes from tall grass and palms to treeless rocks and cacti, and it seems more like Africa than the Caribbean. But the ancient Tainos must have found the terrain hospitable, for numerous artefacts and rock carvings have been found here. The road passes close to **God's Well**, a 50-metre (160-ft)-deep limestone sinkhole with clear turquoise water. It was named by a man who claimed to have been cured of a terminal illness by bathing in its waters.

The chief attraction of this coastline is the colony of manatees which make it their home. At **Canoe Valley** local conservationists will meet your car and guide you to a lookout. The manatee, sometimes called "sea cow", is a sluggish marine vegetarian that frequents shallow coastal waters and estuaries. Adults range from 3 to 5 metres (9 to 15 ft) in length, and attain weights up to 680 kg (1,500 lbs). Once common throughout the Caribbean, this seal-like mammal has been hunted for its meat, hide and fat until it has become rare. You may be lucky enough to see a family of manatees. They neither see nor hear well, so they communicate primarily by nuzzling one another. ❏

INSIGHT GUIDES
TRAVEL TIPS

Simply travelling safely

American Express Travellers Cheques

- are recognised as one of the safest and most convenient ways to protect your money when travelling abroad

- are more widely accepted than any other travellers cheque brand

- are available in eleven currencies

- are supported by a 24 hour worldwide refund service and

- a 24 hour Express Helpline service provides assistance and information when travelling abroad

- are accepted in millions of shops, hotels and restaurants throughout the world

Travellers Cheques

CONTENTS

Getting Acquainted

Area: 10,992 sq. km
(4,244 sq. miles)
Situation: 145 km (90 miles) south
of Cuba and 161 km (100 miles)
west of Haiti
Capital: Kingston
Highest mountain: the Blue
Mountain Peak (2,256 metres/
7,402 ft)
Population: 2.6 million
Language: English, Jamaican patois
Religion: 60 percent Protestant
Christian, 12 percent Roman
Catholic, 18 percent non-religious
and 10 percent other religions
Time zone: Eastern Standard Time,
five hours behind GMT, one hour
behind the Eastern Caribbean
Currency: Jamaican dollar (J$)
(the US dollar (US$) is widely
accepted, with change given in J$)
Electricity: 110 volts/50 cycles
(220 volts also available)
International dialling code: 876

Climate

So many North Americans and
Europeans winter in Jamaica
because there is no winter. The
average temperatures along the
coast and plains range between
27°C and 32°C (80°F and 90°F)
year-round. It's cooler in the hills,
dropping to about 20°C–25°C
(70s and the high 60s°F), while at
the top of the Blue Mountain Peak
temperatures have been known to
drop below 10°C (50°F) on rare
occasions. The coolest months are
November to April.

The rainiest times are May to
June and September to October.
Rain averages 196 cm (77 inches)
annually, although some parts of
the island, notably Portland, can get
three times that amount.

There is a substantial variance
between daytime and night-time
temperatures. Day breezes blow off
the sea to cool the land; night
breezes come in from the mountains,
making conditions a bit chillier.

HURRICANES

When hurricanes are talked about
in Jamaica, people recite a jingle:
June too soon. July stand by.
August prepare you must.
September remember.
October all over.

August is certainly the worst
month for these tropical storms,
but officially the hurricane season
begins on 1 June and continues
into October. Throughout this period
you must be prepared for the
possibility of a hurricane.

The most devastating hurricane
to strike Jamaica this century was
Hurricane Gilbert on 12 September
1988. Gilbert ravaged the entire
island, but saved its worst blows for
Kingston and the eastern parishes.
The banana, coconut, coffee and
chicken industries were damaged to
the tune of millions of dollars.
Before Gilbert, Hurricane Charlie
had scored a direct hit on the island
in 1951, claiming 150 lives and
wreaking the worst damage in
Kingston and Port Royal. Jamaica
was thankful to have been spared a
direct hit from Allen, which crossed
the eastern tip of the island in
1980 with winds of 282 km (175
miles) per hour.

The number of hurricanes that
form in a given year has ranged
from two to 20, but most never
swing into Jamaica. Still, the US
National Hurricane Center in Miami,
Florida, tracks each of the massive
storms carefully with sophisticated
radar detection equipment,
satellites and reconnaissance
planes, issuing warnings throughout
the Caribbean. In Jamaica there is
an official emergency relief service.

A hurricane forms when wind
rushes towards a low-pressure area
and takes on a distinctive swirling
motion. The size of such storms
can range from 97 km (60 miles) in
diameter to monsters more than
1,609 km (1,000 miles) wide.
Despite improved technology, their
patterns and routes remain difficult
to predict.

What to Do

Jamaica residents are well-versed
on precautions that should be taken
when a hurricane approaches.
Newspapers and magazines publish
special sections on the subject at
the beginning of each season. Most
coastal communities publish
information on evacuation planes
and routes.

Needless to say, tourists caught
in Jamaica during an impending
hurricane should drop plans to work
on suntans and follow official
advice and television directives.
Above all, do not take a hurricane

● **Tropical disturbance:** This
phase in a hurricane's
development has no strong
winds, but it may feature a weak
counter-clockwise circulation of
wind. Disturbances of this sort
are common throughout the
tropics in summer.
● **Tropical depression:** A small
low-pressure system develops,
and the counter-clockwise
rotation of air increases to
speeds up to 63 km (39 miles)
per hour.
● **Tropical storm:** By now the low-
pressure system has developed
winds ranging from 63 to 117 km
(39 to 73 miles) per hour and
can be accompanied by heavy
rains.
● **Hurricane:** The low-pressure
system has intensified to the
point where strong winds of more
than 119 km (74 miles) per hour
rotate in a counter-clockwise
direction around an area of calm
called the "eye". Storm tides
may rise as much as 5 metres
(15 ft) above normal and can
surge by as much as 2 metres (6
ft) in minutes.

warning lightly by inviting friends over for a "hurricane party".

Government

Jamaica is a constitutional monarchy with a governor-general who represents the head of state, the British monarch. A multi-party system operates, with the prime minister leading the Government. The judicial system runs on the British model.

Economy

Jamaica is the world's third largest producer of bauxite. In 1998 bauxite and aluminium accounted for just over 50 percent of merchandise exports from the island. Agriculture contributes less to the GDP but, because of the labour-intensive systems used, employs more people than the bauxite-mining companies. Sugar is the most important crop, followed by bananas, coffee and cocoa. Tourism has become the second largest producer of foreign exchange.

Business Hours

Most offices operate from 8.30am until 4.30pm Monday to Friday, with a few open on Saturday. Banks are open Monday to Thursday 9am–2pm, and Friday 9am–4pm.

Public Holidays

Out of all the holidays celebrated in Jamaica, Christmas and Jamaican Independence Day celebrations rank as the most festive occasions. Holidays when businesses are closed include:

New Year's Day	1 January
Ash Wednesday	variable
Good Friday	variable
Easter Monday	variable
Labour Day	23 May
Emancipation Day	1 August
Independence Day	6 August
National Heroes' Day	third Monday in October
Christmas Day	25 December
Boxing Day	26 December

Planning the Trip

Visas & Passports

A passport is the ideal international calling card, and is strongly recommended even for US and Canadian citizens, who in the past have been known to get by with a birth certificate or voter's registration card, as re-entry into North America without a passport is virtually impossible. All other visitors must show passports and in some cases visas, with the same rules applying to children. Check with the authorities in your own country for specifics.

Anyone arriving from a Western country can usually bypass the health clearance in the airports, but all passengers must stop at the Immigration checkpoint to submit proof of citizenship and flash return tickets. Airport officials also stamp the immigration card you fill in on the plane and ask for your Jamaican address. Save the card: it's required for your departure trip, which must be taken within the next six months. Cruise-ship passengers skip this process under blanket ship clearance.

Customs

There is usually quite a pile-up in the incoming Customs Hall due to Jamaicans travelling with huge mounds of luggage. However, there is a queue for those with one piece only, and if you satisfy the watchful officer's quick once-over you may be merely asked for your completed Customs declaration and waved through. Otherwise you may be subjected to a brief but thorough luggage inspection. Regulations prohibit anyone from bringing

flowers, plants and any uncanned fruit and vegetables, honey, coffee, meats, firearms, explosives and dangerous drugs (including marijuana) into the country.

Simply put, an adult 18 years or over can bring in personal belongings, 50 cigars, 200 cigarettes or a half-pound of tobacco, one litre (or one quart) of alcohol, including wine but excluding rum, 6 fluid ounces of perfume or 12 fluid ounces of toilet water.

It's what you can take out, though, that can become rather complicated. The first thing to remember is that, most questions can be answered by calling Norman Manley International Airport in Kingston, tel: 924 8452, Sir Donald Sangster International Airport in Montego Bay, tel: 952 3124, or Customs House, tel: 922 5140 9. General guidelines for US citizens: allow $600 worth of duty-free goods after a 48-hour stay. If you're worried about overstepping that limit you can mail an unlimited number of gifts worth up to $10 each back to the States – provided that one person doesn't get more than $25 worth in a day. Such gifts cannot include perfume, cigars, cigarettes or liquor.

Jamaica is rabies free and has very stringent rules about pets entering the country. Only animals born and bred in the United Kingdom are allowed entry.

A departure tax is levied on everyone leaving the island. This is subject to change, but is likely to be around US$25.

Health

Tropical diseases like smallpox and yellow fever have been stamped out in Jamaica, and all tap water is chlorinated and filtered by modern methods. But even the strongest constitution might not be ready for the spicy island food, so take along an effective antacid. Also bring plenty of high-factor sunscreen, insect repellent and a mosquito coil. See *Practical Tips* for health precautions once you're there.

Money Matters

You can bring in as much of your own money as you please. The Jamaican government has deregulated the currency market, and it is now possible to use US dollars at all but the tiniest establishments. It is legal to use US dollars in markets, shops and hotels where the sign "Authorised Foreign Exchange Dealer" is displayed. You will get your change back in Jamaican dollars, so carry small-denomination notes. You will get the best exchange rates in the banks, not in shops or markets, but for the convenience of using a familiar currency the difference is minimal.

Otherwise, to make island purchases easier you may wish to exchange your US dollars for Jamaican dollars at one of the banks, hotels or international airports, or at one of the licensed exchange bureaux ("cambios") found in all major towns. Hotels tend to give a poorer rate of exchange, so it's better to go elsewhere. Most banks seem to be familiar with the US dollar, and to some extent the English pound, to the exclusion of other foreign currencies. In any event, credit cards and ATM machines make carrying a lot of cash unnecessary. (Of course, a local ATM machine will give you local currency.)

Most credit cards are accepted, and travellers' cheques can be used throughout the island. In banks you will be asked for identification; your passport or travel document will suffice. Most commercial banks offer cash advances on credit cards. You can also get cash through any Western Union office (toll free: 991 2057).

To report lost or stolen travellers' cheques or credit cards, or request replacement, contact:
American Express: tel: 800 327 1267. Local representatives: Kingston, tel: 929 3077; Montego Bay, tel: 929 2586.
Visa: tel: 800 8722 881 (AT&T operator), then place a collect call to tel: 415 574 7700.

MasterCard: tel: 800 8722 881 (AT&T operator), then place a collect call to tel: 314 275 6690.

BANKS

The main offices of some major banks include:
Bank of Commerce, 121 Harbour Street, Kingston; 59 St James Street, Montego Bay.
Citibank, 63-67 Knutsford Blvd, Kingston.
National Commercial Bank, 77 King Street, Kingston; 41 St James Street, Montego Bay.
Scotiabank Jamaica, Duke & Port Royal streets, Kingston; Sam Sharpe Square, Montego Bay.

Internet Jamaica

There are several web sites relating to Jamaica that are worth trying. They include:

The Gleaner on-line: www.jamaica-gleaner.com
Jamaica Tourist Board: www.jamaicatravel.com
The Jamaica Observer www.jamaicaobserver.com
RJR-Radio Jamaica: www.radiojamaica.com
Mona Informatix Ltd: www.informatix.com.jm
National Library of Jamaica: www.nlj.org.jm
Jamaica Information Service (JIS): www.jis.gov.jm
Jamaica Promotions Corporation (JAMPRO): www.investja.com
Aquarius Records: www.aquariushwt.com
Jamaica carnival: www.jamaicacarnival.com
Jamaica Jazz Festival: www.ochoriosjazz.com

● Many hotels also have web sites and online booking – see *Where to Stay*.
● The *Jamaica Internet Guide* (which is by no means exhaustive) is published by Maverick Media, tel: 905 4217; www.maverickmedia.net.

What to Wear

Lightweight tropical clothing is best throughout the year. A light sweater is suggested for evenings, especially in the winter, or for excursions into the hills. If you're climbing in the Blue Mountains, carry a warmer jacket and wear good walking shoes.

On the beaches you can keep cool and comfortable in swimwear, but don't wear the same minimal cover in the business districts of the cities – particularly not in Kingston. Some hotel restaurants require men to wear jackets and ties for dinner.

Useful Addresses

TOURIST OFFICES

Canada: 1 Eglington Avenue East, Suite 616, Toronto, ONT, M4P 3A1, tel: 416 482 7850; fax: 416 482 1730.
United Kingdom: 1–2 Prince Consort Road, London SW7 2BZ, tel: 0171 224 0505; fax: 0171 224 0551.
In the USA:
Boston: 21 Merchants Row, 5th Floor, Boston, MA, tel: 617 248 5811/2.
Chicago: 500 N. Michigan Avenue, Suite 1030, Chicago, IL 60661, tel: 312 527 1296; fax: 312 527 1472.
Los Angeles: 3440 Wilshire Blvd, Suite 1207, Los Angeles, CA 90010, tel: 213 384 1123; fax: 213 384 1780.
Miami: 1320 South Dixie Highway, Suite 1101, Coral Gables, Fla. 33146, tel: 305 665 0557; fax: 305 666 7239.
This office represents Miami and Latin America.
New York: 801 Second Avenue, 20th floor, New York, NY 10017, tel: 212 856 9727; fax: 212 856 9730.

More colour
for the world.

HDCplus. New perspectives in colour photography.

Probably the <u>most</u> <u>important</u> TRAVEL TIP you will ever receive

Before you travel abroad, make sure that you and your family are protected from diseases that can cause serious health problems.

For instance, you can pick up *hepatitis A* which infects 10 million people worldwide every year (it's not just a disease of poorer countries) simply through consuming contaminated food or water!

What's more, in many countries if you have an accident needing medical treatment, or even dental treatment, you could also be at risk of infection from *hepatitis B* which is 100 times more infectious than AIDS, and can lead to liver cancer.

The good news is, you can be protected by vaccination against these and other serious diseases, such as *typhoid, meningitis* and *yellow fever*.

Travel safely! Check with your doctor at least 8 weeks before you go, to discover whether or not you need protection.

Consult your doctor before you go... not when you return!

SB
SmithKline Beecham
V A C C I N E S

Produced as a service to public health

EMBASSIES & CONSULATES

United Kingdom: Jamaican High Commission, 2 Prince Consort Road, London SW7 2BZ, tel: 0171 823 9911; fax: 0171 589 5154.
USA: 1520 New Hampshire Ave NW, Washington, DC 20008–1210, tel: 202 452 0660; fax: 202 452 0081.

Getting There

BY AIR

Most travellers enter Jamaica through one of the two international airports: **Sir Donald Sangster International Airport**, Montego Bay, or **Norman Manley International Airport**, Kingston. Several international airlines serve the island, including Air Jamaica, and numerous charters from North America and Europe.

At either airport it's common to see Jamaicans loaded down with bulging hand luggage. Why? Because they're bringing in goods from other countries priced considerably more cheaply than their Jamaican counterparts. Visitors, however, should keep their carry-on luggage to a minimum in preparation for the lengthy hike between the plane and the Immigration and Customs checkpoints. And if your plane lands during one of the many waves of passengers that descend on the airports, expect a prolonged wait. At the Montego Bay airport you can pass the time spent waiting for your luggage by calling at the Visitor Services booth or sipping the Jamaican rum offered at the Appleton Rum booth.

Airlines

Air Canada, tel: 1 800 776 3000
Air Jamaica, tel: 1 888 FLY AIRJ; 1 800 523 5585; (Kingston) 929 4661; (Montego Bay) 952 4300
ALM, tel: 1 800 327 7230
American Airlines, tel: 1 800 433 7300; (Kingston) 924 830; (Montego Bay) 952 5950
British Airways, tel: 1 800 247

9297; (Kingston) 929 9020; (Montego Bay) 952 3771
BWIA, tel: 1 800 538 2942
Cayman Airways, tel: 1 800 422 9626; (Kingston) 926 1762
Copa, tel: 1 800 359 2672
Cubana Airlines, tel: (Kingston) 978 3406; (Montego Bay) 952 5629
Lan Chile, tel: 1 800 735 5526
LTU, tel: 1 800 888 0200
Martin Air, tel: (Montego Bay) 952 0116
Northwest Airlines, tel: 1 800 225 2525

Flying Times

Approximate flying times to Montego Bay are:

Atlanta	2 hrs 40 mins
Baltimore	3 hrs
Buenos Aires	10 hrs 30 mins
Frankfurt	13 hrs
London	10 hrs 15 mins
Los Angeles	5 hrs 30 mins
Mexico City	5 hrs 30 mins
Miami	1 hr 25 mins
New Orleans	3 hrs
New York	3 hrs 20 mins
Panama City	1 hr 40 mins
Paris	13 hrs 30 mins
Rome	14 hrs 30 mins
Tokyo	19 hrs
Toronto	4 hrs

BY SEA

The seagoing traveller who prefers a leisurely ride coupled with a short stay can select from several cruise ships which include Jamaica on their itineraries.

Ocho Rios in the middle of the north coast is the most popular port of entry, followed by Montego Bay in the north-west.

The main drawback to taking the sea route is the hassle involved in extending your stay beyond the ship's 1–2-day docking time. Most cruise tickets are sold for round-trip voyages, and you'll probably want to avoid the logistical manoeuvring involved in a change. Ensure your ship stops in Jamaica. Cruise lines that include the island on their schedule are:

From Miami
● Carnival Cruises: *Imagination, Destiny, Paradise, Triumph* – Ocho Rios; *Celebration* – Montego Bay. tel: 800 327 9501.
● Costa Cruises (*Costa Romantica, Costa Victoria*). tel: 800 462 6782.
● Dolphin Cruises (*Sea Breeze, Ocean Breeze*) – Montego Bay. tel: 800 999 4299.
● Norwegian Cruise Line (*Norwegian Sky*) – Ocho Rios. tel: 800 327 7030.
● Royal Caribbean (*Majesty, Splendour, Enchantment*) – Ocho Rios. tel: 800 327 6700.
● Sun Line (*Sun Dreams*) – Montego Bay. tel: 800 468 6400.

From Fort Lauderdale
● Celebrity Cruises (*Century*) – Ocho Rios. Tel: 800 437 3111.
● Princess Cruises (*Sea Princess*) – Ocho Rios. Tel: 800 421 0522.

From New Orleans
● Commodore Cruises (*Enchanted Sea*) – Ocho Rios. Tel: 800 237 5361.

From Tampa
● Holland America (*Veendham, Noordam, Volendam*) – Ocho Rios/Montego Bay. Tel: 800 426 0327.

Holidays with a Mission

WEDDINGS

Always popular as a honeymoon destination, Jamaica also beckons as an idyllic spot for the wedding itself. Visitors can be married just 24 hours after arriving in Jamaica. If you want to get married right away (after the 24-hour residency period) you should apply for your licence beforehand. If not, you can apply for your licence in person at the Ministry of National Security, Block 4, 12 Ocean Blvd, Kingston Mail, Kingston, tel: (876) 922 0089. Office hours: Monday to Thursday 9am–5pm, Friday 9am–4pm.

As well as church ministers, there are non-denominational Marriage Officers who can make all the arrangements, and perform the wedding, for a fee which ranges from US$50 to 250. Most officers will perform weddings at their offices, in their homes or at places chosen by the couples, and are able to provide witnesses for the ceremony.

The following documentation is required for all persons wishing to get married in Jamaica:

● Proof of citizenship
● Certified copy of birth certificate which includes father's name
● Parent's written consent if under 18
● Original certificate of divorce if applicable, or certified copy of death certificate for widow or widower.

Italian nationals celebrating their marriage in Jamaica must notify their embassy, and a certified copy of their marriage certificate must be forwarded to their embassy to be legalised and translated. French Canadians need a notarised translated English copy of all documents

Foreign Investment

The Jamaican Government encourages overseas investments and joint ventures, particularly those with export potential such as agriculture, agro-industries, mining, manufacturing (in the Free Zone) and tourism (hotels and resort cottages). There are liberal tax and non-tax incentives.

Potential foreign investors should obtain information and assistance from the **Jamaica Promotions Corporation** (JAMPRO) at 35 Trafalgar Road, Kingston 10, tel: 929 9450/6; www.investjamaica.com. This is the central agency which expediates the process of registration and assists in problem-solving.

Interested prospective overseas investors may also contact the agency's office in New York, or the Jamaican Trade Commissioners in London, Belgium, Germany, Canada and Trinidad.

and a photocopy of the original French documents. No blood test is required.

Some hotels will make all the arrangements for you. Special package prices include performance of the ceremony, government tax, transportation costs and expenses incurred, plus any other special requests.

Marriage Officers

Kingston: Mr Roy Jones, 4 Gibson Drive, tel: (876) 927 2522; Mr H. Blackwood, 15 Hope Blvd, tel: (876) 927 1124; Mr Aubrey Grant, 94A East Street, tel: (876) 922 2717.
Port Antonio: Rev. Delroy Farr, 25 Mount Oakley Road, P.O. Box 229, tel: (876) 933 3369.
Negril: Rev. Winston Barrett, c/o United Church of Jamaica & Grand Cayman, tel: (876) 955 2753; Mr Joseph Campbell, c/o Mahogany Inn Hotel, Wild Things Watersports, tel: (876) 957 5392.
Montego Bay: Mr Percy Thompson, 37 Market Street, tel: (876) 952 3782; Rev. Terrence Gordon, 4 Churchill Ave, tel: (876) 953 3376.
Ocho Rios: Mr Raphael Mason, Exchange District, P.O. Box 274, tel: (876) 974 0479.

Practical Tips

Media

NEWSPAPERS

Two daily newspapers, *The Daily Gleaner* and *The Jamaica Observer*, are published in Kingston and distributed throughout the island. On Sunday there are three national newspapers: *The Sunday Gleaner*, the *Sunday Observer*, and the *Sunday Herald*. *The Star* is a daily afternoon tabloid, and *The X-News*, another tabloid, is published weekly.

In Montego Bay the bi-weekly *Western Mirror* appears on Wednesday and Saturday. Publications for visitors include the *Tourist Guide*, published by the Gleaner Company and *The Visitor*, *Vacation Guide* and *Destination Jamaica*, published by the Jamaica Hotel and Tourist Association (JHTA).

Foreign newspapers are available at hotels, bookshops and better pharmacies. They include the *New York Times*, *Miami Herald*, *Financial Times*, *The Times* of London, *Le Monde* and *Die Welt*.

TELEVISION & RADIO

There are three television stations, TVJ, CVM-TV, and LOVE TV, all based in Kingston.

There is a large number of radio stations: RJR and its FM station FAME, KLAS FM, POWER 106 and LOVE FM (a religious station), all based in Kingston; IRIE FM (the all-reggae station) in Ocho Rios; and HOT 102 in Montego Bay. In addition some community radio stations have joined the band: Kingston-based ROOTS FM, operated by Mustard Seed, a Catholic charitable organisation; TBC, operated by Tarrant Baptist Church, and Bluefields Community Radio in Bluefields, Westmoreland. Several others are likely to join as soon as licences are available.

Postal Services

Most towns and even some villages in Jamaica have a post office or a postal agency. Your hotel will handle your mail or will be able to give you the current postal rates. A telegram service, available at most post offices and offices of **Cable and Wireless Jamaica Ltd** (CWJamaica), is an inexpensive if not totally efficient means of communication.

For courier delivery contact: **TARA Courier Service**, 491/2 Lyndhurst Road, Kingston 5, tel: 926 7982, fax: 968 0711. Island-wide deliveries twice a day; branches in all major towns. **Airpack Express**, Tinson Pen Aerodrome, tel: 923 0371 3. Also provide an island-wide service.

Telephone & Fax

From outside the country add 876 to all Jamaican numbers; inside Jamaica, dial 1 for calls outside your local area.

Please note that 800 numbers are only free if dialled from within the country of origin.

Jamaica's telephone network is controlled by Cable and Wireless Jamaica. High-speed satellite services are provided by Jamaica Digiport International, which operates a teleport in Montego Bay. Lines are open 24 hours, and it is possible to access anywhere in the world any time. However, it is necessary to have an ICAS code to call out of Jamaica, even to make a reversed charges call, so visitors may have some difficulty placing overseas calls directly. If you are not staying in a hotel or guesthouse, several companies can now facilitate you.

You can make reversed charges, or calls, notably through Sprint, tel: 1 800 877 8000; Worldphone, tel: 1 800 888 8000; or through

CWJamaica's own Jamaica LinkUp, tel: 1 800 876 1000. Your AT&T calling card also works.

Reversed charges calls are available to the following countries: Alaska, Anguilla, Antigua & Barbuda, Australia, Barbados, Belgium, Beruda, Canada, Cayman Islands, Guyana, Hawaii, Puerto Rico, St Kitts & Nevis, St Lucia, St Vincent & Grenadines, Trinidad & Tobago, USA, UK and US Virgin Islands.

Jamaica is also linked to the rest of the world by facsimile and cable services, available through CWJamaica or your hotel.

Prepaid Worldtalk Cards can be purchased at hotels, pharmacies and shops and at any CWJamaica office, and can be used to call from Jamaica to anywhere in the world. They can also be used to call Jamaica from the USA, Canada, UK and some Caribbean islands, or for calls within Jamaica.

It is also possible to get prepaid cards for local calls only. Many people just add them to their collection of pretty cards from around the world.

Cable & Wireless Main Offices
Business Offices
(Open to the public Monday–Friday 8am–4pm.)
Kingston: 47 Half Way Tree Road, Kingston 5
Black River: 3 North Street
Falmouth: 23 Market Street
Mandeville: Shop 16, Leaders Plaza
Montego Bay: 20 Church Street
Negril: Shop 27, Plaza de Negril
Ocho Rios: Mutual Life Building, Graham Street
Port Antonio: 4 Allan Avenue
St Ann's Bay: Lot 48, Windsor Road

Cellular Offices
(Open to the public Monday–Friday 8am–4pm, Saturday 8am–noon.)
Kingston: 9 Carlton Crescent, Kingston 5
Mandeville: 24 Hargreaves Avenue
Montego Bay: 36 Fort Street
Ocho Rios: Mutual Life Building, Graham Street

Tourist Information

Over one million people don't just descend on a country in the course of a year. Some organisation must be responsible for the overseeing and marketing of the industry. And in Jamaica, that organisation is the Jamaican Tourist Board.

The Board answers your questions before and after you arrive, issues maps and brochures on the places you want to see, and can even help you meet Jamaicans who shares your interests. It is that last function that has garnered much of the attention since the late 1960s, with the success of the "Meet the People" programme which links island visitors with Jamaicans. For more information you can contact the Tourist Board's local and/or overseas offices.

Tourist Offices

Black River: Hendriks Building, 2 High Street, Black River P.O., tel: 965 2074; fax: 965 2076.
Kingston: ICWI Building, 2 St Lucia Avenue, Kingston 5, tel: 929 9200; fax: 929 9375. Norman Manley Airport, tel: 924 8024; fax: 924 8673.
Montego Bay: Cornwall Beach, P.O. Box 67, Montego Bay, tel: 952 4425; fax: 952 3587. Donald Sangster Airport, tel: 952 3009; fax: 952 2462.
Negril: Shop 20, Villa de Negril, tel: 957 4243; Shop 9, Adrila Plaza, tel/fax: 957 4489.
Ocho Rios: Top Floor, Ocean Village Shopping Centre, tel: 974 2570; fax: 974 2559.
Port Antonio: Top Floor, City Centre Plaza, tel: 993 3051; fax: 993 2117.

Embassies & High Commissions

There are embassies and high commissions of over two dozen countries in Kingston. A few are:
British High Commission: 26 Trafalgar Road, tel: 926 9050/4, 926 1020/3

International Presence

A number of United Nations agencies as well as other multinational organisations are represented in Jamaica. In addition, two organisations concerned with marine affairs, the International Seabed Authority, established under the Convention of the Law of the Sea, and the UN Environment Programme for the Caribbean Sea, have their headquarters in Kingston.

Canadian High Commission: 3 West King's House Road, tel: 926 1500/926 1701
Cuban Embassy: 9 Trafalgar Road, tel: 978 0931
French Embassy: 13 Hillcrest Avenue, tel: 978 4881 3
Germany Embassy: 10 Waterloo Road, tel: 926 6728 /6729
Japanese Embassy: 1 Kensington Crescent, tel: 929 3338 9
Trinidad & Tobago High Commission: 60 Knutsford Blvd, tel: 926 5730/926 5739
United States Embassy: 2 Oxford Road, tel: 929 4850/926 5679

Tipping

Tipping is definitely allowed and encouraged in Jamaica, and is up to the generosity of visitors. However, it is customary to find a 10–15 percent service charge added to your restaurant bill, in addition to 15 per- cent GCT (General Consumption Tax). Since the bill may be higher than anticipated it is advisable to ask beforehand what is the custom of the house.

Religious Services

Kingston
Kingston Parish Church (Anglican), tel: 922 6888.
St Andrew Parish Church (Anglican), tel: 922 6692.
Bethel Baptist Church, tel: 926 8272.
St Peter & Paul (Catholic), tel: 928-6579.

Bethel United Church (Pentecostal), tel: 928 2987.
Webster Memorial Church (Presbyterian), tel: 926 6127.
Jewish Synagogue, tel: 922 5931.

Port Antonio
Christ Church (Anglican), tel: 993 2600.
Port Antonio Baptist Church, tel: 993 2789.
Salvation Army, tel: 993 3155.

Mandeville
Mandeville Baptist Church, tel: 962 3118.
Black River Catholic Church, tel: 965 2209.
St Mark's Parish Church (Anglican), tel: 9622876.

Ocho Rios
St John's Parish Church (Anglican), tel: 972 2305.
Methodist Church, tel: 974 1420.
Church of God of Prophecy, tel: 974 5511.

Montego Bay
St James Parish Church (Anglican), tel: 952 2775.
Holy Trinity (Anglican), tel: 952 1270.
Calvary Baptist Church, tel: 952 4375.
Blessed Sacrament Cathedral (Catholic), tel: 952 1248.

Negril
St Mary's Parish Church (Anlican); United Church of Jamaica & Grand Cayman; Gate of Heaven Catholic Church; Seventh Day Adventist Church; Church of God; Jehovah's Witnesses.

Security & Crime

It's important to use common sense – don't leave home without it. Just because you're on vacation doesn't mean you should shed all normal precautions.

Always place your jewellery and other valuables in the hotel safe until they're needed. When walking in crowds, women should clutch their handbags close to their bodies, and men should transfer their wallets to front pockets. Only carry on your person small amounts of cash or travellers' cheques, never more money than you will need. It's safer not to wear expensive jewellery in plain view – especially thick gold chains, which have on occasion been ripped straight off the neck by thieves.

Carefully scrutinise the goods of all sellers proferring "fantastic deals", and never forget that ganja and cocaine are illegal, for they are very likely to be offered to you.

If you're driving, be particularly vigilant at stop lights in the city. It is advisable, if you are travelling alone, not to drive with your windows open, or your doors unlocked.

Medical Services

For minor illnesses, cuts and bruises, most large hotels employ nurses to treat their guests, and there will be a doctor on call. Major illnesses can be handled by specialists, most of whom practise in Kingston.

All major towns have medical facilities. Large specialist hospitals are located in Kingston and Montego Bay:
Andrews Memorial Hospital, 27 Hope Road, Kingston, tel: 926 7401/2 (daytime) or 926 7403 (9pm–8am). Private.
Bustamante Hospital for Children, Arthur Wint Drive, Kingston, tel: 926-5721/5. Public.
Cornwall Regional Hospital, Mount Salem, Montego Bay, tel: 952 6683. Public.
Kingston Public Hospital, North Street, Kingston, tel: 922 0210; 922 0530/1.
Medical Associates Hospital, 18 Tangerine Place, Kingston, tel: 926 1400. Private.
National Chest Hospital, Liguanea, Kingston, tel: 927 7121/927 6421. Public.
Nuttall Memorial Hospital, 6 Caledonia Avenue, Kingston, tel: 926 2139. Private.
St Joseph's Hospital, Deanery Road, Kingston, tel: 928 4955. Private.

Insight Guides portray destinations in depth, providing the complete picture and the top photography

Insight Pocket Guides focus on the best choices for places to see and things to do and include large fold-out maps

Insight Compact Guides' portability makes them the perfect books to carry with you for on-the-spot reference

Three types of guide for all types of travel

INSIGHT GUIDES Different people need different kinds of information. Some want *background information* to help them prepare for the trip. Others seek *personal recommendations* from someone who knows the destination well. And others look for *compactly presented data* for on-the-spot reference. With three carefully designed series, Insight Guides offer readers the perfect choice. Insight Guides will turn your visit into an experience.

The world's largest collection of visual travel guides

When you're

bitten by the travel bug,

make sure you're protected.

Check into a British Airways Travel Clinic.

British Airways Travel Clinics provide travellers with:
- A complete vaccination service and essential travel health-care items
- Up-dated travel health information and advice

Call **01276 685040** for details of your nearest Travel Clinic.

**BRITISH AIRWAYS
TRAVEL CLINICS**

University Hospital of the West Indies (UHWI), Mona, Kingston, tel: 927 1620 (public); The Tony Thwaites Wing (private patients), tel: 927 6520/927 6555.

In addition, many parish capitals have their own infirmaries.

Jamaica is well served with pharmacies, but antibiotics, tranquilisers and certain other drugs can be bought only on a doctor's prescription. Most pharmacies open late (till 11pm); some in major towns open all night.

Emergencies

EMERGENCY NUMBERS

Police	119
Air-Sea Rescue	119
Ambulance	110
Fire	110
Blood Bank	922 5181/5188
Red Cross	926 7246

Health Precautions

Sunbathing
The first and last rule for sunworshipping is don't overdo it. Yes, the sun is shining; yes, the beach is inviting; yes, the water is sparkling; and yes, the breeze is refreshing. But in your eagerness to purchase that healthy, glowing look, you might emerge looking more like a boiled lobster than a bronzed deity. No matter what your skin colour, first apply a sunscreen and then gradually follow up with a tanning preparation.

Pests
There are two kinds of pests in Jamaica: the human kind and the insect kind. The human kind quickly sum up your tourist status and barrage you with offers of straw goods, wood carvings, cocaine and ganja for sale. The insect kind organise into mosquito squads bent on attacking your blood system. Mount a counter-offensive on the thirsty bloodsuckers with a strong dose of insect repellent spray and a burning mosquito coil. Deal with

Crisis Centres:

(Kingston)	929 2997
(Mo Bay)	852 9533-4
ODPEM	928 5111 4

(Office of Disaster Preparedness & Emergency Management)
Discovery Bay
Marine Lab 973 2241/3272
(for diving emergencies)

AMBULANCE SERVICES

Ambucare, 202 Mountain View Avenue, Kingston, tel: 978 2327, 978 6021; fax 978 8253; email: ambucare@kasnet.com.
Deluxe Ambulance Service, 54 Molynes Road, Kingston 10, tel: 923 7415; fax 923 0310. Island-wide service.
Northborough 24-hour Ambulance and Medical Response Shop, 40 Ocean Village Shopping Centre, Ocho Rios, tel: 974 6403.

the mortal nuisances with a polite but firm "thank you, but no".

Dengue fever still strikes occasionally. This mosquito-borne disease, also called "break bone fever", causes chills, fever and aching joints. In a healthy adult there is usually little cause for concern, but seeing a doctor is a good idea. To reduce the risk, using insect repellent is a must in the rainy seasons.

Hazards in the Sea
A great tip for any type of marine organism sting, including jellyfish and fire coral: if you feel any type of itching or burning when you get out of the sea, quickly douse the area in white vinegar (found at every shop and supermarket – keep a bottle handy in your beach bag) before fresh water. The vinegar doesn't sting and works quicker than anti-histamine creams. If you step on a sea urchin (also called a sea egg), douse the affected area in vinegar or urine – the latter may be more convenient!

Culture & Etiquette

In old-time Jamaica the twin passports to success were "education" and "manners" (see under, *Manners*), and both were in the British tradition, following the format of the colonial masters. Now no more. The education system, as elsewhere, has undergone much revision and would need several chapters. The new manners are everywhere apparent. There are still a few surviving traits of the old manners, particularly in country areas, but by and large Jamaican manners express a great sense of informality and unbridled freedom.

Jamaican Manners
Visitors may be surprised by this "freedom", especially in social interaction and traffic situations. Shop assistants, waiters or other service givers don't necessarily meet your eye when you enter their establishment, and are likely to attend to you when they are good and ready, or have freed themselves from whatever else they may have been doing when you interrupted. Smiles are not freely given, so don't imagine that a stony gaze necessarily means hostility.

You'll notice too that everybody wants to be in the front of the queue, and any space that opens up creates a free-for-all. Open a door, and somebody is likely to enter before you; stop to allow somebody to pass, and somebody else is likely to take over the space.

In traffic, every man (and woman) asserts the right to fend for himself above all others, thereby creating a situation that looks remarkably like chaos. So aggressive/defensive driving and very cool nerves are the order of the day. Horns are likely to start blowing behind you within less than a second of a traffic light changing, and there may be three or four motorists coming through the red light at the opposing intersection. Keep your head!

That's the downside. The upside is that in-your-face aggressiveness and ungovernableness can give rise

Rules of Etiquette

There are still a few iron-clad rules of etiquette the traveller should be concerned with in Jamaica:

● The same individuals who barely acknowledged you when you entered their presence do appreciate the words **"please"** and **"thank you"**, and they may complain that you "don't have no manners" if you don't use them.

● Always **acknowledge a greeting** with a greeting in return, just to show that "where you come from dem still have manners".

● **Mode of Address:**
In spite of the apparent lack of formality, it is still not universally accepted to call an acquaintance by first name immediately. Jamaicans of all classes like to be called by their "handle" and usually identify themselves as, say, Miss Jones or Mr Dalrymple or Mistress

Anderson. The exception is if they are in frequent contact with Americans and understand and accept that cultural norm.

● **Photography:**
Never shove a camera in a person's face and begin snapping away without asking permission first. While you'll want to capture the character-rich visages found in Jamaica, it's easier to find a receptive subject if you offer the right incentive. A few people will accept money, while others will accept a picture of themselves – which makes a Polaroid camera a handy item to carry along with your 35-millimetre camera.
A technical tip: Shoot most of your pictures during the early morning or late afternoon, because the midday sun tends to bleach out colour shots.

to an air of vibrancy, particularly in the cities, that is quite infectious. And visitors who get into the rhythm find that they can go with the flow quite successfully.

Many frequent visitors even get to like the adrenalin rush from this Jamaican infection. And directly opposed to the "me first" grabbiness are frequent acts of astonishing open-heartedness and generosity.

"Soon Come"

Jamaicans are paradoxical people, because these same rushing, impatient, pushy people have another, divergent culture. The bustling activity evident in most of Jamaica's larger cities often belies a laidback attitude that many Jamaicans adopt. It's an attitude that functions as a defence mechanism in the face of frequent breakdowns and long delays in getting things done. Since howls of protest and insistent demands for service generally yield few results, it's best to adopt the Jamaican approach and with a shrug of the

shoulders patiently utter the words, "soon come".

In the same way, Jamaicans complain about everything, yet you can buy T-shirts with the phrase that now passes for a national motto: "Jamaica – no problem." Welcome to ambivalent, paradoxical Jamaica!

Getting Around

By Air

Your international flight will arrive at either the Norman Manley Airport in Kingston or the Sir Donald Sangster Airport in Montego Bay.

There are airports for light domestic aircraft in Negril, Ocho Rios, St Margaret's Bay (for Port Antonio), and Tinson Pen in Kingston. Air Jamaica Express operates from Montego Bay and Tinson Pen to the other points.

For more information call **Air Jamaica Express**, tel: 922 4661, 952 5401 or (800) 523 5585. For schedules and information from the airports: Tinson Pen, Kingston, tel: 923 8680/923 6664; Norman Manley International Airport, tel: 924 8850; Sir Donald Sangster international Airport, Montego Bay, tel: 952 5401/3; Boscobel Aerodrome, Ocho Rios, 975 3254; Port Antonio, tel: 993 2405; Negril, tel: 957 4251.

Air Negril operates flights between Montego Bay and Negril almost every hour, and also flies between Ocho Rios and Negril. It also offers charter flights, tel: 940 7747 or 1 888 884 Negril (toll free from USA and Canada).

Several other companies offer charter flights, priced according to destination:
Airspeed Charter, tel: 937 7072.
Helitours (Ja) Ltd, 120 Main Street, Ocho Rios, tel: 974 2265. Offers helicopter tours of the island as well as charter services.
TIMAIR, tel: 952 2516.
Wings (Ja) Ltd, Tinson Pen Aerodrome, Kingston, tel: 923 5416/923 6573.

By Private Car

In Jamaica you drive on the left – that is the law! Don't be confused if you see other drivers rushing towards you in your lane (hopefully they'll get back into their own lane in time), stopped facing you, or even reversing towards you. A Jamaican driver will try everything that is remotely possible.

The speed limit is 50 kph (30 mph) in towns and 80 kph (50 mph) on highways. Roads are not generally well-maintained, so locals and visitors frequently weave about to avoid pot-holes. Jamaicans seem to favour roundabouts, some of them very difficult to decipher. (Montego Bay is a prime example of a town full of hard-to-comprehend roundabouts.) Roads also tend to be ill-defined: kerbs, soft shoulders and centre strips are often indiscernible, especially at night.

Since the roads, even in cities, are shared by daredevil drivers, pedestrians and animals, all with equal rights, you are advised to drive with extreme caution until you too become a Jamaican-style driver. Even then you are strongly advised not to drive after dark (and to leave plenty of time to return to base before nightfall) as the above-mentioned hazards become all but invisible in areas without street lights and – frighteningly – with some motor vehicles on the road without functioning headlamps, as well as many non-illuminated cyclists and pedestrians.

If you plan to do much touring, be sure to get the detailed *Discover Jamaica* map from the Jamaican Tourist Board, as other maps don't show the minor roads.

Safety belts became mandatory in 1999. Service stations are open daily until midnight, and many open for 24 hours.

CAR HIRE

To hire any vehicle, drivers must be at least 25 years of age, with a valid driver's licence and a major credit card. A North American driver's licence is valid for three months per visit; a UK driver's licence is valid for 12 months per visit; a Japanese driver's licence is valid for up to one month.

Hire-car operations in Jamaica include such big-name agencies as Avis, Budget Rent-A-Car, Hertz and National Car Rental. There are also a number of local agencies. If you are planning to do extensive touring, a four-wheel-drive vehicle is recommended for Jamaica's interior roads (and many of the roads in the cities too!), but only a few hire companies offer them. In any case, try to reserve a car before you arrive on the island, to avoid the frequent surges in demand. If you do wait until your arrival, look for agency representatives at the two international airports, tourist centres and hotel reception desks.

Always check the car over before signing the hire agreement. Report any dents or bumps, and insist that they are recorded, or you may lose some or all of your deposit. Most rental companies accept VISA and some other major credit cards.

By Taxi

You can travel by taxi anywhere, even right across the island from Port Antonio to Negril. However, it is advisable to agree on the price of the journey before you start.

In towns, taxis are summoned either by a telephone call – most are radio controlled – or by hailing them on the street. Generally, they have predetermined rates between one location and another. Before embarking you should first state your destination and ask the cost of the trip and whether the fare is quoted in Jamaican or US dollars. If in doubt, ask the driver to check with his control base, in your hearing, to ascertain the cost.

Legal cabs have red PPV (Public Passenger Vehicle) plates. "Route taxis" also ply the major routes, both in the cities and between towns, and increasingly serve rural areas too. Their rates are much lower than those of regular taxis (since they are shared by three or four, or more, passengers), but more expensive than buses. The route taxis have scheduled and unscheduled stops; you can usually tell where one is when you see a number of people piling in. Anyone else touting for business is likely to be an opportunistic private-car owner.

By Public Bus

The rural areas are served by mini-buses, but the only way to find out where they are going is to ask the driver or another prospective passenger. Few tourists are bold enough to try to tackle the country-bus system.

In the major population centres like Kingston and Montego Bay, the

Driving Times

Kingston–Mandeville	98 km/61 miles	1½ hours
Montego Bay–Negril	84 km/52 miles	1½ hours
Montego Bay–Ocho Rios	108 km/67 miles	2 hours
Negril–Treasure Beach	108 km/67 miles	2 hours
Ocho Rios–Port Antonio	106 km/66 miles	2½ hours
Ocho Rios–Kingston	87 km/54 miles	1½ hours
Port Antonio–Kingston	98 km/61 miles	2 hours
Kingston–Montego Bay	191 km/119 miles	4 hours

● **Rest facilities** are available on some main roads, such as the Rio Bueno and Rio Brac Travel Halts between Falmouth and Runaway Bay; open 9am–8pm. In addition to toilet facilities, light refreshments can be purchased, along with quality local arts and crafts. There is also a rest stop at Bamboo Avenue in St Elizabeth, and an excellent one, Kildare Villa, at Buff Bay halfway between Kingston and Port Antonio.

bus system is no better for the uninitiated. There are established bus routes but frequency is erratic, and the best way to travel is with someone who knows the system.

All in all, the public transport system is only for the intrepid. Fares are low, but there is not much elbow room, the music is loud, and the driving style of minibus drivers in particular can even at its best be described as "hair-raising".

In the resorts, check out free tourist buses connecting hotels with popular beach bars. These save on short-haul taxi fares if you can fit in with the pick-up times.

By Sightseeing Bus

Guided tours are available through your hotel's front desk, or contact JUTAS (Jamaica Union of Travellers Association), tel: 926 1537. It is based in Kingston but there is a, JUTAS stand in most hotels.

By Motorbike

Scooters, mopeds, bicycles and motorcycles can be rented by the day or by the week in most resort locations.

Where to Stay

The Choice

To accommodate the hundreds of thousands of visitors to Jamaica, dozens of hotels, inns and guesthouses have sprung up. They dot the island, with more along the coast in resort areas and fewer as one moves inland. But there is always somewhere to rest your head.

Quality and price vary greatly. Jamaica is the birthplace of the all inclusive hotel resort, and for those who want to live in the lap of luxury there are many all inclusive packages available in ultra-modern resorts which provide food, drink and entertainment for a pre-arranged price. And there are villas as luxurious and spectacular as any you could imagine. There are also tiny guesthouses and villas for those who are happy with fewer comforts than at home.

Children are welcome at all Jamaican hotels, except where it is specifically stated that the hotel/resort is for couples or adults only.

Below is a listing of hotels which gives an idea of what is on offer. The facilities and charges are, of course, always subject to change.

Surrey

KINGSTON & ST ANDREW

Expensive
Crowne Plaza Kingston
211a Constant Spring Road, Manor Park, Kingston 8
Tel: 925 7674
Fax: 905 4425/925 5757
Located on the northern outskirts of Kingston, in the foothills of the surrounding mountains, the hotel is

itself raised above the city on its own summit, giving it commanding views of the city and the spectacular Blue Mountain range. Contemporary furnishings and lots of Jamaican art. Two restaurants; four bars; fitness centre; racquetball; tennis; vita course; pool; special rate for nearby golf course; state-of-the-art conference and business amenities.

Hilton Kingston Hotel
77 Knutsford Blvd, P.O. Box 112, Kingston 5
Tel: 926 5430
Fax: 929 7439
A first-class business hotel in the financial and diplomatic district. Rooms with work desks and lounge area, air conditioning, telephone and private bath/shower. Health club; golf; tennis; swimming pool; nightclub/disco; three bars; two restaurants; shops. Modern business centre over 1,486 sq. metres (16,000 sq. ft) of meeting/convention space.

Le Meridien Jamaica Pegasus
81 Knutsford Blvd, P.O. Box 333, Kingston 5
Tel: 926 3690/9
Fax: 929 5855
Email: jm.pegas@cwjamaica.com
Website: www.meridienjamaica.com
The city's largest and most popular business hotel. More than 300 rooms with air conditioning, telephone and private bath/shower; golf; tennis; gym; swimming pool; nightclub/disco; restaurant and European-style café; two bars; good shops. Still known as The Pegasus following several changes of ownership, this hotel is the focal point of the New Kingston business district. Meeting facilities accommodate up to 1,000 persons; business centre and executive floors; banking facilities in-house. Also contains the Pegasus Art Gallery.

Morgan's Harbour
Port Royal
Tel: 967 8030/8040
Fax: 967 8073
Email: mharbour@casnet.com
Hotel in marina complex. All rooms with air conditioning and cable TV. The restaurant and bar are at the

water's edge with views directly across the harbour. Meeting facilities with capacity of 50. Private beach and swimming pool. Deep-sea fishing, scuba and watersports.

The New Courtleigh
85 Knutsford Blvd, New Kingston
Tel: 929 9000, 968 6339/40
Fax: 926 7744
Email: courtleigh@cwjamaica.com
Upmarket hotel with 88 deluxe rooms, 37 one-bedroom suites and a luxury two-bedroom suite with views of the mountains and sea. An oasis of comfort in the heart of Kingston's financial district, sandwiched between the city's two large business hotels. Small fitness centre; swimming pool and pool bar; business centre; data ports in rooms; gift store; four banquet/meeting rooms (largest seats 80 for dinner). Best known as the home of popular pub bar Mingles, and its good restaurant Alexander's.

Price Guide

Price per person per night including taxes:

Luxury   More than US$500
Expensive   US$150–500
Moderate   US$100–150
Inexpensive Under US$100

● Breakfast may not be included in quoted rates (though it often is in small hotels), so check first. The large hotels usually add on a 10 percent service charge.

Strawberry Hill Hotel & Restaurant
Irish Town, St Andrew
Tel: 944 8400/6
Fax: 944 8408
Email: strawberryhill.cwjamaica.com
Website: www.islandlife.com
Small exclusive hotel with superb architecture, landscaping and setting outside Kingston in the Blue Mountains, with 18 luxury suites and villas with balconies and verandas. Restaurant; bar; telephone and VCRs in rooms; yoga and massage at Strawberry Hill Aveda Concept Spa. Hosts popular

events to mark special occasions, such as Oscar Night Watch; excellent Sunday brunch; friendly staff. Good gift shop and a Japanese-style furniture shop.

Terra Nova
17 Waterloo Road, Kingston 10
Tel: 926 2211, 926 9334
Fax: 929 4933
Email: terranova@cwjamaica.com
Air conditioned junior suites. Close to the major business district, but with an atmosphere more like a country club. Meeting facilities including seven conference rooms. Secluded, quiet elegance. Swimming pool with outdoor bar.

Moderate
Alhambra Inn
1 Tucker Avenue, Kingston 6
Tel: 978 9072/3
Fax: 978 9074
E-mail: alhambra@cwjamaica.com
This hotel may not be as grand as the Moorish castle in Granada, Spain, for which it is named. However, it has a gracious setting and ambience, with great attention to detail. Throw in good Jamaican food at very reasonable prices, plus attentive meal service and a good bar, and you have a winner. Banquet and meeting rooms; Internet access; restaurant serving all meals; bar; swimming pool. Located within minutes of Norman Manley International Airport and the New Kingston commercial district.

Altamont Court Hotel
1–3 Altamont Terrace, Kingston 5
Tel: 929 4497
Fax: 929 2118
Email: altamont@n5.com.1nn
Rooms and suites with air conditioning, telephone, private bath/shower; swimming pool; restaurant. It is 1 minute from one of Kingston's most popular "typically Jamaican" restaurants, Hot Pot, and a few minutes' walk from the most popular theatres.

Christar Villas
99a Hope Road, Kingston 6
Tel: 978 8070/1
The owners have managed to create a comfortable and peaceful atmosphere at one of the busiest and most convenient corners in

Kingston. Rooms, studios and suites, with satellite TV. Traditional Jamaican hospitality with all modern conveniences. Restaurant; bar/lounge; conference facilities; swimming pool; gym. Just a minute away from Kingston's most popular shopping centres, movie houses, restaurants, etc.

Edge Hill Hotel & Apartments
198 Mountain View Avenue, Kingston 6
Tel: 978 0536, 927 9854
Fax: 978 0779
Email: edgehill@infochan.com
This hotel has 24 rooms, (some with air conditioning), with telephone, private bath/shower; restaurant.

Hotel Four Seasons
18 Ruthven Road, Kingston 10
Tel: 929 7655/7
Fax: 929 5964
Located in a lush tropical garden-setting in the heart of all activities. Best known for its restaurant and bar. A European/Jamaican environment. Full room service, satellite TV. Rooms have air conditioning, private bath/shower.

Medallion Hall
53 Hope Road, Kingston 6
Tel: 927 5721
Fax: 927 0048
Centrally located; 13 rooms with air conditioning, private bath/shower; restaurant. Furnished with local antiques.

Pine Grove Guest House
Content Gap, St Andrew
Tel: 922 8705
Mountain setting away from the city action. Breathtaking views. Small place with 20 rooms, (some with air conditioning), private bath/shower; cottages; restaurant.

Kingston/St Andrew contd.

Inexpensive
Indies Hotel
5 Holborn Road
Kingston 10
Tel: 926 2952/926 0989
Fax: 926 2879
Small hotel with 16 rooms, air conditioning, private bath/shower.
Mayfair
4 West King's House Close
P.O. Box 163,
Kingston 10
Tel: 926 1610/2
Fax: 296 7741
Thirty-two bedrooms in eight houses, each in its own garden and graciously comfortable. Centrally located in the New Kingston area. Restaurant, bar, poolside buffets Wednesday and Saturday.
Sandhurst Hotel
70 Sandhurst Crescent
Kingston 6
Tel: 927 7239/8244
Fax: 926 8443
Rooms, (some with air conditioning), private bath/shower; swimming pool; restaurant. Convenient city location.
Sutton Place
11 Ruthven Road
Kingston 10
Tel: 926 2297/4580
Fax: 926 8443
Convenient mid-town location. Air conditioned rooms with telephone, private bath/shower; swimming pool; restaurant.

PORT ANTONIO & EAST COAST

Luxury
Trident Villas & Hotel
P.O. Box 227
Port Antonio
Tel: 993 2602
Fax: 993 2960
Email: trident@infochan.com
Seaside villas, all decorated with antique furniture, which have hosted the rich and famous. Each villa has its own private verandah and balcony; all are air conditioned. Gourmet dining room open daily; two bars; traditional afternoon tea;

nightclub/disco; shops. Manicured grounds; shaded tennis courts; freshwater pool; private beach; watersports; horse-riding. Rooms with telephone, private bath/shower.

Expensive
Dragon Bay Villas
Dragon Bay,
P.O. Box 176
Port Antonio
Tel: 995 8514
Fax: 993 3284
Email: dragonb@cwjamaica.com
Website: www.dragonbay.com
The beaches of Portland are special, and the Dragon Bay beach is one of the best. Large luxury complex with friendly staff. Villas, suites and a penthouses in a magical setting along the craggy cliffs, overlooking a pristine coastline and a calm bay. Air conditioning; TVs in suites and penthouses only. Maid service/cook on request. Sports facilities, watersports, PADI scuba centre with dive packages. A bird-watcher's paradise as well. Popular with German visitors.
Goblin Hill Villas
P.O. Box 26
Port Antonio
Tel: 925 8108
Fax: 925 6248
Charming villa hotel in Jamaican-Georgian style, combining the privacy and personal service of a villa vacation with facilities of a hotel. Spacious one- and two-bedroom villas with ocean views located on a 5-hectare (12-acre) estate. Access to private beach. Pool, floodlit tennis courts, snorkelling. Cook/housekeeper. French and Spanish spoken. Bar.
Jamaica Palace Hotel
Williamsfield, P.O. Box 277
Port Antonio
Tel: 993 2020/1
Fax: 993 3459
Email: jampal@cwjamaica.com
Imagine a palace on a country road. The accommodation is fine, but bring your imagination along as well. Rooms with air conditioning, private bath/shower, telephone; a Jamaica-shaped swimming pool; restaurant; tennis; horse-riding.

Moderate
Bonnie View
P.O. Box 82, Richmond Hill
Tel: 993 2752
Fax: 993 2862
It's a steep drive up to Bonnie View, but worth it for the spectacular bird's eye view of Port Antonio's twin harbours. Modest rooms with air conditioning, telephone, private bath/shower; private beach; swimming pool; tennis; cottages; restaurant; shops.
Fern Hill Club
San San, P.O. Box 100
Port Antonio
Tel: 993 7374
Fax: 993 7373
Rooms with private bath/shower, air conditioning, telephone; swimming pool; gym; restaurant; nightclub/disco; tennis; private beach; watersports; horse-riding.

Price Guide

Price per person per night including taxes:

Luxury	More than US$500
Expensive	US$150–500
Moderate	US$100–150
Inexpensive	Under US$100

● Breakfast may not be included in quoted rates (though it often is in small hotels), so check first. The large hotels usually add on a 10 percent service charge.

Hotel Mocking Bird Hill
P.O. Box 254
Port Antonio
Tel: 993 3370/7134
Fax: 993 7133
Email: mockbrd@cwjamaica.com
This small, cosy hotel aspires to becoming a leader in the "greening" of Jamaica (see box page 336, *Jamaican Hotels Turn Green*). The restaurant specialises in healthy and natural foods, and the owners are committed to tourism that is kind to the environment. Craft workshops; tours and art gallery.

Jamaica Crest Resort
Fairy Hill, P.O. Box 165
Port Antonio
Tel: 993 8400/1
Fax: 993 8432
Small resort with 14 rooms with telephone, air conditioning, private bath/shower; swimming pool; watersports; restaurants; tennis; horse-riding.

Inexpensive
De Montevin Lodge
21 Fort George Street
Port Antonio
Tel: 993 2604
Rooms with private bath/shower; restaurant; foreign languages spoken. One of Jamaica's oldest hospitality institutions; famous for its way with traditional Jamaican food.

Whispering Bamboo Cove
105 Crystal Drive, P.O. Box 2, Retreat, St Thomas
Tel: 982 1788/2912
Fax: 982 2421
Off the beaten track with 10 rooms. Air conditioning, private bath/shower, telephone; private beach; restaurant.

Middlesex

OCHO RIOS & SURROUNDINGS

Luxury
Ciboney Ocho Rios
P.O. Box 728, Ocho Rios P.O.
Tel: 974 1027/9
Fax: 974 5838
Email: ciboney@infochan.com16
Website: www.choicecaribbean.com
A large and luxurious all inclusive villa complex nestled in the hills. Rooms, private bath/shower, air conditioning, telephone. Swimming pool; nightclub/disco; private beach; watersports; restaurants; gym/jacuzzi; tennis.

Jamaica Inn
P.O. Box 1, Main Street
Ocho Rios
Tel: 974 2514
Fax: 974 2449
Email: jamaicainn@infochan.com
Website: www.jamaicainn.com
One of the aristocrats of the North

Coast. A small, grand hotel with a quiet, gracious ambience. Each room furnished with antiques or tasteful reproductions. Rooms have air conditioning, telephone, private bath/shower; 213 metres (700 ft) of private beach; swimming pool; watersports; tennis; golf; horse-riding; orchestra; restaurant. Foreign languages spoken.

Sans Souci Lido
P.O. Box 103, Ocho Rios
Tel: 974 2353
Fax: 974 1544
Email: sslido@cwjamaica.com
One of the SuperClubs all inclusive resorts, with a unique hillside and beach setting. Two pools, one a world-class mineral pool, so not surprising that the hotel has excellent spa treatments. Award-winning cuisine and service. Restaurants and 24-hour service.

Expensive
Boscobel Beach Hotel
Boscobel, P.O. Box 63, Ocho Rios
Tel: 975 7330/6
Fax: 975 7370
Email: bosco@cwjamaica.com
Website: www.superclubs.com
One of the all inclusive SuperClubs resorts, with 207 air conditioned rooms with private bath/shower, telephone. Swimming pool; private beach; watersports; gym/jacuzzi; nightclub; restaurant; tennis; horse-riding. Children under 14 stay free, and they have supervised activities.

Club Jamaica
P.O. Box 342, Ocho Rios
Tel: 974 6632/9
Fax: 974 6644
Email: clubjam@infochan.com
Noted for its setting on Ocho Rios' longest white-sand private beach. All inclusive; 95 rooms with private bath/shower, air conditioning, telephone. Swimming pool; watersports; nightclub/disco; restaurant; gym/jacuzzi.

Comfort Suites (Crane Ridge Club)
17 DaCosta Drive, Ocho Rios
Tel: 974 8050
Fax: 974 8070
Email: calypso@cwjamaica.com
Situated on a bluff overlooking the town, with direct access to the

Ruins Restaurant and Turtle Falls. The hotel has 90 rooms with air conditioning, private bath/shower, telephone; swimming pool; watersports; restaurant; nightclub/disco; horse-riding.

Couples
Tower Isle P.O., St Mary
Tel: 975 4271
Fax: 975 4439
Email: couplesresort@couples
Website: www.couples.com
Jamaica's first all inclusive resort for couples only, and one of the north coast's first resorts. The hotel still retains a romantic air; 212 rooms with air conditioning, telephone, private bath/shower; private beach; swimming pool; watersports; tennis; horse-riding; nightclub/disco; restaurant; shops. No singles or children.

The Enchanted Gardens
P.O. Box 284, Ocho Rios
Tel: 974 1400/9
Fax: 974 5823
all inclusive mountainside active spa and resort set in 20 acres of luxuriant tropical gardens, with 14 waterfalls, two pools, exotic flora and bird life. With 113 rooms with air conditioning, private bath/shower, telephone; swimming pool; private beach; watersports; several restaurants; nightclub/disco; gym/jacuzzi; tennis. And if that is not enough exercise, there are lots of steps to climb if you want to track the waterfalls. If not, transportation is available around the property.

Golden Seas Hotel
P.O. Box 1, Oracabessa, St Mary
Tel: 975 3251, 975 3540/1
Fax: 975 3243
There's a river running down to the sea which gives this 72-room property another dimension; bedrooms have a view of the sea, hills or river. Air conditioning, private bath/shower, telephone; swimming pool; private beach; watersports; restaurant; nightclub/disco; tennis; horse-riding.

Jamaican Hotels Turn Green

Jamaican properties picked up three out of four Caribbean Hotel Association (CHA) environmental awards handed out at the Caribbean Hotel Industry Conference in 1999. The awards are aimed at encouraging hotels to invest in environmentally-friendly technologies.

The **Half Moon Golf, Tennis & Beach Club** near Rose Hall (see page 337) won Green Hotel of the Year from 1995 to 1997; it was the first property to be inducted into the environmental Hall of Fame.

In 1999 the **Hotel Mocking Bird Hill** in Port Antonio (see page 334) won the small-hotel category; and **Negril Cabins Resort** (www.negril-cabins.com) won in the large-hotel category. Both properties have a long history of environmental awareness, and each received Green Globe certification in 1998 in recognition of their commitment to the protection of the environment.

The CHA environmental award winners were judged by a team of experts who inspect and evaluate the properties based on resource conservation, staff awareness of environmental concerns, community stewardship and property infrastructure.

Plantation Inn
P.O. Box 2, Ocho Rios
Tel: 974 5601
Fax: 974 5912
Email: plantationinn@cwjamaica.com
Medium sized hotel with 80 rooms with air conditioning, telephone, private bath/shower; private beach; swimming pool; watersports; tennis; golf; restaurant; shops; foreign languages spoken.

Renaissance Jamaica Grande Resort
P.O. Box 170, Ocho Rios
Tel: 974 2201, 800 228 9898 (reservations)
Fax: 974 2289
Email: jagrande@infochan.com
With 720 rooms, this has been Jamaica's largest hotel for some time. It also claims to be the island's "most complete resort". Three pools; five restaurants; "Club Mongoose" fully-supervised programme for children under 12; private beach; watersports; tennis; nightclub/disco; shops. All rooms have air conditioning, telephone, private bath/shower.

Sandals Dunn's River
P.O. Box 51, by Ocho Rios
Tel: 972 0563
Fax: 972 1611
Email: sdrinet@cwjamaica.com
Website: www.sandals.com
All inclusive, couples only hotel with 256 air conditioned rooms with private bath/shower; private beach; swimming pool; tennis; golf; gym/jacuzzi; nightclub/disco; restaurant; shops.

Sandals Ocho Rios
P.O. Box 771, Ocho Rios
Tel: 974 5691/3
Fax: 974 5700
Email: sorinet@cwjamaica.com
Website: www.sandals.com
More than 200 rooms with air conditioning, private bath/shower, telephone; swimming pool; private beach; watersports; restaurant; nightclub/disco; gym/jacuzzi; tennis; horse-riding. Couples only, all inclusive.

Moderate
Little Pub Inn
59 Main Street, Ocho Rios
Tel: 974 2324
Fax: 974 5826
Email: littlepub@infochan.com
In the heart of the town and allied to a popular entertainment centre in town. Rooms have air conditioning, private bath/shower, telephone; restaurant; nightclub.

Ocean Sands Resort
14 James Avenue, Ocho Rios
Tel: 974 1421
Fax: 974 2605
Rooms with air conditioning, private bath/shower, telephone; swimming pool; restaurant; nightclub; private beach; watersports; horse-riding.

Sand Castles
Main Street, Ocho Rios
Tel: 974 2255/6
Fax: 974 2247
Large child-friendly resort. Rooms with air conditioning, private bath/shower, telephone; swimming pool; restaurant.

Silver Seas
P.O. Box 81, Ocho Rios
Tel: 974 2755/5005
Rooms with air conditioning, telephone, private bath/shower; private beach; swimming pool; watersports; tennis; squash; nightclub/disco; restaurant; shops.

Tower Cloisters Condominiums
Tower Isle P.O., St Mary
Tel/fax: 975 4360
Good Jamaican food and jazz in the evenings, sometimes live. Rooms (some with air conditioning), private bath/shower; swimming pool; restaurant; nightclub/disco.

Inexpensive
Casa Maria
P.O. Box 10, Port Maria
Tel: 994 2323
Fax: 994 2324
Good choice for a quiet holiday. Cottages have rooms (some with air conditioning), with telephone, private bath/shower; swimming pool; tennis; restaurant; shops.

Hibiscus Lodge
P.O. Box 52, Main Street, Ocho Rios
Tel: 974 2676/2594
Fax: 974 1874
Small hotel with 25 rooms with private bath/shower; private beach; restaurant.

Pineapple Penthouse Hotel
Pineapple Place, P.O. Box 263, Ocho Rios
Tel: 974 2727
Fax: 974 1706
Email: rmat@cwjamaica.com
Small hotel, rooms with air conditioning, bath/shower; swimming pool; restaurant.

Sonrise Beach Retreat
Robin's Bay, St Mary
Tel/fax: 999 7169
Cosy place with 6 rooms which have private bath/shower; private beach; restaurant; horse-riding.
Trade Winds Resort
Galina, St Mary
(25 minutes from Ocho Rios; 2½ miles from Port Maria)
Tel: 994 0420/2
Fax: 994 0423
Small friendly inn; only 14 rooms; restaurant serves good Jamaican food at moderate prices, with bar, cocktail terrace and verandah restaurant offering a splendid view of the ocean and the spectacular coastline. A 10-minute drive from Noël Coward's "Firefly"; also close to historic churches and the Galina Lighthouse.

DISCOVERY BAY & RUNAWAY BAY

Expensive
Breezes Runaway Bay
P.O. Box 58, Runaway Bay
Tel: 973 2436
Fax: 973 2352
Email: breezesgolf@jamaica.com
A SuperClubs resort, luxurious rooms and suites with air conditioning, private bath/shower, telephone; restaurant; swimming pool; nude beach (optional); watersports; disco; fitness centre; tennis; golf. No children under 16 years. All inclusive.
Franklyn D. Resort
P.O. Box 201, Runaway Bay
Tel: 973 4591
Fax: 973 3071
Email: fdr@infochan.com
Website: www.fdrholidays.com
All inclusive family resort. Children under 16 stay free all year round. Rooms with air conditioning, private bath/shower, telephone; restaurant; swimming pool; private beach; watersports; nightclub; gym/jacuzzi; tennis; horse-riding.

Moderate
Club Caribbean
P.O. Box 65, Runaway Bay
Tel: 973 3507/9
Fax: 973 4703
Email: clubcar@jamaica.com
Rooms and cottages (some with air conditioning), private bath/shower; private beach; swimming pool; watersports; tennis; golf; horse-riding; nightclub; restaurant. Popular with active young Europeans.

Price Guide

Price per person per night including taxes:

Luxury — More than US$500
Expensive — US$150–500
Moderate — US$100–150
Inexpensive — Under US$100

● Breakfast may not be included in quoted rates (though it often is in small hotels), so check first. The large hotels usually add on a 10 percent service charge.

Tropical Inn
P.O. Box 23, Runaway Bay
Tel: 973 4086
Fax: 973 4089
Small place, all rooms with air conditioning, telephone; swimming pool; watersports; restaurant; gym/jacuzzi; horse-riding.

Inexpensive
Ambiance Jamaica
P.O. Box 20, Runaway Bay
Tel: 973 2066/7
Fax: 973 2067
Email: clubamb@cwjamaica.com
Rooms with air conditioning, telephone, private bath/shower; private beach; swimming pool; fishing; tennis; golf; nightclub/disco; orchestra; restaurant; shops. Bed & breakfast.
Caribbean Isle Hotel
P.O. Box 119, Runaway Bay
Tel: 973 2364
Fax: 973 4835
Email: rivgroup@cwjamaica.com
Rooms with air conditioning, private bath/shower; swimming pool; disco; restaurant.

Portside Resort Villas
Discovery Bay
Tel: 973 2007
Studios and two-bedroom villas with air conditioning, telephone, private bath/shower, kitchen and sitting area, verandah. Two pools; jacuzzi; private beach; watersports; tennis; entertainment. Restaurant and small commissary on premises; supermarket is five minute's walk.
Runaway Bay HEART Hotel & Training Institute
Cardiff Hall, Runaway Bay
Tel: 973 2671/4
Fax: 973 2693
Hospitality training and service institution which has 20 rooms with fans, telephone, TV, private bath/shower; restaurant. Free golf for overnight guests; special rates on green fees. Conference room; audio-visual equipment; typing and photocopying.

MANDEVILLE

Moderate
Astra Country Inn
P.O. Box 60, 62 Ward Avenue
Tel: 962 3725
Fax: 962 1461.
One of the leaders in community tourism and eco-tourism. Rooms have telephone, private bath/shower; private beach; swimming pool; fishing; golf; horse-riding; tennis; restaurant.
Golf View Hotel
51/2 Caledonia Road
Tel: 962 4471
Fax: 962 5640
Rooms which adjoin the oldest golf course in the Caribbean, overlooking the Manchester Club. Wide range of suites. Ground floor is accessible to disabled visitors. All rooms have private bath and satellite TV. Conference facility; swimming pool; golf; tennis; baby-sitting service.
Mandeville Hotel
P.O. Box 78, 4 Hotel Street
Tel: 962 2460
Fax: 962 0700
Email: manhot@cwjamaica.com
Historical hotel with 60 rooms in four acres of tropical garden. Suites

Mandeville contd.

with kitchen facilities. Mahogany
four-poster beds. Two restaurants,
two bars and an authentic English-
style pub. Meeting facilities. Enjoy
the old-world atmosphere and
personalised service. Swimming
pool; tennis; golf nearby. Short walk
to town.

Cornwall

MONTEGO BAY & NORTH COAST

Luxury
Half Moon Golf, Tennis & Beach Club
P.O. Box 80, Rose Hall
Tel: 953 2211
Fax: 953 2731
Email:
reservation@halfmoonclub.com
Website: www.halfmoon.com.jm
Large and luxurious resort, rooms
and cottages with air conditioning,
telephone, private bath/shower;
private beach; swimming pool;
watersports; tennis; squash; golf;
horse-riding; orchestra;
nightclub/disco; restaurant; shops.
The Palms
P.O. Box 186, Rose Hall
Tel: 953 2160
Cottages and rooms with air
conditioning, private bath/shower;
swimming pool; tennis; nightclub;
restaurant.
Round Hill Hotel
P.O. Box 64, Montego Bay
Tel: 952 7050
Fax: 952 7505
Email: roundhill@cwjamaica.com
Website: www.roundhilljamaica.com
Exclusive hotel with unapologetic
old-world, old-style elegance. Rooms
and cottages (some with air
conditioning), with telephone, private
bath/shower; private beach;
swimming pool; tennis; golf; water-
sports; horse-riding; nightclub;
shops.
Sandals Royal Jamaican
P.O. Box 167, Montego Bay
Tel: 953 2231
Fax: 953 2788
Luxurious accommodation. All
inclusive.

Tryall Golf & Beach Club
Sandy Bay P.O., Hanover
Tel: 956 5660/3
Fax: 956 5673
Email: info@tryallclub.com
Rooms and villas with air
conditioning, telephone, private
bath/shower; swimming pool;
watersports; tennis; golf; horse-
riding; nightclub; restaurant.
Wyndham Rose Hall Hotel
P.O. Box 999, Rose Hall
Tel: 953 2650
Fax: 953 2617
Website: www.wyndham.com
Named for the great house. Rooms
with air conditioning, telephone,
private bath/shower; swimming
pool; private beach; orchestra;
watersports; tennis; golf; horse-
riding; nightclub; restaurant; shops.

Price Guide

Price per person per night
including taxes:

Luxury	More than US$500
Expensive	US$150–500
Moderate	US$100–150
Inexpensive	Under US$100

● Breakfast may not be included
in quoted rates (though it often is
in small hotels), so check first.
The large hotels usually add on a
10 percent service charge.

Expensive
Braco Village Resort
Braco, Rio Bueno P.O., Trelawny
Tel: 954 0000 19
Fax: 954 0020
All inclusive in a setting resembling
a traditional village. Rooms have air
conditioning and telephone;
restaurant; swimming pool; private
beach; watersports; gym/jacuzzi;
nightclub/disco; tennis; golf.
**Grand Montego Beach Resort
(Jack Tar Village)**
Gloucester Avenue, Montego Bay
Tel: 952 4340/4
Fax: 952 6633
Email: jtvmbay@cwjamaica.com
Website: www.allegroresorts.com
All inclusive luxury. Rooms with
private bath/shower, air

conditioning, telephone; restaurant;
swimming pool; private beach;
watersports; nightclub; tennis.
Holiday Inn Sunspree Resort
P.O. Box 480, Montego Bay
Tel: 953 2485/6
Fax: 953 2840
Rooms with air conditioning,
telephone, private bath/shower;
swimming pool; private beach; golf;
tennis; horse-riding; watersports;
nightclub/disco; restaurant; shops.
All inclusive.
Pebbles
Trelawny (east of Falmouth)
Tel: (FDR Holidays) 973 4882/4,
1 888 FDR KIDS
Email: fdr@fdrholidays.com
Website: www.fdrholidays.com
Family resort (*see also* Franklyn D.
Resort, Runaway Bay), designed for
families and catering especially to
teenagers. Children under 16 years
are free if sharing with parents.
Camping, hiking, field trips and
watersports available.
Sandals Montego Bay
P.O. Box 100, Montego Bay
Tel: 952 5510
Fax: 952 0816
Rooms and suites. Luxurious
accommodation with air
conditioning, telephone, private
bath/shower; swimming pool;
private beach; watersports; disco;
restaurant. All inclusive.
Trelawny Beach Hotel
P.O. Box 54, Falmouth
Tel: 954 2450
Fax: 954 2173
Email: trelawny-
beach@cwjamaica.com
Rooms and cottages (some with air
conditioning), with telephone,
private bath/shower; swimming
pool; private beach; tennis; horse-
riding; watersports; nightclub;
restaurant.

Moderate
Breezes Montego Bay
Gloucester Avenue, Montego Bay
Tel: 940 1150/7
Fax: 940 1160
Website: www.superclubs.com
A SuperClubs resort, with 124
rooms and suites with private
bath/shower, air conditioning,
telephone; swimming pool;

watersports; restaurant; gym; nightclub; tennis. All inclusive.

Carlyle Beach
P.O. Box 412, Montego Bay
Tel: 952 4140
Rooms with air conditioning, telephone, private bath/shower; pool; restaurant. Children welcome.

Coral Cliff
P.O. Box 253, 165 Gloucester Ave, Montego Bay
Tel: 952 4130/1
Fax: 952 6532
On the "Strip". Rooms with air conditioning, telephone; private bath/shower; swimming pool; tennis; restaurant.

Coyaba Beach Resort & Club
Mahoe Bay, Ironshore, Montego Bay
Tel: 953 9150/3
Fax: 953 2244
Email: coyaba@n5.comirn
Website: www.coyabajamaica.com
Rooms with private bath/shower, air conditioning, telephone; swimming pool; private beach; watersports; gym; nightclub; tennis; horse-riding.

Doctor's Cave Beach
P.O. Box 94, Montego Bay
Tel: 952 4355
Fax: 952 5204
Email: info@doctorscave.com
Website: www.doctorscave.com
Lively hotel with rooms and 10 apartments with air conditioning, telephone, private bath/shower; swimming pool; private beach; watersports; horse-riding; tennis; squash; golf; nightclub; restaurant.

The Gloucestershire Hotel (Quality Inn Montego Bay)
Gloucester Avenue, Montego Bay
Tel: 952 4420
Fax: 952 8088
Email: qualityinn@cwjamaica.com
Website: www.hotelchoice.com
Rooms with private bath/shower, air conditioning, telephone; swimming pool; watersports; gym/jacuzzi; nightclub/disco; horse-riding.

Reading Reef Club
Reading, P.O. Box 225, Montego Bay
Tel: 952 5909
Fax: 952 7217
Email: rrc@n5.com.jm
Website: www.montego-bayjamaica.com/jhta/reefclub
Rooms with private bath/shower, air

conditioning, telephone; swimming pool; restaurant; private beach; watersports.

Richmond Hill Inn
P.O. Box 362, Montego Bay
Tel: 952 3859/2835
Fax: 952 6106
Email: richillin@cwjamaica.com
If you have marriage in mind, Richmond Hill can offer an elegant terrace on a hill overlooking the Caribbean and a honeymoon suite. The hotel organises everything, from the preacher to the confetti. Rooms with air conditioning, private bath/shower; pool; private beach; watersports; restaurant.

Sandals Inn
Kent Avenue, Montego Bay
Tel: 952 4140
Fax: 952 6913
Email: sin.is@cwjamaica.com
Website: www.sandals.com
Rooms with private bath/shower, air conditioning, telephone; swimming pool; private beach; watersports; restaurant; jacuzzi; tennis; horse-riding. Couples only, all inclusive.

Wexford Court Hotel
P.O. Box 239, Montego Bay
Tel: 952 3679/2854
Fax: 952 3637
Email: wexford@cwjamaica.com
Website: www.montego-bay-jamaica.com/wexford
Rooms with air conditioning, telephone, private bath/shower; swimming pool; restaurant.

Inexpensive
Beach View
P.O. Box 86, Montego Bay
Tel: 952 4420/2
Private beach and rooms with air conditioning, telephone, private bath/shower; swimming pool; restaurant.

Blue Harbour
P.O. Box 212, Sewell Avenue, Montego Bay
Tel: 952 5445
Fax: 952 8930
Email: robbyg@cwjamaica.com
Website: www.blueharbourhotel
Rooms with air conditioning, private bath/shower; pool; restaurant.

Private Villas

"Far from the madding crowd", sprinkled all over the island, there are over 350 individual villas and cottages to rent in Jamaica. These are not clustered together, as part of an international holiday ground, but are sited, in some cases, in out-of-the-way places. You will find villas in Negril, Tryall, Rose Hall, Reading, Ironshore (outside Montego Bay), Mammee Bay, Ocho Rios, Oracabessa, Port Antonio, and in more remote places. Some rise dramatically out of a long stretch of beach; others lie in secluded hills; still others overlook the sea from clifftops.

The common attraction of these privately-owned villas is the opportunity to live at your own pace, doing what you want when you want. They offer the privacy and convenience of your own home, together with the promise of romance conjured up by such names as East of Eden and Come What May.

The properties are all fully equipped with linen, towels, cutlery and dishes. Most have private swimming pools and en-suite bathrooms. Full-time maids will do the housework and, on request, do the grocery shopping and prepare tasty meals. Alternatively, you can shop in the local markets for Jamaican foods such as callaloo (Jamaican spinach), ackee, red peas and sugar cane.

Reservations can be made through most travels agent's the Jamaican Tourist Board or the **Jamaican Association of Villas and Apartments** (JAVA), Pineapple Place, P.O. Box 298, Ocho Rios (tel: 974 2508/2763; 1 800 845 5276 or 800 VILLAS-6 from the US and Canada). In the UK you can book through **Just Jamaica**, Suite 607, Langham House, 302–308 Regent Street, London W1 5AL, tel: 0171 436 9292, fax: 0171 580 7220.

Montego Bay/North Coast contd.

Harmony House
P.O. Box 55, Montego Bay
Tel: 952 5710
Rooms with air conditioning,
telephone, private bath/shower;
swimming pool; restaurant.
Ocean View Guest House
P.O. Box 210, 26 Sunset Blvd,
Montego Bay
Tel: 952 2662
Traditional guesthouse with 12
rooms with air conditioning, private
bath/shower; swimming pool;
restaurant.
Royal Court
P.O. Box 195, Montego Bay
Tel: 952 4531
Fax: 952 4532
On the same site as the Royal
Court Health and Wellness Centre.
which specialises in inclusive health
packages. Rooms with air
conditioning, telephone, private
bath/shower; swimming pool;
nightclub; restaurant.
Time 'n' Place Beach Cottages
Trelawny (east of Falmouth)
Tel: 954 4371
Fax: 954 4371
Email: timenplace@cwjamaica.com
Aficionados say the area is what
Negril was like 25 years ago. A
limited number of beach cottages,
magical at full moon. Popular for a
day's hanging out on the beach, or
as a film location – you may
recognise the bar from a movie
you've seen.
Verney House
P.O. Box 18, Montego Bay
Tel: 952 2875
Fax: 979 2944
Small hotel. Rooms (some with air
conditioning), with telephone,
private bath/shower; swimming
pool; private beach; restaurant.

NEGRIL

Luxury
Beaches Negril
P.O. Box 12
Tel: 957 9270/6
Fax: 957 9269, 1 800 beaches
Email: beachesnegril@cwj.com
Large beachfront all inclusive
resort. Good facilities including hot
tubs; diving shop; watersports;
tennis; miniature golf; fitness
centre; nursery and children's
playroom.
Couples Negril
P.O. Box 35
Tel: 957 5960
Fax: 957 5858
Website: www.couples.com
Luxury beachfront all inclusive
resort. Air conditioned rooms and
suites on 18 acres. The place is
artistically decorated with dreamy
silkscreens and designer lighting.
Suites include jacuzzis. Three
speciality restaurants, beach grill,
24-hour food service; bars; live
entertainment; watersports and
sports; tours; golf.
Grand Lido
P.O. Box 88
Tel/fax: 957 5517
Website: www.superclubs.com
A SuperClubs all inclusive
beachfront resort for adult singles
and couples. Luxurious suites and
rooms. Laundry/valet service; 24-
hour room service; bars; live
entertainment; fitness
centre/aerobics; watersports;
sunset cruises on private 147-ft
yacht; golf (includes green fees).
Sandals Negril Beach Resort & Spa
P.O. Box 12
Tel: 957 4216
Fax: 957 5338
Email: sng@cwjamaica.com
Website: www.sandals.com
Luxurious accommodation with 215
rooms and suites with air
conditioning, private bath/shower;
swimming pool; watersports;
tennis; disco; restaurants; bars;
fitness centre; spa facilities; tours;
golf. all inclusive resort for couples
only, on private slice of Negrils 7-
mile beach.

Swept Away
P.O. Box 77
Tel: 957 4061
Fax: 957 4060
Exclusive all inclusive resort
catering for couples and adults, set
in a lush 10-acre tropical garden.
Rooms, in two-storey buildings,
each with spacious verandah.
Restaurants; bars; nightly
entertainment and games room.
Hotel claims to have the largest
sports facility in the Caribbean,
including 25-metre lap pool, jogging
track, aerobics centre, gymnasium,
basketball, squash, racquetball and
10 tennis courts, steam rooms and
saunas. Spa; watersports; golf
(includes green fees); horse-riding.

Expensive
Hedonism II
P.O. Box 25
Tel: 957 5200
Fax: 957 5289
Email: hedoii@cwjamaica.com
Website: www.superclubs.com
A SuperClubs super-inclusive resort
with a party atmosphere. Nude
beach; bars; famous hedonistic
late-opening disco; games room;
freshwater swimming pool; jacuzzis;
air conditioned squash courts;
tennis; watersports.
Poinciana Beach Resort
Norman Manley Blvd
Tel: 957 5100
Fax: 957 5229
Email: beachesnegril@joj.com
All inclusive. One and two-bedroom
villas, superior rooms or spacious
one-bedroom suites. Three
restaurants; two bars; watersports;
tennis; cycling; horse-riding.
Massage and motorised
watersports cost extra.

Moderate/Inexpensive
Unless otherwise stated, all the
following are on Norman Manley
Boulevard.
Bar-B-Barn
Tel: 957 4267
Fax: 957 4679
Email: bar-b-barn@cwjamaica.com
Website: www.bar-b-barn.com
24 rooms set among gardens on
the 7-mile beach. Rooms decorated
in Caribbean colours. Two

restaurants; satellite TV; sports bar; watersports available.

Beachcomber Club
Tel: 957 4170
Fax: 957 4097
Rooms, and spacious suites with large living rooms, fully equipped kitchens, washer/dryer. Bathrooms with soaker tub. Huge covered verandahs with garden/ocean views. Gambino's Italian Restaurant with pasta bar, in intimate setting.

Price Guide

Price per person per night including taxes:

Luxury	More than US$500
Expensive	US$150–500
Moderate	US$100–150
Inexpensive	Under US$100

● Breakfast may not be included in quoted rates (though it often is in small hotels), so check first. The large hotels usually add on a 10 percent service charge.

Charela Inn
Tel/fax: 957 4845
Email: charela@cwjamaica.com
Website: www.negril.com
The inn has a 250 ft private beach. Beachfront/poolside air conditioned rooms, completely renovated. Freshwater pool; inner tropical garden; restaurant and bar. Retreat for couples and families. Baby-sitting available. Free non-motorised watersports; fully equipped gym.

Chuckles
Tel: 957 4250
Fax: 957 9150
Air conditioned rooms. Impressive view of the 7-mile beach. Cable TV, room safes. International and Jamaican cuisine at restaurant. Bar; disco; lively entertainment; two floodlit tennis courts; exercise room; games room; swimming pool; whirlpool. Golf nearby.

Coco LaPalm Seaside Resort
Tel: 957 4277
Fax: 957 3460
Email: cocolap@toj.com
Beachfront location. Big rooms with air conditioning, cable TV, wet bar, coffee-maker with complimentary Blue Mountain coffee. Two restaurants; two bars; swimming pool; jacuzzi. Fitness centre, golf and tennis nearby.

Country Country
Tel: 957 4273/4359
Fax: 957 4342
Rustic, comfortable, colourful Caribbean-style air conditioned cottages on Negril's famous beach. Two restaurants, one on the beach, Jamaican and Chinese cuisine. The Hunan restaurant, with chef from Hong Kong, has become a favourite Negril eating-spot. Bar; watersports; tours available.

Merril's Beach Resort
Tel: 957 4751
Fax: 957 3121
Email: merrils@cw.com
Located on the 7-mile beach, among lush tropical gardens. Air conditioning. Authentic jerk chicken and pork grilled by chef on beach, or dine at full-service restaurant. Two bars; watersports; tours available.

Negril Beach Club
Tel: 957 4220/1
Fax: 957 4364
Email: negrilbeachclub@toj.com
Air conditioned rooms and suites directly on beach. Restaurant; bar; shops; boutique; full watersports rentals; scuba diving and fitness concessions.

Negril Gardens Hotel
Tel: 957 4408
Fax: 957 4374
Email: negrilgardens@cwjamaica.com
Website: www.negrilgardens.com
Tropical garden rooms, and 40 beachside rooms. Two restaurants (one a Jamaican kitchen and jerk centre), beach bar, pool bar. Meeting facilities for 60 people.

Negril Tree House Resort
Tel: 957 4287/8
Fax: 952 4386
Email: jackson@cwjamaica.com
Rooms with air conditioning, private bath/shower, TV, telephone. Swimming pool; private beach; gym/jacuzzi and fitness centre; restaurant; two bars; horse-riding; tennis. Massage therapist and manicurist on site.

Point Village Resort
Tel: 957 5170
Fax: 957 5351
On Rutland Point, between Bloody Bay and Long Bay, apartments and rooms catering for singles, couples, families. Children's centre and activities. Restaurant; two cafés; three bars; swimming pool; jacuzzi; tennis court; watersports; tours available.

Sea Splash Resort
Tel: 957 4041
Fax: 957 4049
Email: seasplashgl@cwjamaica.com
Suites with ocean and garden views. Fully equipped kitchens, telephone, cable TV, air conditioning, private patio/balcony, safety deposit box, hair dryer. Restaurant; beach bar and grill; gift shop; pool and whirlpool; minigym; complimentary bicycles; watersports available. Complimentary access to large sports complex.

Tensing Pen
West End Road
Tel:957 0387
Fax:957 0161
Email: tensingpen@cwjamaica.com
Rustic cottages set in Eden-like garden on the cliffside. Bird-and lizard-watching, or diving off the suspension bridge or cliffside platforms, make a change from basking in the sun. Make and eat your own meals in the communal kitchen/dining room, or hire the services of excellent cooks.

Xtabi Resort
West End Road, P.O. Box 19
Tel: 957 4336
Fax: 957 0121
Email: xtabiresort@cwjamaica.com
Rooms and six quaint octagonal cottages atop rocky terraces overlooking the sea. Restaurant and bar. Caves to explore, snorkelling, beautiful sunsets.

SOUTHWEST COAST

Moderate
Hospitality Inn
66 South Sea Park, Whitehouse,
Westmoreland
Tel: 963 5500/1
Fax: 995 4017
Small cosy inn, rooms with private
bath/shower; restaurant; private
beach.

Jakes Village
Calabash Bay, Treasure Beach,
St Elizabeth
Tel: 965 0635
Fax: 965 0552
Email: jakes@cwjamaica.com
Website: www.islandlife.com
The atmosphere here is relaxed and
laid back. The rooms and colourful
cottages are individually designed in
a whimsical and arty way. Right on
a bay with crashing waves. Excellent
cuisine. No TV.

Natania's Guest House
Culloden, Whitehouse,
Westmoreland
Tel/fax: 963 5342
Rooms with private bath/shower,
telephone; swimming pool; private
beach; watersports; restaurant;
gym/jacuzzi; horse-riding. This small
guesthouse has maintained its
reputation for excellent food.

Treasure Beach Hotel
Treasure Beach, St Elizabeth
Tel: 965 0110/4
Fax: 965 2544
Email:
treasurebhotel@cwjamaica.com
Rooms directly on the beach, with
satellite TV. Dining inside or
seaside bar and grill. Meeting
facilities; swimming pools; jacuzzi;
beach volleyball; snorkelling; boat
trips. Bird-watching tours arranged
for nature lovers.

White House Beach Villa
White House, Shewberry,
Petersfield P.O., Westmoreland
Tel: 955 2033
Tel/fax: (US) 908 654 8129
Villa with 4 rooms; private
bath/shower; private beach; horse-
riding.

Where to Eat

Warning Note: In general, food is
expensive in Jamaica, and dining
out will cost you a pretty penny.
Even "fast food" costs much more
than in the US or some European
cities. With the exception of snacks
from food carts, all dishes cost
more than US$5, and even at very
simple restaurants you will rarely
get a decent lunch for two for less
than US$35.

Surrey

KINGSTON

Akbar
11 Holborn Road, Kingston 10
Tel: 926 3480
Mouthwatering and eye-watering
Indian food. Kingston's only Indian
restaurant of note. **$–$$**

Alexander's
The New Courtleigh, Knutsford Blvd,
New Kingston
Tel: 929 9000
Choose from an array of uniquely
flavoured international and
Caribbean dishes. An innovative
young chef has brought this
restaurant to international
standard. The décor is also
admirable (the restaurant won the
1999 *Jamaica Observer* Award for
Best Décor). Open daily for lunch
noon–3pm and dinner 6–10.30pm.
$$$

Alhambra Inn
1 Tucker Avenue, Kingston 6
Tel: 978 9072
Fax: 978 9074
Generous Jamaican cuisine from
one of the island's best-known
caterers, in an attractive setting.
Breakfast (7–9am), lunch
(noon–2pm) and dinner (7–9pm).
Sunday brunch is sumptuous, and
it's moderately priced. **$$**

Bamboo Village
5, The Village Plaza
20 Constant Spring Road
Kingston 10
Tel: 926 8863/2389
Very comfortable dining room.
Features authentic Chinese cuisine,
specialising in Peking duck, seafood
Warbar and Cantonese dishes. **$$$**

Chasers Café
29 Barbican Road, Kingston 6
Tel: 978 5776
Open 10.30am till late
Monday–Saturday, with evening
entertainment.
Tel: 978 5002
Sunday brunch 9am–1pm with great
Jamaican dishes (corn pork, fried
plantain, bammy, fish, corn etc.).
MasterCard, American Express and
Visa accepted. **$$**

Price Guide

Approximate cost of lunch for
two, including service and tax:

$$$$	More than US$60
$$$	US$50–60
$$	US$35–50
$	US$20–35

● Evening meals normally cost at
least 50 percent more.

Ciao Bella
19 Hillcrest Avenue (corner Hope
Road), Kingston 6
Tel: 978 5002
Pasta, salad and light dishes.
Beautiful setting; fashionable food;
fashionable company. Good value.
$$$

Dragon City Restaurant
17 Northside Drive, Kingston 6
Tel: 927 0939
Good value Chinese cuisine. **$$**

Dragon Court
Dragon Centre, South Avenue,
Kingston 10
Tel: 920 8506
Exceptional Chinese restaurant
offering dim sum daily and BBQ
dishes weekly. Spacious, relaxing,
cosy setting. Attentive service.
Open daily noon–10pm. **$$**

El Dorado
Terra Nova Hotel, 17 Waterloo Road, Kingston 10
Tel: 926 2211/9334
International cuisine and local dishes, especially seafood and soups. Charming hospitality. Open for lunch noon–2.30pm and dinner 7–11pm. **$$$**

Hotel Four Seasons
18 Ruthven Road, Kingston 10
Tel: 926 8805/0682
Dinner menu offers an assortment of continental and Jamaican dishes. For over 20 years the lunch buffet has provided a pleasant midday repast – probably the heartiest lunch you will find. Open daily for breakfast, lunch and dinner. **$$$**

Grog Shoppe Restaurant & Pub
Devon House, 26 Hope Road, Kingston 10
Tel: 929 7027
Indifferent food is compensated for by the relaxed and pleasant atmosphere. Sitting outdoors, under a spreading mango tree, or in the Grog Shoppe (reminiscent of 17th-century Port Royal) is one of the best ways to spend a Kingston evening. Nightly entertainment (jazz, blues, calypso, karaoke, etc.). **$$**

Indies Hotel
5 Holborn Road, Kingston 10
Tel: 926 2952
Fax: 926 2879
English fish and chips and pizza are the favourites. This restaurant does brisk business. (The hotel has: 16 modest but comfortable guest rooms – see page 334). **$$**

Isabella's Restaurant
Crowne Plaza Hotel, 211a Constant Spring Road, Manor Park, Kingston 8
Tel: 925 7676
Fax: 925 4425
Sumptuously decorated restaurant with a view. New World cuisine, featuring American, African, European and Asian culinary delights with distinctly Caribbean flavour and presentation. Dine on the verandah overlooking the city and the harbour, or in the splendid dining room. Open daily noon–11pm. **$$$$**

Jade Garden
106 Hope Road, Sovereign Centre, Kingston 6
Tel: 978 3476/9
Cuisine prepared in a beautiful Oriental setting, with two of the largest sea-water fish tanks on the island. Over 100 exotic dishes. Take-out service with daily lunch special. Open daily noon–10pm; dim sum on last Sunday of month, 10am–9pm. **$$$**

Lillian's Restaurant
University of Technology, 237 Old Hope Road, Kingston 6
Tel: 512 2283
The university's School of Hospitality training restaurant serves an acceptable lunch (noon–2pm) at modest prices, in an elegant Georgian-style building which is a National Heritage Trust property. **$**

Mayfair Hotel
4 West King's House Close, Kingston 10
Tel: 926 1610/2
International and local cuisine served in a colonial-style setting. High ceilings, large mahogany columns and glass-panelled doors open onto wide, shaded verandahs. Open daily for dinner 7–9.30pm. **$$**

Norma's on the Terrace
Devon House, 26 Hope Road, Kingston 10
Tel: 968 5488
Jamaica's most celebrated chef brings her gourmet "nouvelle Jamaican" fare to the veranda at Devon House. Known for her unusual and stylish food presentation; expect innovative food. The Terrace is open for coffee, lunch, tea and dinner (10.30am–11pm). The verandah overlooks the courtyard with all its goings-on, an endlessly fascinating vignette of Jamaican life. **$$$**

Palm Court
Hilton Kingston Hotel, 77 Knutsford Blvd, Kingston 5
Tel: 926 5430
Enjoy a relaxing lunch or dinner on the mezzanine. Quiet ambience,

Vegetarian & "Ital" Restaurants

"Ital" ("natural" — adopted from the Rastafarian faith) is the generic Jamaican vegetarian/fish cooking style. Vegetarian restaurants in Jamaica tend to serve ital food, such as vegetarian stews, soups and fish. Fresh fruit juices are usually available. Most ital and vegetarian restaurants tend to be inexpensive (**$**).

● **Kingston:**
Akbar Indian restaurant (see page 342) will provide vegetarian meals.
Vegetarian restaurants are:
Eden Vegetarian Restaurant, Shop #24, 13c Constant Spring Road, tel: 925 3051; **King Ital**, 4 Caledonia Crescent, Kingston 5, tel: 929 1921 (open 7am–8pm); **Lyn's Vegetarian**, 7 Tangerine Place, Kingston 10, tel: 968 3487; **Queen of Sheba** at the Bob Marley Museum, 56 Hope Road, Kingston 10, tel: 978 0510; **Mother Earth**, 13 Oxford Terrace, Kingston 5, tel: 926 2572 (Monday–Friday 7.30am–5.30pm, specialising in vegetarian and fish).
For the health conscious with a sweet-tooth why not try the ice cream at: **Newberry's Shakes 'n' Cones**, Constant Spring Road/Mary Brown's Corner, Kingston 8, tel: 941 0704/5216. Milk-free, sugar-free, grade A, Kosher, whey and soy protein concentrate "creamy ices". Fresh fruit flavours. (Hot dogs and pastries too.) Open Monday–Saturday noon–11pm, Sunday 1–11pm

● **Ocho Rios:**
Try **Afiya's Island Plaza**, tel: 973 4366, or **Nature's Way**, 2 Rennie Road, tel: 795 3541.

● **Runaway Bay:**
Afiya's, tel: 974 5797.

● **Montego Bay:**
Royal Court, tel: 952 4531.

● **Negril:**
Country Country (see page 347) or **Just Natural**, West End Road, in a lush garden setting.

piano music, excellent Italian and international cuisine. Open daily for lunch noon–2.30pm and dinner 7–10pm. **$$$**

Pegasus Café
Le Meridien Jamaica Pegasus, 81 Knutsford Blvd, Kingston 5
Tel: 926 3690/9
This counter-service continental-style café features waffles, crêpes, delectable pastries, homemade ice cream, light snacks and a variety of freshly brewed coffees and teas. Open daily 7am–11pm (from 10am Sunday). **$$**

Sir Henry's Restaurant
Morgan's Harbour Hotel, Port Royal
Tel: 967 8030
On the waterfront, this marina restaurant specialises in local seafood bought fresh daily, and offers spectacular views of Kingston Bay and the magnificent Blue Mountains in the distance. Relax at the popular Duppy Bar with a cool tropical drink. **$$–$$$**

PORT ANTONIO & NORTHEAST COAST

In addition to those listed below, on the coast road going east out of Port Antonio town towards Boston Beach there are a number of typical, very basic restaurants located right on the seaside. At these places the catch of the day will be cooked while you wait and served with rice 'n' peas or bammy – easy on both palate and pocket. They include the Survival Beach Restaurant and the adjoining KS Coosie Knook Bar & Restaurant.

Further along the coast, Boston Beach is where jerk pork, the flavour for which Jamaica is now famous, originated.

Blue Lagoon
Fairy Hill, west of Boston Bay
Tel: 993 8491
Authentic Jamaican cuisine served against the spectacular backdrop of world-famous Blue Lagoon. Choose your own fresh lobster. Jerk specialities include chicken, pork, fish, sausage, lamb chops and crayfish, complemented with seasonal local vegetables.

Vegetarian pizzas. Live entertainment at weekends. Blue Lagoon party Tuesday nights. Open daily 10am–10pm. **$$**

The Hob
No telephone
By old railway station, Port Antonio
Excellent new restaurant serving traditional Jamaican cuisine. **$**

Kildare Villa
Buff Bay (between Ocho Rios and Port Antonio)
Tel: 996 1240
One of the few places on this coast where you can dine looking out to sea. Located at a spot where the Caribbean is at its most beguiling, this is a perfect rest stop. **$**

Mille Fleurs
Mocking Bird Hill Hotel, Port Antonio
Tel: 993 7267
With a magnificent panoramic view of Port Antonio Bay. The à la carte menu changes daily and features fresh seasonal produce. Praised by *Gourmet* magazine. **$$**

The Pavilion
Dragon Bay Beach Resort
Tel: 993 8514
Nouvelle cuisine with a Jamaican touch. Special themed menus every day. Candlelit evenings with live entertainment. Open daily for dinner 7–10pm. **$$$**

Trident Villas & Hotel Restaurant
Trident Villas & Hotel, Port Antonio
Tel: 993 2602
Candlelit dinners graced with silver service, crystal and pewter stemware. European chefs prepare continental and Jamaican specialities. Jacket required. Open daily 7–10pm. **$$$$**

Middlesex

SPANISH TOWN

Dan's Restaurant
42 King Street
Tel: 984 8642
Chinese Jamaican food at its best. Also serves Jamaican food without the Oriental twist. Open Monday–Saturday 10am–10pm. Very affordable, cash only. **$**

Galaxy Restaurant
Adelaide Street

You can't do better at weekday lunchtimes. But at these prices don't expect any effort with the décor and ambience. **$**

The Sips Lounge
15 Oxford Road
Tel: 984 7459
Inexpensive, but not just a plastic-and-paper "joint"; fresh flowers and real crockery; good mixed drinks. Lunch and dinner menus include Chinese food and local dishes (chop suey, chow mein, fried rice, curried lobster, etc.). Open Monday–Saturday from noon until the last customer leaves. All major credit cards accepted. **$**

The Wine Bar
Next to the Folk Museum on Old King's House grounds, Emancipation Square
Tel: 907 3068
The water wheel, the folk museum and the shadow of Old King's House all set the tone. Traditional Jamaican furniture and an impressive collection of local masters on the walls proclaim the Wine Bar's heritage. But although the setting is colonial "period piece", the fare is wholly contemporary. Good selection of international wines and snacks to satisfy the most cosmopolitan tastes (smoked marlin, stuffed sea-crab backs, vegetarian pâté). Open 11am–11pm Monday–Saturday. **$$**

OCHO RIOS AREA

The following listings cover the stretch of coast from St Ann's Bay to Oracabessa.

Almond Tree
Hibiscus Lodge Hotel, Main Street, Ocho Rios
Tel: 974 2813
Dine by candlelight under the stars while overlooking the Caribbean Sea. A la carte menu features wide variety of fish, seafood and prime meats. Live music three nights a week at swinging bar. Piano bar. Open daily 7am–10pm. **$$$**

Bay Pointe Restaurant
Fisherman's Point Resort, Ocho Rios
Tel: 974 5317/4473

Casual, elegant indoor/outdoor ocean-view dining. Seafood, Jamaican and continental cuisine. Open daily for breakfast, lunch and dinner. Live entertainment Wednesday, Friday and Saturday. **$$**

Bougainvillea Terrace
Plantation Inn, Ocho Rios
Tel: 974 5601
Variety of American, German, Italian and other European dishes. Terrace dining, five-course dinner available. American and buffet breakfasts, changing lunch menu. Open daily for breakfast (7.30–10.30am), lunch (1–3pm) and dinner (7–10pm). **$$$**

Café Aubergine
Moneague
(25 minutes from Ocho Rios, going south on the main road to Kingston)
Tel/fax: 973 0527
French, Italian and nouvelle Jamaican cuisine in a charming cellar-with-garden setting. Open 11.30am–9pm Tuesday–Sunday and holiday Monday. **$$$**

Price Guide

Approximate cost of lunch for two, including service and tax:

$$$$	More than US$60
$$$	US$50–60
$$	US$35–50
$	US$20–35

● Evening meals normally cost at least 50 percent more.

Club House Restaurant
Comfort Suites, 17 DaCosta Drive, Ocho Rios
Tel: 974 8050
Continental cuisine with a local flair and tasty Jamaican dishes. Casual island ambience, lush tropical plants. Open daily 7.30am–10pm. **$$**

Cutlass Bay Palm Terrace
Shaw Park Beach Hotel, Ocho Rios
Te: 974 2552
American, European and Jamaican cuisine. Flambée entrees are prepared tableside. Dine under the stars in this elegant restaurant overlooking the Caribbean Sea. Open daily 7.30am–9.30pm. **$$$**

Dragons
Renaissance Jamaica Grande, Ocho Rios
Tel: 974 2201
Chinese decor. Delicious Cantonese and Szechwan cuisine. Open Tuesday–Sunday for dinner 6–11pm. **$$$**

Evita's Italian Restaurant
Overlooking Ocho Rios
Tel: 974 2333/1012
Authentic Italian food, plus house specialities Rasta Pasta, Pasta Viagra and Jerk Spaghetti. Fresh homemade pasta. Try the "Jamaican Bobsled" for dessert. One of Ocho Rios' most popular restaurants. Elegant but reasonably priced, children half-price. Open daily 11am–11pm. **$$**

Glenn's Jazz Club Restaurant
Tower Cloisters Resort Condominiums, Tower Isle (east of Ocho Rios's, along the coast)
Tel: 975 4360, 975 4763/4
Hearty Jamaican/international cuisine with background jazz; occasional live jazz. Open 9am–10.30pm. **$$**

L'Allegro
Renaissance Jamaica Grande, Ocho Rios
Tel: 974 2201
Italian restaurant with pastas, pizzas, soups, salads and desserts. Open for lunch and dinner noon–11pm; only pizza served 11pm–midnight. **$$$**

The Little Pub
59 Main Street, Ocho Rios
Tel: 974 2324
Set in a Georgian-style complex in the heart of Ocho Rios. In the evenings, the dining area converts to dinner-theatre for cabaret shows. Open daily 7am–midnight. **$$**

The Mug Restaurant
On the Ocho Rios highway, St Ann's Bay
Tel: 972 1018
One of the most pleasant places for lunch in all Jamaica. Right on the water's edge. Fish, conch and other Jamaican favourites. **$$**

Ocean Dock Restaurant
Ocean Sands Resort, 14 James Avenue, Ocho Rios
Tel: 974 1421/3365
A romantic open-air restaurant at the waterside. Sumptuous à la carte or buffet-style cuisine. Cocktails at Ocean Dock Bar. Open daily 7.30am–10.30pm. **$$**

Passage to India
Upstairs, Soni's Centre
Tel: 957 3182
Main Street, Ocho Rios
Indian tandoori cooking in a clay oven. Excellent reputation. Lunch and dinner. **$$**

The Ruins
DaCosta Drive, Ocho Rios
Tel: 974 2442
A waterfall cascades 40 ft into pools surrounding the dining terrace. Jamaican and international cuisine with traditional Jamaican recipes. Open for lunch Monday–Saturday noon–2.30pm, dinner daily 7–10.30pm. **$$$**

Sea Palms
Golden Seas Beach Resort, Oracabessa
Tel: 975 3540/1
International cuisine combined with Jamaican specialities, served in an elegant seaside setting. Open daily for breakfast 7.30–10am, dinner 7–10pm. **$$$**

Toscanini
Harmony Hall
(east of Ocho Rios)
Tel: 975 4785
Stylish Italian restaurant which uses authentic ingredients and also produces innovative dishes. Open Tuesday–Sunday for lunch noon–2.30pm, dinner 7–10.30pm. **$$$**

MANDEVILLE

Bamboo Village
Ward Plaza
Tel: 962 4515/6
Menu features authentic Chinese cuisine. Specialities include house-style beef fillet, seafood served steaming hot, and other Cantonese dishes. Open daily noon–10pm. **$$**

Bloomfield Great House
8 Perth Road
Tel: 962 7130
Email:
bloomfield.g.h@cwjamaica.com
Very grand dining, award-winning contemporary menu. Home-made

pastas are a speciality. Run by husband and wife Ralph Pearce and Pamela Grant. Open noon–11pm, Monday–Saturday. All major credit cards accepted. **$$**

Golf View Restaurant
Golf View Hotel,
51/2 Caledonia Road
Tel: 962 4471
Specialising in Jamaican and international cuisine. Open daily for breakfast 7–10am and dinner 6–9pm. **$$**

Manchester Arms Pub & Restaurant
Mandeville Hotel
Tel: 962 9764/5
Jamaican and international cuisine served in dining room or poolside coffee shop. Pub serves mixed drinks and special rum punch. Poolside barbecue with live music on Wednesday. Authentic Jamaican Sunday brunch, poolside. Open 6.30am–10pm. **$$**

Cornwall

EAST OF FALMOUTH

Nibbles
Silver Sands Villa & Beach Club,
Duncans
Tel: 954 2001
Grill on the beach serving barbecued steaks, ribs and chicken, grilled fish, hot dogs, hamburgers and sandwiches. Open Sunday–Thursday 10am–6pm, Friday and Saturday 10am–9pm. **$**

Palm Terrace
Trelawny Beach Hotel, Falmouth
Tel: 954 2450
Open to non-residents only with a **night pass** (US$35), which includes dinner, drinks and activities from 6pm to 2am. Casual, open-air restaurant serving a variety of European and Jamaican dishes. Entertainment nightly, dancing during dinner. Relaxed ambience, shorts and sandals acceptable.

Rio Brac Rest Stop
Braco, Rio Bueno (between Falmouth and Discovery Bay)
Tel: 954 0269
Hearty Jamaican meals; cool drinks; a true rest stop with good facilities and friendly prices. **$**

MONTEGO BAY AREA

The Atrium at Ironshore
1084 Morgan Road
Tel: 953 2605
Fine European and Jamaican cuisine offered in an intimate, beautiful setting at reasonable prices. Attentive service. Popular Saturday-night barbecue. Open daily 11am–11pm. **$$**

Belfield Restaurant
Barnett Estate
Tel: 952 2382
Step back into Jamaica's history and enjoy fine Jamaican and Caribbean cuisine in a restored sugar mill on the 3,000-acre Barnett Estate. **$$$**

Castles Restaurant
Comfort Suites/Sea Castles,
Rose Hall
Tel: 953 3250
Castles serves dinner from an à la carte menu. Also two open-air cafés on the premises: Poolside Café with buffet dining and Clifftop Café serving grilled lunches and snacks. Open daily: Castles 7.30–9:30pm; Poolside Café 6.30–9:30pm; Clifftop Café during the day. **$$–$$$**

The Greenhouse
Doctor's Cave Beach Hotel,
Gloucester Avenue
Tel: 952 7838
Centrally located. Burgers, pizza and daily Jamaican specials at a price you can afford. Open daily for breakfast, lunch, dinner and snacks, 7am–11pm. **$**

Norma's at The Wharfhouse
Reading
Tel: 979 2745
Dine on the verandah at the historic wharfhouse, chef Norma Shirley's flagship restaurant. Norma has appeared on TV cooking programmes and in international gourmet magazines. You get what you pay for. Closed all summer and on Monday during the winter season. **$$$$**

The Pelican
Gloucester Avenue
Tel: 952 3171
Long favoured by Jamaicans, and now by visitors as well, for hearty Jamaican food, especially

Jerk Centres

"Jerk" pork originates from Boston Beach, Portland. Although jerk pork is the older Jamaican speciality, jerk chicken is now more commonly served. There are jerk restaurants all over Jamaica, most of them inexpensive (**$**). Some of the better known places are:

- **Chelsea Jerk Centre**, Chelsea Avenue, Kingston
- **Ocho Rios Jerk Centre**, DaCosta Drive, Ocho Rios
- **Pork Pit**, Gloucester Avenue, Montego Bay

breakfast. American favourites are here too. Good value. **$$**

Seagrape Terrace
Half Moon Golf, Tennis & Beach Club, Rose Hall
Tel: 953 2211
A gourmet restaurant on an enchanting tree-shaded patio overlooking the Half Moon beach. Specialises in Caribbean nouvelle cuisine. Open daily. **$$$**

Sugarmill Restaurant
Half Moon Golf Course
Tel: 953 2314
An elegant restaurant nestled beside the ancient water wheel of a once well-used sugar mill at the Half Moon Golf Club. Caribbean and continental cuisine with flambée specialities. Open daily for lunch noon–3pm and dinner 7.30–10.30pm. **$$$**

Verandah Restaurant & Bar
Coral Cliff Hotel, 165 Gloucester Avenue
Tel: 952 4130
One of Montego Bay's favourite dining spots since the 1920s. Today the Verandah continues the old tradition of fine dining. **$$**

The Vineyard at Coyaba
Coyaba Beach Resort & Club,
Mahoe Bay, Ironshore
Tel: 953 9150
French-Caribbean cuisine in a garden setting. Enjoy cocktails before or after at The Polo Grounds Lounge. Excellent cuisine, unbeatable charm and old-world grace. Open daily 7–10pm. **$$$**

The Wexford Grill
The Wexford Hotel
Tel: 952-2854
Specialising in ribs and Jamaican cuisine. Open daily for breakfast, lunch and dinner, 7am–11pm. Saturday and Sunday brunch buffet 8–11am. **$$**

NEGRIL

All the following are on Norman Manley Boulevard unless otherwise stated.
Country Country
Tel: 957 4369/4273
Grill situated on the beachfront. Serves a range of food from seafood and meat to vegetarian dishes. There is also a Chinese restaurant at the front of the property. Open daily 10am–8pm. **$$**
Chuckles
Chuckles Negril
Tel: 957 4250/9152
Jamaican and international cuisine. Buffet-style or à la carte. Candlelit dining in a romantic setting. Open daily. **$$**
Gambino's
Beachcomber Club
Tel: 957 4170/1/4
Authentic Italian cuisine along with local favourites. Pasta bar; special Jamaican breakfast every morning. A la carte and buffet dining. Sunset lounge for functions. Open 7.30am–10.30pm. **$$**
La Vendôme
Charela Inn
Tel: 957 4277
Dine under the stars or indoors. French and Jamaican cuisine, wines and champagne. Live traditional Jamaican music on Thursday, cultural folk music show on Saturday. Open daily 6–10pm. **$$$**
Lion's Head Gallery
Bar-B Barn Hotel
Tel: 957 4267/4755
Enjoy dining in a gallery featuring fine pieces of Jamaican art. Jamaican and European cuisine, fresh seafood, beautiful view of sea. Open daily 7am–11pm. **$$**
Merril's Restaurant
Merril's Beach Resort
Tel: 957 4751

Fish, chicken, pork, fresh seafood, grilled lobster. Beach barbecue dinner buffet every night, plus à la carte. Open daily, 7am–10pm. **$$**
Negril Tree House
Tel: 957 4287/8
Inventive Jamaican cuisine. Chicken, fish, pork or lobster any way you like it. Pizza. Sunday jazz and breakfast on the beach. Open daily 7am–11pm. **$$**
Orchid Terrace Restaurant
Negril Gardens Hotel
Tel: 957 4408
Jamaican and international cuisine. Chinese specialities include sweet 'n' sour chicken/pork/fish, choy fan and chop suey. Open daily. **$$**

Price Guide

Approximate cost of lunch for two, including service and tax:

$$$$	More than US$60
$$$	US$50–60
$$	US$35–50
$	US$20–35

● Evening meals normally cost at least 50 percent more.

The Pickled Parrot
West End Road
Tel: 957 4864
Jamaican, Mexican and American cuisine, good for burgers, salads and ribs. Fun clifftop base for daytime, with giant waterslide, rope swing and caves to snorkel through under the restaurant/bar. Open daily 9am–1am. $$
Rondel Village
Rondel Village Resort
Tel: 957 4413
Offering mostly Jamaican dishes, specialising in lobster and fish for dinner. Special Sunday-night barbecue features suckling pig, lobster and chicken. Open until 9.30pm. **$$**
Sandi San Restaurant
Sandi San Beach Hotel
Tel: 957 4487
Specialising in fresh seafood, pasta and jerk chicken, pork and fish. Beach location. Dining inside and outside. Open 7.30am–11pm. **$$**

Seaside Restaurant
Coco LaPalm Resort
Tel: 957 4227
Featuring light California-style cuisine with Jamaican influence. Dishes range from pasta to grilled meats, fresh fish and seafood. Tantalising desserts prepared by Swiss pastry chef. Open daily for breakfast and dinner. **$$**
Sundrenched Bar & Grill
Point Village Resort
Tel: 957 5170/9
A covered, open-air dining facility nestled on a coral reef. Snack on hot dogs, hamburgers, hot or cold sandwiches, 10.30am–6pm, Jamaican specials 7–10pm. **$$**
Tan-Ya's
Sea Splash Resort
Tel: 957 4041
European and classical cuisine accented by the chef's Jamaican nouvelle creations. Island delicacies are prepared with a distinctly European flair. Romantic ambience. Open daily for dinner 6–10pm. **$$$**
Village Connection
Point Village Resort
Tel: 957 5170/9
Open-air dining. International cuisine for breakfast, lunch and dinner. Open for buffet breakfast (7.30–10.30am), lunch and dinner. **$$$**
Xtabi Cliff Restaurant
Xtabi Resort, West End Road
Tel: 957 4336/0121
Lobster, prime meats, chicken and pork, fresh Jamaican seafood. All available chargrilled or any way you like it. Lobster Benedict, conch burgers, many island specialties. Open daily 8am–11pm. **$$**

SOUTHWEST COAST

Yabba
Treasure Beach Hotel
Tel: 965 0110/4
Jamaican and international cuisine and fresh seafood; relaxing atmosphere. The vegetables and citrus fruits are grown on the owner's farm. Open 7am–10pm. **$$**

Culture

Note: Great houses are listed under *Excursions*, page 351. Entry charges and opening times are, of course, subject to change.

Museums

Kingston Area

Bob Marley Museum, 56 Hope Road, Kingston 6, tel: 927 9152. Marley's former residence and site of Tuff Gong recording studio. Open Monday–Saturday 10am–5 pm. Entry fee.

Fort Charles & Maritime Museum, located in former British naval headquarters near Port Royal. Tel: 967 8438. Open daily 9.30am–4.30pm. Guided tours.

Geology Museum, c/o Institute of Jamaica, tel: 922 0620/6.

Institute of Jamaica, 12 East Street, Kingston, tel: 922 0620/6. The largest collection of historical books, articles and prints in the West Indies.

Jamaica Defence Force Museum (The Military Museum), Up Park Camp, tel: 926 8121/8129/8153, ext. 2017. Open Monday–Friday 10am–5pm or by appointment.

National Museum of Historical Archaeology, Port Royal, tel: 922 1287 or 922 0620/6 (c/o Institute of Jamaica).

Natural History Museum, Institute of Jamaica, 12 East Street, Kingston, tel: 922 0620/6. The oldest museum in Jamaica.

Zoology Museum, tel: 927 1202. Open by appointment. Operated by the University of the West Indies.

Spanish Town

Archaeological Museum, Old King's House, Spanish Town Square, tel: 922 0620/6 (c/o Institute of Jamaica). Occupies the former official residence of the governor of Jamaica.

Jamaican People's Museum of Craft and Technology, in the stables of Old King's House, Spanish Town, tel: 922 0620/6 (c/o Institúte of Jamaica).

Ocho Rios Area

Coyaba River Garden & Museum, Shaw Park, P.O. Box 18, Ocho Rios, tel: 974 6235. Includes Taino museums. Open daily 8am–5pm. Entry fee.

Discovery Bay

Columbus Park: Jamaica's only open-air museum is located on a bluff overlooking Discovery Bay, marking the spot where Columbus first landed.

Montego Bay Area

Blue Hole Museum, tel: 909 9602. Also a great house and plantation. Open daily 8am–6pm. Guided tours.

Greenwood Great House Museum, Montego Bay, tel: 953 1077. One of Jamaica's finest collections of antique furniture, musical instruments and maps. Open 9am–6pm.

Galleries

Art galleries normally open Monday–Saturday 10am–5pm, or by special arrangement. Please note, however, that the National Gallery and all exhibitions related to the Institute of Jamaica are closed on Saturday.

Kingston Area

The Art Centre Ltd at Olympia International Art Centre, 202 Old Hope Road, tel: 927 1608.

The Art Gallery, Hilton Shopping Arcade, tel: 960 8939.

Bolivar Gallery & Bookshop, 1D Grove Road, tel: 926 8799.

Chelsea Galleries, 12 Chelsea Avenue, tel: 929 0045.

Contemporary Art Centre, 1 Liguanea Avenue, tel: 927 9958.

Easel Gallery, 134 Old Hope Road, tel: 977 2067.

Frame Art, 7 Belmont Road, tel: 926 5014.

Frame Centre Gallery, 10 Tangerine Place, tel: 926 4644.

Gallery Makonde, Gordon Town Road, tel: 977 4409.

Gallery Pegasus, Jamaica Pegasus, tel: 926 3690.

Grosvenor Galleries, 1 Grosvenor Terrace, tel: 924 6684.

Hi Qo Spanish Court, 19 Spanish Court, tel: 926 4183.

Mutual Life Gallery, 2 Oxford Road, tel: 929 4302.

National Gallery of Art, 12 Ocean Blvd, tel: 922 1561. Open Monday–Friday, 11am–4.30pm (closes at 4pm Friday).

Portland

Carriacou at Mocking Bird Hill Hotel, P.O. Box 254, tel: 993 7267.

Ocho Rios Area

Beautiful Memories, Island Plaza, tel: 974 2374.

Gallery Joe James, Rio Bueno, tel: 954 0046.

Harmony Hall, P.O. Box 192, tel: 975 4222/2870. Open daily 10am–6pm. Shows outstanding Jamaican and Caribbean art.

Montego Bay Area

Ambiente, 9 Forest Street, tel: 952 7919.

Bay Gallery, Westgate Hills, tel: 952 7668.

Gallery Hoffstead, Lucea, tel: 956 2241.

Gallery of West Indian Art, 1 Orange Lane, tel: 952 4547.

Heaven's Art Gallery, 2 Church Lane, tel: 952 2852.

Images, Half Moon Hotel, tel: 953 9043.

Keith Chandler, Rock Wharf, tel: 954 3314.

Neville Budhai Art Gallery, Main Road, Reading, tel: 979 2568.

Sun Art Gallery, Half Moon Shopping Village, tel: 953 3455.

Negril

Gallery Hoffstead, 2 Plaza de Negril, tel: 957 3015.

Geraldine Robins, West End Road.

Kool Brown, West End Road, tel: 957 4361.

Le Bric à Brac, Negril Beach, tel: 957 4277.

Movies

Jamaicans are great movie fans and treat going to the cinema as an interactive experience, so don't be surprised if the audience is rather vocal during a film. American-made films are the most popular, and arrive in Kingston immediately after their release in the USA. The small but thriving local movie industry has tremendous support. Consult the local newspaper or your hotel for details.

Theatre, Dance & Music

Jamaica's lively tradition of performing arts – theatre, dance and music – is surveyed in the features section of this book. There is a lot of live theatre going on in Kingston, the island's cultural hub. Be sure to see the national **Pantomime** at the **Ward Theatre** between December and March/April.

The National Dance Theatre Company, Movements, The Company (also dance) and the Jamaica Musical Theatre, to name a few of the major groups, stage important mini-seasons at Kingston's **Little Theatre**, the dancers in December and the singers in March–April. The Little Theatre is in use all year round. In fact, so great was the demand that the small rehearsal room attached to the theatre was itself converted into the Little Little Theatre, which is now also fully booked year-round.

The **University Singers** (from the University of the West Indies) are excellent and have their season in June at the **Philip Sherlock Centre** on the university campus, a major cultural space renamed after the former vice-chancellor. The **Jamaica School of Music** also hosts classical concerts.

In 1999 a theatre complex, **Centre Stage**, opened in Kingston on the site of a former drive-in cinema. Plays usually run from Wednesday to Sunday.

Festivals

Jamaica carnival: the week after Easter; Kingston and Chukka Cove. Jamaica's biggest festival, established in 1990. "Blow-out" fêtes start in January, but the countdown to the carnival proper starts on Easter Sunday in Chukka Cove, St Ann, then moves to Kingston for a riotous week of fêting and events, culminating in a Road March on the Monday eight days after Easter Sunday.

Manchester Flower Show: in May the venerable Manchester Horticultural Society puts on its annual flower show at the Society's headquarters on Ward Avenue.

Jamaica Festival: May to 6 August (Independence Day), islandwide. Celebrations marking independence, with local activities and children's competitions (song, dance, culinary arts, folk and gospel music, drama etc.). Tel: 926 5726/5729 for details, or ask at your hotel.

Ocho Rios Jazz Festival: June. Also associated events all along the coast from Negril to Ocho Rios, and many in Kingston too. International and local stars are featured. Jazz Centre hotline: tel/fax: 927 3544; website: www.ochoriosjazz.com.

Tastee Talent Contest: Grand Final about a week before Christmas, Tastee Outdoor Theatre, Cross Roads, Kingston. Preliminary rounds take place there also, on the last Thursday of the month through most of the year. Sponsored by Tastee, makers of patties. Attracts performers from all over the island; competitors perform alongside big names. Musicians, dancers, poets, comedians, magicians, etc. Events are free; tel: 926 2834 for details.

Nightlife

Many young visitors to Jamaica are keen to hear some **reggae** music. Nightclubs, bars, discos, open-air stages and basement venues throughout the island offer a regular fare of this rhythmic music, and it's easy to find good live reggae. There are also places where you can seek out a variety of other musical genres.

Negril and Montego Bay are the island's premier nightlife centres.

Kingston

Knutsford Boulevard has become the hottest strip in Kingston. In the space of two blocks, literally around the corner from the city's three major hotels (Le Meridien, The New Courtleigh and the Hilton), Jamaican culture has established a strong presence alongside international fast-food franchises. **Club Asylum** at Number 69 (tel: 906 1828/9) gives asylum to lovers of oldies, dance-hall music, soca etc., on different nights of the week, while the **Halftime Sports Bar** at Number 61 (tel: 906 1452/4) is a refuge for Kingston's most macho.

Kingston Marketplace

This attractive mini-mall on Constant Spring Road, Sandy Gully Bridge (tel: 906 8999), offers nightly entertainment as well as a wide variety of shops and restaurants. Recommended for its relaxed, non-threatening atmosphere. **Megastar Karaoke** is at the Marketplace every Friday and Sunday. (On other nights they play elsewhere; tel: 931 9570 for details.)

Other popular night spots include **Turntable**, **Carlos**, **Chasers** and **Peppers**. Good nights are also to be had at the **Junkanoo Lounge** at the Hilton Hotel, New Kingston, and **Mingles** at The New Courtleigh. The biggest of all is **Cactus** in Portmore.

Ocho Rios

The most popular clubs in Ocho Rios are **The Ruins**, **The Little Pub** and **Silks** (at the Shaw Park Beach Hotel). You might also drop by **Footprints** in the Coconut Grove Shopping Centre, **Jamaica Mi Crazy** (disco in Jamaica Grande Hotel on Mondays), **Parkway Upper Deck**, **Amnesia**, 70 Main Street, and the **Roof Club**, James Avenue. **The Reggae Strip** is an outdoor reggae party where the action stretches from James Avenue at the clock tower to the sea, every Thursday night 8pm till late.

Runaway Bay

In Runaway Bay, look for **Jaws** at Club Caribbean.

Montego Bay

The Witch's Hideaway at the Holiday Inn has been established longer than any other club. Also in the Rose Hall area, try **Disco Inferno** at Holiday Village. The hottest place in town is **Marguueritaville** on Montego Bay Strip; **Walter's Bar & Grill** and **Pier 1** are also popular. For less flamboyant action there's a nightly piano bar at the **Doctor's Cave Beach Hotel**.

Negril

Nightlife is easy to find in Negril. Lively bars in the West End are **Rick's** and the **Pickled Parrot**. On the beachfront are **Margueritaville**, with special events and promotions every night, and for regular big-name reggae events **De-Buss Beach Bar**. There's also the (in)famous **Hedonism II** nightclub attached to the luxury all inclusive resort of the same name.

Excursions

Note: Charges and opening times quoted are, of course, subject to change.

Out of Town

GUIDED TOURS & ACTIVITIES

Birding Tours: Birding in Jamaica is enhanced by the unique richness and variety of the landscape and the beautiful tropical climate. The island supports 256 bird species in total, including 25 species and 21 sub-species which are found nowhere else on earth. For information on birding tours contact the **Touring Society of Jamaica**, tel: 954 2383.

Port Antonio Area
Rio Grande Rafting: A 2-hour cruise on a bamboo raft for two, poled by expert raftsmen through spectacular scenery. Daily, 8.30am–4.30pm. Tel: 993 5778.
Valley Hikes: For history enthusiasts there are tours into the Land of Look Behind and Maroon Country, including a meeting with the "Colonel" (chief of the Maroons, descendants of escaped Spanish slaves). Or venture down trails to tiny villages. Monday–Friday 9am–4.30pm, Saturday and Sunday 9am–noon. Tel: 993 3881.

Ocho Rios Area
Blue Mountain Tours: Downhill rides on mountain bicycles with guides. Meet local coffee farmers. Tuesday–Saturday, 7am–5pm; breakfast, lunch and waterfall swim included. US$80 including transfers, food and equipment. Tel: 974 7075.

Calypso Rafting: 45-minute scenic ride down the White River, with a swim in the cool mountain waters. Daily 8.30am–4.30pm, US$35 per raft. Tel: 974 2527.
Heli Tours: Helicopter tours of the island, 10am–5pm daily. Tel: 974 2265.
Hooves Limited: Guided horseback tours. Learn about medicinal properties of indigenous plants. Choice of two tours, both starting at 9am daily. Tel: 972 0905; fax: 972 0904; e-mail: hooves@cwjamaica.com
Prospect Plantation Tour: Daily tours of a working plantation in an open jitney. Monday–Saturday at 10.30am, 2pm and 3.30pm; Sunday at 11am, 1.30pm and 3pm. US$12. Tel: 994 1058/2058.
Sun Valley Plantation Tour: By Oracabessa. Tells the history of the property from the slave era to present day. Watch the boxing of bananas for export. Open 9am–4pm daily US$12. Tel: 995 3075.

Montego Bay Area
Belvedere Estate Tour: Plantation and heritage tour. Ruined great house 10am–4pm. Tel: 956 7310. US$10 (US$25 with lunch).
Blue Hole Museum, Great House & Plantation: Guided tours and horseriding. Daily 8am–6pm. Tel: 909 9602. Tours are US$15.
Calico Day Cruise: Daily except Mondays and Wednesdays, 10am–5pm, US$35. Tel: 952 5860.
Cockpit Country Adventure Tours: Albert Town, Trelawny. Managed by the South Trelawny Environmental Agency. Several tours available, and personal ones can be arranged. Daily 9.30am–5.30pm. Tours cost up to US$50 including transfers and lunch. Tel: 610 0818; fax: 610 0819; e-mail: stea@cwjamaica.com.
Croydon in the Mountains: Half-day tours of 132-acre working plantation in Catadupa (45 minutes from Montego Bay). Main crops are coffee, pineapples, plantains and citrus. Tuesday, Wednesday and Friday, 10.30am–3pm. Tel: 979 8267.

Evening on the Great River: Sunday and Thursday. Leisurely boat ride downstream, culminating in dinner and local show. Price includes round-trip transfer from Montego Bay hotels, food and open bar. US$60 per person. Tel: 952 3732.
Martha Brae Rafting: River trip lasting just over an hour. Begins at Rafters' Village, 4 miles from Falmouth. 8.30am–4.30pm daily except holidays. Tel: 954 5168.
Miskito Cove Beach Picnic: Daily 9.30am–6pm. US$55. Tel: 953 3506.
MoBay Undersea Tours: Explore Montego Bay's marine sanctuary aboard a modern semi-submarine. Panoramic marine environment and coral reefs. air conditioned cabin holds 50 passengers; narrated by experts. US$35 including transfer from hotel (US$30 without transfer), children US$15. Tel: 979 2281.
Mountain Valley Rafting: One-hour rafting trip on the Great River from Lethe, disembarking at scenic recreation area. Optional hay ride and plantation tour available. 9am–5pm daily. US$45 per person. Tel: 956 4920/6.

Southwest Coast & Inland
Accompong: Tour an old Maroon Town. Tuesday, Thursday and Saturday. Tel: 952 4546/0954.
Appleton Estate Tour: Rum-distillery tour, Monday–Saturday 9am–4pm. Tel: 963 9215.
Black River Safari Boat Tour: Boat tour to see birds and crocodiles, plus YS Falls. Tours at 9am, 11am, 12.30pm, 2pm and 4pm daily. Tel: 965 2513.
Irie Safari: Another Black River boat safari/YS Falls package, with lunch. 8.30am–5pm daily. Tel: 965 2466
St Elizabeth Safaris: 90-minute guided tours up the Black River in motor launches, 8.30am–5pm. Tel: 965 2374.

Great Houses

Kingston Area
Charlottenburgh: Tours Tuesday, Thursday and Saturday, by appointment only. Tel: 994 9265; fax 927 6137.
Craighton House and Estate: Restored great house. By appointment only. Tel: 929 8490/1 or 944 8224.
Devon House: Restored great house. Also three restaurants, a bakery, ice-cream shops, boutiques, craft and souvenir shops. Open 9am–5pm Tuesday–Saturday. Tel: 929 6602/7029.

Ocho Rios Area
Firefly: This property by Oracabessa was the island retreat of the late playwright Noël Coward. Tours, Monday–Saturday 8.30am–5pm; entrance fee. Also musical evenings at full moon in the gardens. Tel: 997 7201.
Seville Great House: House and heritage park 7 miles from Ocho Rios. 9am–5pm daily. Takes you back to the island's early history. Tel: 972 2191.

PLACES TO VISIT

Kingston Area
Boon Hall Oasis: Picnic area with restaurant in the hills of St Andrew, open 7am–5pm daily. Sunday brunch at 11am. Free admission. Tel: 942 3064.
Lime Cay: A glorious sun spot off Kingston's shore. Accessible all day, every day by motorboat from Port Royal.
Rockfort Mineral Bath: Mineral spring open Monday–Friday 6.30am–6pm, weekends and public holidays 8am–6pm. Public (US$2) and private baths.
Serenity Wildlife Park: A 50-acre (20-hectare) wildlife park just outside Spanish Town, with horse-riding, paddle boating, fishing, exotic birds and an animal-petting zoo, among other facilities. Tel: 983 8917 or 983 8607.
Wildflower Lodge & Campsite: Six

Mandeville Area
Marshall's Pen: 18th-century great house in a 300-acre wildlife sanctuary. By appointment only and then only for serious birdwatchers. Tel: 963 8569, 904 5454

Montego Bay Area
Belfield Great House: Daily tours, 10am–5pm. Tel: 952 2382/1709.
Blue Hole Great House: Also museum and plantation. Guided tours daily, 8am–6pm. Tel: 909 9602.
Greenwood Great House: Over 200 years old; once owned by the family of Elizabeth Barrett Browning, the famous English poet. Open daily 9am–6pm. Tel: 953 1077.
Hampden Great House: Tour of House, rum distillery and factory. Tel: 954 6394/5.
Rose Hall Great House: Magnificently restored house and plantation dating from 1760. Fascinating tour and legends surround the house. Open daily 9am–6pm. Tel: 953 2341/ 2456.

miles from Blue Mountain Peak. Open by appointment, tel: 929 5394/5 or 960 4871.

Port Antonio Area
The Blue Lagoon: Formerly known as the Blue Hole, this is a very deep (more than 200 ft) hole, where there's now an excellent restaurant and non-motorised water sports.
Navy Island: A 7-minute boat ride from mainland. Guided tour by reservation. African-style cottages, villas, Admiralty Club restaurant and bar. Ferry operates 7am–10pm. Tel: 993 2667.
Nonsuch Caves: Rich in stalactites and stalagmites. Open 9am–5pm daily. Tel: 993 3740.
Somerset Falls: The Daniels River plunges through a gorge of natural rock in a series of cascades and pools. Restaurant. Open daily, except Christmas and Good Friday,

10am–5pm. Tel: 926 0989 or 913 0108.

Ocho Rios Area
Columbus Park: Historical site near Discovery Bay, open daily 9am–5pm.
Dunn's River Falls & Park: 600 ft of gently terraced cascades for climbing. Open daily 9am–5pm. Tel: 974 2857/5944.
Fern Gully: 3-mile road, built in an old river bed, that winds through a lush valley of ferns.
Sleepy Hollow Park: By St Ann's Bay. Open daily 10am–5pm. Camping, picnic area. Tel: 913 4276/4322.
Wilderness Resort Limited: Sport fishing, mini petting zoo, boat rides on pond. Open 10am–5pm daily. Tel: 974 5189.

Montego Bay Area
Fort Montego: Remains of old fort standing on a hill overlooking the harbour. Crafts market is here.
Rocklands Feeding Station: Bird reserve at Anchovy. Bird feeding daily. Open 2–5pm. Hand-feed the humming birds. Tel: 952 2009.
Tryall Water Wheel: Gigantic water wheel nearly 200 years old and still turning.

Negril Area
Anancy Fun Park: At Poinciana Beach Resort. Open weekdays 1–8pm, weekends 10am–8pm, weather permitting. Tel: 957 5100
Mayfield Falls: waterfalls, camping, picnic area and gift shop. Open daily 9am–6pm. Tel: 957 9185.
Negril Lighthouse: The highest structure in Negril, towering 100 ft above sea level. Open 10am–6pm. Tel: 957 4875.
Roaring River Park: Near Savanna-la-Mar. Tour of blue lagoon, artesian well and river and a picnic area. Cottages. Open daily. Tel: 995 2094.

Southwest Coast & Inland
Apple Valley Park: Park with camping facilities. Tractor tour of farm and waterfall. Also fishing, pedalboat rides, swimming pools and mountain jacuzzi. Open

10am–5pm, closed Monday and Wednesday except public holidays. Tel: 963 9508; fax: 963 9561.
Bamboo Avenue: Road near Lacovia lined with tall bamboo, forming a canopy for miles.
Cashoo Ostrich Park: Lacovia, St Elizabeth. Working 100-acre ostrich farm. Herbal and botanical tours; fishing and kayaking on the river also available. Tel: 961 1960; fax: 961 2132.
High Mountain Coffee Factory: By appointment only. Tour the factory and see the coffee processing. Tel: 963 4211.
Lover's Leap: Scenic view of the South Coast from a sheer 1,500-ft cliff that plunges to the sea. Open 10am–6pm daily. Tel: 965 6634.
Salt Pond: A natural pond and habitat for local birds.
YS Falls: Situated on 2,000 acres of pasture. Waterfall cascades down 120 ft into the YS River.

Tropical Gardens

Kingston Area
Castleton Botanic Gardens: A horticulturalist's dream, on the Junction road between Kingston and the north coast. Open all day, every day. Tel: 927 1257.
Hope Botanical Gardens & Zoo: Largest botanical gardens in the West Indies. Gardens open daily 8.30am–6.30pm; zoo daily 10am–5pm. Tel: 927 1257 (gardens); 927 1085 (zoo).

Ocho Rios Area
Coyaba River Garden: Creekside garden, Shaw Park. Restaurant and museum, fountains and springs. Open daily 8am–5pm. Tel: 974 6235.
Cranbrook Flower Forest: Tropical garden with river path, nature walk, pond fishing, swimming and other activities. Open daily 8.30am–sunset. Tel: 770 8071.
Shaw Park Gardens: Tropical gardens with waterfall overlooking Ocho Rios. Open daily 8am–5pm. Tel: 974 2723.

Closed Mondays and public holidays. Entrance fee includes jitney transport.

Beaches

Port Antonio Area
Portland's beaches are incomparable; those at **Frenchman's Cove** and **Dragons Bay** are considered among the finest in the world. **Boston Beach** is popular for bathing, and the waves are high enough for surfing.

Ocho Rios Area
James Bond Beach Club: Oracabessa. Tel: 975 3665; fax: 975 3399. Open 9am–6pm, closed for clean-up on Mondays except public holidays. Entrance fee US$5. Watersports; Jet Ski Safari. Three magnificent white-sand beaches ring this private peninsula, 20 minutes from Ocho Rios. Restaurant/bar; marina facilities.
Sonrise Beach: Open Tuesday–Sunday 10am–5pm. Entrance fee US$6.

Montego Bay Area
Doctor's Cave Beach: World-famous white-sand and clear-water beach believed to be fed by mineral springs. Open 8.30am–5.30pm daily. Entrance fee. Tel: 952 2566.
Rose Hall Beach Club: Beach with volleyball and other beach games. Also various watersports. Two bars, pavilion and restaurant. Entrance fee. Tel: 953 9982.
Aquasol Theme Park Open 9am–5pm daily. Entrance fee.

Sport

A perfect tropical climate with bright skies and warm weather year-round has spawned a breed of sports enthusiasts. Visitors to the island will therefore find plenty of facilities at hotels, sports associations and health clubs (and of course facilities for all manner of watersports on the beach). Traditional sports for watching range from cricket to horse-racing.

Below is a list of some of the places to go for the most popular sports; your hotel will be able to equip you with further information.

Golf

Kingston: Caymanas Golf Club; Constant Spring Golf Club
Ocho Rios: Sandals Golf & Country Club
Mandeville: Manchester Club
Runaway Bay: Runaway Bay Golf Club
Montego Bay: Tryall Golf Course; Ironshore Golf Club; Half Moon Golf Club

Tennis

Kingston: Liguanea Club; Pegasus Hotel
Port Antonio: Dragon Bay Villas
Mandeville: Manchester Club
Montego Bay: Montego Bay Racquet Club
Negril: Negril Beach Club

Watersports

DEEP-SEA DIVING

Ocho Rios: Sea Jamaica Aquatic Club; Ruddy's Water Sports, Shaw Park Beach
Negril: Aqua Sports

Horse-riding

Montego Bay Area
● Good Hope Great House: Daily except Wednesday, 7.30am–4.30pm. US$30. Tel: 954 3289, 995 2825.
● Orange River Lodge: By appointment. US$20 per hour. Tel: 979 3294/5.
● Try also: Seawind, Montego Freeport; Double A. Ranch; White Witch Stables.

Negril Area
● Country Western Riding Stables: 8am–4pm daily. US$30. Tel: 957 3250.
● Rhodes Hall Plantation: Sunday–Friday, 7am–5pm. (Also scuba-diving tours daily.) Tel: 957 6333/4.

Other Areas
Riding stables are located all over the island, including:
Port Antonio: Errol Flynn's Plantation
Ocho Rios: Prospect Plantation; Dunn's River Stables
Runaway Bay: Chukka Cove Farm
Mandeville: Hotel Astra

● **Horse-racing** takes place at Caymanas Park, Portmore, Kingston, every Wednesday and Saturday and on public holidays, 12.30–6pm. Tel: 988 2523.

JET SKIING

Ocho Rios: Jamaica Grande
Montego Bay: Montego Bay Yacht Club, Montego Freeport

PARASAILING

Ocho Rios: Jamaica Grande
Negril: Ray's Parasailing, Sundowner; Negril Beach Club

SAILING, YACHTING & BOATING

Kingston: Morgan's Harbour Club; Royal Jamaica Yacht Club
Port Antonio: Dragon Bay Villas
Ocho Rios: Sandals Dunn's River Hotel
Montego Bay: Half Moon Club
Negril: Negril Beach Club

SCUBA DIVING & SNORKELLING

Ocho Rios: Sea Jamaica Aquatic Club; Island Dive Shop, Priory, St Ann's Bay
Montego Bay: Sea Crab, Chatham Cottages; Jamaica Reef Divers; Poseidon Divers
Negril: Dive Shop, Rick's Café.

WATERSKIING

Ocho Rios: Club Caribbean; Jamaica Grande; Sandals Dunn's River and Sandals Ocho Rios hotels
Montego Bay: Montego Bay Yacht Club, Montego Freeport; Water Whirl
Negril: Ray's Parasailing; Coconut Grove Hotel

WINDSURFING

Port Antonio: Dragon Bay Villas
Ocho Rios: Shaw Park Beach
Runaway Bay: Jamaica, Jamaica! hotel
Negril: Negril Beach Club

Shopping

What to Buy

All over the island there is a multitude of shopping possibilities. Many shops offer a large variety of merchandise at "in-bond" or duty-free prices. These shops are easily identifiable in the resort towns of Negril, Montego Bay and Ocho Rios. Jamaica is a treasure trove of finer goods like bone china and crystal as well as other merchandise generally found in in-bond stores. These are some of the better buys as they are priced at far less than they would be in the USA and UK. Shopping plazas and complexes make it possible to do all your buying under one roof.

To trigger reminiscences of your visit to the island, look for hand-crafted items made in Jamaica. These include: "Annabella" boxes made of wood and painted, or otherwise adorned, by hand; pimento-filled Spanish jars; beautiful hand-embroidered linens with motifs of birds and flora; silk and cotton hand-painted or batiked in daring colours; wood carvings; paintings; and excellent pottery/ceramics. Lignum vitae, an extremely hard and heavy wood, with a dark-to-black centre and light-to-yellow edge, is used in a lot of the carvings, some excellent, and it makes very useful and unusual cutting boards.

Designer fashion has its place in Jamaica, and for the discerning jewellery collector it will be of interest to note that there are a few world-class jewellers in Jamaica who do fine work in precious metals and gems.

Some visitors favour Jamaican fragrances (White Witch, Pirate's Gold, Khus Khus, Jamaica Island Lyme and Jamaica Island Bay Rum) and handmade soaps in unusual fragrances (cerasee and mint, mint and bay, ortanique). A special favourite is Starfish Aromatic Oils' Blue Mountain-coffee candle, which can permeate your kitchen with the aroma of freshly brewed coffee.

Other home products, a must for visitors either to bring home or to savour across the counters, are Jamaica's famous rums and liqueurs. Take your pick from internationally known names like Appleton – which now has a wide range of fine rums – Coruba, Gold Label, Rumona, Tia Maria and Sangster's Old Jamaican.

Finally, no visit to Jamaica would be complete without purchases of local reggae recordings, Blue Mountain coffee and cigars.

Where to Buy

ART & CRAFTS

Art and artisanal pottery, woodwork and craft items can be bought in all towns. Look for straw goods, wood carvings and beadwork at local markets and roadside craft stalls throughout the island.

For a list of places to buy fine art see *Culture: Galleries*.

Kingston

Craft Cottage, Village Plaza, tel: 926 0719. Very good selection.
Clonmel Potters, 84 Lady Musgrave Road, Kingston 10, tel: 978 3978. High quality stoneware.
Devon House, Nanny's Yard, an outlet for some unusual craft items; Patoo Gallery (see below); Wassi Art (see *Ocho Rios*).

Kingston Crafts Market, downtown Kingston, corner of Pechon and Port Royal streets. Wide selection of crafts, but this is a poor area, and the vendors are especially savvy.
Magic Kitchen, Village Plaza, Kingston 10, tel: 926 8894. Good variety of craft items; coffee; cigars.
Patoo Gallery, Upper Manor Park Plaza, Kingston 8, tel: 924 2552; also at Devon House. The most interesting selection of new and traditional craft items; also a good variety of books and furniture.
Starfish Oils, 5 Bedford Park Avenue, Kingston 10, tel: 920 6974, 968 1198. (Closed weekends.) Wide variety of aromatic oils, soaps and candles.

Port Antonio
Michael Layne Studio Ceramics, 19 Sommers Town Road, tel: 993 3813. Open by appointment. Interesting studio pottery.
St George's Village. Shopping mall housed in a building which incorporates every European architectural style since the Renaissance. Among its shops is the Avant Garde Gallery, which shows the work of some very talented artists.

Ocho Rios
Visit the craft market on Main Street and shops on Pineapple Place.
Art Beat, Walkers Wood, St Ann, tel: 917 2154. Fanciful jewellery made from sticks, stones, bones, shells, seeds, etc.
Calico Jack Treasures, Sonis Plaza, Ocho Rios, tel: 974 6497. Wide assortment of crafts and bric-à-brac. Friendly and helpful staff.
Harmony Hall. Good selection of the best island crafts.
Wassi Art, Bougainvillea Drive, Great Pond, Ocho Rios, tel: 974 5044; fax 974-8096; email: wassiart@cwjamaica.com; website: www.wassiart.com. Original, brightly-coloured handmade pottery. Visit the pottery works at Great Pond or the gallery on the main road in front of the Prospect Plantation (also housing the Ja.Java coffee bar).

Marley Memorabilia

Reggae fans should visit the **Bob Marley Experience** at Half Moon Shopping Village, Rose Hall, Montego Bay. This outlet claims to have the largest collection of Marley memorabilia in the world. Also shows a short film every hour on the hour in the adjoining theatre. Free admission.

Montego Bay
The Art Shop, 31 Gloucester Avenue, tel: 952 7972/7668.
The Gallery of West Indian Art in Montego Bay, 11 Fairfield Road, tel: 952 4547. (Take the Howard Cooke Blvd toward Freeport. Cross the bridge, turn left at the roundabout. The gallery is located before the traffic lights.) Open Monday–Wednesday and Friday 9am–5pm, Thursday 9am–2pm, Saturday 9am–3pm. Diverse and lively collection of Jamaican, Haitian, Cuban and African art, crafts and furniture.
Wassi Art, Golden Triangle Shopping Mall, Ironshore. (See *Ocho Rios*.)

CLOTHING

The popular Jamaican-designed Reggae to Wear line of clothing can be found in shops of all kinds, islandwide. It features soft textiles with vibrant colours in easy-to-wear designs that give a feeling of instant glamour.
Reggae to Wear, Hague Industrial Estates Factory and Retail Outlet, near Martha Brae Rafters' Rest, by Falmouth, tel: 954 3552/3 (weekdays). The factory offers a dazzling array at discount prices.

Kingston
Many Jamaican and international designers have boutiques in the capital. Try the following for easy-to-wear tropical fashions:
Bridget Sandals, 1 Abbeydale Road, Kingston 10, tel: 968 1913. Sexy, sophisticated sandals for sun-tanned feet. Also at Devon House.
Mijan's Caribbean Clothing, 20 Barbican Road, Kingston 6, tel: 977 5133.
Stonewear, 1d Braemar Avenue, tel: 978 4873.

Ocho Rios & St Ann's Bay
For hats in a wide range of styles, from straw hats to fine hats for special occasions:
St Ann Hat Shop Ltd, Island Plaza, Shop #16, Ocho Rios, tel: 974 8398 (open Monday–Thursday 8.30am–7pm, Friday and Saturday 8.30am–8pm); and 64 Main Street, St Ann's Bay, tel: 972 0295.

Montego Bay
The fashion-conscious can browse through the boutiques strung along the Gloucester Avenue hotel strip, and in shopping malls like Beachview Arcade and Casa Montego Arcade.

JEWELLERY

Those with an eye for intricate, delicate jewellery – and a bulging wallet to pay for it – can find a first-class selection at major shopping areas in north-coast resorts, or in the shopping malls and fashion houses in Kingston. Those with less money in their pockets should look for hand-crafted jewellery featuring semi-precious stones, such as the pieces sold at Blue Mountain Gems (below).

Kingston
For original hand-made jewellery:
Italcraft. Highly fashionable shell jewellery created by the former Miss World, Cindy Breakspeare, and colleague Donna Coore.
Jasmin Girvan at Devon House, tel: 927 6642. Top Jamaican jeweller.
L.A. Henriques (Sons), Waterloo Road, Kingston 8, tel: 905 0646.

Montego Bay
Blue Mountain Gems Gallery, Holiday Inn Village, Rose Hall, tel: 953 2338. Famous for semi-precious jewellery, marked by great workmanship and ingenuity.

SKIN CARE

Jencare Skin Farm, Red Hills Mall, Kingston 19, tel: 925 6782, 924 6201. Closed Wednesday and Sunday. Jennifer Samunda is Jamaica's own Elizabeth Arden/Estée Lauder/Christine Valmy. Her products and treatments (facials, massages etc.) are internationally well regarded.

Language

Some colourful Jamaican patois expressions which bear translation are:

Vibes positive vibrations
Bad vibes negative vibrations
Bashment a happening, a dance, a fête
Big up praise, congratulate
Boops a sugar daddy
Bootoo an uncouth person, a yob
Brawta a little extra
Carry go bring come gossip
Chalice a pipe, generally for smoking ganja
Cool runnings Everything's OK
Diss (verb and noun) disrespect, a slight (Dissing is taken seriously in Jamaica)
Don leader, as in *The Godfather*
Hail up to greet
Herb ganja (marijuana)
Hortical authentic, rightful (eg "hortical don")
In foreign abroad
Irie the feeling you get when the vibes are right, cool
Ital natural
Lawn an open place, eg where a bashment is held
Seen? Get it?
Sense seedless herb
Set sound system
Sketel a loose woman
Streggeh a badly behaved woman
Up so the USA
You no seet? Agreed?
Yao! Hail! Hello!
Under manners put under a regime of discipline (eg an errant husband by his wife; the expression came into use in the 1970s, when the Democratic Socialists put society "under manners")

Further Reading

History & Politics

Black, Clinton V. *History of Jamaica.* London: Collins, 1976. *The Story of Jamaica.* London: Collins, 1965. *Tales of Old Jamaica.* Kingston: Sangsters, 1979.

Beckles, Hilary & Shepherd, Verene (ed). *Caribbean Freedom: Economy and Society from Emancipation to the Present.* USA: Markus Wiener Pubs; UK: James Currey Pubs, 1998.

Chevannes, Barry. *Rastafari Roots and Ideology.* The Press UWI/Syracuse Univ Press, 1995.

Craton, Michael. *Empire, Enslavement and Freedom in the Caribbean.* Kingston: Ian Randle Pub., 1997. USA: Markus Wiener Pubs; UK: James Currey Pubs.

Dallas, R.C. *The History of the Maroons.* 2 vols. London: 1803.

Garvey, Amy Jacques (comp). *The Philosophy and Opinion of Marcus Garvey, Vol 1.* The Majority Press, 1986.

Graham, Tom. *Kingston 100: 1872–1972.* Kingston: 1972.

Gunst, Laurie. *Born fi Dead Henry.* Holt and Co, 1995

Hart, Richard. *Towards Decolonisation: Political, Labour and Economic Developments in Jamaica 1938–1945.* Canoe Press, UWI, 1997.

Lacey, Terry. *Violence and Politics in Jamaica 1960–70.* Manchester: Manchester University Press, 1977.

Nugent, Maria, Lady. *Lady Nugent's Journal: Jamaica 150 Years Ago.* London: 1939.

Robinson, Carey. *The Fighting Maroons of Jamaica.* London: Collins/Sangsters, 1969.

Sherlock, Philip & Bennett, Hazel. *The Story of the Jamaican People.* Kingston: Ian Randle Pub., 1998. USA: Markus Wiener Pubs.

Vassell, Linnette (comp). *Voices of Women in Jamaica 1898-1939.* Mona: Dept of History, UWI, 1993.

General

Beckford, William. *A Descriptive Account of the Island of Jamaica.* 2 vols. London: 1796.

Black, Clinton V. *Spanish Town: The Old Capital.* Glasgow: Maclehose, 1960.

Cargill, Morris (ed). *Ian Fleming Introduces Jamaica.* London: André Deutsch, 1965.

Cargill, Morris. *Public Disturbances.* (A collection of writings, 1986–1996). Mill Press, 1998.

Donaldson, Enid. *The Real Taste of Jamaica.* Kingston: Ian Randle Pubs., 1993

Henriques, Fernando. *Jamaica: Land of Wood and Water.* London: MacGibbon & Kee, 1957.

Henry, Mike. *Caribbean Cocktails and Mixed Drinks.* Kingston: Kingston Publishers, 1980.

Miller, Elsa. *Caribbean Cooking and Menus.* Kingston: Kingston Publishers, 1983.

Palladini, David. *Jamaica nice, you know.* Jamaica: Palladin Press, 1997.

Saunders, Dave. *Highlight Jamaica.* (London & Basingstoke) Macmillan Education Ltd, 1997.

Senior, Olive. *A to Z of the Jamaican Heritage.* Kingston: Heinemann, 1984.

Sewell, Tony. *Garvey's Children.* Macmillan Education Ltd, 1990.

Shields, Enid. *Devon House Families.* Kingston: Ian Randle Pub., 1991.

Sibley, Inez. *Place Names of Jamaica.* Kingston: Institute of Jamaica, 1979.

Walsh, Robb & McCarthy, Jay. *Travelling Jamaica with Knife, Fork and Spoon.* The Crossing Press, 1995.

Willinsky, Helen. *JERK – Barbecue from Jamaica.* The Crossing Press, 1990.

The People

Barrett, Leonard E. *The Rastafarians: the Dreadlocks of Jamaica.* London: Heinemann, 1977.

Bennett, Louise, et al. *Anancy Stories and Dialect Verse.*

Kingston: Pioneer Press, 1950. *Aunty Roachy Seh* (ed. by Mervyn Morris). Kingston: Sangsters, 1993.

Brathwaite, Edward. *The Development of Creole Society in Jamaica 1770–1820.* Oxford: Clarendon Press, 1971.

Brown, Aggrey. *Colour, Class and Politics in Jamaica.* New Jersey: Transaction Books, 1979.

Carey, Bev. *The Maroon Story.* Agouti Press, 1997.

Clarke, Edith. *My Mother who Fathered Me* (first published 1957). The Press, UWI, 1997.

Cumper, George E. *The Social Structure of Jamaica.* Mona: UCWI, 1949.

Owens, Joseph. *Dread: the Rastafarians of Jamaica.* Kingston: Sangsters, 1976.

Wynter, Sylvia. *Jamaica National Heroes.* Kingston: Jamaica National Press Commission, 1971.

Biographies

Jarret-Macauley, Delia. *The Life of Una Marson, 1905–1965.* Kingston: Ian Randle Pub., 1998.

Manley, Rachel (ed). *Edna Manley: The Diaries.* Heinemann (Caribbean), 1989. *Drumblair: Memories of a Jamaican Childhood.* Kingston: Ian Randle Pub., 1996.

Prince, Nancy. *A Black Woman's Odyssey Through Russia and Jamaica.* USA: Markus Wiener Publishers.

Seacole, Mary. *Wonderful Adventures Of Mrs Mary Seacole in Many Lands.* Falling Wall Press, 1984 (first published by James Blackwood, 1857).

Taylor, Don. *Marley and Me.* Kingston: Kingston Publishers, 1994.

Thompson, Dudley. *From Kingston to Kenya.* The Majority Press, 1993.

Arts & Culture

Barrow, Steve & Dalton, Peter. *Reggae: The Rough Guide.* UK Rough Guides Ltd, 1997.

Beckwith, Martha. *Jamaican Proverbs*. New York: Negro University Press, 1970.

Boot, Adrian & Thomas, Michael. *Jamaica: Babylon on a Thin Wire*. London: Thames and Hudson, 1976.

Boxer, David & Poupeye, Veerlee *Modern Jamaican Art*. Kingston: Ian Randle Pub., 1998

Chang, Kevin, O'Brien & Chen, Wayne. *Reggae Routes: The Story of Jamaican Music*. Kingston: Ian Randle Pub. USA: Temple University Press, 1998.

Cooper, Carolyn. *Noises in the Blood: Orality, Gender and the "Vulgar" Body of Jamaican Popular Culture*. Basingstoke: Macmillan Press, 1993.

Dalrymple, Henderson. *Bob Marley: Music, Myth and the Rastas*. London: Carib-Arawak, 1976.

Green, Jonathan. *Bob Marley and the Wailers*. London: Wise Publications, 1977.

Larkin, Colin. *Virgin Encyclopaedia of Reggae*. London: Virgin Books, 1998.

Lewin, Olive. *Brown Gal in de Ring: 12 Folk Songs from Jamaica*. London: Oxford University Press, 1974.

Nettleford, Rex. *Inward Stretch Outward Reach* (essays). Basingstoke: Macmillan Press, 1993.

Potash, Chris. *Reggae, Rasta, Revolution* (Jamaican music from ska to dub). Schirmer Books, 1997.

Roots and Rhythms: Jamaica's National Dance Theatre. London: André Deutsch, 1970. *Dance Jamaica*. London: Grove Press, 1985.

Tanna, Laura. *Jamaican Folk Tales and Oral Histories*. Kingston: Institute of Jamaica Publications, 1985.

Religion

Banbury, R. Thomas. *Jamaican Superstitions*. Jamaica: Mortimer C. DeSouza, 1849.

Beckwith, Martha. *Jamaica Forklore*. New York: American Forklore Society, 1928.

Cumper, George E. *The Potential of Rastafarianism as a Modern National Religion*. New Delhi: Recorder Press, 1979.

Seaga, Edward. *Revival Cults in Jamaica*. Kingston: Institute of Jamaica, 1982.

Language

Adams, L. Emilie. *Understanding Jamaican Patois*. Kingston: Kingston Publishers, 1991.

Cassidy, Frederic G. & LePage, R.B. *Dictionary of Jamaican English, 2nd Edition*. Cambridge: Cambridge University Press, 1980.

Lalla, Barbara & D'Costa, Jean. *Lanuage in Exile: 300 Years of Jamaican Creole*. University of Alabama Press, 1990.

Maxwell, Ken. *How to Speak Jamaican*. 50th Printing, 1998.

Morris, Mervyn. *Is English we Speaking* (and other essays). Kingston: Ian Randle Pub., 1998.

Pollard, Velma. *Dread Talk: The Language of Rastafari*. Canoe Press, UWI, 1994.

Williams, Joan. *Original Dancehall Dictionary*. Jamaica: Word Publications.

Fiction

Cumper, Patricia. *One Bright Child*. London: Black Amber Books, 1998.

Delisser, Herbert G. *The White Witch of Rose Hall*. London: Ernert Benn, 1929.

Hearne, John. *The Sure Salvation*. London: Faber and Faber, 1983.

Kennaway, Guy. *One People*. Payback Press, 1997.

Mais, Roger. *Brother Man*. London: Jonathan Cape, 1954.

Patterson, H.O. *Children of Sisyphus*. London: Hutchinson, 1964.

Reid, Victor Stafford. *The Leopard*. New York: Viking Press, 1958.

Winkler, Anthony. *The Painted Canoe*. Kingston: Kingston Publishers, 1985. *The Lunatic*. Kingston Publishers, 1987.

Where to Buy Books & Magazines

The largest concentration of bookshops is in Kingston.

Sangsters have several branches in Kingston: at 97 Harbour Street and 33 King Street (both downtown); on The Mall Plaza on Constant Spring Road; on the lower floor of the Sovereign Shopping Center, 106 Hope Road; and The Bookshop at The Springs Plaza on Constant Spring Road. Elsewhere they have outlets in the Spanish Town Shopping Centre, Spanish Town; at 29 Main Street, Mandeville; and in the Westgate Shopping Centre, Montego Bay.

Kingston Bookshop Limited has two Kingston outlets: at 70b King Street (downtown) and The Pavillion Shopping Centre, Constant Spring Road.

Novelty Trading, a major distributor of books and magazines, has its headquarters at 53 Hanover Street, (tel: 922-5661) and its main retail outlet, **Bookland**, at 53 Knutsford Boulevard, (tel: 926 4035).

The world-famous club poet Mutabaruka runs **Books About Us** at 2 Hillview Avenue (corner Eastwood Park Road), (tel: 929 4651). The other shops mentioned carry a variety of books, including those on all aspects of Jamaican life. They also carry foreign and locally-written novels, and the centrally located outlets carry magazines and newspapers.

In addition to the above-named shops, there are a number of specialist bookshops listed in the Yellow Pages of the local directory, mostly dotted around Kingston. Pharmacies usually carry a selection of foreign and local newspapers and magazines, as well as paperback novels.

Natural History

Adams, C. Dennis. *Flowering Plants of Jamaica*. Mona: UWI, 1972.

Bond, James. *Birds of the West Indies*. London: Collins, 1993 (5th ed).

Fincham, Alan G. *Jamaica Underground – The Caves, Sinkholes and Underground Rivers of the Island*. The Press, UWI, 1997

Gloudon, Ancile & Tobisch, Cicely *Orchids of Jamaica*. The Press, UWI, 1995.

Hodges, Margaret (ed). *Blue Mountain Guide*. Natural History Society of Jamaica, 1993.

Kaye, W.J. *Butterflies of Jamaica*. Transactions of the Entomological Society of London, 1926.

Lack, David. *Island Biology. Illustrated by the Land of Birds of Jamaica*. Berkeley & Los Angeles: University of California Press, 1976.

Stewart, D.B. (ed.) *Gosse's Jamaica 1844–45*. Kingston: Institute of Jamaica Publications, 1985.

Storer, Dorothy. *Familiar Trees and Cultivated Plants of Jamaica*. London: Macmillan for the Institute of Jamaica, 1958.

Photography

Blake, Evon. *Beautiful Jamaica*. 4th Edition. Jamaica: Vista Publications, 1980.

Canetti, Nicolai. *The People and Places of Jamaica*. London: Peebles Press International, 1976.

Egan, Anne. *Jamaica: Story of a People, A Legend and A Legacy*. Kingston: Rose Hall Ltd., 1973.

Ribelli, Piero. *Jah Pickney: Children of Jamaica*. Kingston: Ian Randle Pub., 1995.

Sports

Carnegie, James. *Great Jamaican Olympians*. Stephenson Lithopress, 1996.

Forrester, Claire & Campbell, Alvin. *Unyielding Spirit: Biography of Merlene Ottey*. West Indies Pub., 1996.

Hannau, Michael P. *Fishing in Jamaica*. Hamilton: Buccaneer Publishing House, 1964

Smith, Lloyd S. *Public Life and Sport: Trinidad, Jamaica and Grenada*. Spain, 1941

Other Insight Guides

In Apa Publications' main series of more than 200 Insight Guides, destinations in this region include several to the Caribbean: *Insight Guide: Caribbean, Trinidad and Tobago, Bahamas, Barbados, Bermuda, Cuba* and *Puerto Rico*.

Insight Guide: Caribbean takes readers on a journey from the beauty of a tropical sunset to the charm of the Caribees.

Insight Guide: Puerto Rico takes the adventurous visitor through the colourful streets of San Juan, into the richly populated waters of the Caribbean.

POCKET GUIDES

Apa Publications also has two other series of guidebooks. **Insight Pocket Guides** feature the authors' suggestions for tours, with timed itineraries for the short-stay visitor and a full-size pull-out map. Companion books are: *Insight Pocket Guide: Jamaica, Barbados, Bermuda, Bahamas* and *Puerto Rico*.

COMPACT GUIDES

Insight Compact Guides are handy mini-encyclopedias, whose titles include *Insight Compact Guide: Bahamas, Barbados* and *Dominican Republic*.

ART & PHOTO CREDITS

Picture Spreads

INSIGHT GUIDE Jamaica

Cartographic Editor Zoë Goodwin
Production Stuart A Everitt
Design Consultants
Carlotta Junger, Graham Mitchener
Picture Research
Hilary Genin, Monica Allende

Index

Numbers in italics refer to photographs

New Insight Maps

When you're on the road you sometimes need the big picture that only a large-scale map can provide. This new range of durable Insight Fleximaps has been designed to complement the books and meet that need.

Detailed, clear cartography
produces easy-to-follow route and city maps with main sites highlighted, plus full index

Informative and easy to use
with the top 10 sites listed, plus useful facts about the destination, addresses, handy tips

Laminated finish
makes the maps durable, easy to fold, and allows you to use a non-permanent marker pen.

The World of Insight Guides

400 books in three complementary series cover every major destination in every continent.

Insight Guides

Alaska
Alsace
Amazon Wildlife
American Southwest
Amsterdam
Argentina
Atlanta
Athens
Australia
Austria
Bahamas
Bali
Baltic States
Bangkok
Barbados
Barcelona
Bay of Naples
Beijing
Belgium
Belize
Berlin
Bermuda
Boston
Brazil
Brittany
Brussels
Budapest
Buenos Aires
Burgundy
Burma (Myanmar)
Cairo
Calcutta
California
Canada
Caribbean
Catalonia
Channel Islands
Chicago
Chile
China
Cologne
Continental Europe
Corsica
Costa Rica
Crete
Crossing America
Cuba
Cyprus
Czech & Slovak Republics
Delhi, Jaipur, Agra
Denmark
Dresden
Dublin
Düsseldorf
East African Wildlife
East Asia
Eastern Europe
Ecuador
Edinburgh
Egypt
Finland
Florence
Florida
France
Frankfurt
French Riviera
Gambia & Senegal
Germany
Glasgow

Gran Canaria
Great Barrier Reef
Great Britain
Greece
Greek Islands
Hamburg
Hawaii
Hong Kong
Hungary
Iceland
India
India's Western Himalaya
Indian Wildlife
Indonesia
Ireland
Israel
Istanbul
Italy
Jamaica
Japan
Java
Jerusalem
Jordan
Kathmandu
Kenya
Korea
Lisbon
Loire Valley
London
Los Angeles
Madeira
Madrid
Malaysia
Mallorca & Ibiza
Malta
Marine Life in the South
  China Sea
Melbourne
Mexico
Mexico City
Miami
Montreal
Morocco
Moscow
Munich
Namibia
Native America
Nepal
Netherlands
New England
New Orleans
New York City
New York State
New Zealand
Nile
Normandy
Northern California
Northern Spain
Norway
Oman & the UAE
Oxford
Old South
Pacific Northwest
Pakistan
Paris
Peru
Philadelphia
Philippines
Poland
Portugal
Prague

Provence
Puerto Rico
Rajasthan
Rhine
Rio de Janeiro
Rockies
Rome
Russia
St Petersburg
San Francisco
Sardinia
Scotland
Seattle
Sicily
Singapore
South Africa
South America
South Asia
South India
South Tyrol
Southeast Asia
Southeast Asia Wildlife
Southern California
Southern Spain
Spain
Sri Lanka
Sweden
Switzerland
Sydney
Taiwan
Tenerife
Texas
Thailand
Tokyo
Trinidad & Tobago
Tunisia
Turkey
Turkish Coast
Tuscany
Umbria
US National Parks East
US National Parks West
Vancouver
Venezuela
Venice
Vienna
Vietnam
Wales
Washington DC
Waterways of Europe
Wild West
Yemen

Insight Pocket Guides

Aegean Islands★
Algarve★
Alsace
Amsterdam★
Athens★
Atlanta★
Bahamas★
Baja Peninsula★
Bali★
Bali Bird Walks
Bangkok★
Barbados★
Barcelona★
Bavaria★
Beijing★
Berlin★

Bermuda★
Bhutan★
Boston★
British Columbia★
Brittany★
Brussels★
Budapest &
  Surroundings★
Canton★
Chiang Mai★
Chicago★
Corsica★
Costa Blanca★
Costa Brava★
Costa del Sol/Marbella★
Costa Rica★
Crete★
Denmark★
Fiji★
Florence★
Florida★
Florida Keys★
French Riviera★
Gran Canaria★
Hawaii★
Hong Kong★
Hungary
Ibiza★
Ireland★
Ireland's Southwest★
Israel★
Istanbul★
Jakarta★
Jamaica★
Kathmandu Bikes &
  Hikes★
Kenya★
Kuala Lumpur★
Lisbon★
Loire Valley★
London★
Macau★
Madrid★
Malacca
Maldives
Mallorca★
Malta★
Mexico City★
Miami★
Milan★
Montreal★
Morocco★
Moscow
Munich★
Nepal★
New Delhi
New Orleans★
New York City★
New Zealand★
Northern California★
Oslo/Bergen★
Paris★
Penang★
Phuket★
Prague★
Provence★
Puerto Rico★
Quebec★
Rhodes★
Rome★
Sabah★

St Petersburg★
San Francisco★
Sardinia
Scotland★
Seville★
Seychelles★
Sicily★
Sikkim
Singapore★
Southeast England
Southern California★
Southern Spain★
Sri Lanka★
Sydney★
Tenerife★
Thailand★
Tibet★
Toronto★
Tunisia★
Turkish Coast★
Tuscany★
Venice★
Vienna★
Vietnam★
Yogyakarta
Yucatan Peninsula★

**★ = Insight Pocket Guides
with Pull out Maps**

Insight Compact Guides

Algarve
Amsterdam
Bahamas
Bali
Bangkok
Barbados
Barcelona
Beijing
Belgium
Berlin
Brittany
Brussels
Budapest
Burgundy
Copenhagen
Costa Brava
Costa Rica
Crete
Cyprus
Czech Republic
Denmark
Dominican Republic
Dublin
Egypt
Finland
Florence
Gran Canaria
Greece
Holland
Hong Kong
Ireland
Israel
Italian Lakes
Italian Riviera
Jamaica
Jerusalem
Lisbon
Madeira
Mallorca
Malta

Milan
Moscow
Munich
Normandy
Norway
Paris
Poland
Portugal
Prague
Provence
Rhodes
Rome
St Petersburg
Salzburg
Singapore
Switzerland
Sydney
Tenerife
Thailand
Turkey
Turkish Coast
Tuscany
UK regional titles:
  Bath & Surroundings
  Cambridge & East
    Anglia
  Cornwall
  Cotswolds
  Devon & Exmoor
  Edinburgh
  Lake District
  London
  New Forest
  North York Moors
  Northumbria
  Oxford
  Peak District
  Scotland
  Scottish Highlands
  Shakespeare Country
  Snowdonia
  South Downs
  York
  Yorkshire Dales
USA regional titles:
  Boston
  Cape Cod
  Chicago
  Florida
  Florida Keys
  Hawaii: Maui
  Hawaii: Oahu
  Las Vegas
  Los Angeles
  Martha's Vineyard &
    Nantucket
  New York
  San Francisco
  Washington D.C.
  Venice
  Vienna
  West of Ireland